The Compact Reader

SUBJECTS, STYLES, AND STRATEGIES

Third Edition

The
Compact Reader

SUBJECTS,
STYLES, AND STRATEGIES

Jane E. Aaron

Parsons School of Design
The New School for Social Research

BEDFORD BOOKS OF ST. MARTIN'S PRESS

BOSTON

In memory of Richard S. Beal

For Bedford Books
Publisher: Charles H. Christensen
Associate Publisher: Joan E. Feinberg
Managing Editor: Elizabeth M. Schaaf
Developmental Editor: Karen S. Henry
Production Editor: Tara L. Masih
Copyeditor: Roberta H. Winston
Text Design: Claire Seng-Niemoeller
Cover Design: Michael Mauceri, Independent Design
Cover Art: *Sacramento Mall Proposal #4* by Frank Stella; spine art detail of
Sacramento Mall Proposal #4; National Gallery of Art, Washington, D.C.;
Gift of the Collectors Committee

Library of Congress Catalog Card Number: 88–63046

Manufactured in the United States of America.
4   3   2   1   0
f   e   d   c   b

For information, write: St. Martin's Press, Inc.
175 Fifth Avenue, New York, NY 10010

Editorial Offices: Bedford Books *of* St. Martin's Press
29 Winchester Street, Boston, MA 02116

ISBN: 0–312–02850–4

ACKNOWLEDGMENTS

Mortimer J. Adler, from "How to Mark a Book," *Saturday Review*, July 6,
1940. Reprinted by permission.
Nelson W. Aldrich, Jr., from *Old Money: The Mythology of America's Upper
Class*. Copyright © 1988 by Nelson W. Aldrich, Jr. Reprinted by permission of Alfred A. Knopf, Inc.

*Acknowledgments and copyrights are continued at the back of the book on
pages 384–87, which constitute an extension of the copyright page.*

Preface

This third edition of *The Compact Reader* contains almost one-half new selections and a new chapter, among other changes, but its purpose remains the same. It is designed for composition instructors who want a manageable collection of essays to illustrate the rhetorical methods and for students who can use clear, concrete guidance on reading and writing.

Of the thirty-six essays (compared with fifty or more in most composition readers), many are familiar and many, deliberately, are not. Alongside classics by E. B. White, Judy Syfers, Richard Rodriguez, and Maxine Hong Kingston are pieces reprinted for the first time in a composition reader, by Peter Schjeldahl, George F. Will, John Berger, Margarita Chant Papandreou, Barbara Ehrenreich, and others. Many of the selections, both new and otherwise, address issues of contemporary interest or urgency, such as sex roles, homelessness, terrorism, the messages of the media, and the war against drugs. And complementing the essays are twenty-two paragraphs, two representing each rhetorical method (eight of them new), by such distinctive voices as Sallie Tisdale, Charles Kuralt, Alice Walker, Berton Roueché, and Jan Morris.

The book's new chapter actually results from splitting an old chapter, "Division and Classification," into Chapter 4, "Division or Analysis," and Chapter 5, "Classification." Now a single chapter no longer has to do the work of two. And, more important, the new arrangement stresses the analytical nature of division—usually treated as a mere adjunct of classification—and shows analysis to be as fundamental as it is to most of the other methods of development, to critical thinking and writing, to all academic and professional work. By explaining and illustrating rudimentary division or analysis and more sophisticated critical thought, the chapter introduction, paragraph examples, selections, and questions provide basic training in an essential skill. Chapter 5 then does the same for classification. (Process analysis now follows rather than precedes these methods because it depends in part on analytical skills. Nonetheless, the needed skills are not assumed, so that instructors who wish to cover process analysis before division or analysis may safely do so.)

This change in organization is the most recent of *The Compact Reader*'s efforts to treat the rhetorical methods not as forms to be filled out but as ways of thinking and writing about experience and ideas. As before, each chapter introduction explains the uses and principles of one method and provides detailed advice for developing an essay using the method. In this edition, the two paragraphs illustrating each method are extensively annotated (rather than commented on), so that the relation between principle and example is more immediate. The same goal informed the new annotations on the three essays in the final chapter, which are chosen to illustrate the tenet, central to *The Compact Reader*, that writers rarely use the methods of development in isolation but combine them as needed. (This point is discussed throughout the book and driven home with a question labeled "Other Methods" following every essay.)

Besides the detailed chapter introductions, *The Compact Reader* includes abundant editorial aids. As before, the general introduction, "Reading and Writing," discusses the value of reading, shows how to read critically (including a detailed analysis of a new sample essay), and presents a specific introduction to the writing process, culminating in three drafts of a student's paper written in response to the sample essay. Also as before, each essay in the book is preceded by two headnotes, one on the author and one on the essay itself. Each essay is also followed by a full set of discussion questions designed to help students analyze the essay and by several specific writing topics. (The three essays in the final chapter are free of questions and topics in the book itself, but this supporting material appears in the instructor's manual.) A long list of possible writing topics concludes each method chapter. And finally, a glossary defines the terms used in the book and provides advice on such matters as writing an introduction and using transitions.

Instructors reading this preface are probably holding the special Instructor's Edition of *The Compact Reader*—the book itself bound with its instructor's manual. The manual, prepared by Kathleen Shine Cain of Merrimack College, suggests other course materials the essays can be combined with, recommends classroom uses for the various parts of the book, and, for each essay, provides teaching ideas as well as possible answers to the end-of-essay questions.

ACKNOWLEDGMENTS   Many instructors who used the second edition of *The Compact Reader* responded generously to a detailed questionnaire on the book, and their comments helped set the course of this revision. Deep thanks to H. Dirksen L. Bauman, University of Northern Colorado; Joseph Brogunier, University of Maine, Orono; Annette Conn, Bucks County Community College; Patricia B. del Rio, Philadelphia Community College; Bruce Gospin, Union County College; Amy Grat, San Diego State University; Rebecca Kanost, University of Oklahoma; Marianne H. Knowlton, University of Lowell; C. Lawrence, Nova College; Beverly A. McCrellis, Onondaga Community College; Howard A. Mayer, University of Hartford; Joan Meehan, City College of San Francisco; Elizabeth Metzger, University of South Florida; Virginia Meyn, Saddleback College; Robert A. Morace, Daemen College; Joyce Nower, San Diego State University; John Ohst, State University of New York College of Technology; Karen L. Regal, Mankato State University; Loren F. Schmidtberger, Saint Peter's College; Patricia Stewart, C. S. Mott Community College; Eve M. Stwertka, State University of New York, Farmingdale; Judith Vidal, Delaware Technical and Community College; John Vulcmirovich, Loyola University of Chicago; Alan T. Watters, California State University, Sacramento; Sarah W. Wheeler, Castleton State College; Roger E. Wiche, University of Lowell; Marjorie Williams, Baptist Bible College of Pennsylvania; and Robert Zweig, Manhattan Community College.

In addition to preparing an excellent instructor's manual, Kathleen Cain was a cheerful sounding board. At Bedford Books, as usual, good ideas and supportiveness reigned. Thanks especially to Charles H. Christensen, Karen S. Henry, Jane Betz, and Tara L. Masih. Thanks also to Andrew Christensen and John Christensen, two loyal student users of the book. And grateful appreciation to the late Richard S. Beal, whose contributions to the field of composition and to his friends in it cannot adequately be commemorated by the dedication of this book to him.

Contents

2

Narration

57

3

Example

87

4
Division or Analysis
110

5
Classification
137

6
Process Analysis
161

7
Comparison and Contrast
196

8

Analogy

229

9

Definition

250

10
Cause-and-Effect Analysis
275

11
Argument and Persuasion
308

12
Combining Methods of Development
ESSAYS FOR FURTHER READING
357

The Compact Reader

SUBJECTS, STYLES, AND STRATEGIES

Introduction

Reading
and Writing

This collection of essays has one purpose: to help you become a more proficient writer. It combines examples of good writing on diverse subjects with explanations of the writers' methods, questions on their work, and ideas for your own writing. In doing so, it shows how you can adapt the processes and techniques of people who write for a living as you learn to communicate clearly and effectively on paper.

Writing well is not an inborn skill but an acquired one: you will become proficient only by writing and writing, experimenting with different strategies, listening to the responses of readers. How, then, can it help to read the work of other writers? First, reading others' ideas can introduce you to new information, open your mind to new associations, give you new perspectives on your own experience. Many of the essays collected here demonstrate that personal experience is a rich and powerful source of material for writing. But the knowledge gained from reading can help pinpoint just what is remarkable in your experience. And by introducing varieties of behavior and ways of thinking that would otherwise remain unknown to you, reading can also help you understand where you fit in the scheme of things. Such insight not only reveals subjects for writing but also improves your ability to communicate with others whose experiences naturally differ from your own.

A second benefit of reading for writing is that it exposes you to a broad range of strategies and styles. Just seeing that these vary as much as the writers themselves should assure you that there is no fixed standard of writing, no perfect all-occasion model, while it should also encourage you to find your own strategies, your own style. At the same time, you will see that writers do make choices to suit their subjects, their purposes, and especially their readers. Writing is rarely easy, even for the pros; but the more options you have to choose from, and the more you understand the reasons for your choices and their effects on readers, the more likely you are to succeed at it.

Reading makes a third contribution to writing. As you become adept at reading the work of other writers critically, discovering intentions and analyzing choices, you will also become increasingly sensitive to the role of audience in writing. You will see how the writer's decisions affect you as audience: how a clearly defined, consistent purpose makes your reading more interesting and rewarding; how the arrangement of ideas focuses and channels your attention; how details and examples help you understand explanations; how sentences and words give you pleasure and shape your responses to ideas. Training yourself to read consciously and critically is a first step to becoming a more objective reader of your own writing. And objectivity—the ability to disengage from your work and imagine readers' responses—is crucial to effective writing.

Before we explore some strategies for reading and writing that will help you make the best use of this book, you should understand the book's organization. The essays are arranged in twelve chapters. Eleven of them introduce methods of developing a piece of writing.

description	comparison and contrast
narration	analogy
example	definition
division or analysis	cause-and-effect analysis
classification	argument and persuasion
process analysis	

These methods correspond to basic and familiar patterns of thought and expression, common in our daily musings and conversations as well as in writing for all sorts of purposes and audiences: college term papers, lab reports, and examinations; business memos and reports; letters to the editors of newspapers; articles in popular magazines. The methods provide a context for critical reading and also stimulate writing by helping you generate and shape ideas. Detailed chapter introductions explain each method, show it at work in paragraphs, and give advice for using it to develop your own essays. Then the essays in each chapter provide clear examples that you can analyze and learn from (with the help of specific questions) and can refer to while writing (with the help of specific writing suggestions). In the twelfth chapter, three additional essays illustrate how writers combine the methods of development to suit their subjects and purposes.

Reading

When we look for something to watch on television or listen to on the radio, we often tune in one station after another, pausing just long enough each time to catch the program or music being broadcast before settling on one choice. Much of the reading we do is similar: perusing a newspaper or magazine, for instance, we skim the pages, noting headings and scanning paragraphs to get the gist of the content. But such skimming is not really reading, for it neither involves us deeply in the subject nor engages us in interaction with the writer. To get the most out of reading, we must invest something of ourselves in the process, applying our own ideas and emotions and attending not just to the substance but to the writer's interpretation of it.

Reading in this way can be enormously rewarding, but of course it takes care and time. A good method for developing your own skill in critical reading is to prepare yourself beforehand and then read the work at least twice to uncover what it has to offer. Preparation need involve no more than a few minutes as you form some ideas about the author and the work.

1. What is the author's background, what qualifications does he or she bring to the subject, and what approach is he or she likely to take? The biographical information provided before each essay in this book should help answer these questions; and many periodicals and books include similar information on their authors.

2. What does the title convey about the subject and the author's attitude toward it? Note, for instance, the quite different attitudes

conveyed by these three titles on the same subject: "Safe Hunting," "In Touch with Ancient Spirits," and "Killing Animals for Fun and Profit."

3. For your reading in this book, what does the method of development suggest about how the author will handle the subject? Annie Dillard's "In the Jungle," for instance, appears in the chapter on description, so you know in advance that her essay describes the jungle.

After developing some expectations about the piece of writing, read it through carefully to acquaint yourself with the subject, the author's reason for writing about it, and the way the author presents it. (Each essay in this book is short enough to be read at one sitting.) Try not to read passively, letting the words wash over you, but instead interact directly with the work to discover its meaning, the author's intentions, and your own responses. One of the best aids to active reading is to make notes on separate sheets of paper or, preferably (if you own the book), on the pages themselves. As you practice making notes, you will probably develop a personal code meaningful only to you.

As a start, however, try this system:

1. Underline or bracket passages that you find particularly effective or that seem especially important to the author's purpose.
2. Circle words you don't understand so that you can look them up when you finish.
3. Put question marks in the margins next to unclear passages.
4. Jot down associations that occur to you, such as examples from your own experience or disagreements with the author's assumptions or arguments.

When you have finished such an active reading, your annotations might look like those below. (The paragraph is from the end of the essay reprinted on the next four pages.)

The first half of our lives is spent stubbornly denying it. As children we acquire language to make ourselves understood and soon learn from the blank stares in response to our babblings that even these, our saviors, our parents, are strangers. In adolescence when we replay earlier dramas with peers in the place of parents, we begin the quest for the best friend, that person who will receive all thoughts as if they were ~~her~~ own. Later we assert

(margin annotations:) What about his own? Audience= women? true?

that true love will find the way. True love finds many ways, but no escape *[margin note: Ophelia + Juliet from Shakespeare. Others also?]* from exile. The shores are littered with us, Annas and Ophelias, Emmas and Juliets, all outcasts from the dream of perfect understanding. We might as well draw the night around us and find solace there and a friend in our own voice. *(Just give up?)*

Before leaving the essay after such an initial reading, try to answer your own questions by looking up unfamiliar words and figuring out the meaning of unclear passages. Then let the essay rest in your mind for at least an hour or two before approaching it again. When rereading it, write a one- or two-sentence summary of each paragraph—in your own words—to increase your mastery of the material. Aim to answer the following questions:

1. Why did the author write about this subject?
2. What impression did the author wish to make on readers?
3. How do the many parts of the work—for instance, the sequencing of information, the tone, the evidence—contribute to the author's purpose?
4. How effective is the essay, and why?

A procedure for such an analysis—and the insights to be gained from it—can best be illustrated by examining an actual essay. The paragraph above comes from "The Box Man" by the American writer Barbara Lazear Ascher. Born in 1946, Ascher attended Bennington College (B.A., 1968) and Cardozo School of Law (J.D., 1979) and practiced law for two years. Then she turned to writing full-time, publishing essays in *The New York Times*, *Vogue*, *The Yale Review*, and other periodicals. "The Box Man" comes from Ascher's book *Playing After Dark* (1986). The scene is New York City, where Ascher lives with her family.

—————— *Barbara Lazear Ascher* ——————

The Box Man

The Box Man was at it again. It was his lucky night. 1

The first stroke of good fortune occurred as darkness fell and the night 2
watchman at 220 East Forty-fifth Street neglected to close the door as he

slipped out for a cup of coffee. I saw them before the Box Man did. Just inside the entrance, cardboard cartons, clean and with their top flaps intact. With the silent fervor of a mute at a horse race, I willed him toward them.

It was slow going. His collar was pulled so high that he appeared head-   *3*
less as he shuffled across the street like a man who must feel Earth with his toes to know that he walks there.

Standing unselfconsciously in the white glare of an overhead light, he   *4*
began to sort through the boxes, picking them up, one by one, inspecting tops, insides, flaps. Three were tossed aside. They looked perfectly good to me, but then, who knows what the Box Man knows? When he found the one that suited his purpose, he dragged it up the block and dropped it in a doorway.

Then, as if dogged by luck, he set out again and discovered, behind the   *5*
sign at the parking garage, a plastic Dellwood box, strong and clean, once used to deliver milk. Back in the doorway the grand design was revealed as he pushed the Dellwood box against the door and set its cardboard cousin two feet in front—the usual distance between coffee table and couch. Six full shopping bags were distributed evenly on either side.

He eased himself with slow care onto the stronger box, reached into one   *6*
of the bags, pulled out a *Daily News*, and snapped it open against his card-board table. All done with the ease of IRT Express passengers whose white-tipped, fair-haired fingers reach into attaché cases as if radar-directed to the *Wall Street Journal*. They know how to fold it. They know how to stare at the print, not at the girl who stares at them.

That's just what the Box Man did, except that he touched his tongue to   *7*
his fingers before turning each page, something grandmothers do.

One could live like this. Gathering boxes to organize a life. Wandering   *8*
through the night collecting comforts to fill a doorway.

When I was a child, my favorite book was *The Boxcar Children*. If I   *9*
remember correctly, the young protagonists were orphaned, and rather than live with cruel relatives, they ran away to the woods to live life on their own terms. An abandoned boxcar was turned into a home, a bubbling brook became an icebox. Wild berries provided abundant desserts and days were spent in the happy, adultless pursuit of joy. The children never worried where the next meal would come from or what February's chill might bring. They had unquestioning faith that berries would ripen and streams run cold and clear. And unlike Thoreau,[1] whose deliberate living was self-conscious and purposeful, theirs had the ease of children at play.

Even now, when life seems complicated and reason slips, I long to live   *10*
like a Boxcar Child, to have enough open space and freedom of movement to arrange my surroundings according to what I find. To turn streams into

[1] Henry David Thoreau (1817–1862) was an American essayist and poet who for two years lived a solitary and simple life in the woods. He wrote of his experiences in *Walden* (1854). [Editor's note.]

iceboxes. To be ingenious with simple things. To let the imagination hold sway.

Who is to say that the Box Man does not feel as Thoreau did in his doorway, not ". . . crowded or confined in the least," with "pasture enough for . . . imagination." Who is to say that his dawns don't bring back heroic ages? That he doesn't imagine a goddess trailing her garments across his blistered legs? 11

His is a life of the mind, such as it is, and voices only he can hear. Although it would appear to be a life of misery, judging from the bandages and chill of night, it is of his choosing. He will ignore you if you offer an alternative. Last winter, Mayor Koch[2] tried, coaxing him with promises and the persuasive tones reserved for rabid dogs. The Box Man backed away, keeping a car and paranoia between them. 12

He is not to be confused with the lonely ones. You'll find them every-where. The lady who comes into our local coffee shop each evening at five-thirty, orders a bowl of soup and extra Saltines. She drags it out as long as possible, breaking the crackers into smaller and smaller pieces, first in halves and then halves of halves and so on until the last pieces burst into salty splinters and fall from dry fingers onto the soup's shimmering surface. By 6 P.M., it's all over. What will she do with the rest of the night? 13

You can tell by the vacancy of expression that no memories linger there. She does not wear a gold charm bracelet with silhouettes of boys and girls bearing grandchildren's birthdates and a chip of the appropriate birthstone. When she opens her black purse to pay, there is only a crumpled Kleenex and a wallet inside, no photographs spill onto her lap. Her children, if there are any, live far away and prefer not to visit. If she worked as a secretary for forty years in a downtown office, she was given a retirement party, a cake, a reproduction of an antique perfume atomizer and sent on her way. Old col-leagues—those who traded knitting patterns and brownie recipes over the water cooler, who discussed the weather, health, and office scandal while applying lipstick and blush before the ladies' room mirror—they are lost to time and the new young employees who take their places in the typing pool. 14

Each year she gets a Christmas card from her ex-boss. The envelope is canceled in the office mailroom and addressed by memory typewriter. Within is a family in black and white against a wooded Connecticut landscape. The boss, his wife, who wears her hair in a gray page boy, the three blond daugh-ters, two with tall husbands and an occasional additional grandchild. All assembled before a worn stone wall. 15

Does she watch game shows? Talk to a parakeet, feed him cuttlebone, and call him Pete? When she rides the buses on her Senior Citizen pass, does she go anywhere or wait for something to happen? Does she have a niece like 16

[2] Edward Koch was the mayor of New York City from 1978 through 1989. [Editor's note.]

the one in Cynthia Ozick's story "Rosa," who sends enough money to keep her aunt at a distance?

There's a lady across the way whose lights and television stay on all   17
night. A crystal chandelier in the dining room and matching Chinese lamps on Regency end tables in the living room. She has six cats, some Siamese, others Angora and Abyssinian. She pets them and waters her plethora of plants— African violets, a ficus tree, a palm, and geraniums in season. Not necessarily a lonely life except that 3 A.M. lights and television seem to proclaim it so.

The Box Man welcomes the night, opens to it like a lover. He moves in   18
darkness and prefers it that way. He's not waiting for the phone to ring or an engraved invitation to arrive in the mail. Not for him a P.O. number. Not for him the overcrowded jollity of office parties, the hot anticipation of a singles' bar. Not even for him a holiday handout. People have tried and he shuffled away.

The Box Man knows that loneliness chosen loses it sting and claims no   19
victims. He declares what we all know in the secret passages of our own nights, that although we long for perfect harmony, communion, and blending with another soul, that this is a solo voyage.

The first half of our lives is spent stubbornly denying it. As children we   20
acquire language to make ourselves understood and soon learn from the blank stares in response to our babblings that even these, our saviors, our parents, are strangers. In adolescence when we replay earlier dramas with peers in the place of parents, we begin the quest for the best friend, that person who will receive all thoughts as if they were her own. Later we assert that true love will find the way. True love finds many ways, but no escape from exile. The shores are littered with us, Annas and Ophelias, Emmas and Juliets,[3] all outcasts from the dream of perfect understanding. We might as well draw the night around us and find solace there and a friend in our own voice.

One could do worse than be a collector of boxes.   21

Even read quickly, Ascher's essay would not be difficult to comprehend: the author draws on examples of three people to make a point at the end about solitude. In fact, a quick reading might give the impression that Ascher produced the essay effortlessly, artlessly. But close reading and analysis reveal a carefully conceived work whose parts work independently and together to achieve the author's pur-

---

[3] These are all doomed heroines of literature. Anna is the title character of Leo Tolstoy's novel *Anna Karenina* (1876). Emma is the title character of Gustave Flaubert's novel *Madame Bovary* (1856). Ophelia and Juliet are in Shakespeare's plays— the lovers, respectively, of Hamlet and Romeo. [Editor's note.]

pose. One way to uncover the underlying intentions and relations is to work through a series of questions that proceed from the general to the specific—from overall meaning to particular word choices. Such a set of questions appears below, interspersed with possible answers for Ascher's essay. (The paragraph numbers can help you locate the appropriate passages in Ascher's essay as you follow the analysis.)

MEANING

What is the main idea of the essay—the chief point the writer makes about the subject, to which all other ideas and details relate? What are the subordinate ideas that contribute to the main idea?

Ascher states her main idea near the end of her essay: in choosing solitude, the Box Man confirms the essential aloneness of human beings (paragraph 19) but also demonstrates that we can "find solace" within ourselves (20). (Writers sometimes postpone stating their main idea, as Ascher does here. Perhaps more often, they state it near the beginning of the essay. See p. 17–18.) Ascher leads up to and supports her idea with three examples—the Box Man (paragraphs 1–7, 11–12) and, in contrast, two women whose loneliness seems unchosen (13–16, 17). These examples are developed with specific details from Ascher's observations (such as the nearly empty purse, 14) and from the imagined lives these observations suggest (such as the remote, perhaps nonexistent children, 14).

PURPOSE AND AUDIENCE

Why did the author write the essay? What did the author hope readers would gain from it? What did the author assume about the knowledge and interests of readers, and how are these assumptions reflected in the essay?

Ascher seems to have written her essay for two interlocking reasons: to show and thus explain that solitude need not always be lonely and to argue gently for defeating loneliness by becoming one's own friend. In choosing the Box Man as her main example, she reveals perhaps a third purpose as well—to convince readers that a homeless person can have dignity and may achieve a measure of self-satisfaction lacking in some people who do have homes.

Ascher seems to assume that her readers, like her, are people with homes, people to whom the Box Man and his life might seem completely foreign: she comments on the Box Man's slow shuffle (paragraph 3), his mysterious discrimination among boxes (4), his "blistered legs" (11), how miserable his life looks (12), his bandages (12), the cold night he inhabits (12), the fearful or condescending approaches of strangers (12, 18). Building from this assumption that her readers will find the Box Man strange, Ascher takes pains to show the dignity of the Box Man—his "grand design" for furniture (5), his resemblance to commuters (6), his grandmotherly finger licking (7), his refusal of handouts (18).

Several other apparent assumptions about her audience also influence Ascher's selection of details, if less significantly. First, she assumes some familiarity with literature—at least with the writings of Thoreau (9, 11) and the characters named in paragraph 20. Second, Ascher seems to address women: in paragraph 20 she speaks of each person confiding in "her" friend, and she chooses only female figures from literature to illustrate "us, . . . all outcasts from the dream of perfect understanding." Finally, Ascher seems to address people who are familiar with, if not actually residents of, New York City: she refers to a New York street address (2); alludes to a New York newspaper, *The Daily News*, and a New York subway line, the IRT Express (6); and mentions the city's mayor (12). However, readers who do not know the literature Ascher cites, who are not women, and who do not know New York City are still likely to understand and appreciate Ascher's main point.

METHOD AND STRUCTURE

What method or methods does the author use to develop the main idea, and how do the methods serve the author's purpose? How does the organization serve the author's purpose?

As nonfiction writers often do, Ascher develops her main idea with a combination of the methods discussed in this book. Her primary support for her idea consists of three examples (Chapter 3)— specific instances of solitary people. These examples are developed with description (Chapter 1), especially of the Box Man and the two women (as in paragraphs 6–7), and with narration (Chapter 2) of the Box Man's activities (1–7). Narration figures as well in the summary of the lifelong search for understanding (20). In addition, Ascher uses division or analysis (Chapter 4) to tease apart the elements of her three characters' lives. And she relies on comparison and contrast

(Chapter 7) to show the differences between the Box Man and the other two (13, 17–18).

While using many methods to develop her idea, Ascher keeps her organization fairly simple. She does not begin with a formal introduction or a statement of her idea but instead starts right off with her main example, the inspiration for her idea. In the first seven paragraphs she narrates and describes the Box Man's activities. Then, in paragraphs 8–12, she explains what appeals to her about circumstances like the Box Man's and she applies those thoughts to what she imagines are his thoughts. Still delaying a statement of her main idea, Ascher contrasts the Box Man with two other solitary people, whose lives she sees as different from his (13–17). Finally, she returns to the Box Man (18–19) and zeroes in on her main idea (19–20). Though she has withheld this idea until the end, we see that everything in the essay has been controlled by it and directed toward it.

LANGUAGE

How are the author's main idea and purpose revealed at the level of sentences and words? How does the author use language to convey his or her attitudes toward the subject and to make meaning clear and vivid?

Perhaps Ascher's most striking use of language to express and support her idea is in paragraph 20, where she paints a picture of isolation with such words as "blank stares," "strangers," "exile," "littered," and "outcasts." But earlier she also depicts the Box Man's existence and her feeling for it in much warmer terms: she watches him with "silent fervor" (paragraph 2); he seems "dogged by luck" (5); he sits with "slow care" and opens the newspaper with "ease" (6); his page turning reminds Ascher of "grandmothers" (7); it is conceivable that, in Thoreau's words, the Box Man's imagination has "pasture" to roam, that he dreams of "heroic ages" and a "goddess trailing her garments" (11). The contrast between these passages and the later one is so marked that it emphasizes Ascher's point about the individual's ability to find comfort in solitude.

In describing the two other solitary people—those who evidently have not found comfort in aloneness—Ascher uses words that emphasize the heaviness of time and the sterility of existence. The first woman "drags" her meal out and crumbles crackers between "dry fingers" (13), a "vacancy of expression" on her face (14). She lacks even the trinkets of attachment—a "gold charm bracelet" with pictures of grandchildren (14). A vividly imagined photograph of her boss and his family (15)—the wife with "her hair in a gray page boy," "the three blond daughters"—emphasizes the probable absence of such scenes in the woman's own life.

Ascher occasionally uses incomplete sentences (or sentence fragments) to stress the accumulation of details or the quickness of her impressions. For example, in paragraph 10 the incomplete sentences beginning "To . . . " sketch Ascher's dream. And in paragraph 18 the incomplete sentences beginning "Not . . . " emphasize the Box Man's withdrawal. Both of these sets of incomplete sentences gain emphasis from **parallelism**, the use of similar grammatical form for ideas of equal importance. (See the Glossary.) The parallelism begins in the complete sentences preceding each set of incomplete sentences—for example, ". . . I long to live like a Boxcar Child. . . . To turn streams into iceboxes. To be ingenious with simple things. To let the imagination hold sway." Although incomplete sentences can be unclear, these and the others in Ascher's essay are clear: she uses them deliberately and carefully, for a purpose. (Inexperienced writers usually find it safer to avoid any incomplete sentences until they have mastered the complete sentence.)

These notes on Ascher's essay show how one can arrive at a deeper, more personal understanding of a piece of writing by attentive, thoughtful analysis. Every other essay in this book will also repay such close analysis. To guide your reading, all the essays (except those in the final chapter) are followed by more specific versions of the questions posed above, arranged in the same categories of meaning, purpose and audience, method and structure, and language. Aided by these questions, you will find that each essay contains its own lessons and pleasures.

Writing

An analysis like the one above clearly provides insights into a writer's meaning, purpose, and strategies for achieving that purpose. The analysis is valuable in itself, for it helps you better understand and appreciate whatever you read. But it can also contribute to your growth as a writer by showing you how to read your own work critically, by broadening the range of strategies available to you, and by suggesting subjects for you to write about.

Accompanying the questions on the essays in this book are "Writing Topics"—ideas for you to adapt and develop into essays of your own. Sometimes one of these suggestions calls for your analysis of the writer's ideas or some aspect of his or her strategy. Such a suggestion for Barbara Ascher's essay might lead you to analyze the different vocabularies Ascher uses to contrast the Box Man and the other two solitary people. In this kind of analysis, you would use quotations from the essay itself as evidence for your interpretations. The other writing suggestions after each essay generally lead you to examine your own experiences and observations in light of the essay's ideas. For instance, with regard to Ascher's essay, you might explore your own attitudes toward solitude or your understanding of homelessness. (A student essay in response to Ascher's begins on p. 25.)

Most of these suggestions draw on the resources of your mind or your powers of observation, but some encourage or require you to consult other sources in order to develop and support your ideas. Often, too, these suggestions recommend that you use the method of development illustrated by the essay both to generate ideas and to write your essay. In addition, a list of topics suitable for development by each method, without reference to any particular essay in the book, appears at the end of each chapter.

To help you develop essays using the various methods, the last section of each chapter introduction gives specific advice arranged by stages of the writing process: getting started, organizing, drafting, and revising. Actually, these stages are quite arbitrary, for writers do not move in straight lines through fixed steps, like locomotives over tracks. Instead, just as they do when thinking, writers continually circle back over covered territory, each time picking up more information or seeing new relationships, until their meaning is clear to themselves and can be made clear to readers. No two writers proceed in exactly the same way, either. One writer may plan everything she wants to say, down to the last detail, before beginning a draft, and then concentrate on clarity and tone in revision. Another may jot down three or four key points, write without stopping until their possibilities seem exhausted, and then spend the bulk of his time cutting, adding, reshaping, and rewording. Yet another writer may sketch a rough outline and then write and revise at the same time, getting every sentence right before beginning a new one, developing every idea fully before tackling the next one.

The purpose of dividing the writing process into stages, then, is not to tell you how you *must* proceed. Rather, the purpose is twofold: to identify what all writers need to consider while developing an essay, and to arrange these considerations in some practical order that will at least start you on evolving your own unique writing process.

GETTING STARTED

This first stage involves finding a subject, discovering your purpose in writing about the subject, and generating some ideas for achieving that purpose. A subject may arise from any source, including your own experience or reading, a suggestion in this book, or an assignment specified by your instructor. (Barbara Ascher's essay demonstrates how an excellent subject can be found from observing one's surroundings.) Whatever its source, the subject should be something you care enough about to probe deeply and to stamp with your own perspective.

This personal stamp comprises both your main idea, the central point you want to make about the subject, and your purpose, your reason for writing. The purpose may be to explain the subject so that readers understand it or see it in a new light; to persuade readers to accept or reject an opinion or to take a certain action; to entertain readers with a humorous or exciting story; or to express the thoughts and emotions triggered by a revealing or instructive experience. A single essay may sometimes have more than one purpose, too: for instance, a writer might both explain what it's like to be handicapped and try to persuade readers to respect special parking zones for the handicapped. Your purpose and your main idea may occur to you early on, arising almost inevitably out of the subject and its significance for you. But you may need to explore your subject for a while— even to the point of writing a draft—before it becomes clear to you.

Writers use a variety of techniques for probing their subjects. Some concentrate on the subject for, say, an hour, writing down every thought, no matter how irrelevant it seems. Others incubate the subject, carrying it in mind while pursuing other activities, making notes of useful ideas and details as they occur. Still others force themselves to write for ten or fifteen minutes, following ideas wherever they lead, paying no attention to completeness or correctness. Here is an example of this kind of exploratory writing, called **freewriting**. The writer, a student named Grace Patterson, was responding to Ascher's essay.

> Something in Ascher's essay keeps nagging at me, almost ticks me off. What she says about the Box Man is based on certain assumptions. Like she knows what he's been through, how he feels. Can he be as content as she says? or is that my own assumption about life on the street—how awful it must be?? What bothers me is, how much choice does the guy

really have? Just because he manages to put a little dignity into his life on the street and refuses handouts—does that mean he *chooses* homelessness? Life in a shelter might be worse than life on the street.

Freewriting like this or any of the other techniques mentioned may help you discover what you want to say. In addition, the methods of development discussed in this book can be useful tools for probing a subject. They suggest questions that can spark ideas by opening up different approaches.

Description: How does the subject look, sound, smell, taste, and feel?

Narration: How did the subject happen?

Example: How can the subject be illustrated?

Division or analysis: What are the subject's parts, and what is their relationship or significance?

Classification: What groups can the subject be sorted into?

Process analysis: How does the subject work?

Comparison and contrast: How is the subject similar to or different from something else?

Analogy: How is the subject like something else that is more familiar to readers?

Definition: What are the subject's characteristics and boundaries?

Cause-and-effect analysis: Why did the subject happen? What were its consequences?

Argument and persuasion: Why do I believe as I do about the subject? Why do others have different opinions? How can I convince others to accept my opinion or believe as I do?

If your subject does not suggest a particular method of development or you are not assigned one, then you can run through each of the methods in turn to open up a wide range of possibilities.

When your purpose and main idea are clear, you should try to state them in a **thesis sentence**, an assertion about the subject. Barbara Ascher's thesis sentence, actually two sentences, comes at the end of her essay (paragraph 20):

[We are] all outcasts from the dream of perfect understanding. We might as well draw the night around us and find solace there and a friend in our own voice.

It's not unusual for a thesis sentence to change over the course of the writing process, sometimes considerably, as the writer works to discover and express meaning. The following thesis sentences show how one writer shifted his opinion and moved from an explanatory to a persuasive purpose between the early stages of the writing process and the final draft.

Tentative: With persistence, adopted children can often locate information about their birth parents.

Final: Adopted children are unfairly hampered in seeking information about their birth parents.

Even though your thesis sentence may change, it's a good idea to draft it early on because it can help keep you focused as you generate more ideas, seek information, organize your thoughts, and so on. If you state it near the beginning of your essay, the thesis sentence can also serve as a promise to readers—a commitment to examine a specific subject from a particular perspective—that can help control your writing and revising. (However, as Ascher's essay demonstrates, the thesis sentence may come elsewhere as long as it still controls the whole essay.) Writers do not always state a thesis sentence in their finished work, as some of the essays in this book illustrate. But a thesis governs these essays nonetheless: every element, from ideas to individual words, is guided by the writer's purpose and main idea, and these are evident to us.

Either very early, when you first begin exploring your subject, or later, as a check on what you have generated, you may want to make a few notes on your anticipated audience. The notes are optional, but thinking about audience definitely is not. Your purpose and main idea as well as supporting ideas, details and examples, organization, style, tone, and language—all should reflect your answers to the following questions:

1. What impression do you want to make on readers?
2. What do readers already know about your subject? What do they need to know?
3. What are readers' likely expectations and assumptions about your subject?
4. How can you build on readers' previous knowledge, expectations, and assumptions to bring them around to your view?

These considerations are obviously crucial to achieve the fundamental purpose of all public writing: communication. Accordingly, they come up again and again in the chapter introductions and the questions after each essay.

ORGANIZING

As indicated above, writers vary in the extent to which they arrange their material before they begin writing, but most do establish some plan. For you the plan may take the form of a list of key points, a fuller list including specifics as well, or even a detailed formal outline—whatever provides direction for your essay and thus promises to relieve some of the pressure of writing. You will find that some subjects and methods of development demand fuller plans than others: a chronological narrative of a personal experience, for instance, would not require as much prearrangement as a comparison of two complex social policies. Most of the methods of development also suggest specific structures, as you will find in reading the chapter introductions and essays.

As you plan the organization of your essay, you should also be thinking of how you want to begin and end it. This is not to suggest that you must draft a conclusion or even an introduction before drafting the body of the essay. In fact, effective openings and closings often do not become apparent until after the main part has been drafted. But by considering at this stage how you want to approach readers and what you want to leave them with, you may find it easier to channel your thoughts while writing. The basic **introduction** draws readers into the essay and focuses their attention on the main idea and purpose—often stated in a thesis sentence. The basic **conclusion** ties together the elements of the essay and provides a final impression for readers to take away with them. But these basic forms allow considerable room for variation. Especially as you are developing your writing skills, you will find it helpful to state your thesis sentence near the beginning of the essay; but sometimes you can place it effectively at the end, or you can let it direct what you say in the essay but never state it at all. One essay may need two paragraphs of introduction but only a one-sentence conclusion, whereas another essay may require no formal introduction but a lengthy conclusion. How you begin and end depends on your subject and purpose, the kind of essay you are writing, and the likely responses of your readers. Specific ideas for opening and closing essays are included in each chapter introduction and in the Glossary under **introductions** and **conclusions**.

DRAFTING

However detailed your organizational plan is, you should not view it as a rigid taskmaster while you are drafting your essay. If you are like most writers, you will discover much of what you have to say while drafting. Not even the most elaborate outline can anticipate how ideas will shift and rearrange themselves when a few words must be expanded into complete sentences, when thoughts that were once listed must be linked smoothly and logically, and when general state-ments and supporting details must be shaped into paragraphs. In fact, if your subject is complex or difficult for you to write about, you may need several drafts just to work out your ideas and their relationships.

While drafting, concentrate on *what* you are saying, not on *how* you are saying it. Awkwardness, repetition, wrong words, grammati-cal errors, spelling mistakes—these and other more superficial con-cerns can be attended to in a later draft. The same goes for considering your readers' needs. Like many writers, you may find that attention to readers during the first draft inhibits the flow of ideas. If so, then postpone that attention until the second or third draft.

You may find it helpful to start your draft with your thesis sen-tence—or to keep it in front of you as you write—as a reminder of your purpose and main idea. But if you find yourself pulled away from the thesis by a new idea, you may want to let go and follow, at least for a while. After all, drafting is your opportunity to find what you have to say. If your purpose and main idea change as a result of such exploration, you can always revise your thesis accordingly.

Here is the first draft of Grace Patterson's essay on homelessness, written in response to Ascher's essay. The draft is very rough, with frequent repetitions, wandering paragraphs, and many other flaws. But these weaknesses are not important. The draft gave Patterson the opportunity to discover what she had to say, fill out her ideas, and link them in rough sequence.

First Draft

Title?

In the essay, "The Box Man," Barbara Ascher says that a homeless man who has chosen solitude can show the rest of us how to "find . . . a friend in our own voice." Maybe. But her case depends on the Box Man's choice, her assumption that he had one.

Discussions of the homeless often use the word choice. Many people with enough money can accept the condition of the homeless in America when they tell themselves that many of the homeless chose their lives. That the streets are in fact what they want.

But its not fair to use the word <u>choice</u> here: the
homeless don't get to choose their lives the way most
of the rest of us do. For the homeless people in
America today, there are no good choices.

     What do I mean by a "good choice"? A good choice
is made from a variety of options determined and narrowed down by the chooser. There is plenty of room
for the chooser to make a decision that he will be
satisfied with. When I choose a career, I expect to
make a good choice. There is plenty of interesting
fields worth investigating, and there is lots of rewarding work to be done. It's a choice that opens the
world up and showcases its possibilities. But if it
came time for me to choose a career, and the mayor of
my town came around and told me that I had to choose
between a life of cleaning public toilets and operating a jackhammer on a busy street corner, I would object. That's a lousy choice, and I wouldn't let
anyone force me to make it.

     When the mayor of New York tried to take the
homeless off the streets, some of them didn't want to
go. People assumed that the homeless people who did
not want to get in the mayor's car for a ride to a
city shelter <u>chose</u> to live on the street. But just
because some homeless people chose the street over the
generosity of the mayor does not necessarily mean that
life on the streets is their ideal. We allow ourselves as many options as we can imagine, but we allow
the homeless only two: go to a shelter, or stay where
you are. Who narrowed down the options for the homeless? Who benefits if they go to a shelter? Who suf-
fers if they don't?

     Homeless people are not always better off in

shelters. Last Sunday, I had a conversation with a
man who had lived on the streets for a long time. He
said that he had spent some time in those shelters for
the homeless, and he told me what they were like.
They're crowded and dirty and people have to wait in
long lines for everything. People are constantly being herded around and bossed around. It's dangerous--
drug dealers, beatings, theft. Dehumanizing. It
matches my picture of hell. Some homeless people prefer to have some space to breathe, some autonomy, some
peace for sleeping.

When homeless people sleep in the street, though,
that makes the public uncomfortable. People with
enough money wish the homeless would just disappear.
They don't care where they go. Just out of sight.
I've felt this way too but I'm as uneasy with that reaction as I am at the sight of a person sleeping on
the sidewalk. And I tell myself that this is more
than a question of my comfort. By and large I'm comfortable enough.

The homeless are in a difficult enough situation
without having to take the blame for making the rest
of us feel uncomfortable with our wealth. If we cannot offer the homeless a good set of choices, the opportunity to choose lives that they will be truly
satisfied with then the least we can do is stop dump-
ing on them (?). They're caught between a rock and a
hard place: there are not many places for them to go,
and the places where they can go afford nothing but
suffering.

REVISING

In a rough draft like that above, you have the chance to work out
your meaning without regard for what others may think. Eventually,

though, you must look critically at a draft, seeing it as a reader sees it, mere words on a page that are only as clear, interesting, and significant as you have made them. For most writers, this stage, **revision**, actually divides in two: a phase for fundamental changes in content and structure; and a phase for more superficial changes in style, grammar, and the like. In the first phase, you might ask yourself the following questions:

1. Is your purpose clear and consistent?
2. Do subordinate points relate to the thesis sentence and support it fully?
3. Have you provided enough facts, examples, and other evidence for readers to understand your meaning and find your ideas convincing?
4. Does your organization channel readers' attention as you intended?
5. Does each sentence and each paragraph relate clearly and logically to the ones before and after?

Considering questions like these led Grace Patterson to revise her first draft as shown below. Notice that she made substantial cuts, especially of a digression near the end of the draft. She also revamped the introduction, tightened many passages, and wrote a wholly new conclusion to sharpen her point.

Revised Draft

A Rock and a Hard Place
~~Title?~~

In the essay~~/~~ "The Box Man~~/~~" Barbara Ascher says that a homeless man who has chosen solitude can show the rest of us how to "find . . . a friend in our own voice." Maybe. But ~~her~~ Ascher's case depends on the Box Man's choice, her assumption that he <u>had</u> one.

Discussions of the homeless often use the word <u>choice</u>. Many ~~people with enough money can accept the~~ of us with homes would like to think ~~condition of the homeless in America when they tell themselves~~ that many of the homeless chose their lives. ~~That the streets are in fact what they want. But its not fair to use the word~~ <u>choice</u> ~~here: the~~

~~homeless don't get to choose their lives the way most
of the rest of us do.~~ But ^ For the homeless people in
America today, there are no good choices.

What do I mean by a "good choice"? A good choice
is made from a variety of options determined and narrowed down by the chooser. There is plenty of room
for the chooser to make a decision that he will be
satisfied with. When I choose a career, I expect to
make a good choice. There is plenty of interesting
fields worth investigating, and there is lots of rewarding work to be done. ~~It's a choice that opens the
world up and showcases its possibilities.~~ But if ~~it
came time for me to choose a career, and~~ the mayor of
my town came around and told me that I had to choose
between a life of cleaning public toilets and operating a jackhammer on a busy street corner, I would object. That's a lousy choice, and I wouldn't let
anyone force me to make it.

When the mayor of New York tried to take ~~the~~
homeless ^people off the streets, he likewise offered them a bad choice. ~~some of them didn't want to~~
They could ^ ~~go. People assumed that the homeless people who did
not want to~~ get in the mayor's car for a ride to a
city shelter, or they could stay ~~chose to live~~ on the street. People assumed ~~But just
that the homeless people who refused a ride to the shelter wanted to live
because some homeless people chose the street over the
on the street. But that assumption~~ is not necessarily true. ~~generosity of the mayor does not necessarily mean that
life on the streets is their ideal.~~ We allow our-
selves as many options as we can imagine, but we allow
the homeless only two/, both unpleasant. ~~go to a shelter, or stay where
you are. Who narrowed down the options for the home-
less? Who benefits if they go to a shelter? Who suf-
fers if they don't?~~

Homeless people are not always better off in
shelters. Last Sunday, I had a conversation with a
man who had lived on the streets for a long time. He

said that he had spent some time in those shelters for
the homeless, and he told me what they were like.
~~They're crowded and dirty and people have to wait in~~ **dangerous and dehumanizing. Drug dealing, beatings, and theft are common. The shelters are dirty and crowded, so that residents have to wait in long** ~~long lines for everything. People are constantly be-~~ **lines for everything and are constantly being** ~~ing herded around and~~ bossed around. ~~It's dangerous--~~
~~drug dealers, beatings, theft. Dehumanizing. It~~
~~matches my picture of hell.~~ **No wonder** ~~S~~ome homeless people prefer ~~to have~~ **the street:** some space to breathe, some autonomy, some
peace for sleeping.

~~When homeless people sleep in the street, though,~~
~~that makes the public uncomfortable. People with~~
~~enough money wish the homeless would just disappear.~~
~~They don't care where they go. Just out of sight.~~
~~I've felt this way too but I'm as uneasy with that re-~~
~~action as I am at the sight of a person sleeping on~~
~~the sidewalk. And I tell myself that this is more~~
~~than a question of my comfort. By and large I'm com-~~
~~fortable enough.~~

~~The homeless are in a difficult enough situation~~
~~without having to take the blame for making the rest~~
~~of us feel uncomfortable with our wealth. If we can-~~
~~not offer the homeless a good set of choices, the op-~~
~~portunity to choose lives that they will be truly~~
~~satisfied with then the least we can do is stop dump-~~
~~ing on them (?). They're caught between a rock and a~~
~~hard place: there are not many places for them to go,~~
~~and the places where they can go afford nothing but~~
~~suffering.~~

Focusing on the supposed choices the homeless have may make us feel better, but it distracts attention from the kinds of choices that are really being denied the homeless. The options we take for granted — a job with decent pay, an affordable home — do not belong to the homeless. They're caught between no shelter at all and shelter that dehumanizes, between a rock and a hard place.

As this draft indicates, in revision you consider your readers constantly, for this is your chance to reach them. Having someone read your essay for unclear or unconvincing passages can be very helpful. But since such help isn't always available, you need to develop some method for seeing your work from the point of view of your readers. Try to put your first draft aside for at least a few hours before attempting to revise it; you may have further thoughts in the interval, and you will be able to see your work more objectively when you return to it. To gain even more objectivity, you could try reading the draft aloud, for speaking the words often creates some distance from them. Or you could imagine you are someone else—a friend, perhaps, or a particular person in your intended audience—and read the draft through that person's eyes, as if for the first time. The method itself is unimportant—every writer's is probably unique—but the mental operation of stepping outside yourself and into the minds of your readers is fundamental to good writing.

Focusing on your readers' needs is crucial also in the second phase of revision, **editing**. In editing, however, you turn from what the text says to how it sounds and looks.

1. Are transitions smooth between paragraphs and sentences?
2. Are sentences clear and concise, and do their lengths and structures vary to suit your meaning and purpose?
3. Do concrete, specific words sharpen your meaning?
4. Are details vivid enough to help your readers see your subject as you want them to?
5. Are grammar, punctuation, and spelling correct?

Here is an edited paragraph from Patterson's essay, in which she has responded to questions like these.

Edited Paragraph

~~What do I mean by~~ **A** **a** "good choice"~~?~~ ~~A good choice~~
is **one** made from a variety of options determined and narrowed down by the chooser. ~~There is plenty of room for the chooser to make a decision that he will be satisfied with.~~ When I choose a career, I expect to make a good choice. There **are many** ~~is plenty of~~ interesting fields ~~worth~~ **to** investigating**,** and there is ~~lots of~~ **much** re-

warding work to ~~be done.~~ do. But if the mayor of my town suddenly ~~came around and~~ told me that I ~~had~~ would have to choose between a career ~~life~~ of cleaning public toilets and one of operating a jack-hammer on a busy street corner, I would object. That's a ~~lousy~~ bad choice. ~~and I wouldn't let anyone force me to make it.~~

Once you are satisfied that your essay achieves your purpose and is as clear as possible, prepare the final draft, the one you will submit. Proofread the draft carefully to correct spelling errors, typographical mistakes, and other minor problems. The final draft of Patterson's essay appears below. Compared with the first draft (p. 18), it is not only briefer and easier to read but also clearer and more interesting— all improvements achieved during revision and editing.

Final Draft

A Rock and a Hard Place

In the essay "The Box Man" Barbara Ascher says that a homeless man who has chosen solitude can show the rest of us how to "find . . . a friend in our own voice." Maybe he can. But Ascher's case depends on the Box Man's choice, her assumption that he <u>had</u> one. Discussions of the homeless often involve the word <u>choice</u>. Many of us with homes would like to think that many of the homeless chose their lives. But for the homeless people in America today, there are no good choices.

A "good choice" is one made from a variety of options determined and narrowed down by the chooser. When I choose a career, I expect to make a good choice. There are many interesting fields to investigate, and there is much rewarding work to do. If the mayor of my town suddenly told me that I would have to choose between a career of cleaning public toilets and

one of operating a jackhammer on a busy street corner,
I would object. That's a <u>bad</u> choice.

When the mayor of New York tried to remove the
homeless people from the streets, he offered them a
similarly bad choice. They could get in the mayor's
car for a ride to a city shelter, or they could stay
on the street. People assumed that the homeless people who refused a ride to the shelter <u>wanted</u> to live
on the street. But that assumption is not necessarily
true. We allow ourselves as many options as we can
imagine, but we allow the homeless only two, both
unpleasant.

The fact is that homeless people are not always
better off in shelters. I recently had a conversation
with a man named Alan who had lived on the streets for
a long time. He said that he had spent some time in
shelters for the homeless, and he told me what they
are like. They're dangerous and dehumanizing. Drug
dealing, beatings, and theft are common. The shelters
are dirty and crowded, so that residents have to wait
in long lines for everything and are constantly being
bossed around. No wonder some homeless people, including Alan, prefer the street: it affords some space
to breathe, some autonomy, some peace for sleeping.

Focusing on the supposed choices the homeless
have may make us feel better. But it distracts our
attention from something more important than our comfort: the options we take for granted—a job with decent pay, an affordable home—are denied the homeless.
These people are caught between no shelter at all and
shelter that dehumanizes, between a rock and a hard
place.

In finishing with revision and editing, we have circled back to the beginning of this chapter. Good writers are good readers. Reading the essays in this book will give you pleasure and set you thinking. But analyzing and writing about them will also increase your flexibility as a writer and train you to read your own work critically.

Chapter 1

Description

Understanding the Method

Whenever we use words to depict or re-create a scene, object, person, or feeling, we use **description**. We draw on the perceptions of our five senses—sight, hearing, smell, taste, and touch—to understand and communicate our experience of the world. Description is a mainstay of conversation between people, and it is likely to figure in almost any writing situation: a letter home may describe a new roommate's spiky yellow hair; a laboratory report may describe the colors and odors of chemicals; a business memo may distinguish between the tastes of two competitors' chicken potpies.

The writer's purpose in writing and involvement with the subject will largely determine how objective or subjective a description is. In **objective description** the writer strives for precision and objectivity, trying to convey the subject impersonally, without emotion. This is the kind of description required in scientific writing—for instance, a medical diagnosis or a report on an experiment in psychology—where cold facts and absence of bias are essential for readers to judge the accuracy of procedures and results. It is also the method of news reports and of reference works such as encyclopedias. **Subjective description**, in contrast, draws explicitly on the writer's biases, giving an impression of the subject filtered through the writer's emotional experience of it. Instead of withdrawing to the background, the writer invests his or her feelings in the subject and lets those feelings determine which details to describe and how to describe them. The writer's state of mind—perhaps loneliness, anger, joy—can be re-created by reference to sensory details such as numbness, heat, or sweetness.

In general, writers favor objective description when their purpose is explanation and subjective description when their purpose is self-expression or entertainment. But the categories are not exclusive, and most descriptive writing mixes the two. A news report on a tropical storm, for instance, might objectively describe bent and broken trees, fallen wires, and lashing rains, but the writer's selection of details would give a subjective impression of the storm's fearsomeness.

Whether objective or subjective or a mixture of the two, effective description requires a **dominant impression**—a central theme or idea about the subject to which readers can relate all the details. The dominant impression may be something the writer sees in the subject, such as the apparent purposefulness of city pedestrians or the expressiveness of an actor. Or it may derive from the writer's emotional response to the subject, perhaps pleasure (or depression) at all the purposefulness, perhaps admiration (or disdain) for the actor's technique. Whatever its source, the dominant impression serves as a unifying principle that guides the writer's selection of details and the reader's understanding of the subject.

To help readers imagine the subject, writers use specific, concrete language that appeals directly to readers' experiences and senses. The description that relies entirely on general or abstract words either leaves readers with no distinct impressions at all or forces them to supply their own meanings from their own experiences of the words. Saying that "Beautiful, scented wildflowers were in the field," for instance, leaves readers to imagine the color and size of the flowers, their odor, the size of the field, and so on—an assignment most readers will not bother to tackle. To see and smell flowers and the field as the writer did, readers need words more concrete than *beautiful*, more specific than *wildflowers* and *field*. They need something like this: "Backlighted by the sun and smelling faintly sweet, an acre of tiny lavender flowers spread away before me." Much description depends on **figures of speech,** expressions that use words in other than their literal meanings. Most figures of speech compare two unlike subjects to achieve special vividness. The field of wildflowers, for instance, might be described as "a giant's bed covered in a quilt of lavender dots" (a metaphor), or the backlighted flowers might be said to "glow like tiny lavender lamps" (a simile). (See the Glossary under *figures of speech* for fuller discussions of metaphor, simile, and others.)

Besides specific, concrete language, another aid to creating a dominant impression is a consistent **point of view,** a position from which the writer approaches the subject. Point of view is partly the writer's real or imagined *physical* relation to the subject: a mountain could be viewed from the bottom looking up, from fifteen miles away across a valley, or from an airplane passing overhead. The first two points of view are fixed because the observer stands in one position and scans the scene from there; the third is moving because the observer changes position.

Point of view also involves the writer's *psychological* relation to the subject, a relation partly conveyed by pronouns. In subjective description, where the writer's feelings are part of the message, *I* and *you* are often used freely to narrow the distance between writer and subject and writer and reader. But in the most objective, impersonal description, the writer may use *one* ("One can see the summit . . .") or avoid self-reference altogether in order to appear distant from and unbiased toward the subject.

Once a writer establishes a physical and psychological point of view, readers come to depend on it. Thus a sudden and inexplicable shift from one view to another—zooming in from fifteen miles away to the foot of a mountain, abandoning *I* for the more removed *one*—can disorient readers and distract them from the dominant impression the writer is trying to create.

Analyzing Description in Paragraphs

George Packer (born 1960) writes nonfiction and fiction, mostly about the people and places of the Third World. The following paragraph comes from Packer's *The Village of Waiting* (1988), an account of his experience as a Peace Corps volunteer in Togo, West Africa. The subject, Christine, was Packer's landlady in the small village of Lavié. The description is both objective (in most of its details) and subjective (in its impression).

Christine's French came from the market women of Abidjan, Ivory Coast, where the family had spent some years. She was a woman of real beauty: the high, shiny cheekbones that give some Africans an Oriental look; dark, underslept, abstracted eyes; a full and expressive mouth; skin the color of rosewood. At thirty-five, after nine children in fifteen years (a twin of Atsu had died), her body was thin and strong and exhausted. Sometimes when she wasn't wearing a scarf, and her long hair was unbraided and uncombed, she had a wild gypsy look. And something about that look, and her shouts during the day at the children, and the nighttime quarrels with Benjamin that I began to overhear, usually about money, and then the tired smile she put on for me the next morning, said that she wasn't happy here.

Specific, concrete details (underlined)

Point of view: fixed; psychologically somewhat distant

Dominant impression: fatigue, strength, unhappiness

Sallie Tisdale (born 1957) is a registered nurse and a writer of nonfiction about the nursing profession and other subjects. The paragraph below is from "The Only Harmless Great Thing" (1989), an essay about elephants that was printed in *The New Yorker* magazine. Belle is a female Asian elephant (called a "cow") in the Washington Park Zoo in Portland, Oregon. The description is largely subjective, with the emphasis on Tisdale's response to Belle.

Down the hall, Belle has planted her face against the crack of a door. Behind her in the room is a trio of younger cows. The elephant guards the tree of life; the elephant worships the moon and stars. Elephants were once supposed to have had wings. Belle greets me with a grim stare, blocking me like a house matron uncertain whether I'm fit to be let in. I stand quietly for the inspection. Her trunk slides up, loose and confident, and rapidly slips under my collar, through my hair, down my sleeve, my pant leg. This close, her trunk is enormous, the two huffing nostrils at the end strangely naked and pink, vacuuming in my smell, my volatiles, my

Specific, concrete details (underlined once)

Figures of speech (underlined twice)

Point of view: fixed, with simultaneous memory of photographs (next page); psychologically close

self. All the while, she fixes her <u>moist brown eye</u>
on mine. I remember—because I can't forget—
photographs I've seen of butchered elephants.
What was left of one bull <u>knelt in apparent</u>
<u>calm</u>. The <u>body, its head missing</u>, was eerily
<u>still</u>, as though waiting. John Donne called the
elephant "Nature's great masterpiece . . . the
only harmless great thing." As I submit to
Belle's <u>precise, intelligent examination</u>, I remember that and the dead elephant's calm, and
look straight back into her <u>cautious and curious</u>   *Dominant impression:*
<u>eye</u>.   *guardedness, calm, and*
    grandeur

Developing a Descriptive Essay

GETTING STARTED

The subject for a descriptive essay may be any object, place, person, or state of mind that you have observed closely enough or experienced sharply enough to invest with special significance. A chair, a
tree, a room, a shopping mall, a movie actor, a passerby on the street,
a feeling of fear, a sense of achievement—anything you have a strong
impression of can prompt effective description.

When you have your subject, specify in a sentence the impression
that you want to create for readers. The sentence will help keep you
on track while you search for details, and later it may serve as the
thesis of your essay. It should evoke a quality or an atmosphere or an
effect, as these examples do: "His fierce anger at the world shows in
every word and gesture"; "The mall is a thoroughly unnatural place,
like a space station in a science-fiction movie."

A sentence like these should give you a good start in choosing the
sensory details that will make your description concrete and vivid.
Observe your subject directly, if possible, or recall it as completely as
you can. Whether it is in front of you or in your mind, you may find it
helpful to consider the subject one sense at a time—what you can see,
hear, smell, touch, taste. Of course, not all senses will be applicable to
all subjects; a chair, for instance, may not have a noticeable odor, and
you're unlikely to know its taste. But proceeding sense by sense can
help you uncover details, such as the smell of a tree or the sound of a
person's voice, that you might otherwise have overlooked. Examining

one sense at a time is also one of the best ways to conceive of concrete words and figures of speech to represent sensations and feelings. For instance, does *acid* describe the taste of fear? Does an actor's appearance suggest the smell of soap? Does a shopping mall smell like new dollar bills? In creating distinct physical sensations for readers, such representations make meaning inescapably clear.

Opening your mind to the possibilities of your subject may distract you from the dominant impression you originally decided to create. At some point, then, you will want to recall that impression, revise it if your collection of details seems to create a different impression, and trim away the details that add little or nothing to the whole. Also at this stage, if you have not done so already, you should consider the needs and expectations of your readers. If the subject is something readers have never seen or felt before, you will need enough objective details to create a complete picture in their minds. A description of a friend, for example, might focus on his distinctive voice and laugh, but readers will also want to know something about his appearance. If the subject is essentially abstract, like an emotion, you will need details to make it concrete for readers. And if the subject is familiar to readers, as a shopping mall or an old spruce tree on campus probably would be, you will want to skip obvious objective information in favor of fresh observations that will make readers see the subject anew.

ORGANIZING

Though the details of a subject may not occur to you in any particular order, you should arrange them so that readers are not confused by rapid shifts among features. You can give readers a sense of the whole subject in the introduction to the essay: objective details of location or size or shape, the incident leading to a state of mind, or the reasons for describing a familiar object. In the introduction, also, you may want to state your thesis—the dominant impression you will create. An explicit thesis is not essential in description; sometimes you may prefer to let the details build to a conclusion. But the thesis should hover over the essay nonetheless, governing the selection of every detail and making itself as clear to readers as if it were stated outright.

The organization of the body of the essay depends partly on point of view and partly on dominant impression. If you take a moving point of view—say, strolling down a city street—the details will probably arrange themselves naturally. But a fixed point of view, scanning a subject from one position, requires your intervention. When the subject is a landscape, a person, or an object, a spatial organization may be appropriate: near to far, top to bottom, left to right, or vice versa. Other subjects, such as a shopping mall, might be better treated in groups of features: shoppers, main concourses, insides of stores. Or a description of an emotional state might follow the chronological sequence of the event that aroused it (thus overlapping description and narration, the subject of the next chapter). The order itself is not important, as long as there is an order that channels readers' attention.

DRAFTING

With your details listed and arranged, the challenge of drafting your description will be finding the concrete and specific words to make the subject live in readers' minds. To describe a man's walk, for instance, you could write simply, "He walked funny"; but that sentence creates no picture in readers' minds. What's needed is language that *shows* the man's walk much as a film would—perhaps "With each bowlegged step he rolled from heel to toe on the outside edge of the shoe." When you are trying to describe something abstract, such as an emotion, work for figures of speech that appeal to the senses. Instead of "I felt remote," for instance, you might write "I felt as if I were a hundred feet down a well."

A thesaurus or dictionary of synonyms can help you find the precise word to express your meaning, but be careful not to abuse reference books. *Concrete* and *specific* do not mean "fancy": good description does not demand five-dollar words when nickel equivalents are just as informative. The writer who uses *rubiginous* instead of *rusty red* actually says less because fewer readers will understand the less common word. When you get stuck for a word, conjure up your subject and see it, hear it, touch it, smell it, taste it. Then try to help your readers do the same with the clearest, sharpest sensory details.

REVISING

When you are ready to revise, use the following questions as a guide.

1. *Have you in fact created the dominant impression you intended*

to create? Check that every detail helps to pin down one crucial feature of your subject. Cut irrelevant details that may have crept in. What counts is not the number of details but their quality and the strength of the impression they make.

2. *Are your point of view and organization clear and consistent?* Watch for confusing shifts from one vantage point or organizational scheme to another. Watch also for confusing and unnecessary shifts in pronouns, such as from *I* to *one* or vice versa. Any shifts in point of view or organization should be clearly essential for your purpose and for the impression you want to create.

3. *Have you used the most specific, concrete language you can muster?* Keep a sharp eye out for vague words like *delicious, handsome, loud,* and *short* that force readers to create their own impressions or, worse, leave them with no impression at all. Using details that call on readers' sensory experiences, say why delicious or why handsome, how loud or how short. At the same time, cut or change fancy language that simply calls attention to itself without adding to your meaning.

Annie Dillard

A poet and essayist, Annie Dillard is part naturalist, part philosopher, part mystic. She was born in 1945 in Pittsburgh. Growing up in that city, she was an independent child given to exploration and reading. (As an adult, she reads nearly a hundred books a year.) After graduating from Hollins College in the Blue Ridge Mountains of Virginia, Dillard settled in the area to investigate her natural surroundings and to write. Her first book was a collection of poems, Tickets for a Prayer Wheel *(1974). It was closely followed by* Pilgrim at Tinker Creek *(1974), a series of related essays that demonstrate Dillard's intense, passionate involvement with the world of nature and the world of the mind. The book earned her national recognition and a Pulitzer Prize. Partly to escape the resulting attention, she says, Dillard moved to Puget Sound in Washington State, where she taught at Western Washington University.* Holy the Firm *(1977), a prose poem, and* Teaching a Stone to Talk *(1982), a collection of essays, followed her move and revealed more of her open-eyed encounters with nature. She has also published* Living by Fiction *(1982), a collection of critical essays;* Encounters with Chinese Writers *(1984); the autobiography* An American Childhood *(1987); and* The Writing Life *(1989). Dillard currently lives in Connecticut and teaches at Wesleyan University.*

In the Jungle

"We are here to witness," Dillard has written. "If we were not here, material events like the passage of the seasons would lack even the meager meanings we are able to muster for them. The show would play to an empty house." In this essay from Teaching a Stone to Talk, *Dillard witnesses the jungle of Ecuador, a country on the northwestern edge of South America.*

Like any out-of-the-way place, the Napo River in the Ecuadorian 1
jungle seems real enough when you are there, even central. Out of the way of *what?* I was sitting on a stump at the edge of a bankside palm-thatch village, in the middle of the night, on the headwaters of the Amazon. Out of the way of human life, tenderness, or the glance of heaven?

A nightjar in deep-leaved shadow called three long notes, and 2
hushed. The men with me talked softly in clumps: three North Americans, four Ecuadorians who were showing us the jungle. We were

holding cool drinks and idly watching a hand-sized tarantula seize moths that came to the lone bulb on the generator shed beside us.

It was February, the middle of summer. Green fireflies spattered ³ lights across the air and illumined for seconds, now here, now there, the pale trunks of enormous, solitary trees. Beneath us the brown Napo River was rising, in all silence; it coiled up the sandy bank and tangled its foam in vines that trailed from the forest and roots that looped the shore.

Each breath of night smelled sweet, more moistened and sweet ⁴ than any kitchen, or garden, or cradle. Each star in Orion seemed to tremble and stir with my breath. All at once, in the thatch house across the clearing behind us, one of the village's Jesuit priests began playing an alto recorder, playing a wordless song, lyric, in a minor key, that twined over the village clearing, that caught in the big trees' canopies, muted our talk on the bankside, and wandered over the river, dissolving downstream.

This will do, I thought. This will do, for a weekend, or a season, ⁵ or a home.

Later this night I loosed my hair from its braids and combed it ⁶ smooth—not for myself, but so the village girls could play with it in the morning.

We had disembarked at the village that afternoon, and I had ⁷ slumped on some shaded steps, wishing I knew some Spanish or some Quechua so I could speak with the ring of little girls who were alternately staring at me and smiling at their toes. I spoke anyway, and fooled with my hair, which they were obviously dying to get their hands on, and laughed, and soon they were all braiding my hair, all five of them, all fifty fingers, all my hair, even my bangs. And then they took it apart and did it again, laughing, and teaching me Spanish nouns, and meeting my eyes and each other's with open delight, while their small brothers in blue jeans climbed down from the trees and began kicking a volleyball around with one of the North American men.

Now, as I combed my hair in the little tent, another of the men, a ⁸ free-lance writer from Manhattan, was talking quietly. He was telling us the tale of his life, describing his work in Hollywood, his apartment in Manhattan, his house in Paris. . . . "It makes me wonder," he said, "what I'm doing in a tent under a tree in the village of Pompeya, on the Napo River, in the jungle of Ecuador." After a pause he added, "It makes me wonder why I'm going *back*."

The point of going somewhere like the Napo River in Ecuador is   9
not to see the most spectacular anything. It is simply to see what is
there. We are here on the planet only once, and might as well get a feel
for the place. We might as well get a feel for the fringes and hollows in
which life is lived, for the Amazon basin, which covers half a continent, and for the life that—there, like anywhere else—is always and
necessarily lived in detail: on the tributaries, in the riverside villages,
sucking this particular white-fleshed guava in this particular pattern
of shade.

What is there is interesting. The Napo River itself is wide (I mean   10
wider than the Mississippi at Davenport) and brown, opaque, and
smeared with floating foam and logs and branches from the jungle.
White egrets hunch on shoreline deadfalls and parrots in flocks dart in
and out of the light. Under the water in the river, unseen, are anacondas—which are reputed to take a few village toddlers every year—
and water boas, stingrays, crocodiles, manatees, and sweet-meated
fish.

Low water bares gray strips of sandbar on which the natives build   11
tiny palm-thatch shelters, arched, the size of pup tents, for overnight
fishing trips. You see these extraordinarily clean people (who bathe
twice a day in the river, and whose straight black hair is always
freshly washed) paddling down the river in dugout canoes, hugging
the banks.

Some of the Indians of this region, earlier in the century, used to   12
sleep naked in hammocks. The nights are cold. Gordon MacCreach,
an American explorer in these Amazon tributaries, reported that he
was startled to hear the Indians get up at three in the morning. He was
even more startled, night after night, to hear them walk down to the
river slowly, half asleep, and bathe in the water. Only later did he
learn what they were doing: they were getting warm. The cold woke
them; they warmed their skins in the river, which was always ninety
degrees; then they returned to their hammocks and slept through the
rest of the night.

The riverbanks are low, and from the river you see an unbroken   13
wall of dark forest in every direction, from the Andes to the Atlantic.
You get a taste for looking at trees: trees hung with the swinging nests
of yellow troupials, trees from which ant nests the size of grain sacks
hang like black goiters, trees from which seven-colored tanagers flutter, coral trees, teak, balsa and breadfruit, enormous emergent silk-
cotton trees, and the pale-barked *samona* palms.

When you are inside the jungle, away from the river, the trees *14*
vault out of sight. It is hard to remember to look up the long trunks
and see the fans, strips, fronds, and sprays of glossy leaves. Inside the
jungle you are more likely to notice the snarl of climbers and creepers
round the trees' boles, the flowering bromeliads and epiphytes in every bough's crook, and the fantastic silk-cotton tree trunks thirty or
forty feet across, trunks buttressed in flanges of wood whose curves
can make three high walls of a room—a shady, loamy-aired room
where you would gladly live, or die. Butterflies, iridescent blue,
striped, or clearwinged, thread the jungle paths at eye level. And at
your feet is a swath of ants bearing triangular bits of green leaf. The
ants with their leaves look like a wide fleet of sailing dinghies—but
they don't quit. In either direction they wobble over the jungle floor as
far as the eye can see. I followed them off the path as far as I dared,
and never saw an end to ants or to those luffing chips of green they
bore.

Unseen in the jungle, but present, are tapirs, jaguars, many species *15*
of snake and lizard, ocelots, armadillos, marmosets, howler monkeys,
toucans and macaws and a hundred other birds, deer, bats, peccaries,
capybaras, agoutis, and sloths. Also present in this jungle, but var-
iously distant, are Texaco derricks and pipelines, and some of the
wildest Indians in the world, blowgun-using Indians, who killed mis-
sionaries in 1956 and ate them.

Long lakes shine in the jungle. We traveled one of these in dugout *16*
canoes, canoes with two inches of freeboard, canoes paddled with
machete-hewn oars chopped from buttresses of silk-cotton trees, or
poled in the shallows with peeled cane or bamboo. Our part-Indian
guide had cleared the path to the lake the day before; when we
walked the path we saw where he had impaled the lopped head of a
boa, open-mouthed, on a pointed stick by the canoes, for decoration.

The lake was wonderful. Herons, egrets, and ibises plodded the *17*
sawgrass shores, kingfishers and cuckoos clattered from sunlight to
shade, great turkeylike birds fussed in dead branches, and hawks
lolled overhead. There was all the time in the world. A turtle slid into
the water. The boy in the bow of my canoe slapped stones at birds
with a simple sling, a rubber thong and leather pad. He aimed bril-
liantly at moving targets, always, and always missed; the birds were
out of range. He stuffed his sling back in his shirt. I looked around.

The lake and river waters are as opaque as rain-forest leaves; they *18*
are veils, blinds, painted screens. You see things only by their effects. I

saw the shoreline water roil and the sawgrass heave above a thrashing *paichi,* an enormous black fish of these waters; one had been caught the previous week weighting 430 pounds. Piranha fish live in the lakes, and electric eels. I dangled my fingers in the water, figuring it would be worth it.

We would eat chicken that night in the village, and rice, yucca, *19* onions, beets, and heaps of fruit. The sun would ring down, pulling darkness after it like a curtain. Twilight is short, and the unseen birds of twilight wistful, uncanny, catching the heart. The two nuns in their dazzling white habits—the beautiful-boned young nun and the warm-faced old—would glide to the open cane-and-thatch schoolroom in darkness, and start the children singing. The children would sing in piping Spanish, high-pitched and pure; they would sing "Nearer My God to Thee" in Quechua, very fast. (To reciprocate, we sang for them "Old MacDonald Had a Farm"; I thought they might recognize the animal sounds. Of course they thought we were out of our minds.) As the children became excited by their own singing, they left their log benches and swarmed around the nuns, hopping, smiling at us, every-one smiling, the nuns' faces bursting in their cowls, and the clear-voiced children still singing, and the palm-leafed roofing stirred.

The Napo River: it is not out of the way. It is *in* the way, catching *20* sunlight the way a cup catches poured water; it is a bowl of sweet air, a basin of greenness, and of grace, and, it would seem, of peace.

Meaning

1. In the last paragraph of her essay, Dillard says that the Napo River jungle "is a bowl of sweet air, a basin of greenness, and of grace, and, it would seem, of peace." To what extent does this sentence summarize the dominant impression of Dillard's description? What would you add to the sentence or delete from it to state the dominant impression Dillard creates for you?

2. What commonly understood meanings does Dillard imply for the expression "out-of-the-way place"—especially in paragraphs 1, 8, 9, and 20? What features of the Napo River jungle and the people who live there lead her to insist that the jungle is *not* out of the way?

3. If you do not know the meanings of the following words, look them up in a dictionary: illumined (paragraph 3); twined (4); disembarked (7); tributaries (9); goiters (13); boles, buttressed, flanges, loamy, iridescent, swath, dinghies, luffing (14); impaled (16); roil (18); wistful, uncanny, reciprocate, cowls (19).

Purpose and Audience

1. Why did Dillard travel to the Napo River jungle? Why do you think she wrote about it? How are her reasons for traveling to the jungle and her purpose in writing the essay related?
2. Dillard presents contrasting images of the jungle; for instance, a description of the jungle's startling beauty is closely followed by a brief tale of murderous Indians (paragraphs 14–15). How do these contrasting details serve Dillard's purpose?
3. Why does Dillard mention so many animals and plants? In paragraph 10, for instance, she mentions egrets, parrots, anacondas, boas, stingrays, crocodiles, and manatees; and other paragraphs are similar. Does she expect readers to be familiar with the animals and plants and their names? If so, is that a reasonable expectation? If not, what effect might Dillard want to achieve by including them? Do you think they strengthen the essay or weaken it? Why?

Method and Structure

1. Why is description a particularly appropriate way for Dillard to develop her subject and achieve her purpose?
2. Locate several examples of objective description and several of subjective description in Dillard's essay. What does each type of description contribute to the essay? What about her purpose leads Dillard to rely chiefly on subjective description?
3. Dillard's essay is divided into three sections; two short ones (paragraphs 1–5, 6–8) and then a third longer one (9–20). What purpose does each section serve? What is the relationship of each section to the others? Why do the lengths of the sections vary?
4. **Other Methods** Dillard's description is filled with examples (Chapter 3), as noted in the last question under Purpose and Audience. Dillard also provides brief narratives (Chapter 2), such as the story of the girls braiding her hair (paragraph 7). What other examples of narrative do you find in the essay? What does each contribute to Dillard's description?

Language

1. What is Dillard's apparent attitude toward the jungle and its human inhabitants: delight? fear? awe? serenity? curiosity? a combination? Support your answer with specific words and phrases from the essay.
2. Dillard re-creates her impressions with concrete words that appeal to

readers' senses. Look, for instance, at the verbs "plodded," "clattered," "fussed," "lolled," "slid," and "slapped" in paragraph 17. Locate ten or twelve other examples of concrete language. What sense or senses does each one appeal to?

3. Dillard uses several figures of speech, such as the Napo River's "catching sunlight the way a cup catches poured water" (paragraph 20). Find two or three other figures of speech and analyze how each one contributes to Dillard's meaning and helps convey her attitude toward the jungle. (If necessary, consult *figures of speech* in the Glossary.)

4. Dillard occasionally shifts from *I* or *we* with past-tense verbs (*was, called*) to *you* with present-tense verbs (*see, look*). See, for instance, paragraph 14. Does Dillard seem to have a reason for using *you* and present-tense verbs? If so, what is it? If not, do you think the inconsistency weakens the essay?

Writing Topics

1. Think of an out-of-the-way place to which you feel a special connection. The place may be rural or urban or suburban, and it need not be far away. In an essay, describe the place for readers who are completely unfamiliar with it and who may be skeptical about your enthusiasm for it. Use concrete, specific details and, if appropriate, figures of speech to show clearly why you value the place.

2. Reread Dillard's essay, paying particular attention to her use of concrete words and figures of speech that appeal to the senses. Choose the sensory details and language that you find most powerful or suggestive, and write a brief essay explaining how they contribute to Dillard's dominant impression of the Napo River jungle.

3. In a travel magazine or the travel section of a newspaper, read a description of a place you are unfamiliar with. Then write a comparison of that piece and Dillard's essay, explaining which you find more interesting and why. To what extent do the authors' different purposes and audiences account for the differences you perceive in the essays?

——— Joan Didion ———

One of America's leading nonfiction writers, Joan Didion consistently applies a journalist's eye for detail and a terse, understated style to the cultural dislocation pervading modern American society. She was born in 1934 in Sacramento, a fifth-generation Californian, and she has attended closely to the distinctive people and places of the American West. After graduating from the University of California at Berkeley in 1956, Didion lived for nearly a decade in New York City before returning permanently to California. She has contributed to many periodicals, including Vogue, Life, Esquire, *and* The American Scholar, *and her essays have been collected in* Slouching Towards Bethlehem *(1968),* The White Album *(1979), and* Essays and Conversations *(1984). Didion has also published four novels:* Run River *(1963),* Play It as It Lays *(1970),* A Book of Common Prayer *(1977), and* Democracy *(1984). With her husband, the writer John Gregory Dunne, she has written screenplays for movies, among them* Panic in Needle Park *(1971),* A Star Is Born *(1976), and* True Confessions *(1981). Didion's latest book,* Miami *(1987), takes a level look at that fast-growing and intense city.*

Death in El Salvador

El Salvador is a small Central American country where political unrest and violence grew out of a protracted civil war between leftist guerrillas and rightist military and civilian regimes. American support for the Salvadoran government has generated controversy in the United States as well, and in 1982 Didion visited the country to see for herself what was going on. In Salvador *(1983), the book from which the following selection is taken, Didion etches a memorable picture of a nightmarish place.*

The three-year-old El Salvador International Airport is glassy and white and splendidly isolated, conceived during the waning of the Molina "National Transformation"[1] as convenient less to the capital (San Salvador is forty miles away, until recently a drive of several

---

[1] Colonel Arturo Armando Molina became president of El Salvador in 1972. His "National Transformation," following economic depression and a war with neighboring Honduras in the late 1960s, included removal of political opponents from the government and the National University. General Carlos Humberto Romero, mentioned later in the sentence, succeeded Molina as president in 1977. [Editor's note.]

hours) than to a central hallucination of the Molina and Romero regimes, the projected beach resorts, the Hyatt, the Pacific Paradise, tennis, golf, water-skiing, condos, *Costa del Sol*; the visionary invention of a tourist industry in yet another republic where the leading natural cause of death is gastrointestinal infection. In the general absence of tourists these hotels have since been abandoned, ghost resorts on the empty Pacific beaches, and to land at this airport built to service them is to plunge directly into a state in which no ground is solid, no depth of field reliable, no perception so definite that it might not dissolve into its reverse.

The only logic is that of acquiescence. Immigration is negotiated   2
in a thicket of automatic weapons, but by whose authority the weapons are brandished (Army or National Guard or National Police or Customs Police or Treasury Police or one of a continuing proliferation of other shadowy and overlapping forces) is a blurred point. Eye contact is avoided. Documents are scrutinized upside down. Once clear of the airport, on the new highway that slices through green hills rendered phosphorescent by the cloud cover of the tropical rainy season, one sees mainly underfed cattle and mongrel dogs and armored vehicles, vans and trucks and Cherokee Chiefs fitted with reinforced steel and bulletproof Plexiglas an inch thick. Such vehicles are a fixed feature of local life, and are popularly associated with disappearance and death. There was the Cherokee Chief seen following the Dutch television crew killed in Chalatenango province in March of 1982. There was the red Toyota three-quarter-ton pickup sighted near the van driven by the four American Catholic workers on the night they were killed in 1980. There were, in the late spring and summer of 1982, the three Toyota panel trucks, one yellow, one blue, and one green, none bearing plates, reported present at each of the mass detentions (a "detention" is another fixed feature of local life, and often precedes a "disappearance") in the Amatepec district of San Salvador. These are the details—the models and colors of armored vehicles, the makes and calibers of weapons, the particular methods of dismemberment and decapitation used in particular instances—on which the visitor to Salvador learns immediately to concentrate, to the exclusion of past or future concerns, as in a prolonged amnesiac fugue.

Terror is the given of the place. Black-and-white police cars cruise   3
in pairs, each with the barrel of a rifle extruding from an open window. Roadblocks materialize at random, soldiers fanning out from trucks and taking positions, fingers always on triggers, safeties click-

ing on and off. Aim is taken as if to pass the time. Every morning *El Diario de Hoy* and *La Prensa Gráfica* carry cautionary stories. "*Una madre y sus dos hijos fueron asesinados con arma cortante (corvo) por ocho sujetos desconocidos el lunes en la noche*": A mother and her two sons hacked to death in their beds by eight *desconocidos*, unknown men. The same morning's paper: the unidentified body of a young man, strangled, found on the shoulder of a road. Same morning, different story: the unidentified bodies of three young men, found on another road, their faces partially destroyed by bayonets, one face carved to represent a cross.

It is largely from these reports in the newspapers that the United States embassy compiles its body counts, which are transmitted to Washington in a weekly dispatch referred to by embassy people as "the grimgram." These counts are presented in a kind of tortured code that fails to obscure what is taken for granted in El Salvador, that government forces do most of the killing. In a January 15 1982 memo to Washington, for example, the embassy issued a "guarded" breakdown on its count of 6,909 "reported" political murders between September 16 1980 and September 15 1981. Of these 6,909, according to the memo, 922 were "believed committed by security forces," 952 "believed committed by leftist terrorists," 136 "believed committed by rightist terrorists," and 4,889 "committed by unknown assailants," the famous *desconocidos* favored by those San Salvador newspapers still publishing. (The figures actually add up not to 6,909 but to 6,899, leaving ten in a kind of official limbo.) The memo continued:

> The uncertainty involved here can be seen in the fact that responsibility cannot be fixed in the majority of cases. We note, however, that it is generally believed in El Salvador that a large number of the unexplained killings are carried out by the security forces, officially or unofficially. The Embassy is aware of dramatic claims that have been made by one interest group or another in which the security forces figure as the primary agents of murder here. El Salvador's tangled web of attack and vengeance, traditional criminal violence and political mayhem make this an impossible charge to sustain. In saying this, however, we make no attempt to lighten the responsibility for the deaths of many hundreds, and perhaps thousands, which can be attributed to the security forces. . . .

The body count kept by what is generally referred to in San Salvador as "the Human Rights Commission" is higher than the embassy's, and documented periodically by a photographer who goes out looking for bodies. These bodies he photographs are often broken into unnatural positions, and the faces to which the bodies are attached (when they are attached) are equally unnatural, sometimes unrecognizable as human faces, obliterated by acid or beaten to a mash of misplaced ears and teeth or slashed ear to ear and invaded by insects. *"Encontrado en Antiguo Cuscatlán el día 25 de Marzo 1982: camison de dormir celeste,"* the typed caption reads on one photograph: found in Antiguo Cuscatlán March 25 1982 wearing a sky-blue nightshirt. The captions are laconic. Found in Soyapango May 21 1982. Found in Mejicanos June 11 1982. Found at El Playón May 30 1982, white shirt, purple pants, black shoes. . . .

All forensic photographs induce in the viewer a certain protective   6 numbness, but dissociation is more difficult here. In the first place these are not, technically, "forensic" photographs, since the evidence they document will never be presented in a court of law. In the second place the disfigurement is too routine. The locations are too near, the dates too recent. There is the presence of the relatives of the disappeared: the women who sit every day in this cramped office on the grounds of the archdiocese, waiting to look at the spiral-bound photo albums in which the photographs are kept. These albums have plastic covers bearing soft-focus color photographs of young Americans in dating situations (strolling through autumn foliage on one album, recumbent in a field of daisies on another), and the women, looking for the bodies of their husbands and brothers and sisters and children, pass them from hand to hand without comment or expression.

Meaning

1. In the last sentence of paragraph 2 Didion says that the visitor to El Salvador focuses on certain hard and gory details "to the exclusion of past or future concerns, as in a prolonged amnesiac fugue." *Amnesia*, as you probably know, is a loss of memory. A *fugue* is a psychological condition in which one flees an unbearable situation by becoming someone else, with no knowledge of one's real self. How does this sentence forecast and capture the dominant impression created by Didion's description?

2. What does Didion mean by "The only logic is that of acquiescence" (paragraph 2)? Acquiescence to what or to whom? Why is it the "only logic"?

3. If you do not know the meaning of the following words, look them up in a dictionary: gastrointestinal (paragraph 1); acquiescence, brandished, scrutinized, phosphorescent, dismemberment, decapitation (2); extrud-

ing (3); limbo, vengeance, mayhem (4); obliterated, laconic (5); forensic, induce, dissociation (6).

Purpose and Audience

1. What seems to be Didion's purpose in this selection: to explain the roots of the violence in El Salvador? to generate readers' sympathy toward the victims? to convince readers to oppose U.S. involvement in El Salvador? to make readers see the situation there in unaccustomed ways? What passages support your answer?
2. Given her purpose, why does Didion ignore the social, economic, and political causes of the situation in El Salvador?
3. Do the grisly details in paragraph 3 and especially paragraph 5 shock or revolt you? If so, did Didion intend for you to have this reaction? Why, or why not?

Method and Structure

1. Didion does not make herself a direct participant in the situation she describes, and many of her details and her quotations from newspapers suggest the objective approach of the news reporter. In which sentences, then, it is especially apparent that Didion is interpreting the situation subjectively?
2. How does Didion's organization—first scene and mood (paragraphs 1–3), then the "official" scope of violence (4), then its effects in detail (5–6)—contribute to her dominant impression and purpose?
3. **Other Methods** Paragraphs 2, 3, 5, and 6 are developed largely by example (see Chapter 3). What do the examples in each paragraph contribute to Didion's dominant impression and purpose?

Language

1. Didion's tone is almost matter-of-fact, but occasionally she introduces a wry, drily amused note, as in "the famous *desconocidos* favored by those San Salvador newspapers still publishing," presumably government-approved newspapers (paragraph 4). What other similarly wry details or comments do you find in the essay? What do these touches convey about Didion's attitude toward her subject? (If necessary, consult the Glossary for an explanation of *tone*.)
2. What effect does Didion achieve by avoiding the first-person *I*, referring to herself as "one" and "the visitor" (paragraph 2) and "the viewer" (6)?

And why does she describe the situation in the present tense ("is," "learns")? How do these choices contribute to Didion's "amnesiac fugue"?

3. Didion peppers her description with nouns and verbs of threat, force, and violence (see, for instance, paragraph 3). Locate these nouns and verbs, and consider their cumulative effect. How would the essay be different if Didion had omitted many of these words or used milder substitutes?

Writing Topics

1. Focus on a thing or place or situation that you have found horrifying or outrageous, and write a description designed to elicit similar feelings from your readers. Your topic may be quite different from Didion's: emotional abuse, for instance, can have the same power as physical abuse.

2. Read the first paragraph of Didion's essay and examine each descriptive detail closely. Pay special attention to the connotations of words such as "glassy," "hallucination," and "ghost." Write a paragraph explaining how the opening description reflects, supports, and leads the reader into Didion's dominant impression of El Salvador. (If necessary, consult the Glossary for an explanation of *connotation*.)

3. In paragraphs 2, 4, and 5 Didion gives dates of several events in El Salvador. Using periodical indexes such as *The New York Times Index* or *The Readers' Guide to Periodical Literature*, locate at least one article in a newspaper or magazine that describes one of the same incidents or another incident of violence in El Salvador. Write an essay comparing the report with Didion's essay, concentrating on differences and similarities in descriptive details, language, and overall tone.

4. Didion's "Death in El Salvador" (paragraph 6) and Annie Dillard's "In the Jungle" (paragraph 19, p. 40) both end with descriptions of the local people engaged in everyday activities. Write an essay explaining how the ending of each essay reflects each author's view of her subject. Support your explanation with specific words and details from each essay.

Peter Schjeldahl

An art critic and a poet, Peter Schjeldahl was born in 1942 in North Dakota and attended Carleton College in Minnesota. His poetry has been collected in several volumes, including White Country *(1968),* Dreams *(1973), and* Since 1964 *(1978). He is currently the art critic for the New York City weekly* 7 Days *but has also contributed to* The Village Voice, The New York Times, Vanity Fair, Art News, *and other publications. Schjeldahl has written, by his own estimate, "many dozens" of catalogs to accompany exhibits of the work of such artists as Ad Reinhardt, Joan Miró, David Salle, and Cindy Sherman. His latest books are a monograph on the artist Eric Fischl (1988) and a collection of his writings,* The Hydrogen Jukebox *(1990). In 1982 Schjeldahl received the Frank Jewett Mather award for art criticism from the College Art Association. He lives in New York City.*

Cyclone!

In the following essay Schjeldahl describes an experience familiar to most Americans: a roller-coaster ride. The roller coaster is a special one—the Cyclone at Coney Island, the public beach and amusement area in Brooklyn, New York City. The essay first appeared in Harper's Magazine *in 1988.*

The Cyclone is art, sex, God, the greatest. It is the most fun you can 1
have without risking bad ethics. I rode the Cyclone seven times one afternoon last summer, and I am here to tell everybody that it is fun for fun's sake, the pure abstract heart of the human capacity for getting a kick out of anything. Yes, it may be anguishing initially. (I promise to tell the truth.) Terrifying, even, the first time or two the train is hauled upward with groans and creaks and with you in it. At the top then—where there is sudden strange quiet but for the fluttering of two tattered flags, and you have a poignantly brief view of Brooklyn, and of ships far out on the Atlantic—you may feel very lonely and that you have made a serious mistake, cursing yourself in the last gleam of the reflective consciousness you are about, abruptly, to leave up there between the flags like an abandoned thought-balloon. To keep yourself company by screaming may help, and no one is noticing: try it. After a couple of rides, panic abates, and after four or five you aren't even frightened, exactly, but *stimulated,* blissed, sent. The squirt of adrenaline you will never cease to have at

the top as the train lumbers, wobbling slightly, into the plunge, finally fuels just happy wonderment because you can't, and never will, *believe* what is going to happen.

Every roller coaster has that first, immense drop. In practical 2 terms, it provides the oomph for the entire ride, which is of course impelled by nothing but ecologically sound gravity, momentum, and the odd slingshot of centrifugal force. The coaster is basically an ornate means of falling and a poem about physics in parts or stanzas, with jokes. The special quality of the Cyclone is how different, how *articulated*, all the components of its poem are, the whole of which lasts a minute and thirty-some seconds—exactly the right length, composed of distinct and perfect moments. By my fifth ride, my heart was leaping at the onset of each segment as at the approach of a dear old friend, and melting with instantaneous nostalgia for each at its finish.

I think every part of the Cyclone should have a name, the better 3 to be recalled and accurately esteemed. In my mind, the big drop is Kismet—fate, destiny. I can't think of what to call the second, a mystery drop commenced in a jiffy after we have been whipped around, but good, coming out of Kismet. (Someday soon I will devote particular attention to the huge and violent but elusive second drop.) I do know that the third drop's name can only be Pasha.[1] It is so round and generous, rich and powerful, looking like a killer going in but then actually like a crash landing in feathers that allows, for the first time in the ride, an instant for luxuriating in one's endorphin rush.

This brings me to another important function of the first drop, 4 which (I firmly contend) is to trigger the release of endorphins, natural morphine, into the bloodstream by persuading the organism that it is going to die. I know all about endorphins from reading *The New York Times* science section, and from an accident a few years ago. I broke my elbow, which is something not to do. It hurts. Or let me put it this way: in relation to what I had previously understood of pain, the sensation of breaking an elbow was *a whole new idea*, a new continent suddenly—whole unknown worlds of pain out there over the horizon. I was aghast, when I broke my elbow, at the extent of my naiveté about pain—but only for a second. Then I was somewhere else, pain-free, I think it was a cocktail party, but confusing, I didn't recognize anybody. On some level I knew the party wasn't real, that I was in another, real place which had something unpleasant about it

---

[1] *Pasha* was a title of honor for Turkish officials. [Editor's note.]

that made me not want to be there, but then I began to be afraid that if I stayed at the party I would be unable ever to be real again, so with an effort of will I returned to my body, which was sitting up with family members leaning over. The pain returned, but muffled and dull, drastically lessened. Endorphins.

Other things than breaking an elbow can give you an endorphin high, and one of them is suddenly falling ninety-some feet, seeing the ground charge directly at you. I think the forebrain, loaded with all sorts of chemical gimmicks we don't suspect, just there for special occasions, registers the situation, and, quick, pours a last-minute, bon voyage endorphin highball: "Hey, [*your name here*], this one's for you!" That's why it's important to ride the Cyclone many times, to comb out the distraction of terror—which gradually yields to the accumulating evidence that you are not dead—in order to savor the elixir for its own sake and for the sake of loving God or whatever—Nature—for cunningly secreted kindnesses. But Kismet is such a zonk, and the anonymous second drop is so perplexing and a zonk, too, that it isn't until mid-Pasha, in great fleshy Pasha's lap, that consciousness catches up with physiologic ravishment. Some part of my soul, because of the Cyclone, is still and will remain forever in that state, which I think is a zone of overlap among the heavens of all the world's mystic religions, where transcendent swamis bump around with freaked Spanish women saints. Blitzed in Pasha permanently, I have this lasting glimpse into the beyond that is not beyond, and you know what I'm talking about, or you don't.

Rolling up out of Pasha, we enter the part of the Cyclone that won't quit laughing. First there's the whoop of a whipping hairpin curve, which, if someone is sitting with you, Siamese-twins you. (Having tried different cars in different company, I prefer being alone at the very front—call me a classicist.) The ensuing dips, humps, dives, and shimmies that roar, chortle, cackle, and snort continue just long enough to suggest that they may go on forever—as worrisome as the thought, when you're laughing hard, that maybe you can never stop—and then it's hello, Irene. Why do I think Irene is the name of the very sharp drop, not deep but savage, that wipes the grin off the laughing part of the Cyclone? (Special about it is a crosspiece, low over the track at the bottom, that you swear is going to fetch you square in the eyebrows.) Irene is always the name—or kind of name, slightly unusual but banal—of the ordinary-seeming girl whom a young man may pursue idly, in a bored time, and then *wham!* fall horribly in love with, blasted in love with this person he never bothered to even particularly look at and now it's too late, she's his universe, Waterloo,[2] *personal* Kismet. This is one good reason I can think of for growing older: learning an aversion reflex for girls named something like Irene. In this smallish but vicious, sobering drop, abstract shapes of my own youthful romantic sorrows do not fail to flash before my inner eye ... but then, with a jarring zoom up and around, I am once more grown-up, wised-up me, and the rest of the ride is rejoicing.

The Cyclone differs from other roller coasters in being (a) a work 7 of art and (b) old, and not only old but old-looking, decrepit, rusting in its metal parts and peeling in its more numerous wooden parts, filthy throughout and jammed into a wire (Cyclone!) fence abutting cracked sidewalks of the Third World sinkhole that Coney Island is, intoxicatingly. Nor is it to be denied or concealed that the Cyclone, unlike newer coasters, tends to run *rough*, though each ride is unique and some are inexplicably velvety. One time the vibration, with the wheels shrieking and the cars threatening to explode with strain, made me think, "This is *no fun at all!*" It was an awful moment, with a sickening sense of betrayal and icy-fingered doubt: was my love malign?

That was my worst ride, which left me with a painfully yanked 8 muscle in my shoulder, but I am glad to say it wasn't my last. I got back on like a thrown cowboy and discovered that the secret of handling the rough rides is indeed like riding a horse, at trot or gallop— not tensing against it, as I had, but posting and rolling. It's all in the thighs and rear end, as I especially realized when—what the hell—I joined pimpled teenagers in the arms-raised *no hands!* trick. I should mention that a heavy, cushioned restraining bar locks down snugly into your lap and is very reassuring, although, like everything upholstered in the cars, it may be cracked or slashed and leaking tufts of stuffing from under swatches of gray gaffer's tape. One thing consistently disquieting is how, under stress, a car's wooden sides may *give* a bit. I wish they wouldn't do that, or that my imagination were less vivid. If a side did happen to fail on a curve, one would depart like toothpaste from a stomped-on tube.

I was proud of braving the *no hands!* posture—as trusting in the 9 restraining bar as a devout child in his heavenly Father—particularly

---

[2] Waterloo, a town in Belgium, was the site in 1815 of the crushing defeat of the French emperor Napoleon by the English. [Editor's note.]

the first time I did it, while emerging from the slinging turn that succeeds Irene into the long, long career that bottoms out at absolute ground level a few feet from the fence where pedestrians invariably gather to watch, transfixed. I call this swift, showy glide Celebrity: the ride's almost over, and afflatus swells the chest. But going *no hands!* soon feels as cheap and callow as it looks, blocking with vulgar self-centeredness the wahoo-glimmering-away-of-personality-in-convulsive-Nirvana[3] that is the Cyclone's essence. A righteous ride is hands on, though lightly, like grace. The payoff is intimacy in the sweet diminuendo, the jiggling and chuckling smart little bumps and dandling dips that bring us to a quick, pillowy deceleration in the shed, smelling of dirty machine oil, where we began and will begin again. It is a warm debriefing, this last part: "Wasn't that *great*?" it says. "Want to go again?"

Of course I do, but first there is the final stage of absorption, 10 when you squeeze out (it's easy to bang a knee then, so watch it) to stand wobbly but weightless, euphoric, and then to enjoy the sensation of walking as if it were a neat thing you had just invented. Out on the sidewalk, the object of curious gazes, you see that they see that you see them, earthlings, in a diminishing perspective, through the wrong end of the telescope of your pleasure, and your heart is pitying. You nod, smiling, to convey that yes, they should ride, and no, they won't regret it.

Meaning

1. Schjeldahl's opening paragraph briefly describes his reaction to the Cyclone ride in its entirety, before breaking the ride down into segments. What dominant impression does his overview establish?
2. According to Schjeldahl, what makes the Cyclone ride a different and thus more desirable experience than the ride offered by other roller coasters? Why does he find these differences significant?
3. If you do not know the meanings of the following words, look them up in a dictionary: poignantly (paragraph 1); centrifugal, articulated, nostalgia (2); elusive (3); naiveté (4); elixir, physiologic (5); classicist, banal (6); decrepit, malign (7); transfixed, afflatus, callow, diminuendo, dandling, debriefing (9); euphoric (10).

---

[3] In Buddhism, Nirvana is the state of blessedness in which the self is suppressed. [Editor's note.]

Purpose and Audience

1. In his first paragraph Schjeldahl says, "I promise to tell the truth." This confidence, placed in parentheses, establishes a relationship between writer and reader. Briefly characterize that relationship, citing examples from the essay to support your view.
2. Why does the Cyclone so interest Schjeldahl, a poet and art critic? Where in the essay do readers get a glimpse of the poet and critic speaking?
3. Most of us have experienced a ride on something like the Cyclone. What details of Schjeldahl's evoked your own experiences on roller coasters? What details caused you to rethink the experience?

Method and Structure

1. Schjeldahl digresses from his description of the roller-coaster ride to talk about breaking his elbow (paragraph 4). Often, such a digression can detract from an essay. What purpose does this digression serve? How does it contribute to the effectiveness of Schjeldahl's description?
2. Schjeldahl's description of the Cyclone is mainly subjective. Why is subjectivity essential to the essay? What would happen to the essay if the description were mainly objective?
3. Schjeldahl occasionally uses objective description—plain, precise details. Find two or three examples of objective description, and explain their contribution to the effectiveness of the essay.
4. **Other Methods**   Schjeldahl's description involves other methods of development as well: paragraphs 3, 5–6, and 9–10 analyze the parts of the ride (Chapter 4); paragraph 7 contrasts the Cyclone with other roller coasters (Chapter 7); and the essay contains numerous narratives (Chapter 2), not only of the whole Cyclone ride but also of particular experiences outside the ride (as in paragraph 4) and on one ride or another. How does the narrative of one of these particular experiences—the worst ride (paragraphs 7 and 8)—serve Schjeldahl's purpose?

Language

1. Much of Schjeldahl's language is sophisticated, even poetic—for example, "In this smallish but vicious, sobering drop, abstract shapes of my own youthful romantic sorrows do not fail to flash before my inner eye" (paragraph 6). But he also uses colloquial language and slang, such as "the greatest" (1) and "oomph" (2). Find five or six other instances of

    such informal language, and explain how they interact with the more formal language to emphasize the experience of the Cyclone.

2. Schjeldahl's essay is filled with concrete words and figures of speech that evoke the physical sensations of sound, sight, and touch. In paragraph 1, for example, we hear the cars groan and creak, see the flags flutter, and feel the squirt of adrenaline. Locate three or four figures of speech and five or six words or phrases that convey sharp sensory impressions. Explain how each contributes to Schjeldahl's description of the effect of the ride. (If necessary, consult *abstract and concrete words* and *figures of speech* in the Glossary.)

3. Schjeldahl uses the first-person *I* and the second-person *you* throughout his essay. How does this choice affect the tone of the essay?

4. In paragraph 1 the long, complex sentence beginning "At the top" uses interruptions and descriptive phrases to create the same tension and suspense felt by the rider anticipating the Cyclone's first big drop. Find two or three similar sentences, and explain how their structures mimic the sensations of the ride itself. How does Schjeldahl's unusual sentence structure contribute to the effect of his essay? What kinds of essays is such a style appropriate for? Why?

Writing Topics

1. Think about an experience that you consider the ultimate combination of fear and excitement—for instance, an athletic performance, an amusement park ride other than a roller coaster, or perhaps a horror movie. Write an essay in which you convey the experience, using sensory detail as Schjeldahl does.

2. The difference between subjective and objective description can be profound. Rewrite a paragraph of Schjeldahl's description of the Cyclone from an objective point of view, avoiding *I* and *you* and emotional language. Be as clear and concrete as you can. Then write an analysis of the differences between the two treatments in length, purpose, and effect.

3. Reread Schjeldahl's essay for instances of personification in the description of the Cyclone. (If necessary, consult "personification" under *figures of speech* in the Glossary.) Write an essay analyzing his use of personification, concentrating on how that figure of speech contributes to the overall effect of the essay.

Writing Topics

Description

Choose one of the following topics, or any other topic they suggest, for an essay developed by description. The topic you decide on should be something you care about so that description is a means of communicating an idea, not an end in itself.

1. A natural disaster that you witnessed
2. A work of art
3. A happy family
4. An adventurous person
5. A pet or an animal in a zoo
6. Waiting for important news
7. A neighborhood playground
8. A shopping mall
9. The hands of a grandparent or other relative
10. A garden or backyard
11. A frightening place
12. A favorite childhood toy
13. A used car lot
14. A place near water (ocean, lake, pond, river, swimming pool)
15. A place you daydream about
16. A person whose appearance and mannerisms are at odds with his or her real self
17. A person you admire or respect
18. A irritating child
19. A person who intimidates you (teacher, salesperson, doctor, police officer, fellow student)
20. The sensations of skating, running, body surfing, skydiving, or some other activity
21. A prison cell, police station, or courtroom
22. A cellar, attic, or garage
23. A yard sale or flea market
24. Your room
25. Late night or early morning
26. The look and sound of a musical instrument
27. The feeling of extreme hunger, thirst, cold, heat, or fatigue
28. A prized possession
29. The look and taste of a wonderful or terrible food
30. The scene at a concert (rock, country, folk, jazz, classical)

Chapter 2

Narration

Understanding the Method

To **narrate** is to tell a story, to relate a sequence of events that are linked in time. We narrate when we tell of a funny experience, report a baseball game, or trace a historical event. By arranging events in an orderly progression, we illuminate the stages leading to a result.

Sometimes the emphasis in narration is on the story itself, as in fiction, biography, autobiography, some history, and much journalism. But often a narrative serves some larger point: a paragraph relating a meeting of Japanese factory workers may help explain the Japanese practice of involving workers in their jobs; or a brief story about an innocent person's death may help strengthen an argument for stricter handling of drunk drivers. When used as the primary means of developing an essay, such pointed narration usually relates a sequence of events that led to new knowledge or had a notable outcome. The point of the narrative—the idea the reader is to take away—then determines the selection of events, the amount of detail devoted to them, and their arrangement.

Though narration arranges events in time, narrative time is not real time. An important event may fill whole pages, even though it took only minutes to unfold; and a less important event may be dispensed with in a sentence, even though it lasted hours. Suppose, for instance, that a writer wants to narrate the experience of being mugged in order to show how courage came unexpectedly to his aid. He might provide a slow-motion account of the few minutes' encounter with the muggers, including vivid details of the setting and of the attackers' appearance, a moment-by-moment replay of his emotions, and exact dialogue. At the same time, he will compress events that merely fill in background or link main events, such as how he got to the scene of the mugging or the follow-up questioning by a police detective. And he will entirely omit many events, such as a conversation overheard at the police station, that have no significance for his point.

The point of a narrative influences not only which events are covered and how fully but also how the events are arranged. A straight chronological sequence is usually the easiest to manage because it relates events in the order of their actual occurrence. It is particularly useful for short narratives, for those in which the last event is the most dramatic, or for those in which the events preceding and following the climax contribute to the point being made (for instance, a police detective's comments on what could have happened to the mugging victim if he had panicked). But other arrangements are also possible. The writer may start with the final event—a self-revelation, the results of an election—and then explain how it came about. Or the entire story may be summarized first and then examined in detail. Or the writer may use **flashbacks**—shifts backward rather than forward in time—to recall events whose significance would not have been apparent earlier. Flashbacks are common in movies and fiction: a character in the midst of one scene mentally replays another. In narrating the mugging, the writer might replay an earlier experience of panic for the purpose of explaining the source of his newfound courage.

Whatever the organization of a narrative, the writer needs to help readers through the sequence of events with **transitional expressions**, words and phrases that signal relationships. Some transitional expressions, such as *afterward* or *earlier,* signal the order of events. Others, such as *for an hour* or *in that time*, signal the duration of events. And still others, such as *the next morning* or *a week later*, signal the amount of time between events. In any narrative such expressions serve the dual purpose of keeping the reader on track and linking sentences and paragraphs so that they flow smoothly.

In addition to providing a clear organization aided by informative transitional expressions, the writer of a narrative also helps readers by adopting a consistent **point of view**, a position relative to the events. One aspect of point of view, the writer's place in the story, is conveyed by pronouns: the first-person *I* if the writer is a direct participant; the third-person *he, she, it,* and *they* if the writer is an observer or reporter. Another aspect, the writer's relation in time to the sequence of events, is conveyed by verb tense: present (*is, run*) or past (*was, ran*). Combining the first-person pronoun with the present tense can create great immediacy ("I feel the point of the knife in my back"). At the other extreme, combining third-person pronouns with the past tense creates more distance and objectivity ("He felt the point of the knife in his back"). In between extremes, the writer can combine first person with past tense ("I felt . . .") or third person with present tense ("He feels . . ."). The choice depends on the writer's actual involvement in the narrative and on his or her purpose. The only requirements are two: the chosen person should be consistent throughout the essay; and verb tense should not shift unnecessarily from present to past or vice versa. (Sometimes verb tense shifts out of necessity, to reflect real time. In the following sentence, for instance, *have felt* indicates action occurring earlier than the present of *know* and *is*: "I *know* what the prick in my back *is*, even though I *have* never *felt* it before.")

Analyzing Narration in Paragraphs

Andrea Lee (born 1953) is a journalist and fiction writer. The following paragraph is from "The Blues Abroad," an essay in Lee's book *Russian Journal* (1981), which records a year spent in the Soviet Union. Here Lee tells of attending a concert by the great American blues musician B. B. King, given at the Gorky Palace of Culture in Leningrad.

A slick-haired Soviet M.C. announced B. B. King ("A great *Negritanski* musician"), and <u>then</u> King was onstage with his well-known guitar—Lucille—and a ten-man ensemble. <u>As</u> King and the ensemble swung into "Why I Sing the Blues," one could sense the puzzlement of the	*Chronological order (almost minute by minute)* *Past tense* *Transitional expressions (underlined)*

Soviet audience. "Negro" music to them meant
jazz or spirituals, but this was something else.
Also, there was the question of response.
B. B. King is a great, warm presence when he
performs, and he asks his audiences to pour
themselves out to him in return. King teases his
audiences, urging them to clap along, to whistle,
to hoot their appreciation, like the congrega-
tions in the Southern churches in which he grew
up. But to Russians, such behavior suggests a
lack of culture and an almost frightening disor-
der. Though obviously impressed, the audience
at first kept a respectful silence during the numbers, as it might at the symphony. (Only the
foreigners shouted and stomped out the beat;
we found the Russians around us staring at us
open-mouthed.) Then King played an irresistible riff, stopped, and leaned toward the audience with his hand cupped to his ear. The
audience caught on and began to clap. King
changed the beat, and waited for the audience
to catch up. Then he changed it again. Soon the
whole place was clapping along to "Get off My
Back, Woman," and there were even a few
timid shouts and whistles. King, who has carried the blues to Europe, Africa, and the Far
East, had broken the ice one more time.

Interruption for necessary background (present tense for recurring actions and general truths)

Point of view: direct participant

Purpose: to relate how King broke through the Russians' reserve

Benjamin Capps (born 1922) has written eight novels and three
books of nonfiction, all placed in the Great Plains in the nineteenth
century. One of his nonfiction books, *The Great Chiefs* (1975), is the
source of the following paragraph. Capps is telling the story of the
Sioux Indians in an area that is now South Dakota.

The next year [1874], the federal government
itself set its sights on a precious chunk of the
Sioux reservation. The Army decided that, to
guard Northern Pacific workers when the construction got under way, a new fort should be
erected in the Black Hills—a well-watered and
heavily timbered region of granite crags on the
western edge of the reservation. A reconnais-
sance team under Lieutenant Colonel George

Chronological order (five significant events in more than a year)

Past tense

Point of view: reporter

Armstrong Custer was sent out to locate a suitable site. Custer, a reckless glorymonger, found a way to win himself national headlines while on the mission. When geologists with the party detected traces of gold in the hills, Custer sent glowing reports to the East which led the press to hail his discovery as the new golconda [source of great wealth]. By the middle of 1875, nearly a thousand prospectors were illegally camped in the Black Hills, which the Sioux regarded as a sacred dwelling place of spirits.

Transitional expressions (underlined)

Jump ahead to next relevant event

Purpose: to relate how the U.S. government encroached on Indian lands

Developing a Narrative Essay

GETTING STARTED

To find a subject for a narrative essay, probe your own experiences for a situation such as an argument involving strong emotion, a humorous or embarrassing incident, a dramatic scene you witnessed, or a learning experience like a job. If you have the opportunity to do research, you might choose a topic dealing with the natural world (such as the Big Bang scenario for the origin of the universe) or an event in history (such as the negotiation of a peace treaty). Whatever your subject, you should have some point to make about it: Why was the incident or experience significant? What does it teach or illustrate? Phrasing this point in a sentence will keep you focused while you generate ideas, and later the sentence may serve as the thesis of your essay. For instance: "I used to think small-town life was boring, but one taste of the city made me appreciate the leisurely pace of home"; or "A recent small earthquake demonstrated the hazards of inadequate civil-defense measures."

When you have your thesis, explore the subject by listing all the major and minor events in sequence as they happened. At this stage you may find the traditional journalist's questions helpful:

Who was involved?
What happened?
When did it happen?
Where did it happen?
Why did it happen?
How did it happen?

Not all of these questions will produce useful answers, but asking each of them in turn will force you to examine your subject from all angles. Then you need to decide which events should be developed in great detail because they are central to your point; which merit compression because they merely contribute background or tie the main events together; and which should be omitted altogether because they add nothing to your point and might clutter your narrative.

While you are weighing the relative importance of events, consider also what your readers need to know in order to understand and appreciate your narrative. What information will help locate them in the narrative's time and place? How will you expand and compress events to keep their attention? What details about people, places, and feelings will make the events vivid for them? What is your attitude toward the subject—lighthearted, sarcastic, bitter, serious?—and how will you convey it to readers in your choice of events and details? Think of your readers as well in deciding on your point of view. Do you want to involve them intimately by using the first person and the present tense? Or does that seem overdramatic, less appropriate than the more detached, objective view that would be conveyed by the past tense or the third person or both?

ORGANIZING

Narrative essays often begin without formal introductions, instead drawing the reader in with one of the more dramatic events in the sequence. But you may find an introduction useful to set the scene for your narrative, summarize the events leading up to it, or otherwise establish the context for it. Such an opening may lead to your thesis so that readers know why you are bothering to tell them your story. Even if you later decide to omit the thesis in order to intensify the drama of your narrative, you may want to include it in early drafts as a reminder of your point.

The arrangement of events in the body of your essay depends on the actual order in which they occurred and the point you want to make. To narrate a trip during which one thing after another went wrong, you might find a strict chronological order most effective. To narrate an earthquake that began and ended in an instant, you might sort simultaneous events into groups—say, what happened to buildings and what happened to people—or you might arrange a few people's experiences in order of increasing drama. To narrate your experience of city life, you might interweave events in the city with contrasting flashbacks to your life in a small town, or you might start by relating one especially bad experience in the city, drop back to explain how you ended up in that situation, and then go on to tell what happened afterward. Narrative time can be manipulated in any number of ways, but your scheme should have a purpose that your readers can see, and you should stick to it.

Let the ending of your essay be determined by the effect you want to leave with readers. You can end with the last event in your sequence, or the one you have saved for last, if it conveys your point and provides a strong finish. Or you can summarize the aftermath of the story if it contributes to the point. You can also end with a formal conclusion that states your point—your thesis—explicitly. Such a conclusion is especially useful if your point unfolds gradually throughout the narrative and you want to emphasize it at the finish.

DRAFTING

While you are drafting your essay, think of your readers. Help them experience events by providing ample descriptive details. (See the previous chapter.) If appropriate, tell what the people in your narrative were wearing, what expressions their faces held, how they gestured, what they said. Specify the time of day, and describe the weather and the surroundings (buildings, vegetation, and the like). Rely on precise, strong verbs to make your meaning clear and to move the action along—verbs such as *sprints* or *lopes* instead of *runs*, *crashed* or *tumbled* instead of *fell*, *shattered* or *splintered* instead of *broke*.

In your draft you might want to experiment with dialogue—quotations of what participants said, in their words. Dialogue can add immediacy and realism as long as it advances the narrative and doesn't ramble beyond its usefulness. In reconstructing dialogue from memory, try to recall not only the actual words but also the sounds of speakers' voices and the expressions on their faces—information that will help you represent each speaker distinctly. And keep the dialogue natural sounding by using constructions typical of speech. For instance, most speakers prefer contractions like *don't* and *shouldn't* to the longer forms *do not* and *should not*; and few speakers begin sentences with *although*, as in the formal-sounding "Although we could hear our mother's voice, we refused to answer her."

Whether you are relating events in strict chronological order or manipulating them for some effect, try to make their sequence in real time and the distance between them clear to readers. Instead of signaling sequence with the monotonous *and then . . . and then . . . and then . . .* or *next . . . next . . . next,* use informative transitional expressions such as *meanwhile* and *within minutes.* (See the Glossary under *transitions* for a list of such expressions.) Watch your verb tenses, too. Unnecessary shifts in tense can make it difficult for the reader to follow the sequence.

REVISING

When your draft is complete, revise it by answering the following questions.

1. *Is the point of your narrative clear, and does every event you relate contribute to it?* Whether or not you state your thesis, it should be obvious to readers. They should be able to see why you have lingered over some events and compressed others, and they should not be distracted by insignificant events and details.

2. *Is your organization clear?* Be sure that your readers will understand any shifts backward or forward in time. And be sure that transitional expressions let readers know exactly where they are in the sequence.

3. *Is your point of view consistent?* If you started with the first or third person, you should stay with it to avoid confusing readers. For the same reason, if you started with verbs in the present tense or past tense, you should stay with that tense unless a shift is necessary to reflect real time.

4. *If you have used dialogue, is it purposeful and natural?* Be sure all quoted speeches move the action ahead. And read all dialogue aloud to check that it sounds like something someone would actually say.

Langston Hughes

A poet, fiction writer, playwright, critic, and humorist, Langston Hughes described his writing as "largely concerned with depicting Negro life in America." He was born in 1902 in Joplin, Missouri, and grew up in Illinois, Kansas, and Ohio. After dropping out of Columbia University in the early 1920s, Hughes worked at odd jobs while struggling to gain recognition as a writer. His first book of poems, The Weary Blues *(1925), helped seed the Harlem Renaissance, a flowering of black music and literature centered in the Harlem district of New York City during the 1920s. The book also generated a scholarship that enabled Hughes to finish college at Lincoln University. In all of his work—including* The Negro Mother *(1931),* The Ways of White Folks *(1934),* Shakespeare in Harlem *(1942),* Montage of a Dream Deferred *(1951),* Ask Your Mama *(1961), and* The Best of Simple *(1961)—Hughes captured and projected the rhythms of jazz and the distinctive speech, subtle humor, and deep traditions of black people. He died in New York City in 1967.*

Salvation

A chapter in Hughes's autobiography, The Big Sea *(1940), "Salvation" is a simple yet compelling narrative about a moment of deceit and disillusionment for a boy of twelve.*

I was saved from sin when I was going on thirteen. But not really 1 saved. It happened like this. There was a big revival at my Auntie Reed's church. Every night for weeks there had been much preaching, singing, praying, and shouting, and some very hardened sinners had been brought to Christ, and the membership of the church had grown by leaps and bounds. Then just before the revival ended, they held a special meeting for children, "to bring the young lambs to the fold." My aunt spoke of it for days ahead. That night, I was escorted to the front row and placed on the mourner's bench with all other young sinners, who had not yet been brought to Jesus.

My aunt told me that when you were saved you saw a light, and 2 something happened to you inside! And Jesus came into your life! And God was with you from then on! She said you could see and hear and feel Jesus in your soul. I believed her. I have heard a great many old people say the same thing and it seemed to me they ought to know. So I sat there calmly in the hot, crowded church, waiting for Jesus to come to me.

The preacher preached a wonderful rhythmical sermon, all moans 3
and shouts and lonely cries and dire pictures of hell, and then he sang
a song about the ninety and nine safe in the fold, but one little lamb
was left out in the cold. Then he said: "Won't you come? Won't you
come to Jesus? Young lambs, won't you come?" And he held out his
arms to all us young sinners there on the mourner's bench. And the
little girls cried. And some of them jumped up and went to Jesus right
away. But most of us just sat there.

A great many old people came and knelt around us and prayed, 4
old women with jet-black faces and braided hair, old men with work-
gnarled hands. And the church sang a song about the lower lights are
burning, some poor sinners to be saved. And the whole building
rocked with prayer and song.

Still I kept waiting to *see* Jesus.   5

Finally all the young people had gone to the altar and were saved, 6
but one boy and me. He was a rounder's son named Westley. Westley
and I were surrounded by sisters and deacons praying. It was very hot
in the church, and getting late now. Finally Westley said to me in a
whisper: "God damn! I'm tired o' sitting here. Let's get up and be
saved." So he got up and was saved.

Then I was left all alone on the mourner's bench. My aunt came 7
and knelt at my knees and cried, while prayers and songs swirled all
around me in the little church. The whole congregation prayed for me
alone, in a mightly wail of moans and voices. And I kept waiting
serenely for Jesus, waiting, waiting—but he didn't come. I wanted to
see him, but nothing happened to me. Nothing! I wanted something
to happen to me, but nothing happened.

I heard the songs and the minister saying: "Why don't you come? 8
My dear child, why don't you come to Jesus? Jesus is waiting for you.
He wants you. Why don't you come? Sister Reed, what is this child's
name?"

"Langston," my aunt sobbed.   9

"Langston, why don't you come? Why don't you come and be 10
saved? Oh, Lamb of God! Why don't you come?"

Now it was really getting late. I began to be ashamed of myself, 11
holding everything up so long. I began to wonder what God thought
about Westley, who certainly hadn't seen Jesus either, but who was
now sitting proudly on the platform, swinging his knickerbockered
legs and grinning down at me, surrounded by deacons and old women
on their knees praying. God had not struck Westley dead for taking
his name in vain or for lying in the temple. So I decided that maybe to

save further trouble, I'd better lie, too, and say that Jesus had come, and get up and be saved.

So I got up. 12

Suddenly the whole room broke into a sea of shouting, as they 13 saw me rise. Waves of rejoicing swept the place. Women leaped in the air. My aunt threw her arms around me. The minister took me by the hand and led me to the platform.

When things quieted down, in a hushed silence, punctuated by a 14 few ecstatic "Amens," all the new young lambs were blessed in the name of God. Then joyous singing filled the room.

That night, for the last time in my life but one—for I was a big 15 boy twelve years old—I cried. I cried, in bed alone, and couldn't stop. I buried my head under the quilts, but my aunt heard me. She woke up and told my uncle I was crying because the Holy Ghost had come into my life, and because I had seen Jesus. But I was really crying because I couldn't bear to tell her that I had lied, that I had deceived everybody in the church, that I hadn't seen Jesus, and that now I didn't believe there was a Jesus any more, since he didn't come to help me.

Meaning

1. What is the main point of Hughes's narrative? What change occurs in him as a result of his experience?
2. What finally makes Hughes decide to get up and be saved? How does this decision affect him afterward?
3. What do you make of the title and the first two sentences? What is Hughes saying here about "salvation"?
4. If you do not know the meanings of the following words, look them up in a dictionary: dire (paragraph 3); rounder, deacons (6).

Purpose and Audience

1. Why do you think Hughes wrote "Salvation" as part of his autobiography more than two decades after the experience? Was his purpose simply to express feelings prompted by a significant event in his life? Did he want to criticize his aunt and the other adults in the congregation? Did he want to explain something about childhood or about the distance between generations? What passages support your answer?
2. What does Hughes seem to assume about his readers' familiarity with the kind of service he describes? What details help make the procedure clear?

3. How do dialogue, lines from hymns, and details of other sounds (paragraphs 3–10) help re-create the increasing pressure Hughes feels? What other details contribute to this sense of pressure?

Method and Structure

1. Where in his narrative does Hughes insert explanations, compress time by summarizing events, or jump ahead in time by omitting events? Where does he expand time by drawing moments out? How does each of these insertions and manipulations of time relate to Hughes's main point?
2. In paragraph 1, Hughes uses several transitional words and expressions to signal the sequence of events and the passage of time: "for weeks," "Then just before," "for days ahead," "That night." Where does he use similar signals in the rest of the essay?
3. **Other Methods**   Hughes's narrative also explains a process (Chapter 6): we learn how a revival meeting works. In addition, Hughes uses description (Chapter 1) to capture the sights and sounds of the meeting. Notice the different ways in which Hughes describes the noise of the congregation in paragraphs 4, 7, and 13. Why does he focus on this sense?

Language

1. What does Hughes's language reveal about his adult attitudes toward his experience: does he feel anger? bitterness? sorrow? guilt? shame? amusement? What words and passages support your answer?
2. Hughes relates his experience in an almost childlike style, using many short sentences and beginning many sentences with *And*. What effect do you think he is trying to achieve with this style?
3. Hughes expects to "see" Jesus when he is saved (paragraphs 2, 5, 7), and afterward his aunt thinks that he has "seen" Jesus (15). What does each of them mean by *see*? What is the significance of the difference in Hughes's story?

Writing Topics

1. Think of an incident in your own life that led to strong discomfort, disappointment, or disillusionment. Then write a narrative essay that explains to your readers exactly how the experience affected you.
2. Hughes's decision to be saved is influenced partly by Westley (paragraphs 6 and 11). Think of a situation when your actions were influenced

by some sort of pressure from your peers—with good results or bad. Write a narrative essay telling what happened and making it clear why the situation was important to you.

3. Hughes says, "I have heard a great many old people say the same thing and it seemed to me they ought to know" (paragraph 2). Think of a piece of information or advice that you heard over and over again from adults when you were a child. Write a narrative essay about an experience in which you were helped or misled by that information or advice.

4. Do you have childhood memories of one or more experiences with religion that comforted, distressed, confused, bored, or challenged you? If so, write a narrative essay about your experiences, making sure the reader understands why they were important. Or, if you prefer, write an essay in which you argue for or against introducing children to religious beliefs and practices.

E. B. White

With an infallible ear for language and a keen eye for detail, Elwyn Brooks White earned a place among America's finest writers. White was born in 1899 in Mount Vernon, New York, and there he also grew up. After graduating from Cornell in 1921, he traveled for a time in the West before heading back to settle in Manhattan. In 1927 he joined the staff of The New Yorker, *which was a little over a year old, and for decades his contributions of essays, poems, editorials, and cartoon captions helped shape the magazine. With his wife, Katharine Sergeant White (herself an influential* New Yorker *editor), and their son, Joel, White moved in 1938 to Maine, where he took up farming and animal husbandry while continuing to write. Among his nineteen books are many essay collections; three works for children, including the classic* Charlotte's Web *(1952); and* The Elements of Style *(3rd ed., 1979), his revision of the composition textbook he used at Cornell, by his teacher William Strunk, Jr. In his last decade, White published his* Letters *(1976),* Essays *(1977), and* Poems and Sketches *(1981), and he edited a collection of Katharine White's essays on gardening, published two years after her death in 1977. White died in 1985 on the Maine farm they had shared.*

Once More
to the Lake

Probably White's best-known essay, "Once More to the Lake" was written in 1941 and collected in One Man's Meat *(1944) along with White's other contributions to* Harper's Magazine. *Mingling past and present, reflection and observation, poetic images and spoken rhythms, the essay recounts White's visit to a scene of his boyhood, a place "linking the generations in a strong indestructible chain."*

One summer, along about 1904, my father rented a camp on a lake in Maine and took us all there for the month of August. We all got ringworm from some kittens and had to rub Pond's Extract on our arms and legs night and morning, and my father rolled over in a canoe with all his clothes on; but outside of that the vacation was a success and from then on none of us ever thought there was any place in the world like that lake in Maine. We returned summer after summer— always on August 1 for one month. I have since become a salt-water man, but sometimes in summer there are days when the restlessness of the tides and the fearful cold of the sea water and the incessant wind that blows across the afternoon and into the evening make me wish for the placidity of a lake in the woods. A few weeks ago this feeling got so strong I bought myself a couple of bass hooks and a spinner and returned to the lake where we used to go, for a week's fishing and to revisit old haunts.

I took along my son, who had never had any fresh water up his 2 nose and who had seen lily pads only from train windows. On the journey over to the lake I began to wonder what it would be like. I wondered how time would have marred this unique, this holy spot— the coves and streams, the hills that the sun set behind, the camps and the paths behind the camps. I was sure that the tarred road would have found it out, and I wondered in what other ways it would be desolated. It is strange how much you can remember about places like that once you allow your mind to return into the grooves that lead back. You remember one thing, and that suddenly reminds you of another thing. I guess I remembered clearest of all the early mornings, when the lake was cool and motionless, remembered how the bedroom smelled of the lumber it was made of and of the wet woods whose scent entered through the screen. The partitions in the camp were thin and did not extend clear to the top of the rooms, and as I was always the first up I would dress softly so as not to wake the others, and sneak out into the sweet outdoors and start out in the canoe, keeping close along the shore in the long shadows of the pines. I remembered being very careful never to rub my paddle against the gunwale for fear of disturbing the stillness of the cathedral.

The lake had never been what you would call a wild lake. There 3 were cottages sprinkled around the shores, and it was in farming country although the shores of the lake were quite heavily wooded. Some of the cottages were owned by nearby farmers, and you would live at the shore and eat your meals at the farmhouse. That's what our family did. But although it wasn't wild, it was a fairly large and undisturbed lake and there were places in it that, to a child at least, seemed infinitely remote and primeval.

I was right about the tar: it led to within half a mile of the shore. 4 But when I got back there, with my boy, and we settled into a camp near a farmhouse and into the kind of summertime I had known, I could tell it was going to be pretty much the same as it had been before—I knew it, lying in bed the first morning, smelling the bedroom and hearing the boy sneak quietly out and go off along the shore in a boat. I began to sustain the illusion that he was I, and

therefore, by simple transposition, that I was my father. This sensation persisted, kept cropping up all the time we were there. It was not
an entirely new feeling, but in this setting it grew much stronger. I
seemed to be living a dual existence. I would be in the middle of some
simple act, I would be picking up a bait box or laying down a table
fork, or I would be saying something, and suddenly it would be not I
but my father who was saying the words or making the gesture. It
gave me a creepy sensation.

We went fishing the first morning. I felt the same damp moss 5
covering the worms in the bait can, and saw the dragonfly alight on
the tip of my rod as it hovered a few inches from the surface of the
water. It was the arrival of this fly that convinced me beyond any
doubt that everything was as it always had been, that the years were a
mirage and that there had been no years. The small waves were the
same, chucking the rowboat under the chin as we fished at anchor,
and the boat was the same boat, the same color green and the ribs
broken in the same places, and under the floorboards the same fresh-
water leavings and débris—the dead helgramite, the wisps of moss,
the rusty discarded fishhook, the dried blood from yesterday's catch.
We stared silently at the tips of our rods, at the dragonflies that came
and went. I lowered the tip of mine into the water, tentatively, pen-
sively dislodging the fly, which darted two feet away, posed, darted
two feet back, and came to rest again a little farther up the rod. There
had been no years between the ducking of this dragonfly and the other
one—the one that was part of memory. I looked at the boy, who was
silently watching his fly, and it was my hands that held his rod, my
eyes watching. I felt dizzy and didn't know which rod I was at the end
of.

We caught two bass, hauling them in briskly as though they were 6
mackerel, pulling them over the side of the boat in a businesslike
manner without any landing net, and stunning them with a blow on
the back of the head. When we got back for a swim before lunch, the
lake was exactly were we had left it, the same number of inches from
the dock, and there was only the merest suggestion of a breeze. This
seemed an utterly enchanted sea, this lake you could leave to its own
devices for a few hours and come back to, and find that it had not
stirred, this constant and trustworthy body of water. In the shallows,
the dark, water-soaked sticks and twigs, smooth and old, were undulating in clusters on the bottom against the clean ribbed sand, and the
track of the mussel was plain. A school of minnows swam by, each
minnow with its small individual shadow, doubling the attendance, so

clear and sharp in the sunlight. Some of the other campers were in swimming, along the shore, one of them with a cake of soap, and the water felt thin and clear and unsubstantial. Over the years there had been this person with the cake of soap, this cultist, and here he was. There had been no years.

Up to the farmhouse to dinner through the teeming, dusty field, the road under our sneakers was only a two-track road. The middle track was missing, the one with the marks of the hooves and the splotches of dried, flaky manure. There had always been three tracks to choose from in choosing which track to walk in; now the choice was narrowed down to two. For a moment I missed terribly the middle alternative. But the way led past the tennis court, and something about the way it lay there in the sun reassured me; the tape had loosened along the backline, the alleys were green with plantains and other weeds, and the net (installed in June and removed in September) sagged in the dry noon, and the whole place steamed with midday heat and hunger and emptiness. There was a choice of pie for dessert, and one was blueberry and one was apple, and the waitresses were the same country girls, there having been no passage of time, only the illusion of it as in a dropped curtain—the waitresses were still fifteen; their hair had been washed, that was the only difference—they had been to the movies and seen the pretty girls with the clean hair. [7]

Summertime, oh, summertime, pattern of life indelible, the fade-proof lake, the woods unshatterable, the pasture with the sweetfern and the juniper forever and ever, summer without end; this was the background, and the life along the shore was the design, the cottagers with their innocent and tranquil design, their tiny docks with the flagpole and the American flag floating against the white clouds in the blue sky, the little paths over the roots of the trees leading from camp to camp and the paths leading back to the outhouses and the can of lime for sprinkling, and at the souvenir counters at the store the miniature birch-bark canoes and the postcards that showed things looking a little better than they looked. This was the American family at play, escaping the city heat, wondering whether the newcomers in the camp at the head of the cove were "common" or "nice," wondering whether it was true that the people who drove up for Sunday dinner at the farmhouse were turned away because there wasn't enough chicken. [8]

It seemed to me, as I kept remembering all this, that those times and those summers had been infinitely precious and worth saving. There had been jollity and peace and goodness. The arriving (at the [9]

beginning of August) had been so big a business in itself, at the rail-
way station the farm wagon drawn up, the first smell of the pine-
laden air, the first glimpse of the smiling farmer, and the great
importance of the trunks and your father's enormous authority in
such matters, and the feel of the wagon under you for the long ten-
mile haul, and at the top of the last long hill catching the first view of
the lake after eleven months of not seeing this cherished body of
water. The shouts and cries of the other campers when they saw you,
and the trunks to be unpacked, to give up their rich burden. (Arriving
was less exciting nowadays, when you sneaked up in your car and
parked it under a tree near the camp and took out the bags and in five
minutes it was all over, no fuss, no loud wonderful fuss about trunks.)

   Peace and goodness and jollity. The only thing that was wrong   10
now, really, was the sound of the place, an unfamiliar nervous sound
of the outboard motors. This was the note that jarred, the one thing
that would sometimes break the illusion and set the years moving. In
those other summertimes all motors were inboard; and when they
were at a little distance, the noise they made was a sedative, an ingredient of summer sleep. They made one-cylinder and two-cylinder en-
gines, and some were make-and-break and some were jump-spark,
but they all made a sleepy sound across the lake. The one-lungers
throbbed and fluttered, and the twin-cylinder ones purred and purred,
and that was a quiet sound, too. But now the campers all had out-
boards. In the daytime, in the hot mornings, these motors made a
petulant, irritable sound; at night, in the still evening when the after-
glow lit the water, they whined about one's ears like mosquitoes. My
boy loved our rented outboard, and his great desire was to achieve
single-handed mastery over it, and authority, and he soon learned the
trick of choking it a little (but not too much), and the adjustment of
the needle valve. Watching him I would remember the things you
could do with the old one-cylinder engine with the heavy flywheel,
how you could have it eating out of your hand if you got really close
to it spiritually. Motorboats in those days didn't have clutches, and
you would make a landing by shutting off the motor at the proper
time and coasting in with a dead rudder. But there was a way of
reversing them, if you learned the trick, by cutting the switch and
putting it on again exactly on the final dying revolution of the flywheel, so that it would kick back against compression and begin
reversing. Approaching a dock in a strong following breeze, it was
difficult to slow up sufficiently by the ordinary coasting method, and

if a boy felt he had complete mastery over his motor, he was tempted to keep it running beyond its time and then reverse it a few feet from the dock. It took a cool nerve, because if you threw the switch a twentieth of a second too soon you would catch the flywheel when it still had speed enough to go up past center, and the boat would leap ahead, charging bull-fashion at the dock.

We had a good week at the camp. The bass were biting well and the sun shone endlessly, day after day. We would be tired at night and lie down in the accumulated heat of the little bedrooms after the long hot day and the breeze would stir almost imperceptibly outside and the smell of the swamp drift in through the rusty screens. Sleep would come easily and in the morning the red squirrel would be on the roof, tapping out his gay routine. I kept remembering everything, lying in bed in the mornings—the small steamboat that had a long rounded stern like the lip of a Ubangi, and how quietly she ran on the moonlight sails, when the older boys played their mandolins and the girls sang and we ate doughnuts dipped in sugar, and how sweet the music was on the water in the shining night, and what it had felt like to think about girls then. After breakfast we would go up to the store and the things were in the same place—the minnows in a bottle, the plugs and spinners disarranged and pawed over by the youngsters from the boys' camp, the Fig Newtons and the Beeman's gum. Outside, the road was tarred and cars stood in front of the store. Inside, all was just as it had always been, except there was more Coca-Cola and not so much Moxie and root beer and birch beer and sarsaparilla. We would walk out with the bottle of pop apiece and sometimes the pop would backfire up our noses and hurt. We explored the streams, quietly, where the turtles slid off the sunny logs and dug their way into the soft bottom; and we lay on the town wharf and fed worms to the tame bass. Everywhere we went I had trouble making out which was I, the one walking at my side, the one walking in my pants. **11**

One afternoon while we were there at the lake a thunderstorm came up. It was like the revival of an old melodrama that I had seen long ago with childish awe. The second-act climax of the drama of the electrical disturbance over a lake in America had not changed in any important respect. This was the big scene, still the big scene. The whole thing was so familiar, the first feeling of oppression and heat and a general air around camp of not wanting to go very far away. In midafternoon (it was all the same) a curious darkening of the sky, and a lull in everything that had made life tick; and then the way the boats **12** suddenly swung the other way at their moorings with the coming of a breeze out of the new quarter, and the premonitory rumble. Then the kettle drum, then the snare, then the bass drum and cymbals, then crackling light against the dark, and the gods grinning and licking their chops in the hills. Afterward the calm, the rain steadily rustling in the calm lake, the return of light and hope and spirits, and the campers running out in joy and relief to go swimming in the rain, their bright cries perpetuating the deathless joke about how they were getting simply drenched, and the children screaming with delight at the new sensation of bathing in the rain, and the joke about getting drenched linking the generations in a strong indestructible chain. And the comedian who waded in carrying an umbrella.

When the others went swimming, my son said he was going in, *13* too. He pulled his dripping trunks from the line where they had hung all through the shower and wrung them out. Languidly, and with no thought of going in, I watched him, his hard little body, skinny and bare, saw him wince slightly as he pulled up around his vitals the small, soggy, icy garment. As he buckled the swollen belt, suddenly my groin felt the chill of death.

Meaning

1. The main idea of White's essay is fully revealed only in the last paragraph. What is this idea? Why, after White had identified so closely with his son, reliving his own boyhood, does he suddenly feel the "chill of death"?

2. In the opening paragraph White mentions that he sought escape from "the restlessness of the tides and the fearful cold of the sea water and the incessant wind" to the "placidity of a lake in the woods." His escape seems complete but for the "creepy sensation" (paragraph 4) and the "dizzy" feeling (5) accompanying the illusion that time has stood still since his boyhood. What causes these uneasy feelings, and how do they relate to the main idea of the essay?

3. Why do you think it disturbs White momentarily that the road offers only two tracks to choose from, not the three of his boyhood (paragraph 7)? How does this observation relate to the main idea of the essay?

4. If you do not know the meanings of the following words, look them up in a dictionary: incessant, placidity (paragraph 1); desolated, gunwale (2); primeval (3); transposition (4); chucking (5); undulating (6); indelible (8); petulant (10); imperceptibly, sarsaparilla (11); melodrama, premonitory, perpetuating (12); languidly (13).

Purpose and Audience

1. Do you think White's purpose is solely to express his feelings, or does he want to explain something as well? If so, what does he want to explain?
2. To what extent does White seem to consider readers unlike himself—say, young adults with no children and no experience of lakeside vacations? Does he succeed in making you identify with the perceptions and feelings prompted by his experience? If so, what details or passages do you find particularly effective, and why? If not, what details or passages do you have particular difficulty relating to, and why?
3. Why do you think White devotes such detail to boat handling (paragraph 10)? In answering, consider especially the significance of the idea of getting "really close to [the boat] spiritually," the many undefined boating terms, and the context of comparison between inboard and outboard motors and between his son's experiences and his own.

Method and Structure

1. Whereas the previous narrative essay, Langston Hughes's "Salvation," proceeds in simple chronological sequence, White's narrative is a more complex interweaving of the present and the past. To discover the essay's basic chronological framework, trace the events of the present by starting with "A few weeks ago" in paragraph 1 and finding similar transitional expressions that signal the passage of time during the week-long vacation. Then locate the many flashbacks in which White remembers being a boy at the lake, and examine what events in the present trigger them. Note that in some passages (paragraph 8, for instance) the time is neither clearly present nor clearly past. Why?
2. **Other Methods**   Though primarily a narrative essay, "Once More to the Lake" is also developed by description (see Chapter 1) and by comparison and contrast (see Chapter 7). Locate examples of both methods just in paragraph 9, and analyze what they contribute to the essay as whole.

Language

1. How would you characterize White's tone? What, for example, is the effect of "holy," "sweet," and "cathedral" (paragraph 2), "sleepy" (10), and similar words throughout the essay? And what is the effect of the many long sentences containing series of observations or recollections, such as in paragraphs 7, 8, and 9? (If necessary, see *tone* in the Glossary.)
2. White's sense that time has stood still is repeated or restated many times

throughout the essay—not only explicitly, as in "There had been no years" (paragraph 5), but also in single words, such as "indelible" (8). Locate both the restatements and the single words in paragraphs 4–11. How does White intensify this theme in his description of the oncoming storm (12)? How do the figures of speech in the description of the storm and the lingering over the "deathless joke" forecast the essay's last sentence? (If necessary, consult the Glossary for *figures of speech*.)

Writing Topics

1. Think of a situation in which you have observed a child undergoing an experience or making a decision that recalls your own childhood. (The child may be a brother, sister, son, daughter, cousin, neighbor, or even a stranger.) Write a narrative essay linking your observations with your memories, making sure that you lead the reader to see the insights you gained.

2. Recall a time when you accompanied a parent or other adult (aunt, uncle, grandparent, and so on) to a place he or she knew well but you were seeing for the first time. It could be a place where the person grew up, went to school, lived for a time, or vacationed. Write an essay in which you compare your reactions to the place with what you remember of the adult's reactions or what, with hindsight, you think the adult's reactions might have been.

3. In "Salvation" Langston Hughes takes a child's perspective, whereas in "Once More to the Lake" White takes the adult's perspective. To experiment with how much a perspective affects the selection of details and the attitude toward them, rewrite part of Hughes's and White's narratives from the opposite perspective. For instance, tell of Hughes's crying in bed (paragraph 15) from the perspective of his aunt, or tell of swimming after the rainstorm (paragraph 12) from the perspective of White's son.

Scott MacLeod

*Scott MacLeod is a journalist with broad experience in international affairs.
He was born in 1954 in Rochester, Pennsylvania, and grew up in suburban
Pittsburgh. After obtaining a B.A. from the University of Pittsburgh in 1976,
MacLeod served as a correspondent with United Press International, first in
Pennsylvania and then in London, England, and Beirut, Lebanon. In 1985 he
moved to* Time *magazine as a reporter in the Middle East bureau, and in
1988 he became a staff writer on the magazine's "World" section. He is now*
Time's *bureau chief in Johannesburg, South Africa. In addition, MacLeod has
contributed articles to* The New York Review of Books, *including a two-part
interview in 1989 with Yasser Arafat, the leader of the Palestine Liberation
Organization; and he is writing a book on the Middle East.*

The Lost Life
of Terry Anderson

*Assembling bits of information from many sources, MacLeod here provides a
tense and unsettling narrative of the ordeal suffered by an American hostage
in Beirut. MacLeod knew his subject when they were both journalists in
Beirut and was in the city when the kidnaping occurred. The essay first appeared in* Time *in March 1989.*

Imagine it. You are chained to a radiator in a bare, dank room. You 1
never see the sun. When your captors fear that a noise in the night is
an impending rescue attempt, you are slammed up against the wall,
the barrel of a gun pressed against your temple. Each day you have 15
minutes to shower, brush your teeth, and wash your underwear in the
bathroom sink. Your bed is a mat on the floor. One of your fellow
hostages tries to escape, and the guards beat him senseless. Another
tries to commit suicide. One day you too reach the edge of your
sanity. You begin furiously pounding your head against a wall. Blood
oozes from your scalp and smears down your face.

Life has been like that for Terry Anderson ever since March 16, 2
1985, when the chief Middle East correspondent for the Associated
Press was kidnaped in West Beirut. The men who grabbed him, members of the Shi'ite Muslim fundamentalist group called Hizballah,
were intent on swapping Western hostages for 17 comrades impris-

oned in Kuwait for a terrorist spree. Four long years later, Anderson is still held hostage. From accounts by his former fellow captives, *Time* has pieced together a glimpse of the life he has led.

The first day: Terry Anderson lies on a cot in a dingy apartment   3 in Beirut's sprawling, bomb-ravaged Shi'ite slums. A blindfold is tightly wrapped around his head, and chains shackle a wrist and ankle, biting into the flesh. He can hear the roar of jets; Beirut airport is near. The former U.S. Marine is stunned and sobs constantly, frustrated, angry, and afraid that the kidnapers intend to execute him. A guard bursts in and threatens him merely because he creaked the bedsprings. "I am a friend of the Lebanese," Anderson had told his family. "They won't kidnap me. I tell their story to the world."

Anderson is lost in the bowels of Beirut, but he is not alone. In the   4 same 12-ft. by 15-ft. bedroom, also shackled hand and foot and crouching on the floor of a dirty clothes closet, Father Lawrence Martin Jenco of Catholic Relief Services (kidnaped Jan. 8, 1985) peers under his blindfold at the new arrival. A month later, they are led down to the dungeon, a basement partitioned into cramped cells with thin plasterboard, and held prisoner with others: William Buckley, Beirut station chief of the CIA (kidnaped March 16, 1984), the Rev. Benjamin Weir, a Presbyterian missionary (kidnaped May 8, 1984), and eventually David Jacobsen, director of American University Hospital (kidnaped May 28, 1985).

The hostages are repeatedly theatened with death. Their meals   5 consist of Arabic bread, foul-tasting cheese, and tea. Buckley's treatment reveals the full cruelty of the kidnapers. He catches a bad cold that develops into pneumonia, but the guards show him no mercy. "Mr. Buckley is dying," Father Jenco pleads one day. "He is sick. He has dry heaves. Give us liquids."

Speaking to one another in whispers, the hostages listen to Buck-   6 ley's moans as he grows weaker, and finally delirious. On June 3, Buckley squats on the tile floor believing that he is sitting on a toilet seat, and food fantasies fill his head. "I'd like some poached eggs on toast, please," he mumbles. "I'd like an order of pancakes." That night Buckley starts making strange grunts and the others realize they are hearing the rattle of death, and a guard comes and drags Buckley's body away. Anderson's first letter to his family contains his last will and testament.

Out of the blue comes hope. At the end of June Anderson learns   7 that TWA Flight 847 has been hijacked and 39 American passengers are being held. Hajj, the chief guard, arrives with word that a package deal is in the works. "You will be going home," he says.

Nothing happens. The guards, however, improve living condi-   8
tions for Anderson and the others, apparently in fear they might fall
sick and die like Buckley. "Christmas in July" brings dinner of Swiss
steak, vegetables and fruit, medical checkups by a kidnaped Lebanese
Jewish doctor, and the chance to start worshiping together. Anderson,
once a lapsed Catholic whose faith now grows stronger by the day,
wheedles permission from Hajj to make his confession to Father
Jenco. Later, all the hostages are allowed to hold daily services in their
"Church of the Locked Door." They celebrate Communion with
scraps of Arabic bread. Anderson tells the guards to shut up when
they mock the Christian service.

After the first worship, Pastor Weir reaches out and grasps An-   9
derson, and the two men hug. Perhaps worried that the frail minister
might be slipping, Anderson urges him to be strong. "Don't give up,"
he tells him. "Keep going."

Another new hostage has arrived, Thomas Sutherland, dean of   10
agriculture at American University (kidnaped June 9, 1985). Eventually the captors permit their prisoners to be together all the time and
to remove their blindfolds when the guards are out of the room.

One day in September, Hajj raises everybody's hopes again by   11
announcing that a hostage will finally be released. He has them play a
cruel game: they must choose for themselves who will go free. "Think
it over," he commands as he walks away.

The hostages drag their agonizing discussion late into the night.   12
Pastor Weir and Father Jenco make no effort to put themselves forward, and Sutherland is too much of a gentleman. But Anderson
nearly takes a swing at Jacobsen as the two men engage in a bitter
contest to be chosen. Anderson wins the vote, but then is devastated
when Hajj refuses to abide by the decision. "Terry Anderson will not
be the first to be released," he snaps. "He might be the last one." A
few nights later, Hajj tells Pastor Weir he is going home.

On Christmas Eve the hostages hear on the radio that Church of   13
England envoy Terry Waite has failed to negotiate their freedom, and
has returned to London. Anderson is crushed. Father Jenco tries to
sing carols but is too depressed. Jacobsen draws a crude Christmas
tree on a piece of cardboard and sticks it on the wall.

Anderson fights back boredom and depression by throwing him-   14
self into habits and hobbies. Each morning he obsessively cleans the
sleeping mats and takes spirited 40-minute walks around and around
the room. When he fashions a chess set from scraps of tinfoil, the
guards take the game away. Anderson takes French lessons from

Sutherland, and stays up all night reading the Bible and novels by
Charles Dickens that the guards provide.

After solitary confinement, the camaraderie is energizing. From *15*
memory Sutherland recites the poetry of his beloved Robert Burns, in
the brogue of his native Scotland (he once played professional football
with the Glasgow Rangers). Father Jenco takes the hostages on an
imaginary tour of Rome and the Vatican. Anderson makes a deck of
cards from paper scraps, and they all play cutthroat games of hearts.

Like sophists, Anderson the liberal Democrat and Jacobsen the *16*
Reagan Republican constantly provoke each other into arguments to
keep their minds alive.

More than the others, Anderson challenges the guards, although *17*
for some reason he is beaten less frequently. He goes on a seven-day
hunger strike when they suddenly ban the radio and the occasional
copies of the *International Herald Tribune*. He does not know it, but
the news blackout is imposed so he will not learn of the deaths of his
father and brother back in the U.S. He does find out, however, that
since his kidnaping his second daughter, Sulome, has been born.

In July 1986 Father Jenco is freed. Jacobsen goes home in No- *18*
vember, but the public revelation of a secret U.S. arms-for-hostages
deal with Iran torpedoes any further releases. Two months later,
Waite the mediator is himself kidnaped.

Feeling increasingly abandoned by his government, Anderson *19*
spends much of 1987 in isolation. In December he gets a new roommate, French diplomat Marcel Fontaine (kidnaped March 22, 1985).
Anderson is denied permission to send out a videotaped Christmas
message to his family. The frustration becomes unbearable, and one
day he walks over to a wall and beats his head against it. Blood seeps
from Anderson's scalp. "Terry!" Fontaine pleads. "Think of your
family!"

All the hostages find the cruelty too much to take. Sutherland, *20*
who had gone to Beirut passionately hoping to help Lebanese farmers,
is treated worse than the others. He tries to kill himself by putting a
nylon sack over his head. A more recent kidnap victim, Frank Reed,
director of the Lebanese International School (kidnaped Sept. 9,
1986), attempts to escape but is caught. The guards beat him viciously
and break his spirit, leaving him prostrate on the floor.

In 1988 Anderson and Fontaine find themselves in an apartment *21*
that has carpeting, heat, and hot food. Are they being fattened up in
preparation for their release? Despite the constant disappointments,
Anderson is determined to think about his future. He ponders quitting

journalism to take up farming. At last on May 3, after he has spent more than three years as a hostage, his time appears to have come when a guard tells him to get ready.

"You should do the same as I'm doing," Anderson says, trying to improve the Frenchman's chances. At midnight they come and take Anderson away. Two hours later, Fontaine learns that it is he who is being freed. 22

Fontaine remembers a conversation with Anderson. Feeling ill and more depressed than usual, he had turned to Anderson and said, "Terry, I am not afraid to die. But I don't want to die here and have them throw my body into the sea like they did with Buckley." 23

Anderson thought for a moment and replied, "I don't want to die anywhere." 24

Five months ago, Anderson's most recent videotaped message was dropped off at a Western news agency in Beirut. Signing off, he said to his family, "Kiss my daughters. Keep your spirits up, and I will try to do the same. One day soon, God willing, this will end." 25

Meaning

1. What is the meaning of "lost" in MacLeod's title? In what ways is Anderson's life "lost"?
2. Working for the Associated Press in Lebanon, Anderson was convinced that his safety was ensured. According to MacLeod's essay, why was he so confident? From what you know of the Middle East situation, what factors may have put Anderson in danger?
3. What evidence does MacLeod present that indicates malicious cruelty on the part of Anderson's captors?
4. How do the hostages try to maintain their spirits? What events trigger sudden bouts of despair?
5. If you do not know the meanings of the following words, look them up in a dictionary: abide (paragraph 12); camaraderie (15); sophists (16); prostrate (20).

Purpose and Audience

1. The story of Terry Anderson's captivity is powerful, but is that MacLeod's only reason for telling it? What other purpose(s) might he have had, given Anderson's situation as a hostage?
2. Instead of providing a general chronicle of Anderson's four years in cap-

tivity, MacLeod elaborates on several incidents. Why do you think he chooses this approach and these incidents? Select two incidents and explain their effect on you.
3. MacLeod assumes that his audience has a general understanding of the Middle East situation. Where in the article does he mention names, events, and situations that need little or no explanation?

Method and Structure

1. What is the function of MacLeod's first two paragraphs? How is each different from the rest of the essay, and why?
2. **Other Methods** MacLeod's narrative contains considerable description (Chapter 1)—for example, in paragraph 4 MacLeod gives the precise dimensions of the bedroom in which Anderson is first held. Find four or five other instances of such precise detail, and explain their effect on MacLeod's story.

Language

1. In paragraphs 3 through 22, the entire narrative is in the present tense, as in "Terry Anderson *lies* on a cot" and "A blindfold *is* tightly wrapped around his head" (paragraph 3). How does this choice of tense affect MacLeod's point of view? How would the essay differ if it were in the past tense? What is the effect of the past tense in paragraphs 23–25?
2. MacLeod uses the second-person *you* rather than the third-person *he* throughout paragraph 1, addressing the reader directly. As a reader, how effective do you find this stylistic choice, and why?
3. MacLeod's narrative is filled with vivid, concrete words designed to evoke particular images in the mind of the reader—for example, "slammed" (paragraph 1); "biting" (3); and "bowels" (4). Find ten or twelve such words, and explain their effect.

Writing Topics

1. If you know someone who has been through an ordeal, interview him or her to find out particular details. (The ordeal need not be as drastic as Anderson's. Consider such traumas as divorce, illness, prolonged unemployment, or service in a war.) If necessary, augment your interview with other research (in the case of combat service, for example, by reading about particular battles in newspapers or books). Then compose an ac-

count of the ordeal, following MacLeod's organization: invite the reader to identify with the main character, give the background of the story, and then tell the story through incidents.

2. Moorehead Kennedy, one of the hostages captured by the Iranian students at the American embassy in 1979, wrote an article titled "The Root Causes of Terrorism" for the October 1986 issue of *The Humanist*, a periodical available in most college libraries. Read Kennedy's explanation, and consider how his characterization of terrorists contrasts with MacLeod's characterization of Anderson's captors. Write an essay in which you first identify two perspectives on terrorism and then assess Kennedy's attempt to analyze the problem from the terrorists' perspective.

3. Choose one of the events mentioned in MacLeod's chronicle: Terry Waite's negotiations for the release of the hostages (December 1985), Lawrence Jenco's release (July 1986), the arms-for-hostages deal (November 1986), Terry Waite's kidnaping (January 1987), or Marcel Fontaine's release (May 1988). Using *The New York Times Index,* consult one or more newspaper accounts of the event you choose. Write an essay comparing the objective journalistic treatment of the newspaper account(s) to MacLeod's more subjective account. Focusing on the different purposes of each account, consider how each makes use of detail and language.

Writing Topics

Narration

Choose one of the following topics, or any other topic they suggest, for an essay developed by narration. The topic you decide on should be something you care about so that narration is a means of communicating an idea, not an end in itself.

1. A significant trip with your family
2. A wedding or funeral
3. An interaction you witnessed while taking public transportation
4. Your first day of school, as a child or more recently
5. A family reunion
6. Acquiring and repaying a debt, either psychological or financial
7. An episode of extrasensory perception
8. An especially satisfying run, tennis match, bicycle tour, one-on-one basketball game, or other sports experience
9. The first time you met someone who became important to you
10. A time when you confronted authority
11. A time when you had to deliver bad news
12. A performance you gave
13. Moving to a new residence
14. A time when a new, eagerly anticipated possession proved disappointing
15. A time when a fear proved unfounded
16. The most important minutes of a particular game in baseball, football, basketball, or other sport
17. Your biggest social blunder
18. An incident from family legend
19. An argument you had years ago that you would not have today
20. A close encounter with the police
21. A lesson you learned from someone younger than you
22. A great or a terrible party
23. An act of generosity
24. A reunion of long-separated friends or relatives
25. A bad day in school
26. A harrowing experience in a car, airplane, bus, or train, or on an amusement-park ride
27. A time when a poem, story, film, song, or other work left you feeling changed

Chapter 3

Example

Understanding the Method

An **example** represents some general group or some abstract concept or quality. Steven Spielberg is an example of the group of movie directors. A friend's calling at 2:00 A.M. is an example of her inconsiderateness. We habitually use examples to bring our general and abstract statements down to earth so that our listeners or readers will take an interest in them and understand them.

As this definition indicates, the chief purpose of examples is to make the general specific and the abstract concrete. Since these operations are among the most basic in writing, it is easy to see why illustration or exemplification (the use of example) is among the most common methods of writing. Examples appear frequently in essays developed by other methods. In fact, as diverse as they are, all the essays in this book employ examples for clarity, support, and liveliness. If the writers had not used examples, we might have only a vague sense of their meaning or, worse, might supply mistaken meanings from our own experiences.

While nearly indispensable in any kind of writing, examples may also serve as the sole method of developing ideas that can be explained as effectively by illustration as by any other means. Such ideas include generalizations about trends ("The television monitor is fast becoming the most useful machine in the house"), events ("Some members of the audience at *The Rocky Horror Picture Show* were stranger than anything in the movie"), institutions ("A mental hospital is no place for the mentally ill"), behaviors ("The personalities of parents are sometimes visited on their children"), and rituals ("A funeral benefits the dead person's family and friends"). Each of these ideas could form the central assertion (the thesis) of an essay, and as many examples as necessary would then support it.

How many examples are necessary? That depends on the subject, the writer's purpose, and the intended audience. Some ideas can be developed with a single **extended example** of several paragraphs or several pages that fills in needed background and gives the reader a complete view of the subject from one angle. For instance, the advantages of a funeral might be made clear with a narrative and descriptive account of a particular funeral, the family and friends who attended it, and the benefits they derived from it. In contrast, other ideas require **multiple examples**. Illustrating the strangeness of a movie's viewers might require only a couple of very strange examples, or it might require six or eight examples to show range of peculiarity. Supporting the generalization about mental hospitals might demand many examples of patients whose illnesses worsened in the hospital or (from a different angle) many examples of hospital practices that actually harm patients. Sometimes a generalization merits support from both an extended example and several briefer examples, a combination that provides depth along with range. For instance, half the essay on mental hospitals might be devoted to one patient's experiences and the other half to brief summaries of others' experiences.

Analyzing Examples in Paragraphs

Charles Kuralt (born 1934) is a well-known journalist on CBS television. During the 1970s he broadcast his impressions of mostly small-town America over a national radio show called *Dateline America*. The following paragraph appears in his book of the same title, published in 1979.

Example 89

Poll takers and soothsayers, their eyes upon the box office, proclaim baseball to be a dying sport. They should travel the land in the spring and shift their gaze to the vacant lots. <u>Nothing, nothing has changed.</u> Nine-year-olds still take mighty practice swings holding the bat at the very end, for to choke up on the handle is to admit you are not yet a man. The ball is wrapped in the black friction tape to keep it from unraveling. The catcher wears his cap backwards but takes the pitch on the first bounce, because who has a mask or chest protector? The ten-year-old shortstop still talks it up to the eleven-year-old pitcher—"Make him hit it to us, baby!"—and prays to God that if he does hit it, it doesn't come too low and hard to handle. The fat, slow kid still plays right field.

Generalization (underlined)

Five specific, concrete examples

Alice Walker (born 1944) is a teacher, essayist, poet, and fiction writer, the winner of a Pulitzer Prize for her novel *The Color Purple* (1982). The following paragraph comes from Walker's essay "The Black Writer and the Southern Experience," which appears in a collection of her essays, *In Search of Our Mothers' Gardens* (1983).

<u>What the black Southern writer inherits as a natural right is a sense of *community,*</u> something simple but surprisingly hard, especially these days, to come by. My mother, who is a walking history of our community, tells me that when each of her children was born the midwife accepted as payment such home-grown or homemade items as a pig, a quilt, jars of canned fruits and vegetables. But there was never any question that the midwife would come when she was needed, whatever the eventual payment for her services. I consider this each time I hear of a hospital that refuses to admit a woman in labor unless she can hand over a substantial sum of money, cash.

Generalization (underlined)

Single extended example of first part of generalization

Specific examples within example

Example of second part of generalization

Developing an Essay by Example

GETTING STARTED

An appropriate subject for an example paper is likely to be a general idea you have formed on the basis of your experiences or observations. Say, for instance, that over the past several years you have seen one made-for-television movie after another dealing effectively with a sensitive issue such as incest, spouse abuse, or AIDS. There is your subject: some TV movies do a good job of dramatizing and explaining difficult social issues. It is a generalization about TV movies based on what you know of individual movies. Or suppose you've just survived a summer living with a friend and his cat despite your allergy to cats. The experience has taught you a lesson: make the best of a bad situation by cooperation and compromise. Again, you've found a subject in an idea based on an incident. Either of these generalizations could serve as the thesis of your essay, the point you want readers to take away. A clear thesis is crucial for an example paper because without it readers can only guess what your illustrations are intended to show.

After arriving at your thesis, you should make a list of all the pertinent examples or all the pertinent features of a single extended example. This stage may take some thought and even some further reading or observation. While making the list, keep your intended readers at the front of your mind: what do they already know about your subject, and what do they need to know in order to accept your thesis? In developing the example of living with a roommate's cat, you might assume that your readers can imagine the situation easily enough as long as you provide a clear, well-detailed narration of your initial difficulties and how you and your roommate (and his cat) resolved them. In contrast, illustrating the social value of TV movies would require a different approach for readers who are indifferent to television or who believe television is worthless or even harmful. Then you might concentrate on the movies that are most relevant to readers' lives, providing enough detail about each to make readers see the relevance.

ORGANIZING

Most example essays open with an introduction that engages readers' attention and gives them some context to relate to. You might begin the paper on TV movies, for instance, by briefly narrating

Example 91

the plot of one movie. Or you might begin the paper on living with a cat by describing yourself gasping and scratching when you first moved in with your roommate. The opening should lead into your thesis so that readers know what to expect from the rest of the essay.

Organizing the body of the essay may not be difficult if you use a single example, for the example itself may suggest a distinct method of development and thus an arrangement. The experience of living with a cat, for instance, strongly suggests development by narration and a chronological order. In contrast, an essay presenting a building as an example of a style of architecture suggests development by description and a spatial organization (say, from the ground up, or from the roof down) or an arrangement by parts of the building (door, windows, corners, roof, and so on).

An essay using multiple examples usually requires more attention to arrangement so that readers experience not a list but a pattern. If you're using a limited number of examples—say, four or five—they may be arranged in order of increasing importance, interest, or complexity, with the strongest and most detailed one providing a dramatic finish. But with very many examples—perhaps ten or fifteen—the climactic order probably will not work by itself, either to help you organize (most of the examples may seem roughly equal in importance) or to help readers keep track of individual instances. In that case you should find some likenesses among examples that will allow you to treat them in groups. For instance, instead of covering fourteen TV movies in a shapeless list, you might group them by subject into movies dealing with family relations, those dealing with illness, and the like. (This is the method of classification discussed in Chapter 5.) Covering each group in a separate paragraph or two would avoid the awkward string of choppy paragraphs that might result from covering each example independently. And arranging the groups themselves in order of increasing interest or importance would further structure your presentation.

To conclude your essay, you may want to summarize by elaborating on the generalization of your thesis now that you have supported it. But the essay may not require a conclusion at all if you believe your final example emphasizes your point and provides a strong finish.

DRAFTING

While you draft your essay, remember that your examples must be plentiful and specific enough to support your generalization. If you use fifteen different examples, their range should allow you to treat each one briefly, in one or two sentences. But if you use only three examples, say, you will have to describe each one in sufficient detail to make up for their small number. And, obviously, if you use only a single example, you must be as specific as possible so that readers see clearly how it alone illustrates your generalization.

REVISING

To be sure you've met the expectations that most readers hold for examples, revise your draft against the following questions.

1. *Are all examples, or all parts of a single example, obviously pertinent to your generalization?* Be careful not to get sidetracked by peripheral information, such as your sister's allergy to cats or theatrical films about social issues.

2. *Do the examples, or the parts of a single example, cover all the territory mapped out by your generalization?* To support your generalization, you need to present a range of instances that fairly represents the whole. An essay on the social value of TV movies would be misleading if it failed to acknowledge that not *all* TV movies have social value. It would also be misleading if it presented several TV movies as representative examples of socially valuable TV when in fact they were the *only* instances of such TV.

3. *Do your examples support your generalization?* You should not start with a broad statement and then try to drum up a few examples to prove it. A thesis such as "Children do poorly in school because they watch too much television" would require factual support gained from research, not the lone example of your little brother. If your little brother performs poorly in school and you attribute his performance to his television habits, then narrow your thesis so that it accurately reflects your evidence—perhaps "In the case of my little brother, at least, the more time spent watching television the poorer the grades."

Perri Klass

Perri Klass is a doctor and a writer of both fiction and nonfiction. She was born in 1958 in Trinidad and grew up in New York City and New Jersey. After obtaining a B.A. from Harvard University in 1979, she began graduate work in biology but then switched to medicine. Klass finished Harvard Medical School in 1986 and is now a resident in pediatrics in a Boston hospital. Meanwhile, she has published short stories in Mademoiselle, Antioch Review, *and other magazines; published a novel,* Recombinations *(1985), and a collection of stories,* I Am Having an Adventure *(1986); written essays for* The New York Times, Discover, *and other periodicals; and published a collection of essays,* A Not Entirely Benign Procedure *(1987). She has also taught freshman composition at Harvard and helped raise her son, born in 1984—"just after finals," Klass says, "and just before next semester's hospital duties began."*

She's Your Basic
L.O.L. in N.A.D.

Most of us have felt excluded, confused, or even frightened by the jargon of the medical profession—that is, by the special terminology and abbreviations for diseases and other ailments. In this essay Klass uses examples of such jargon, some of it heartless, to illustrate the pluses and minuses of becoming a doctor. The essay first appeared as a 1984 "Hers" column in The New York Times.

"Mrs. Tolstoy is your basic L.O.L. in N.A.D., admitted for a soft 1
rule-out M.I.," the intern announces. I scribble that on my patient list. In other words Mrs. Tolstoy is a Little Old Lady in No Apparent Distress who is in the hospital to make sure she hasn't had a heart attack (rule out a myocardial infarction). And we think it's unlikely that she has had a heart attack (a *soft* rule-out).

If I learned nothing else during my first three months of working 2
in the hospital as a medical student, I learned endless jargon and abbreviations. I started out in a state of primeval innocence, in which I didn't even know that "s̄ C.P., S.O.B., N/V" meant "without chest pain, shortness of breath, or nausea and vomiting." By the end I took the abbreviations so for granted that I would complain to my mother

the English Professor, "And can you believe I had to put down *three* NG tubes last night?"

"You'll have to tell me what an NG tube is if you want me to 3 sympathize properly," my mother said. NG, nasogastric—isn't it obvious?

I picked up not only the specific expressions but also the patterns 4 of speech and the grammatical conventions; for example, you never say that a patient's blood pressure fell or that his cardiac enzymes rose. Instead, the patient is always the subject of the verb: "He dropped his pressure." "He bumped his enzymes." This sort of construction probably reflects that profound irritation of the intern when the nurses come in the middle of the night to say that Mr. Dickinson has disturbingly low blood pressure. "Oh, he's gonna hurt me bad tonight," the intern may say, inevitably angry at Mr. Dickinson for dropping his pressure and creating a problem.

When chemotherapy fails to cure Mrs. Bacon's cancer, what we 5 say is, "Mrs. Bacon failed chemotherapy."

"Well, we've already had one hit today, and we're up next, but at 6 least we've got mostly stable players on our team." This means that our team (group of doctors and medical students) has already gotten one new admission today, and it is our turn again, so we'll get whoever is next admitted in emergency, but at least most of the patients we already have are fairly stable, that is, unlikely to drop their pressures or in any other way get suddenly sicker and hurt us bad. Baseball metaphor is pervasive: A no-hitter is a night without any new admissions. A player is always a patient—a nitrate player is a patient on nitrates, a unit player is a patient in the intensive-care unit and so on, until you reach the terminal player.

It is interesting to consider what it means to be winning, or doing 7 well, in this perennial baseball game. When the intern hangs up the phone and announces, "I got a hit," that is not cause for congratulations. The team is not scoring points; rather, it is getting hit, being bombarded with new patients. The object of the game from the point of view of the doctors, considering the players for whom they are already responsible, is to get as few new hits as possible.

These special languages contribute to a sense of closeness and 8 professional spirit among people who are under a great deal of stress. As a medical student, it was exciting for me to discover that I'd finally cracked the code, that I could understand what doctors said and wrote and could use the same formulations myself. Some people seem to become enamored of the jargon for its own sake, perhaps because they are so deeply thrilled with the idea of medicine, with the idea of themselves as doctors.

I knew a medical student who was referred to by the interns on the team as Mr. Eponym because he was so infatuated with eponymous terminology,[1] the more obscure the better. He never said "capillary pulsations" if he could say "Quincke's pulses." He would lovingly tell over the multinamed syndromes—Wolff-Parkinson-White, Lown-Ganong-Levine, Henoch-Schonlein—until the temptation to suggest Schleswig-Holstein or Stevenson-Kefauver or Baskin-Robbins became irresistible to his less reverent colleagues. 9

And there is the jargon that you don't ever want to hear yourself using. You know that your training is changing you, but there are certain changes you think would be going a little too far. 10

The resident was describing a man with devastating terminal pancreatic cancer. "Basically he's C.T.D.," the resident concluded. I reminded myself that I had resolved not to be shy about asking when I didn't understand things. "C.T.D.?" I asked timidly. 11

The resident smirked at me. "Circling The Drain." 12

The images are vivid and terrible. "What happened to Mrs. Melville?" 13

"Oh, she boxed last night." To box is to die, of course. 14

Then there are the more pompous locutions that can make the beginning medical student nervous about the effects of medical training. A friend of mine was told by his resident, "A pregnant woman with sickle-cell represents a failure of genetic counseling." 15

Mr. Eponym, who tried hard to talk like the doctors, once explained to me, "An infant is basically a brainstem preparation." A brainstem preparation, as used in neurological research, is an animal whose higher brain functions have been destroyed so that only the most primitive reflexes remain, like the sucking reflex, the startle reflex, and the rooting reflex. 16

The more extreme forms aside, one most important function of medical jargon is to help doctors maintain some distance from their patients. By reformulating a patient's pain and problems into a language that the patient doesn't even speak, I suppose we are in some sense taking those pains and problems under our jurisdiction and also reducing their emotional impact. This linguistic separation between 17

[1] *Eponymous* means "named after"—in this case, medical terminology is named after researchers. [Editor's note.]

doctors and patients allows conversations to go on at the bedside that are unintelligible to the patient. "Naturally, we're worried about adeno-C.A.," the intern can say to the medical student, and lung cancer need never be mentioned.

I learned a new language this past summer. At times it thrills me to hear myself using it. It enables me to understand my colleagues, to communicate effectively in the hospital. Yet I am uncomfortably aware that I will never again notice the peculiarities and even atrocities of medical language as keenly as I did this summer. There may be specific expressions I manage to avoid, but even as I remark them, promising myself I will never use them, I find that this language is becoming my professional speech. It no longer sounds strange in my ears—or coming from my mouth. And I am afraid that as with any new language, to use it properly you must absorb not only the vocabulary but also the structure, the logic, the attitudes. At first you may notice these new alien assumptions every time you put together a sentence, but with time and increased fluency you stop being aware of them at all. And as you lose that awareness, for better or for worse, you move closer and closer to being a doctor instead of just talking like one. 18

Meaning

1. What point does Klass make about medical jargon in this essay? Where does she reveal her main point explicitly?
2. What useful purposes does medical jargon serve, according to Klass? Do the examples in paragraphs 9–16 serve these purposes? Why or why not?
3. If you do not know the meanings of the following words, look them up in a dictionary: primeval (2); terminal (6); perennial (7); syndromes, reverent (9); pompous, locutions (15); jurisdiction (17).

Purpose and Audience

1. What does Klass imply when she states that she began her work in the hospital "in a state of primeval innocence" (paragraph 2)? What does this phrase suggest about her purpose in writing the essay?
2. From what perspective does Klass write this essay: that of a medical professional? someone outside the profession? a patient? someone else? To what extent does she expect her readers to share her perspective? What evidence in the essay supports your answer?

3. Given that she is writing for a general audience, does Klass take adequate care to define medical terms? Support your answer with examples from the essay.

Method and Structure

1. Why does Klass begin the essay with an example rather than a statement of her main idea? What effect does this example produce? How does this effect support her purpose in writing the essay?
2. Although Klass uses many examples of medical jargon, she avoids the dull effect of a list by periodically stepping back to make a general statement about her experience or the jargon—for instance, "I picked up not only specific expressions but also the patterns of speech and the grammatical conventions" (paragraph 4). Locate other places—not necessarily at the beginnings of paragraphs—where Klass breaks up her examples with more general statements.
3. **Other Methods** Klass uses several other methods besides example, among them narration (Chapter 2), definition (Chapter 9), and cause-and-effect analysis (Chapter 10). In paragraphs 6–7 the "baseball metaphor" Klass explains adds up to an analogy—that is, a comparison of two unlike subjects (tending the sick and playing baseball) that uses some actual similarities as the basis for establishing other similarities (see Chapter 8). What actual similarities does Klass suggest between doctors' work and playing ball? How does the "game" differ among doctors?

Language

1. Klass refers to the users of medical jargon as both *we/us* (paragraphs 1, 5, 6, 17) and *they/them* (7); and sometimes she shifts from *I* to *you* within a paragraph (4, 18). Do you think these shifts are effective or distracting? Why? Do the shifts serve any function?
2. Klass obviously experienced both positive and negative feelings about mastering medical jargon. Which words and phrases in the last paragraph (18) reflect positive feelings, and which negative?

Writing Topics

1. Klass likens her experience learning medical jargon to that of learning a new language (paragraph 18). If you are studying or have learned a second language, write an essay in which you explain the "new alien

assumptions" you must make "every time you put together a sentence."
Draw your examples not just from the new language's grammar and
vocabulary but from its underlying logic and attitudes. For instance, does
one speak to older people differently in the new language? make requests
differently? describe love or art differently?

2. Most groups focused on a common interest have their own jargon. If you
belong to such a group—for example, runners, football fans, food serv-
ers, engineering students—spend a few days listening to yourself and
others use this language and thinking about the purposes it serves. In an
essay, explain what this jargon reveals about the group and its common
interest, using as many specific examples as you can.

3. Klass's essay explores the "separation between doctors and patients"
(paragraph 17). Has this separation affected you as a patient or as the
relative or friend of a patient? If so, write an essay about your experiences. Did the medical professionals rely heavily on jargon? Was their
language comforting, frightening, irritating? Based on your experience
and on Klass's essay, do you believe that the separations between doctors
and patients is desirable? Why, or why not?

Neil Postman

A cultural critic focusing on education and communication, Neil Postman was born in 1931 in Brooklyn, New York. He was educated at the State University of New York at Fredonia (B.S., 1953) and Columbia University (M.A., 1955; Ed.D., 1958). Starting in the late 1960s, Postman and a coauthor, Charles Weingartner, earned reputations as educational reformers with several influential books, including Teaching as a Subversive Activity *(1969) and* The Soft Revolution *(1971). Then, in 1979, Postman shifted positions with* Teaching as a Conserving Activity, *arguing that increasingly rapid social change and intense media bombardment now demanded schools providing stability and continuity. Meanwhile, he was also writing about communication and development, publishing numerous articles and such books as* Crazy Talk, Stupid Talk: How We Defeat Ourselves by the Way We Talk and What to Do About It *(1976),* The Disappearance of Childhood *(1982), and* Amusing Ourselves to Death: Public Discourse in the Age of Show Business *(1985). Postman lives in New York City and is an award-winning teacher of communication arts and sciences at New York University.*

Megatons for Anthromegs

In this essay from his latest book, Conscientious Objections *(1988), Postman uses examples within examples to skewer our use of language to conceal rather than reveal meaning. When it comes to nuclear war, says Postman, "the language of everyday political commentary is incapable of expressing what is at stake."*

Now that we know how much our children's dreams are plagued by   1
fears of a nuclear holocaust, it is time we adults did something about it. Since it would be immature, not to mention irresponsible, to actually eliminate nuclear weapons, what is needed is a new vocabulary of nuclear war, a vocabulary uncluttered by the associations which generate fear and trembling.

This I have begun to do. I hope my lexicon, when completed, will   2
form the basis of a rhetoric of reassurance that will pacify our children's dreams and help the rest of us contemplate with courage and dignity the realities of nuclear war.

Below, I have placed currently used terms on the left. To the right 3
of each is the term I offer in its place. I have also included some small
elaboration of the superiority of my term over the one it would
replace.

ONE MILLION PEOPLE   ANTHROMEG

It is disconcerting and unnecessarily emotional to talk of millions 4
of people, especially if they are going to die. What could be more
objective and detached, and at the same time more calming, than the
statement, "Ten megatons kills twenty anthromegs"? Ask any man if
he is willing to lose, say, 65 anthromegs if he could thereby defeat the
Russians, and he will immediately say "Yes." If you ask him if he is
willing to lose 65 million people, he will become confused and
depressed.

NUCLEAR ATTACK   AERIAL VISITATION

If the Russians attack us, they will not come with ice pellets. 5
"Attack" *means* "nuclear attack." Why provide ourselves with a double reminder, especially one so anxiety-producing? "Aerial visitation"
will help to eliminate unreasonable fears about the future and will do
more to encourage us to plan ahead with enthusiasm. Who could
possibly get upset by a sign which says: "In Case of Aerial Visitation,
Drive over Bridge"? Tell a man that in the event of an aerial visitation
his child will be kept at school, and he will probably ask, "And when
may I come to get him?"

KILLING BY NUCLEAR WEAPONS   THERMALICIDE

Men have invented an illustrious list of technical words to de- 6
scribe with precision and detachment the various types of killing.
"Thermalicide" extends the list by one by providing us with an un-
emotional, scientific denotation of a perfectly natural, albeit unpleasant, human activity. Besides, there are far too many disgusting
associations attached to "genocide."

DEATH BY NUCLEAR WEAPONS   CULMINATING EXPERIENCE

"To culminate" means to reach one's highest point, a virtual cer- 7
tainty when one has been exploded by a nuclear weapon. "To experience" means to undergo actively, another certainty when within range
of a nuclear explosion. "Culminating experience" is, therefore, a perfectly precise description of the process.

RADIATION   FILTERATION

Who would not prefer being filterated as against radiated, even if 8
the effect is the same? One filters cigarette smoke or swimming pools
or lubricating oil. The word forcefully suggests that the result of the
process is some sort of purity, a most apt connotation. For, after all, is
it not purifying to suffer?

FALLOUT SHELTER   PROTECTIVE RESIDENCE

Although not much has been said about it lately, when the subject 9
of fallout shelters comes up there is usually a considerable amount of
hysteria. It is to be expected. What man would desire to live in a
"shelter" even for a day? The word is ominous. It hints at alienation
and ultimate isolation. "Protective residence" is another matter. The
term suggests an extension of one's home—comfy, warm, intimate,
familiar. Moreover, the moral question of whether or not you are
obligated to allow others entrance is easily settled. A "shelter" connotes public domain, but a man's "residence" is his castle. That's that.

SURVIVORS   THE UNCULMINATED

Is there a more desperate-sounding word in our language than 10
"survivors"? It conjures up visions of groping, disoriented people and
surrounding chaos. "The unculminated" logically follows from "culminating experience" and at the same time suggests unfulfilled ambi-
tions, unsatisfied desires; in short, the continuation of life.

The vocabulary presented above is, of course, only a beginning— 11
basic talk, as it were. In order to suggest how such a vocabulary might
be used to create a new rhetoric of reassurance, I have composed
below a short paragraph which describes in inoffensive language the
realities of thermonuclear war:

American scientists assure us that our capacity for thermalicide is 12
the greatest in the world. This fact will, of course, deter our enemies
from attempting it on us. But should our enemies decide to make
aerial visitations, we will persevere. If every family has provided itself
with a protective residence, the extent of filteration will be sharply
minimized. And even if our enemies should launch a 300-megaton
aerial visitation, probably no more than 50 or 60 anthromegs will
have a culminating experience. Those who are unculminated may re-
main in their protective residences until all danger of thermalicide is
past.

Sleep in peace, my children. 13

Meaning

1. Why does Postman say a new vocabulary of nuclear war is needed? Is his reason serious? How do you know?
2. Explain what you think Postman means by his phrase "rhetoric of reassurance" (paragraph 2). In what ways do his new terms promote a false reassurance? Where in the essay do you find evidence of Postman's awareness of this false reassurance?
3. If you do not know the meanings of the following words or parts of words, look them up in a dictionary: lexicon, rhetoric, pacify (paragraph 2); disconcerting, anthro- or anthropo-, meg- or mega- (4); thermal- or thermo-, -cide, denotation, albeit, genocide (6); connotation (8); persevere (12).

Purpose and Audience

1. If we rely solely on what Postman says, his purpose is to create a "rhetoric of reassurance that will . . . help . . . us contemplate with courage and dignity the realities of nuclear war" (paragraph 2). However, the essay is ironic—Postman says one thing but means another. (See *irony* in the Glossary.) How would you describe Postman's real purpose in writing this essay? Why do you think he believes that the only way we can talk about nuclear war is to "speak about how we speak about [it]"?
2. Based on his treatment of the subject, how would you characterize Postman's attitude toward nuclear arms?
3. Is Postman writing to an audience whose views are similar to his own, or different? On what evidence do you base your response?

Method and Structure

1. Postman's essay consists of examples within examples: the new words themselves are examples of a new vocabulary; most of the new words are explained with examples of their use (as in paragraph 4); and the essay ends with an extended example using the words (12). How do both the particular examples of the words' use and the final extended example contribute to Postman's main idea? How to they reinforce each other?
2. At the end of his essay Postman brings us full circle to the opening image of children asleep and dreaming. Why do you suppose Postman returns to that image? What is the difference between these two references to children?
3. **Other Methods**   Besides example, two other methods of development

figure prominently in paragraphs 4–11 of Postman's essay: definition (Chapter 9) and comparison and contrast (Chapter 7). What is Postman's reason for comparing old and new terms? How does the use of comparison support his point?

Language

1. Postman's "rhetoric of reassurance" is made up of carefully constructed euphemisms. If necessary, look up the word *euphemism* in the dictionary, and then explain how each of Postman's words is a euphemism. What associations does each word have?
2. Part of Postman's reassurance comes from his use of the first-person *I* and *we* in his introductory paragraphs. How does this choice help to create the desired effect?

Writing Topics

1. Consider an issue, situation, or behavior that you find silly, irritating, or potentially harmful—for example, campus parking problems, residence hall rules, a personal relationship (parent-child, sibling, and so on), a popular advertising campaign, or professional athletes' salaries. Invent examples of a language to use when discussing the subject, using Postman's essay as a model. Begin with an introduction explaining the need for your new vocabulary, and provide explanations and examples of the new words. Use understatement, exaggeration, reversal, and other techniques to establish irony (see *irony* in the Glossary). Use your new words in an extended example at the end of your essay.
2. Rewrite Postman's extended example of his new, inoffensive language (paragraph 12), using the actual terms that his euphemisms are meant to replace. Then write a comparison of Postman's original and your rewrite, paying special attention to the logic and effect of each.
3. Look up the terms *irony* and *satire* in the Glossary, and read Jonathan Swift's "A Modest Proposal" (p. 345) for another example of ironic satire in which the author clearly separates himself from the character he pretends to be in making his recommendations. Then write an essay analyzing how Postman the author separates himself from Postman the character who is advocating this vocabulary. Concentrate on how his examples reveal the difference between his real and his stated self and purpose.

George F. Will

George F. Will, born in 1941 in Champaign, Illinois, is a nationally known political columnist and television commentator. He was educated at Trinity College (B.S., 1962), Oxford University, and Princeton University (Ph.D., 1967). He taught politics at Michigan State University and the University of Toronto, served as an aide to a United States senator, and then in 1972 became Washington editor of The National Review. *Since the mid-1970s he has been a contributing editor of* Newsweek, *writing a biweekly column, and the author of a syndicated newspaper column that now appears in more than 450 papers across the country. His essays—notable for their wit, eloquence, and conservative political stance—have been collected in several volumes, including* The Pursuit of Happiness and Other Sobering Thoughts *(1978) and* The Pursuit of Virtue and Other Tory Notions *(1982). He has also written* Statecraft as Soulcraft: What Government Does *(1983) and* The New Season: A Spectator's Guide to the 1988 Election *(1988). In 1977 Will received the Pulitzer Prize for commentary. He lives outside Washington, D.C.*

When Homicide
Is Noble

In the essay below, Will uses a single extended example, laid out with meticulous care, to support a claim likely to be controversial among his readers. The piece first appeared in April 1983 and was collected in The Morning After: American Successes and Excesses, 1981–1986 *(1986).*

It is said that hard cases make bad law. But bad law can be made by   1
pretending that hard cases are not cases.

Consider the case of Hans Florian, who on March 18 [1983] shot   2
to death the woman to whom he had been married for 33 years. His act was loving, brave, even noble. Nevertheless, it was not an act about which society should be indifferent or permissive, or about which the law should be agnostic. Yet a Florida grand jury refused to indict him.

Alzheimer's disease began destroying his wife's mind in the late   3
1970s. There is no known cause or cure for the disease. It causes the brain to shrivel and fill with bubbles and granules. Soon his wife

could not drive or write, and would panic when he stepped away from her. He and his son by an earlier marriage cared for her, forcing her mouth open for food, and bathing her and changing her clothes five or six times a day as she soiled them.

For most of the past two years, whenever she was not heavily 4 drugged she howled constantly, and screamed two words, "fire" and "pain," in her native German. Finally, she had to be put in a nursing home for her own safety. Hans Florian is 17 years older than she was and he did not want to die leaving her alone.

This case did not involve any of the multiplying dilemmas occa- 5 sioned by the sophistication of modern medicine, the mechanical and pharmacological technologies that can prolong a painful process of dying, without altering the prognosis. This was not the sort of case for which hospice care is most suited. Such care is designed for the predictable final period of a terminal disease, during which the patient can lead a tolerable life enhanced by pain management. Alzheimer's disease can run on and on.

This was not a case where a person had sunk into a condition 6 where, by some arguable definition, death could be said to have occurred. Mrs. Florian's mind was destroyed, but brain death had not happened. Because Alzheimer's disease is terrifying, irreversible and protracted, Florian's case underscores this fact: There is no way entirely to exclude "quality of life" considerations from all controversies in biomedical ethics.

Many persons feel proper anxiety about casual, incoherent injec- 7 tions of "meaningful life" rhetoric in the 1973 Supreme Court abortion ruling,[1] and in rationalizations for infanticide even against newborns with easily remediable physical defects. Therefore, many persons have tried to assert "sanctity of life" criteria that would enable all decision-making to proceed without consideration of the quality of life a subject can lead.

Quality of life assessments are fraught with difficulties and dan- 8 gers. Current practices offer abundant examples of mistakes and abuses. However, when "heroic" medical measures are employed, or when there is a decision to intervene in a person's life to alter the

---

[1] In 1973 the Supreme Court ruled, in *Roe v. Wade*, that a state may not prevent a woman from having an abortion during the first six months of pregnancy. The issue of when life becomes "meaningful" was often raised in the arguments and in the final decision. [Editor's note.]

course nature would take in "taking its course," this is true: You cannot judge the morality of what is done without reference to the quality of life that has been extended by heroic medicine or ended by extreme action.

However, the law cannot quite countenance such extreme measures as Florian's, even when, as in this case, the situation is extreme. Obviously Florian was in an unsettled frame of mind when carrying out his considered decision to shoot the woman he loved. But he did not try to diminish his responsibility for his action. And there was no ambiguity concerning competent consent: Florian obviously substituted his judgment for that of a person incapable of choosing.   *9*

It is, therefore, hard to see how the grand jury can have properly refused to indict. Surely there was probable cause for finding that a crime—homicide—had been committed. Grand juries require less to indict (a finding of probable cause to believe that a crime has been committed) than a trial jury requires to convict (proof of guilt beyond reasonable doubt).   *10*

The proper place for society to express compassionate understanding in cases such as Florian's is at the sentencing stage. There should be ample discretion at that stage to enable society to avoid the practice of not indicting when a homicide undoubtedly has occurred. Such a practice would express the dangerous doctrine that certain homicides are matters of indifference to society.   *11*

Some cases are hard because this is true: A homicide can be noble without properly being, in the eyes of the law, permissible.   *12*

Meaning

1. Explain what Will means by his first two sentences. What is a "hard case"? How does Will's extended example illustrate that "bad law can be made by pretending that hard cases are not cases"?
2. According to Will, how does the Florian case differ from other current medical/legal dilemmas?
3. What is the distinction between the requirements for indictment and those for conviction that Will makes in paragraph 10? What is the significance of this distinction to Will's point?
4. If you do not know the meanings of the following words, look them up in a dictionary: agnostic, indict (paragraph 2); granules (3); pharmacological, prognosis, hospice (5); protracted, biomedical (6); infanticide, remediable (7); fraught (8); countenance, ambiguity (9); discretion (11).

Purpose and Audience

1. Will wrote this essay for a general audience, many members of which would not be familiar with the legal and medical implications of this case. Find several places where he explains terms and concepts that the general reader may not know. Where does he assume understanding on the part of the reader?
2. What is Will's purpose, besides explaining the Florian case? Why do you think he used only the one example to achieve that purpose?
3. What side is Will on in this essay: that of the individual faced with a painful decision? that of the medical establishment dealing with a difficult case? that of the legal system charged with maintaining society's order? Where in the essay does he make his alignment clear?

Method and Structure

1. Will opens his essay with an abstract legal concept (paragraph 1), and then provides an extended example. How would the essay have differed if Will had withheld his initial statement until after introducing Florian's case?
2. In relating his example, Will tells the whole story of Florian's act before analyzing its implications. Why do you suppose he chose not to interject analysis into the story? For example, why did he not discuss the possible care and prognosis of Alzheimer's disease (paragraph 5) immediately after explaining the disease medically (3)?
3. **Other Methods** Will employs other methods besides example in his essay: for instance, in paragraphs 5–6 and 9 he contrasts Florian's case with other cases (Chapter 7); in paragraph 3 he defines Alzheimer's disease (Chapter 9); and in paragraphs 3–4 he analyzes the causes of Florian's act (Chapter 10). Most notable, however, is the use of argument and persuasion (Chapter 11), which here becomes the main purpose of the essay. Why is the use of example essential to the argument Will is making?

Language

1. In his last paragraph Will repeats key words from the first two paragraphs: "hard cases," "noble," and "permissive/permissible." How does this repetition reinforce his main point?

2. Analyze Will's use of language when he refers to Hans Florian. What attitude does Will convey?

3. Several times Will uses a sentence pattern like that at the end of paragraph 6: "... Florian's case underscores this fact: There is no way entirely to exclude 'quality of life' considerations. . . ." Locate two patterns similar to this one. Why do you think Will uses this pattern? How effective or ineffective do you think it is, and why?

Writing Topics

1. Think of a point you would like to make about a controversial issue. The issue need not be a matter of life and death; you may consider, for example, your college's plagiarism policy, an instructor's attendance policy, your state's drunk-driving laws, or your family's rules for behavior. After stating your point generally, use an extended example to illustrate the point. Follow Will's example as closely as possible in looking at the case from all angles and progressing logically from step to step.

2. Will states that the quality of a life saved by heroic measures or ended by extreme action must be considered before the morality of the action can be judged (paragraph 8). Write a brief essay in which you analyze this statement as objectively as you can, considering not only possible support for it (including Will's argument) but also possible opposition: for instance, what of the opinion Will alludes to in paragraph 7, that the sanctity of life should always take precedence over the quality of life, regardless of other circumstances? Your purpose is not to argue for any one position but to present all possible positions fairly and clearly.

3. Try to find a newspaper account of the grand jury's decision in the Florian case by consulting *The New York Times Index* from mid-March to mid-April 1983. In an essay, compare the grand jury's apparent reading of the case with Will's, noting especially the interpretation of the law in each account. In the conclusion of your essay, state your view of the case, offering reasons why you agree with either the grand jury or Will.

Writing Topics

Example

Choose one of the following statements, or any other statement they suggest, and agree *or* disagree with it in an essay developed by one or more examples. The statement you decide on should concern a topic you care about so that the example or examples are a means of communicating an idea, not an end in themselves.

1. Bumper stickers are a form of conversation among Americans.
2. Advertisements contain messages that are not always obvious.
3. Sometimes the press misleads the public.
4. Good art can be ugly.
5. These days, politics seems to be the art of acquiring wealth.
6. In happy families, talk is the main activity.
7. A craze or fad reveals something about the culture it arises in.
8. Drug or alcohol addiction does not happen just to "bad" people.
9. The best rock musicians treat social and political issues in their songs.
10. Violence on TV and in movies harms the children who see it.
11. Grandparents relate more closely to their grandchildren than to their children.
12. Rock music fosters bad behavior.
13. Students at schools with enforced dress codes behave better than students at schools without such codes.
14. Television news programs are beauty pageants for untalented journalists.
15. Unemployment is hardest on those over 50 years old.
16. Murphy's Law: If anything can go wrong, it will go wrong, and at the worst possible moment.
17. With enough motivation, a person can accomplish anything.
18. Religion may be a source of comfort for some, but it can be a source of misery for others.
19. Lying is often justified by the circumstances.
20. Friends are people you can't always trust.
21. Gestures and facial expressions often communicate what words cannot say.
22. Sooner or later, children take on the personalities of their parents.
23. The most rewarding books are always easy to read.
24. Our natural surroundings when we are growing up contribute to our happiness or unhappiness as adults.

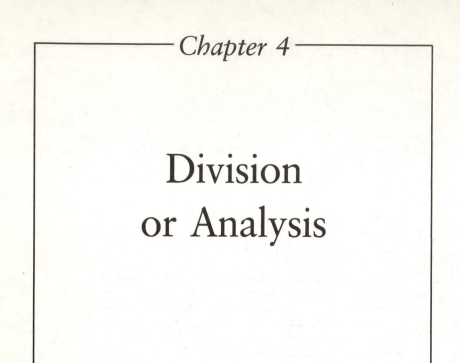

Chapter 4

Division
or Analysis

Understanding the Method

The word *division* comes from a Latin word meaning "to force asunder or separate." The word *analysis* comes from a Greek word meaning "to undo." Thus **division** and **analysis** name the same method: we separate a whole into its elements, examine the relations of the elements to one another and to the whole, and reassemble the elements into a new whole informed by the examination. The method is essential to understanding and evaluating objects, works, and ideas.

At its simplest, division or analysis looks closely at a subject for the knowledge to be gained and perhaps put to use. We take this simple approach in everyday life, as when we ponder our relationships with others or try to understand a politician's campaign promise. We also use analysis throughout this book, when looking at paragraphs or answering questions about essays. And it is the basic operation in at least five other methods discussed in this book: classification (Chapter 5), process analysis (Chapter 6), comparison and contrast (Chapter 7), analogy (Chapter 8), and cause-and-effect analysis (Chapter 10).

A more complex kind of division or analysis also builds on this basic operation: the separation into elements leads to a conclusion about the meaning, significance, or value of the whole. This approach is essential to college learning, whether in discussing literature, reviewing a psychology experiment, or interpreting a business case. It is fundamental to work, from choosing a career to making sense of market research. And it informs and enriches life outside school or work, in buying a car, looking at art, or deciding whom to vote for. The method is the foundation of **critical thinking**, the ability to see beneath the surface of things, images, events, and ideas; to uncover and test assumptions; to see the importance of context; and to draw and support independent conclusions.

The subject of any division or analysis is usually singular—a freestanding, coherent unit, such as a bicycle or a poem, with its own unique constitution of elements. (In contrast, classification, the subject of the next chapter, usually starts with a plural subject, such as bicycles or the poems of the Civil War, and groups them according to their shared features.) The writer of division or analysis chooses the subject and with it a **principle of division or analysis**, a framework or criterion that determines how the subject is divided and thus what elements are identified.

Sometimes the principle of division or analysis is self-evident, especially when the subject is an object, such as a bicycle or a camera, that can be "undone" in only a limited number of ways. Most of the time, however, the principle depends on the writer's view of the whole. In academic disciplines, businesses, and the professions, distinctive analytical perspectives—distinctive principles—are part of what the field is about and are often the subject of debate within the field. In art, for instance, some critics see a painting primarily as a visual object and concentrate on its composition, color, line, and other formal qualities; other critics see a painting primarily as a social object and concentrate on its content and context (cultural, economic, political, and so on). Both groups use a principle of division or analysis that is a well-established way of looking at painting; yet each group finds different elements and thus meaning in a work.

There is, then, a great deal of flexibility in choosing a principle of division or analysis. But it should be appropriate for the subject and the field or discipline; it should be significant; and it should be applied thoroughly and consistently. Division or analysis is not done for its own sake but for a larger goal of illuminating the subject, perhaps concluding something about it, perhaps evaluating it. But even when the method culminates in evaluation—in the writer's judgment of the subject's value—the analysis should represent the subject as it actually is, in all its fullness and complexity. In analyzing a movie, for instance, a writer may emphasize one element, such as setting, and even omit some elements, such as costumes; but the characterization of the whole must still apply to *all* the elements. If it does not, readers can be counted on to notice; so the writer must single out any wayward element(s) and explain why they do not substantially undermine the framework and thus weaken the opinion.

Analyzing Division or Analysis in Paragraphs

Margaret Visser (born 1940) is a Canadian teacher and radio commentator and the author of *Much Depends on Dinner* (1986), a survey of facts, rituals, and myths concerning some of our most common foods. The paragraph below comes from the chapter on lemons and follows a discussion of the uses of lemon juice. Visser's analysis is simple and straightforward: each part is named and its uses are described.

The principle of division or analysis: the useful parts of a lemon (minus the juice)

Absolutely every part of a lemon is useful in some way, from its seeds to its outermost peel. Lemon-pip oil, unsaturated and aromatic, is important in the soap industry and in special diets. *1. Pips (or seeds)*

The pulp left over from squeezed lemons is *2. Pulp* evaporated and concentrated into "citrus molasses" which is sold as a base for making vinegar and as an ingredient in bland syrups and alcohol. The remains of the "rag" or pulp is also sold as cattle feed. Most of the pectin used to *3. Pith* thicken and solidify jams, jellies, and marmalades comes from the white pith of citrus fruits. Among these, lemon and lime pectin has the highest "jelly grade" or capacity to thicken liquids. It is widely used in medicines taken to combat diarrhea. The flavedo, or outer yellow *4. Flavedo* layer of lemon peel, is invaluable for its intense taste and scent. (The word *zest*, which originally meant "skin or peel," then specifically "citrus peel," is now in common use as signifying "lively enjoyment.")

The new whole: a thoroughly useful lemon

Luci Tapahonso (born 1953) is a poet and teacher at the University of New Mexico at Albuquerque. This paragraph is from an essay by Tapahonso, "The Way It Is," in *Sign Language*, a book of photographs (by Skeet McAuley) of life on the reservation for some Navajo and Apache Indians. Tapahonso's analysis is more complex than Visser's: she draws a conclusion about the commercial she analyzes.

It is rare and, indeed, very exciting to see an Indian person in a commercial advertisement. Word travels fast when that happens. Nunzio's Pizza in Albuquerque, New Mexico, ran commercials featuring Jose Rey Toledo of Jemez Pueblo talking about his "native land—Italy" while wearing typical Pueblo attire—jewelry, moccasins, and hair tied in a chongo. Because of the ironic humor, because Indian grandfathers specialize in playing tricks and jokes on their grandchildren, and because Jose Rey Toledo is a respected and well-known elder in the Indian communities, word of this commercial spread fast among Indians in New Mexico. It was the cause of recognition and celebration of sorts on the reservations and in the pueblos. His portrayal was not in the categories which the media usually associate with Indians but as a typical sight in the Southwest. It showed Indians as we live today—enjoying pizza as one of our favorite foods, including humor and fun as part of our daily lives, and recognizing the importance of preserving traditional knowledge.

The principle of division or analysis: the elements of the commercial that appealed to Indians

1. Rarity of an Indian in a commercial

2. Indian dress

3. Indian humor
4. Indian tradition

5. Respected Indian spokesperson

6. Indian life

The new whole: a realistic, positive commercial sensitive to Indians

Developing an Essay by Division or Analysis

GETTING STARTED

Division or analysis is one of the readiest methods of development: almost anything whole can be separated into its elements, from a lemon to a play by Shakespeare to an economic theory. In college and work, many writing assignments will demand analysis with verbs such as *analyze, criticize, discuss, evaluate, interpret,* or *review.* If you need to develop your own subject for division or analysis, think of something whose meaning or significance puzzles or intrigues you and whose parts you can distinguish and relate to the whole—an object such as a machine, an artwork such as a poem, a media product such as a news broadcast, an institution such as a hospital, a relationship such as stepparenting, a social issue such as sheltering the homeless.

If you begin division or analysis by seeking meaning or significance, you will be more likely to find a workable principle of division and less likely to waste time on a hollow exercise. To what extent is the enormously complex hospital you work in a community in itself? What is the appeal of the front-page headlines in the local tabloid newspaper? Why did a certain movie have such a powerful effect on you and your friends? Each of these questions dictates a distinct approach to the subject's elements—a distinct principle—that makes it easier to isolate the elements and show their connection to one another.

Each question also suggests a thesis that states an opinion and reveals the principle of division: for instance, "The hospital encompasses such a wide range of personnel and services that it resembles a good-sized town"; "The newspaper's front page routinely appeals to readers' fear of crime, anger at criminals, and sympathy for victims"; "The film is a unique and important statement of the private terrors of adolescence." Note that all three of these theses imply an explanatory purpose—an effort to understand something and share that understanding with the reader. The third thesis, however, conveys an evaluative purpose as well: the writer hopes to persuade readers to accept her judgment of the film.

In truth, your thesis may not come to you until you have drafted your analysis: you may have to perform the division in pursuit of your interest before you can say what the subject's meaning or significance is. The thesis will be essential to the final essay, however, for it is where you reintegrate the elements into a new whole. When you state, for example, that a film uniquely represents adolescent terrors, you transform a roll of celluloid into a critique.

Of course, the thesis must develop from and be supported by the evidence of the division or analysis—the elements of the subject, their interconnections, and their relation to the whole. Dissect your subject, looking at the actual, physical thing if possible, imagining it in your mind if necessary. Make detailed notes of all the elements you see, their distinguishing features, and how they help answer your starting question about meaning or significance. In analyzing someone's creation (including an artwork, a political policy, a report on an experiment), tease out the creator's influences, assumptions, intentions, conclusions, and evidence. You may have to go outside the work for some of this information—researching an author's background, for instance, to uncover the political biases that may underlie his or her opinions. Even if you do not use all this information in your final draft, it will help you see the elements and help keep your analysis true to the subject. (If your subject is a written work, such as a short story or a journal article, summarize it in writing so that you're sure of the elements and how they work together.) Include examples whenever relevant—instances of the hospital's support services, say, or specific headlines from the tabloid newspaper.

At this point you should consider your readers' needs as well as the needs of your subject and your own framework. If the subject is likely to be familiar to readers (as, say, the newspaper's headlines might be), then your principle of division may not require much justification (as long as it's clear), but your details and examples must be vivid and convincing. If the subject is unfamiliar, then you should carefully explain your principle of division, define all specialized terms, distinguish parts from one another, and provide ample illustrations. If readers know your subject but may dispute your way of looking at it, then you should justify as well as explain your principle of division; and you should account for any evidence that may seem not to support your opinion by showing either why, in fact, the evidence is supportive or why it is unimportant. If contrary evidence refuses to be dispensed with, you may have to rethink your approach. Though the method of division or analysis gets easier with practice, each new subject demands a fresh start, and a certain amount of experimentation is inevitable.

ORGANIZING

In the introduction to your essay, let readers know why you are bothering to analyze your subject: Why is the subject significant? How might the essay relate to the experiences of readers or be useful to them? A subject unfamiliar to readers might be summarized or described, or part of it (an anecdote or quotation, say) might be used to tantalize readers. A familiar subject might be introduced with a surprising fact or unusual perspective. An evaluative analysis might open with an opposing viewpoint. Ending the introduction with your thesis will focus readers' attention and advise them of what to expect. (Occasionally, you may want to let your analysis build to a statement of your thesis at the end, but the thesis must still control the essay.)

In the body of the essay you'll need to explain your principle of division or analysis—only briefly if readers know your subject and aren't likely to disagree with your approach; more extensively under the opposite conditions. The arrangement of elements and analysis should suit your subject and purpose: you can describe the elements and then offer your analysis, or you can introduce and analyze elements one by one. You can arrange the elements themselves from least to most important, least to most complex, most to least familiar, spatially, or chronologically. Devote as much space to each element as it demands: there is no requirement that all elements be given equal space and emphasis if their complexity or your framework dictates otherwise.

Most division or analysis essays need a conclusion that reassembles the elements, returning readers to a sense of the whole subject. If the thesis was not expressed in the introduction, it should be stated clearly in the conclusion. But even if it is already known, the thesis might be restated. It can be accompanied by a summary of what the essay has contributed, a consideration of the influence of the subject or its place in a larger picture, or (especially in an evaluation) an assessment of the effectiveness or worth of the subject.

DRAFTING

If your subject or your view of it is complex, you may need at least two drafts of a division or analysis essay—one for yourself, to discover what you think, and one for your readers, to clarify your principle, cover each element, and support your points with concrete details and vivid examples (including quotations if the subject is a written work). Plan on two drafts if you're uncertain of your thesis when you begin: you'll probably save time in the long run by attending to one goal at a time. Especially because the division or analysis essay says something about the subject by explaining its structure, you need to have a clear picture of the whole and relate each part to it.

REVISING

When you revise your essay, ask the following questions to uncover any weaknesses remaining in your analysis.

1. *Does your essay have a clear thesis?* Will it be clear to your readers what the subject is, why you are analyzing it (your purpose), and what your principle of analysis is? The significance of your analysis and your view of the subject should be apparent throughout your essay.

2. *Is your division or analysis complete?* Have you identified all elements according to your principle of division and determined their relations to one another and to the whole? If you have omitted some elements from your discussion, will the reason for their omission be clear to readers?

3. *Is your division or analysis consistent?* Is your principle of division applied consistently to the entire subject (including any elements you have omitted)? Do all elements reflect the same principle, and are they clearly separate rather than overlapping? You may find it helpful to check your draft against your list of elements or your outline or to outline the draft itself.

4. *Is your division or analysis well supported?* Is the thesis supported by clear assertions, and are the assertions supported by concrete, specific evidence (sensory details, facts, quotations, and so on)? Do not rely on your readers to prove your thesis.

5. *Is your division or analysis true to the subject?* Is your thesis unforced, your analysis fair? Is your new whole (your reassembly of the elements) faithful to the original? Be wary of leaping to a conclusion that distorts the subject.

Ray Allen Billington

Ray Allen Billington was a leading historian of the American frontier. Born in 1903 in Bay City, Michigan, he attended the University of Wisconsin, the University of Michigan, and Harvard University, from which he earned a Ph.D. in 1933. He began teaching American history at Clark University in 1931, then moved to Smith College in 1937. From 1944 until his retirement from teaching in 1963, he was professor of history at Northwestern University, and then he served for fifteen years as a senior research associate at the Huntington Library in California. The author of numerous scholarly articles and several textbooks on the American West, Billington also wrote The Protestant Crusade, 1800–1860: A Study of the Origins of American Nativism *(1938);* The Far Western Frontier, 1830–1860 *(1956);* America's Frontier Heritage *(1966);* Frederick Jackson Turner *(1973), a biography of the influential American historian; and* Land of Savagery, Land of Promise: The European Image of the American Frontier in the Nineteenth Century *(1981). Billington died in 1981 in California.*

The Frontier Disappears

The winning of the American West did more than merely expand the boundaries of the United States. As Billington explains in this essay, it also stamped the American character with its distinctive and enduring traits. After providing some background on the frontier experience, Billington looks at these traits one by one, in a clear example of division or analysis. The essay first appeared in The American Story *(1956), a collection of pieces by noted historians on facets of our past.*

The director of the census made a dramatic announcement in 1890. 1
The nation's unsettled area, he revealed, "has been so broken into by isolated bodies of settlement that there can hardly be said to be a frontier line." These words sounded the close of one period of America's history. For three centuries before men had marched westward, seeking in the forests and plains that lay beyond the settled areas a chance to begin life anew. For three centuries they had driven back the wilderness as their conquest of the continent went on. Now, in 1890,

they were told that a frontier line separating the settled and unsettled portions of the United States no longer existed. The West was won, and the expansion that had been the most distinctive feature of their country's past was at an end.

The story of that westward march begins in the early 17th Century, when Englishmen began their assault on the deep forests of America at Jamestown and Plymouth. For the next years the advance was slow, as Europeans learned the technique of subduing a wilderness; by 1776 the line of settlements extended only to the crest of the Appalachians. With independence won, and a sympathetic national government ready to provide the frontiersman with self-government and cheap lands, the pace of migration accelerated. Across the broad valley of the Ohio and along the Gulf plains the pioneers marched, until by 1850 their settlements filled the first tier of states lying beyond the Mississippi. There they halted, for ahead lay the unfamiliar environment of the Great Plains, a giant grassland that provided neither timber for homes nor adequate rainfall for crops. Yet so strong was the expansionist urge that even now bolder frontiersmen leaped across this barrier to fill the interior valleys of California and the Oregon country. After the Civil War, when railroads and other man-made devices allowed the conquest of the semiarid plains country, the march was resumed, this time to end only with the West occupied and the continent settled.

Opportunity was the magnet that drew men westward during those three centuries, for nature's untapped riches promised pioneers the fortunes that fate had denied them in older societies. There, where a king's ransom in furs could be had for the taking, where lush grasslands beckoned the herdsman, where fortunes in gold and silver lay scarcely hidden, where virgin soils awaited only the magic touch of man to yield their wealth, men and women could begin life anew with only their brains and brawn and courage to sustain them. There they could realize the social equality that was the goal of every democratically inclined American. These were the lures that drew the frontiersmen ever westward toward the Pacific.

They moved in an orderly procession. The fur trappers came first, roaming far in advance of the settled areas as they gathered the bales of shiny beaver peltry that would gladden the hearts of Europe's elite. Then came the miners, who also left civilization far behind as they prospected mountain streams and desert wastes in their endless quest for gold or silver. Behind them were the cattlemen, seeking the grassy pastures where their herds could graze without the confinement of fences. Cowboys were a familiar sight on the frontiers of Virginia or Kentucky or Illinois long before they won their place in the sun and cinema on the High Plains of the Far West. These shock troops of civilization made little impression on the wilderness; instead they adapted themselves so completely to the forest environment that they altered the face of the country but slightly.

Not so the farmers who moved westward on the heels of the   5 cattlemen. To them nature was an enemy; every tree was a barrier that stood before the advance of civilization and must be removed. This process was begun by the "pioneer farmers." Nomadic, restless men, they half-cleared the forests, built their cabins, raised a few crops, and then moved on again as neighbors came uncomfortably near. When they moved, they sold their improvements to "equipped farmers" with some capital, who continued cutting away the forests until their clearings met. Behind them came the frontier of villages and towns, where adventuresome merchants and editors and lawyers completed the transformation of the wilderness into a civilized land.

The civilization emerging in this way, however, differed from that   6 of Europe or even of the eastern United States, for as the pioneers moved westward they found that the habits, the institutions, and the cultural baggage of the older societies they had known were out of place in their primitive forest clearings. Highly developed political institutions designed to operate in compact cities were unnecessary in a tiny frontier outpost; complex economic controls were useless in an isolated community geared to an economy of self-sufficiency; rigid social customs were outmoded in a land where prestige depended on skill with the ax or rifle rather than on hereditary glories. So there occurred in each of these frontier communities a reversion toward the primitive. The settlers met together to provide such governmental controls as existed; each man cared for his own economic needs without dependence on his fellows; cultural progress halted as the frontiersmen concentrated on the primal tasks of providing food, clothing, and shelter for their families. In this reversion toward a state of nature, the habits and customs of older civilizations were momentarily forgotten.

Gradually, newcomers drifted in to swell the population of each   7 wilderness outpost. As their numbers increased, the community began a slow climb back toward civilization once more. Governmental controls were tightened and extended, economic specialization set in, social stratification began, and cultural activities quickened. The process continued until eventually a fully developed society evolved. This new society, however, differed from the old from which it had sprung. The accident of separate evolution, the borrowings from the different lands represented among its founders, the influence of the physical environment in which it developed, all played their part in creating a unique social organism. It was similar to but different from the older civilizations that lay to the east.

As this process went on, over and over again, during the three 8 centuries required to settle the continent, these minute societies slowly merged to form a nation as unique as the units from which it was formed. The characteristics of its people and the nature of its institutions reflected their primitive origin long after the frontier had passed on westward. An "Americanization" of both men and society had taken place. The distinctive traits that are associated with the American people today stem at least partly from the frontier experience of our ancestors.

This fact does not mean, of course, that our characteristics and 9 institutions are solely the result of that frontier heritage. The United States of today is the product of a variety of forces: its European origins, the continuing impact of ideas from abroad, the constant mingling of peoples, and the changes wrought by the Industrial Revolution. Yet none of these forces was more significant than the frontier in endowing the Americans with the traits that distinguish them from other peoples of the world. Down to the present time many of our basic attitudes toward society and the world around us reflect that pioneer background.

What are the characteristics that are traceable to this unique fea- 10 ture of our inheritance?

We are a mobile people, constantly on the move, and but lightly 11 bound to home or community. If you were to ask any group of Americans today how many live in the homes where they were born, or where their parents were born, only a handful would reply in the affirmative. If you asked the same question of a group of Englishmen or Frenchmen or Italians, an opposite answer would be given. Like our frontier ancestors, who shifted about so regularly that mobility became a habit, we are always ready for any change that promises to better our lives.

We are a wasteful people, unaccustomed to thrift or saving. The 12 frontiersmen established that pattern, for nature's resources were so plentiful that no one could envisage their exhaustion. Within a few years of the first Virginia settlement, for example, pioneers burned down their houses when ready to move west; thus they were allowed to retrieve nails, and none gave thought to the priceless hardwoods that went up in smoke. As a people we still destroy much that others would save. I had this driven home to me when, during a year's residence in England, I received a letter from one of that nation's largest banks, enclosed in a secondhand envelope that had been read-dressed to me. Such saving would be unthinkable in the United States, where even the most insignificant bank would never address a client save on elaborately engraved stationery, usually with the names of all twenty-eight vice presidents parading down one side of the page.

We are a practical, inventive people on whom the weight of tradi-   13
tion rests but lightly. In many lands of the world, people confronted with an unpleasant situation will quietly adjust themselves; in the United States, a man's first impulse is to change things for the better. This willingness to experiment came naturally to the pioneers, who had no precedents on which to build. It has remained a trait of the industrial pioneers whose ability to adapt and change has laid the basis for America's supremacy as a manufacturing nation.

We are individualistic people, deeply resentful of any intrusion   14
into our affairs by government or society, also a basic attitude among frontiersmen. Aware that they were living in a land where resources were so abundant that only their own energies were necessary for success, they wanted to be left alone above all else. This trait has persisted in American thought, even though the passing of the frontier has forced the government to adopt a more positive social role. Even today such activity is more resented in the United States than else-where; and this resentment also helps explain the almost fanatical American hatred of political systems such as fascism or communism that are based on the subjugation of the individual.

We are a democratic people. Our pioneering forefathers origi-   15
nated neither the theory nor the practice of democracy; the western world was well on its way to political equalitarianism when the conti-nent was settled. But conditions in frontier communities vastly stimu-lated this trend. There nature reduced men to equality by dimming the importance of wealth or hereditary privilege. There poverty served as a great leveler. There the demand for self-rule was particularly strong, for frontiersmen knew that their problems were unique and must be solved locally. And so on the frontier the democratic tradition was strengthened, until it became a part of the American creed. The undy-ing hatred of the United States for all forms of totalitarianism only mirrors the strength of this faith.

Thus has the frontier placed its stamp on America and its people. *16* In the continuing rebirth of civilization during the three centuries required to settle the continent, nature modified the characteristics of its conquerors, even in the midst of their conquest. There emerged a new people, robust and strong, with an unwavering faith in the merits of the individual and an unswerving allegiance to the principles of democracy. The frontier is no more, but its heritage remains to give strength as well as individuality to the civilization of the United States.

Meaning

1. Where does Billington state the main idea that encompasses his entire essay? What is the main idea?
2. Summarize Billington's ideas about the civilization of the frontier (paragraphs 6–7). What features of older civilizations were abandoned on the frontier, and why? What forces caused the evolving frontier civilization to be unique?
3. What aspects of the frontier experience shaped each of the distinctive American traits that Billington identifies (paragraphs 11–15)?
4. If you do not know the meanings of the following words, look them up in a dictionary: semiarid (paragraph 2); peltry (4); nomadic (5); primal (6); stratification (7); envisage (12); fanatical, subjugation (14); equalitarianism, totalitarianism (15).

Purpose and Audience

1. What is the specific purpose of each part of Billington's essay in relation to his main idea: the story of westward expansion (paragraphs 2–5), the analysis of why and how a new civilization emerged in the West (6–7), and the analysis of the unique traits of the American character (8–16)?
2. What assumptions does Billington seem to make about his readers' knowledge of frontier history? How are these assumptions reflected in each part of the essay?
3. How clear and convincing do you find Billington's analysis of the unique traits of the American character? Do you think the five traits are typical of most Americans? Should Billington have strengthened his analysis with more or different examples at any point? Explain your answers.

Method and Structure

1. The most significant part of Billington's essay is the division of the American character into five traits (paragraphs 8–16). What principle does he use as the basis for division or analysis—that is, what perspective on the American character leads him to identify these five traits?
2. Billington uses division or analysis as well in discussing the evolution of society in the West (paragraphs 6–7). What similar elements does he identify both in the civilization left behind by the pioneers and in the new civilization they evolved?
3. What, if anything, does Billington gain by beginning his essay as he does? Would you have found the essay more or less clear if Billington had stated his main idea near the beginning of the essay instead of saving it for later? Why?
4. **Other Methods**   In addition to division or analysis, Billington also relies on two methods of development that are favored by historians: narration (Chapter 2), as in paragraph 2; and cause-and-effect analysis (Chapter 10), as in paragraph 14. Locate at least one other example of each method. What does each method contribute to Billington's essay?

Language

1. Starting with the words "marched," "driven back," and "won" in paragraph 1, Billington uses a metaphor of an army advancing in battle to explain the pioneers' westward movement. What words in paragraphs 2–5 and 16 continue this metaphor? What "enemy" were the pioneers marching against? (If necessary, consult the Glossary under *figures of speech* for a definition of *metaphor*.)
2. Though in paragraphs 11–15 Billington does not state outright that he values some traits of the American character more than others, many of the words he uses do convey a sense of approval or disapproval. Locate these words, and analyze what they suggest about Billington's attitudes toward each trait.

Writing Topics

1. Focus on a subgroup of Americans that you are familiar with—for example, your family, rock musicians, professional athletes, college freshmen—and write an essay analyzing the traits that distinguish that group from other groups. If you can, follow Billington's example in explaining the reasons for the distinctive traits as well.

2. Billington identifies five distinguishing traits of the American character: mobility, wastefulness, practicality and inventiveness, individualism, and democracy (paragraphs 11–15). Write an essay on the trait that you find most interesting—most important, perhaps, or most positive or least positive. Use your own examples and details to support your thesis.

3. Billington's example of American wastefulness—a bank's "elaborately engraved stationery, usually with the names of all twenty-eight vice presidents parading down one side of the page" (paragraph 12)—could also be said to illustrate the preoccupation of Americans with the images they project to others. Consider some of the ways in which Americans forsake comfort, practicality, or money to make an impression with the clothes they wear or the cars they drive. Choose four or five peculiarities of clothes or of cars and write an essay explaining what each one symbolizes for and about the wearer or driver and what impression it makes on others. Or, if you prefer, choose a particular image—such as playboy or playgirl, teenage rebel, or outdoors type—and explain what peculiarities of clothes and cars help project the image.

A teacher and cultural critic, Mark Crispin Miller was born in 1949 in Chicago and grew up there and in Boston. He received a B.A. from Northwestern University (1971) and an M.A. and Ph.D. from The Johns Hopkins University (1973, 1977). He taught for several years at the University of Pennsylvania and now teaches in the writing seminars at Johns Hopkins. While studying the literature of the Renaissance for his advanced degrees, Miller says, he was increasingly "struck by the possibility of close reading for an understanding of the images of contemporary mass culture." Such close reading has informed Miller's contributions to The New York Review of Books, The Nation, Mother Jones, *and* The New Republic. *Many of his essays on television were collected in* Boxed In: The Culture of TV *(1988). He is currently editing a book on the movies and writing a book on modern advertising.*

Getting Dirty

In this essay from Boxed In, *originally printed in* The New Republic *in 1982, Miller offers a complex analysis of a run-of-the-mill television commercial for soap. Most people, Miller says, think that such advertisements mean nothing more than their explicit messages say they do: in this case, "feel cleaner." Miller maintains that this attitude benefits advertisers but harms those who hold it.*

We are outside a house, looking in the window, and this is what we see: a young man, apparently nude and half-crazed with anxiety, lunging toward the glass. "Gail!" he screams, as he throws the window open and leans outside, over a flower box full of geraniums: "The most important shower of my life, and you switch deodorant soap!" He is, we now see, only half-naked, wearing a towel around his waist; and he shakes a packaged bar of soap—"Shield"—in one accusing hand. Gail, wearing a blue man-tailored shirt, stands outside, below the window, clipping a hedge. She handles this reproach with an ease that suggests years of contempt. "Shield is better," she explains patiently, in a voice somewhat deeper than her husband's. "It's extra strength." (Close-up of the package in the husband's hand, Gail's efficient finger gliding along beneath the legend, THE EXTRA

1

STRENGTH DEODORANT SOAP.) "Yeah," whimpers Mr. Gail, "but my first call on J. J. Siss [*sic*], the company's *toughest customer*, and now *this*!" Gail nods with broad mock-sympathy, and stands firm: "Shield fights odor better, so you'll feel *cleaner*," she assures her husband, who darts away with a jerk of panic, as Gail rolls her eyes heavenward and gently shakes her head, as if to say, "What a half-wit!"

Cut to our hero, as he takes his important shower. No longer 2 frantic, he now grins down at himself, apparently delighted to be caked with Shield, which, in its detergent state, has the consistency of wet cement. He then goes out of focus, as if glimpsed through a shower door. "Clinical tests prove," proclaims an eager baritone, "Shield fights odor better than the *leading* deodorant soap!" A bar of Shield (green) and a bar of that other soap (yellow) zip up the screen with a festive toot, forming a sort of graph which demonstrates that Shield does, indeed, "fight odor better, so you'll feel *cleaner*!"

This particular contest having been settled, we return to the major 3 one, which has yet to be resolved. Our hero reappears, almost transformed: calmed down, dressed up, his voice at least an octave lower. "I *do* feel cleaner!" he announces cheerily, leaning into the doorway of a room where Gail is arranging flowers. She pretends to be ecstatic at this news, and he comes toward her, setting himself up for a profound humiliation by putting on a playful air of suave command. Adjusting his tie like a real man of the world, he saunters over to his wife and her flower bowl, where he plucks a dainty purple flower and lifts it to his lapel: "And," he boasts throughout all this, trying to make his voice sound even deeper, "with old J. J.'s business and my brains—" "—you'll . . . *clean up again?*" Gail asks with suggestive irony, subverting his authoritative pose by leaning against him, draping one hand over his shoulder to dangle a big yellow daisy down his chest. Taken aback, he shoots her a distrustful look, and she titters at him.

Finally, the word SHIELD appears in extreme close-up and the 4 camera pulls back, showing two bars of soap, one packaged and one not, on display amidst an array of steely bubbles. "Shield fights odor better, so you'll feel *cleaner*!" the baritone reminds us, and then our hero's face appears once more, in a little square over the unpackaged bar of soap: "I feel *cleaner* than *ever before*!" he insists, sounding faintly unconvinced.

Is all this as stupid as it seems at first? Or is there, just beneath the 5 surface of this moronic narrative, some noteworthy design, intended to appeal to (and to worsen) some of the anxieties of modern life? A serious look at this particular trifle might lead us to some strange discoveries.

We are struck, first of all, by the commercial's pseudofeminism, 6 an advertising ploy with a long history, and one ubiquitous on television nowadays. Although the whole subject deserves more extended treatment, this commercial offers us an especially rich example of the strategy. Typically, it woos its female viewers—i.e., those who choose the soap in most households—with a fantasy of dominance; and it does so by inverting the actualities of woman's lot through a number of imperceptible details. For instance, in this marriage it is the wife, and not the husband, who gets to keep her name; and Gail's name, moreover, is a potent one, because of its brevity and its homonymic connotation. (If this housewife were more delicately named, called "Lillian" or "Cecilia," it would lessen her illusory strength.) She is also equipped in more noticeable ways: she's the one who wears the button-down shirt in this family, she's the one who's competent both outdoors and in the house, and it is she, and only she, who wields the tool.

These visual details imply that Gail is quite a powerful housewife, 7 whereas her nameless mate is a figure of embarrassing impotence. This "man," in fact, is actually Gail's *wife*: he is utterly feminized, striking a posture and displaying attributes which men have long deplored in women. In other words, this commercial, which apparently takes the woman's side, is really the expression (and reflection) of misogyny. Gail's husband is dependent and hysterical, entirely without that self-possession which we expect from solid, manly types, like Gail. This is partly the result of his demeanor: in the opening scene, his voice sometimes cracks ludicrously, and he otherwise betrays the shrill desperation of a man who can't remember where he left his scrotum. The comic effect of this frenzy, moreover, is subtly enhanced by the mise-en-scène,[1] which puts the man in a conventionally feminine position—in dishabille, looking down from a window. Thus we infer that he is sheltered and housebound, a modern Juliet calling for his/her Romeo; or—more appropriately—the image suggests a scene in some suburban red-light district, presenting this husband as an item on display, like the flowers just below his stomach, available for anyone's enjoyment, at a certain price. Although in one way contradic-

---

[1] French for "putting on stage": the arrangement of actors and props. [Editor's note.]

tory, these implications are actually quite congruous, for they both serve to emasculate the husband, so that the wife might take his place, or play his part.

Such details, some might argue, need not have been the conscious 8 work of this commercial's makers. The authors, that is, might have worked by instinct rather than design, and so would have been no more aware of their work's psychosocial import than we ourselves: they just wanted to make the guy look like a wimp, merely for the purposes of domestic comedy. While such an argument certainly does apply to many ads, in this case it is unlikely. Advertising agencies do plenty of research, by which we can assume that they don't select their tactics arbitrarily. They take pains to analyze the culture which they help to sicken, and then, with much wit and cynicism, use their insights in devising their small dramas. This commercial is a subtle and meticulous endorsement of castration, meant to play on certain widespread guilts and insecurities; and all we need to do to demonstrate this fact is to subject the two main scenes to the kind of visual analysis which commercials, so brief and broad, tend to resist (understandably). The ad's visual implications are too carefully achieved to have been merely accidental or unconscious.

The crucial object in the opening shot is that flower box with its 9 bright geraniums, which is placed directly in front of the husband's groin. This clever stroke of composition has the immediate effect of equating our hero's manhood with a bunch of flowers. This is an exquisitely perverse suggestion, rather like using a cigar to represent the Eternal Feminine: flowers are frail, sweet, and largely ornamental, hardly an appropriate phallic symbol, but (of course) a venerable symbol of *maidenhood*. The geraniums stand, then, not for the husband's virility, but for its absence.

More than a clever instance of inversion, futhermore, these phal- 10 lic blossoms tell us something odd about this marital relationship. As Gail, clippers in hand, turns from the hedge to calm her agitated man, she appears entirely capable of calming him quite drastically, if she hasn't done so already (which might explain his hairless chest and high-pitched voice). She has the power, that is, to take away whatever slender potency he may possess, and uses the power repeatedly, trimming her husband (we infer) as diligently as she prunes her foliage. And, as she can snip his manhood, so too can she restore it, which is what the second scene implies. Now the flower bowl has replaced the flower box as the visual crux, dominating the bottom center of the frame with a crowd of blooms. As the husband, cleaned and dressed, comes to stand beside his wife, straining to affect a new authority, the flower bowl too appears directly at his lower center; so that Gail, briskly adding flowers to the bouquet, appears to be replenishing his vacant groin with extra stalks. He has a lot to thank her for, it seems: she is his helpmate, confidante, adviser, she keeps his house and grounds in order, and she is clearly the custodian of the family jewels.

Of course, her restoration of his potency cannot be complete, or   11
he might shatter her mastery by growing a bit too masterful himself. He could start choosing his own soap, or take her shears away, or—worst of all—walk out for good. Therefore, she punctures his momentary confidence by taunting him with that big limp daisy, countering his lordly gesture with the boutonniere by flaunting that symbol of his floral status. He can put on whatever airs he likes, but she still has his fragile vigor firmly in hand.

Now what, precisely, motivates this sexless battle of the sexes?   12
That is, what really underlies this tense and hateful marriage, making the man so weak, the woman so contemptuously helpful? The script, seemingly nothing more than a series of inanities, contains the answer to these questions, conveying, as it does, a concern with cleanliness that amounts to an obsession: "Shield fights odor better, so you'll feel cleaner!" "I *do* feel cleaner!" "Shield fights odor better, so you'll feel *cleaner!*" "I feel *cleaner* than *ever before!*" Indeed, the commercial emphasizes the feeling of cleanliness even more pointedly than the name of the product, implying, by its very insistence, a feeling of dirtiness, an apprehension of deep filth.

And yet there is not a trace of dirt in the vivid world of this   13
commercial. Unlike many ads for other soaps, this one shows no sloppy children, no sweatsoaked workingmen with blackened hands, not even a bleary housewife in need of her morning shower. We never even glimpse the ground in Gail's world, nor is her husband even faintly smudged. In fact, the filth which Shield supposedly "fights" is not physical but psychological besmirchment: Gail's husband feels soiled because of what he has to do for a living, in order to keep Gail in that nice big house, happily supplied with shirts and shears.

"My first call on J. J. Siss, the company's *toughest customer*, and   14
now *this!*" The man's anxiety is yet another feminizing trait, for it is generally women, and not men, who are consumed by doubts about the sweetness of their bodies, which must never be offensive to the guys who run the world. (This real anxiety is itself aggravated by commercials.) Gail's husband must play the female to the mighty J. J.

Siss, a name whose oxymoronic character implies perversion: "J. J." is a stereotypic nickname for the potent boss, while "Sis" is a term of endearment, short for "sister" (and perhaps implying "sissy," too, in this case). Gail's husband must do his boyish best to please the voracious J. J. Siss, just as a prostitute must satisfy a demanding trick, or "tough customer." It is therefore perfectly fitting that this employee refer to the encounter, not as a "meeting" or "appointment," but as a "call"; and his demeaning posture in the window—half dressed and bent over—conveys, we now see, a definitive implication.

Gail's job as the "understanding wife" is not to rescue her hus- 15 band from these sordid obligations, but to help him meet them successfully. She may seem coolly self-sufficient, but she actually depends on her husband's attractiveness, just as a pimp relies on the charm of his whore. And, also like a pimp, she has to keep her girl in line with occasional reminders of who's boss. When her husband starts getting uppity *après la douche*,[2] she jars him from the very self-assurance which she had helped him to discover, piercing that "shield" which was her gift.

"And, with old J. J.'s business and my brains—" "—you'll . . . 16 *clean up again?*" He means, of course, that he'll work fiscal wonders with old J. J.'s account, but his fragmentary boast contains a deeper significance, upon which Gail plays with sadistic cleverness. "Old J. J.'s business and my brains" implies a feminine self-description, since it suggests a variation on the old commonplace of "brains vs. brawn": J. J.'s money, in the world of this commercial (as in ours), amounts to brute strength, which the flexible husband intends to complement with his mother wit. Gail's retort broadens this unconscious hint of homosexuality: "—you'll . . . *clean up again?*" Given the monetary nature of her husband's truncated remark, the retort must mean primarily, "You'll make a lot of money." If this were all it meant, however, it would not be a joke, nor would the husband find it so upsetting. Moreover, we have no evidence that Gail's husband ever "cleaned up"—i.e., made a sudden fortune—in the past. Rather, the ad's milieu and *dramatis personae*[3] suggest upward mobility, gradual savings and a yearly raise, rather than one prior killing. What Gail is referring to, in fact, with that "again," is her husband's shower: she implies that what he'll have to do, after his "call" on J. J. Siss, is, quite

---

[2] French: "after the shower." [Editor's note.]
[3] *Milieu* comes from the French and means "environment." *Dramatis personae* is Latin, meaning "persons of the drama." [Editor's note.]

literally, wash himself off. Like any other tidy hooker, this man will have to clean up after taking on a tough customer, so that he might be ready to take on someone else.

These suggestions of pederasty are intended, not as a literal char-   *17*
acterization of the husband's job, but as a metaphor for what it takes to get ahead: Gail's husband, like most white-collar workers, must debase himself to make a good impression, toadying to his superiors, offering himself, body and soul, to the corporation. Maybe, therefore, it isn't really Gail who has neutered him: it may be his way of life that has wrought the ugly change. How, then, are women represented here? The commercial does deliberately appeal to women, offering them a sad fantasy of control; but it also, perhaps inadvertently, illuminates the unhappiness which makes that fantasy attractive.

The husband's status, it would seem, should make Gail happy,   *18*
since it makes her physically comfortable, and yet Gail can't help loathing her husband for the degradations which she helps him undergo. For her part of the bargain is, ultimately, no less painful than his. She has to do more than put up with him; she has to prepare him for his world of affairs, and then must help him to conceal the shame. Of course, it's all quite hopeless. She clearly despises the man whom she would bolster; and the thing which she provides to help him "feel cleaner than ever before" is precisely what has helped him do the job that's always made him feel so dirty. "A little water clears us of this deed" is her promise, which is false, for she is just as soiled as her doomed husband, however fresh and well-ironed she may look.

Of course, the ad not only illuminates this mess, but helps perpet-   *19*
uate it, by obliquely gratifying the guilts, terrors, and resentments that underlie it and arise from it. The strategy is not meant to be noticed, but works through the apparent comedy, which must therefore be studied carefully, not passively received. Thus, thirty seconds of ingenious advertising, which we can barely stand to watch, tell us something more than we might want to know about the souls of men and women under corporate capitalism.

Meaning

1. What point does Miller make about the Shield advertisement? On the surface, what impression of male-female relationships does the commercial seem to create? What, according to Miller, is the deeper meaning?

2. Why does Miller refer to the placement of the flower box as "an exquisitely perverse suggestion" (paragraph 9)? How does Gail's behavior contribute to this suggestion?

3. According to Miller (paragraph 13), how does the treatment of dirt in this commercial differ from that found in commercials for other products? How does this difference support his final statement that the Shield advertisement reveals "something more than we might want to know about the souls of men and women under corporate capitalism"(19)?

4. If you do not know the meanings of the following words or parts of words, look them up in the dictionary: contempt (paragraph 1); baritone (2); octave, suave, saunters, subverting (3); trifle (5); pseudo-, ubiquitous, inverting, homonymic, illusory, wields (6); deplored, misogyny, demeanor, ludicrously, scrotum, dishabille, congruous, emasculate (7); psychosocial, arbitrarily, cynicism, castration (8); perverse, phallic, virility (9); inversion, potency, crux, replenishing (10); boutonniere (11); contemptuously, inanities (12); besmirchment (13); oxymoronic, voracious, definitive (14); sordid (15); fiscal, sadistic, truncated (16); pederasty, metaphor, debase, toadying (17); degradations, bolster (18); perpetuate, obliquely (19).

Purpose and Audience

1. What is Miller's purpose in analyzing the Shield commercial? What advice does he want to share with his readers? Where in the essay is his purpose made clear?

2. In a comment on this essay, Miller has written that "most Americans still perceive the media image as transparent, a sign that simply says what it means and means what it says." Close analyses of media images like Miller's are thus dismissed, he says, as "reading too much into it." Where, if at all, do you think Miller is guilty of this charge? Be specific, giving particular claims and stating why you find each one far-fetched. Do any weaknesses you identify undermine Miller's entire analysis? To what extent do you accept or reject Miller's analysis, and why?

3. What was your attitude toward commercials before reading this essay? Has the essay changed your attitude? How and why, or why not? Be specific.

Method and Structure

1. What elements of the Shield commercial does Miller focus on in his analysis? How does his analysis of these features help create a new whole? How does the new whole differ from the original?

2. Miller's essay is divided into four distinct sections, two of them signaled by questions. What are those sections? How does each contribute to Miller's conclusions about the commercial?

3. **Other Methods**   Miller uses several other methods of development: for example, he describes the room in which the second half of the action takes place (Chapter 1), narrates the exchange between Gail and her husband (Chapter 2), and compares the Shield commercial with other soap commercials (Chapter 7). Also important to Miller's analysis is the analogy he makes in paragraphs 14–16 (Chapter 8). What is the analogy, and how does it support Miller's analysis? Do you find the analogy convincing? Why, or why not?

Language

1. In retelling the story of Gail and her husband, Miller chooses expressions to suggest his distaste for the commercial before he begins his analysis. For example, he describes the husband as "half-crazed with anxiety" in the opening line, while Gail's look indicates "years of contempt" (paragraph 1). Locate eight or ten other examples of suggestive language, and explain how each supports Miller's negative impression of the commercial.

2. Miller's writing style is sometimes academic, with long, formal sentences and words, such as "Typically, [the commercial] woos its female viewers—i.e., those who choose the soap in most households—with a fantasy of dominance; and it does so by inverting the actualities of woman's lot through a number of imperceptible details" (paragraph 6). Yet the style is also at times quite informal, as in "Is all this as stupid as it seems at first?" (5). Locate additional examples of both styles. What do each and their combination contribute to the essay?

3. In paragraphs 9–11, Miller points out an extended metaphor that he claims is central to the underlying meaning of the commercial. What is the metaphor, and how does it contribute to his analysis? (If necessary, see *figures of speech* in the Glossary.)

Writing Topics

1. Organize your answers to questions 2 and 3 under Purpose and Audience into an analysis essay that supports or rebuts Miller's claims. Clearly identify the elements of Miller's essay (the specific claims and the support for them), and deal with them one by one, offering support from your

own experience of television advertising, if you like, as well as from Miller's essay. Make sure your readers understand the goal of your analysis and the new whole—the vision of the essay—that you have in mind.

2. Consider a television commercial that presents a brief situation similar to that in the Shield commercial. (If possible, record the commercial so that you can view it many times.) Using Miller's essay as a model, analyze the commercial by narrating the story and subjecting it to careful scrutiny and interpretation. Focus on the names (if any) of the characters, their behavior and demeanor, their dress, their dialogue, the mise-en-scène (arrangement of actors and props), the music (if any), and anything else that you feel contributes to a "hidden message." Conclude by stating what you think that message is.

3. Write an essay in which you view Miller's essay through the perspective of Robert Reich's parable of Rot at the Top in "The Four Parables of American Politics" (p. 144, paragraph 3). In your essay, consider the following questions: Who, according to Miller, fills the role of Reich's "powerful elites"? How do they undermine society? In what role does Miller cast himself? What means does he use to attack the rot? How does his essay attempt to support the moral of Reich's parable, that "Americans must not allow any privileged group to amass too much power"?

Writing Topics

Division or Analysis

Choose one of the following topics, or any other topic they suggest, for an essay developed by division or analysis. The topic you decide on should be something you care about so that division or analysis is a means of communicating an idea, not an end in itself.

1. The personality of a friend or relative
2. A machine or appliance such as a car engine, harvesting combine, computer, hair dryer, toaster, or sewing machine
3. A nonmotorized vehicle such as a skateboard, roller skate, bicycle, or sled
4. A style of dress or "look" such as that associated with the typical businessperson, jock, punk rocker, or outdoors enthusiast
5. An organization or institution such as a sports league or club, labor union, church, synagogue, school, or government agency
6. An animal such as a cat, dog, horse, cow, spider, or bat
7. A typical hero or villain in science fiction, romance novels, war movies, or movies or novels about adolescents
8. A theory or concept in a field such as psychology, sociology, economics, biology, physics, engineering, or astronomy
9. A television or film comedy
10. A literary work: short story, novel, poem, essay
11. A visual work: painting, sculpture, building
12. A musical work: song, concerto, symphony, opera
13. A performance: sports, acting, dance, music, speech
14. The slang of a particular group or occupation
15. The evidence in a political argument (written, spoken, or reported in the news)

Chapter 5

Classification

Understanding the Method

We **classify** when we sort things into groups: kinds of cars, styles of writing, types of psychotherapy. Because it creates order, classification helps us make sense of our physical and mental experience. With it, we see the correspondences among like things and distinguish them from unlike things. We can name things, remember them, discuss them.

As we saw in the previous chapter, classification draws on division or analysis: using that method, we separate things into their elements; then we isolate the similarities in those elements and group or classify the things based on those similarities. A familiar example of classification—at least in its broad outlines—is the system of ordering all living things into categories. The primary groups are the animals and the plants. Then each divides into subclasses, each of which in turn divides into smaller subclasses, and so on. For instance:

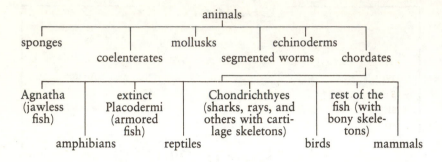

All the members of the overall group—the animals—share at least one characteristic (the need to obtain food instead of manufacturing it themselves, as all the plants do). The animals in each subcategory also share at least one characteristic: they are jawless, for instance, or have cartilage skeletons. The animals in each subcategory are also independent of one another, and none of them is essential to the existence of the category; indeed, as the extinct armored fish indicate, a category continues to exist as a slot even when no representatives fill it at the moment.

The number of groups in a classification scheme depends entirely on the basis for establishing the classes in the first place. In a system like that used for the animal kingdom, called a **complex classification,** each animal fits firmly into one class because it shares at least one distinguishing feature with all members of that class but *not* with any members of any other classes. Another kind of classification is **binary,** or **two-part:** two classes are set up, one with a certain characteristic, the other without it. For instance, the animals might have been classified as those with bony skeletons and those without. Such binary schemes can be adequate when a writer wants to emphasize the possession of a particular characteristic. But, as the example of the animals shows, many binary classifications are not very informative because they create broad categories and specify nothing about the members of the "other" class except that they lack a certain trait. (An old joke claims that there are two kinds of people in the world—those who classify, and all others.)

Sorting items demands a **principle of classification** that determines the groups. The principle in sorting the animals, for instance, is their anatomy—the structures of their bodies. Principles for sorting a year's movies might be genre (action-adventures, comedies, dramas);

place of origin (domestic, foreign); or cost of production (low-budget, medium-priced, high-budget). The writer's choice would depend on his or her interest.

As the examples so far indicate, classification is used almost exclusively for explanation. Thus, though a writer may emphasize one class over the others, the classification itself must be complete and consistent. A classification of movies by genre would be incomplete if it omitted comedies. It would be inconsistent if it included action-adventures, comedies, dramas, low-budget films, and foreign films: such a system mixes *three* principles (genre, cost, origin); it omits whole classes (what of high-budget domestic dramas?); and it overlaps other classes (a low-budget foreign action-adventure would fit in three different groups).

Analyzing Classification in Paragraphs

Mortimer J. Adler (born 1902) is a philosopher, critic, and educator, the author of many essays and forty-four books. The following paragraph is from "How to Mark a Book" (1940), an essay urging readers to mark their books as a way of conversing with the author.

There are three kinds of book owners. The first has all the standard sets and best-sellers—unread, untouched. (This deluded individual owns woodpulp and ink, not books.) The second has a great many books—a few of them read through, most of them dipped into, but all of them as clean and shiny as the day they were bought. (This person would probably like to make books his own, but is restrained by a false respect for their physical appearance.) The third has a few books or many—every one of them dog-eared and dilapidated, shaken and loosened by continual use, marked and scribbled in from front to back. (This man owns books.)

Principle of classification (revealed gradually): how hard book owners use their books
1. Those who do not truly own books

2. Those who want to own books

3. Those who truly own books

William H. Calvin (born 1939) is a neurobiologist who teaches at the University of Washington in Seattle. The following paragraph appeared in "Aplysia, the Hare of the Ocean," an essay in Calvin's book

The Throwing Madonna: Essays on the Brain (1983). *Aplysia* is a large, sluglike sea mollusk whose nervous system is unusually well understood by neurobiologists.

There are only two identified nerve cells in the fish brain, and none yet in higher animals. In *Aplysia,* there are almost a hundred identified cells—still only a small fraction of the total number of *Aplysia* nerve cells, but an especially useful subset. Some of them are sensory cells, detecting a touch or water current, conveying electrical impulses from the skin into a ganglion of many hundreds of nerve cells where decisions are made. Some of the identified neurons [nerve cells] are the motor neurons in the ganglia which send electrical impulses out to a muscle, causing contraction and movement. But some neurons are simply decision-makers, interneurons with no branches coming or going from the skin and muscles. So sensory neurons deliver impulses to interneurons and motor neurons; interneurons affect the motor neurons and modify the messages sent by the sensory neuron endings upon the motor neurons. As more and more of these interneurons have become identified, neurobiologists have been able to figure out some of the basis for learning and memory in these animals.

Principle of classification (revealed gradually): the functions of the known Aplysia *nerve cells*

1. Sensory cells

2. Motor neurons

3. Interneurons

How the classes work together

Developing an Essay by Classification

GETTING STARTED

Classification essays are often assigned in college courses. When you need to develop your own subject for a classification essay, think of one large class of things whose members can be sorted into sub-classes, such as study habits, midnight grocery shoppers, or political fund-raising appeals. Be sure that your general subject forms a class in its own right—that all its members share at least one important quality. Then discover the qualities that distinguish some members from others, providing poles for the members to group themselves around. One such scheme for political fund-raising appeals might be the different methods of delivery, including letters, telephone calls, advertisements, telethons, social gatherings, and rallies. This principle of classification suggests a thesis—"Political fund-raising appeals are delivered in any of six ways"—but not a very interesting one. The thesis should also convey a reason for the classification so that the essay does not become a mere list of categories and their features: for instance, "Of the six ways to deliver political fund-raising appeals, the three that rely on personal contact are generally the most effective." (Note that this thesis implies a further classification based on whether the appeals involve personal contact or not.)

While generating ideas for your classification, keep track of them in a list, diagram, or outline to ensure that your principle is applied thoroughly (all classes) and consistently (each part or each class relating to the principle, without gaps or overlaps). Fill in the list, diagram, or outline with the distinguishing features of each class and with examples that will clarify your scheme. Be sure to consider your readers' needs. The principle for classifying a familiar subject such as study habits might need little justification, although the classes themselves would need to be enlivened with vivid examples. An unfamiliar subject, in contrast, might require considerable care in explaining the principle of classification as well as attention to the details.

ORGANIZING

The introduction to a classification essay should make clear why the classification is worthwhile: What situation prompted the essay? What do readers already know about the subject? What use might they make of the information you will provide? Unless your principle of classification is self-evident, you may want to explain it briefly—though save extensive explanation for the body of the essay. Do state your principle in a thesis, so that readers know where you're taking them.

In the body of the essay the classes may be arranged in order of decreasing familiarity or increasing importance or size—whatever pattern provides the emphasis you want and clarifies your scheme for readers. You should at least mention each class, but some may demand more space and detail than others to make your point.

Like a division or analysis essay, a classification essay should end with a conclusion that restores the wholeness of the subject. Among other uses, the conclusion might summarize the classes, comment on the significance of one particular class in relation to the whole, or point out a new understanding of the whole subject gained from the classification.

DRAFTING

While drafting the essay, picture each class clearly in your mind so that your details are concrete and your examples vivid. Take care to distinguish each one from the others, not only implicitly, by choosing effective details and examples, but also explicitly, by stating differences outright. At the same time, don't lose sight of the subject itself. How does each class contribute to the subject as a whole?

REVISING

The following questions can help you revise your classification.

1. *Will readers see the purpose of your classification?* Let readers know early why you are troubling to classify your subject, and keep this purpose evident throughout the essay.

2. *Is your classification complete?* Your principle of classification should create categories that encompass every representative of the general subject. If some representatives will not fit the scheme, you may have to create a new category or revise the existing categories to include them.

3. *Is your classification consistent?* Consistency is essential to save readers from confusion or irritation. Make sure all the classes reflect the same principle and that they do not overlap. Remedy flaws by adjusting the classes or creating new ones.

4. *Are your classes well detailed?* Provide plenty of examples of each class so that readers know exactly what its boundaries are—what's counted in, what's counted out, and why.

Robert B. Reich

Robert Reich was born in 1946 in Scranton, Pennsylvania. He received a B.A. from Dartmouth College (1968), attended Oxford University as a Rhodes Scholar, and earned a law degree from Yale Law School (1973). After working for some time as a lawyer, Reich joined the Federal Trade Commission, the government agency responsible for business regulation. There he was struck by the absence of a "holistic view" of government policy toward business, an impression that has influenced his current work as a writer, a consultant, and a teacher of business, political economy, and public policy at Harvard University's John F. Kennedy School of Government. Along with articles in The Atlantic Monthly, The New York Times Book Review, *and other periodicals, Reich has written several books, including* Minding America's Business *(1982, with Ira Magaziner),* The Next American Frontier *(1983),* New Deals: The Chrysler Revival and the American System *(1985, with John D. Donahue),* Tales of a New America *(1987), and* The Power of Public Ideas *(1988). He is considered an intellectual leader of the "neoliberals," politicians, economists, and business and labor leaders who seek ways for the government to foster economic growth along with social justice.*

The Four Parables
of American Politics

Reich often looks to American history for explanations of current attitudes and problems. In the following essay he classifies political views and messages into four groups, each represented by an American parable, or moral tale. The essay first appeared in The New York Times Magazine *in 1985 and was revised by Reich especially for this book.*

The next presidential race will start remarkably soon. In short order, 1
we will be treated to a new round of speeches, debates, and interviews concerning America's most pressing problems. Some of the proposals will be original, a few of the perspectives even novel. But underlying the rhetoric will be stories we have heard many times before. They are the same stories we tell and retell one another about our lives together in America; some are based in fact, some in fiction, but most lie in between. They are our national parables.

These parables are rooted in the central experiences of American 2
history: the flight from an older culture, the rejection of central au-

thority and aristocratic privileges, the lure of the unspoiled frontier, the struggles for social equality. One can distill four central themes:

1. *The Rot at the Top.* This parable is about the malevolence of   3
powerful elites, be they wealthy aristocrats, rapacious business leaders, or imperious government officials. It is the story of corruption in high places, of conspiracy against the public. At the end of the century, muckrakers like Upton Sinclair and Ida Tarbell uncovered sordid tales of corporate malfeasance; their modern heirs are called investigative reporters. The theme arises from the American detective story whose hero—such as Sam Spade, Serpico, or Jack Nicholson in *Chinatown*—traces the rot directly to the most powerful members in the community. The political moral is clear: Americans must not allow any privileged group to amass too much power.

2. *The Triumphant Individual.* This is the story of the little person   4
who works hard, submits to self-discipline, takes risks, has faith in himself, and is eventually rewarded with wealth, fame, and honor. Consider Benjamin Franklin's *Autobiography*, the first in a long line of American manuals on how to become rich through self-denial and diligence. The theme recurs in the tale of Abraham Lincoln, log-splitter from Illinois who goes to the White House; in the hundred or so novellas of Horatio Alger, whose heroes all rise promptly and predictably from rags to riches; and in modern success stories, such as *Rocky* and *Iacocca*. Regardless of the precise form, the moral is the same: Anyone can "make it" in America through hard work and perseverance.

3. *The Benign Community.* The third parable is about the Ameri-   5
can community. It is the story of neighbors and friends rolling up their sleeves and pitching in to help one another, of self-sacrifice, community pride, and patriotism. The story is rooted in America's religious traditions, and its earliest formulations are found in sermons like John Winthrop's "A Model of Christian Charity," delivered on board ship in Salem Harbor just before the Pilgrims landed in 1630. He envisioned a "city set upon a hill" whose members would "delight in each other" and be "of the same body." Three hundred years later, these sentiments echoed in Robert Sherwood's plays, John Steinbeck's novels, Aaron Copland's music, and Frank Capra's films. The last scene in *It's a Wonderful Life* conveys the lesson: Jimmy Stewart learns that he can count on his neighbors' generosity and goodness, just as they had counted on him. They are bound together in a spirit of dependence and compassion. The principle: We must nurture and preserve genuine community.

4. *The Mob at the Gates.* The fourth parable is about social   6

disintegration that lurks just below the surface of democracy. It is the tale of mob rule, violence, crime, and indulgence—of society coming apart from an excess of democratic permissiveness. It gives voice to the fear that outsiders will exploit the freedom and openness of America. The story shows up in Federalist writings about the instabilities of democracy, in Whig histories of the United States, and in the anti-immigration harangues of the late 19th and 20th centuries. Its most dramatic appearance in recent years has come in fictionalized accounts of vigilante heroes who wreak havoc on muggers—like Clint Eastwood's Dirty Harry or Charles Bronson in *Death Wish*—and in Rambo's messy eradication of platoons of Communist fighters. The lesson: We must impose social discipline, lest the rabble overrun us.

These four parables are completely familiar to most of us. They 7 shape our political discourse. They confirm our ideologies. Every American retells and listens repeatedly to all four stories; every politician and social commentator borrows, embellishes, and seeks legitimacy from them.

But the parables can be linked together in different ways, each 8 arrangement suggesting a distinct political message. At any given time in our nation's history one particular configuration has been dominant, eventually to be replaced by another. The art of political rhetoric has been to reconfigure these stories in a manner that affirms and amplifies the changes already occurring in the way Americans tell the tales.

In the early part of the century, for example, leaders of the Pro- 9 gressive era emphasized the link between the parables of Rot at the Top and the Triumphant Individual. Big business—the trusts—blocked worthy citizens from their rightful places in society; corruption at the top was thwarting personal initiative. Woodrow Wilson put the matter succinctly in a speech during the 1912 presidential campaign, promising to wage "a crusade against the powers that have governed us . . . that have limited our development . . . that have determined our lives . . . that have set us in a straitjacket to do as they please." In his view, the struggle against the trusts would be nothing less than "a second struggle for emancipation."

By the 1930s, the parables had shifted. Now the key conceptual 10 link was between Rot at the Top and the Benign Community. The liberties of common people were under attack by leaders of big business and finance. In the 1936 presidential campaign, Franklin D. Roosevelt warned against the "economic royalists" who had impressed the whole of society into "royal service."

"The hours men and women worked, the wages they received, the   *11*
conditions of their labor . . . these had passed beyond the control of
the people, and were imposed by this new industrial dictatorship," he
warned in one speech. "The royalists of the economic order have
conceded that political freedom was the business of the Government,
but they have maintained that economic slavery was nobody's business." What was at stake, he concluded, was the "survival of
democracy."

The shift from the Progressives' emphasis on the Triumphant In-   *12*
dividual to the New Deal's Benign Community was more than an
oratorical device. It represented a change in Americans' understanding of social life. The Great Depression had provided a national lesson
in social solidarity; nearly every American family felt the effects of
poverty. The Benign Community became intimately relevant as relatives and neighbors sought to help one another, as Government became the insurer of last resort, and then as Americans turned together
to win the "good war" against fascism. The Benign Community embraced the entire nation.

In the decades following World War II, however, the Benign   *13*
Community became a less convincing parable. Much of the country's
middle class began to enjoy a scattered suburban affluence, far removed from the experiences of mutual dependence that had characterized American life a generation before. The prewar images of the
common people and the forgotten man were less compelling now that
most Americans felt prosperous and not at all forgotten; the story of
Rot at the Top was less convincing now that life at the top was within
plain sight.

The descendant of the Benign Community was a feeble impulse   *14*
toward social altruism. Lyndon Johnson's War on Poverty was sold to
the American public as being relatively costless. The idea was that
proper Keynesian management of the economy required substantial
public expenditures, which might as well be for the benefit of the
poor. The economy was buoyant enough that America could afford to
enlarge its welfare state; the "fiscal dividend" could be spent on the
less fortunate. And in any event, "we" were only giving "them" an
"equal opportunity," simply allowing the Triumphant Individuals
among them to come forth and find their true potential. Under the
banner of civil rights and social justice, Triumphant Individuals joined
the nation's Benign Community.

Once again, the configuration of stories Americans told one an-   *15*
other began to shift. As the economy slowed in the 1970s, a public
tired of belt tightening became less tolerant of social altruism.

Enter Ronald Reagan, master storyteller. His parables drew upon 16
the same four American tales, but substantially recast. This time the
Rot at the Top referred to career bureaucrats in government and
liberal intellectuals. The Triumphant Individuals were America's business entrepreneurs. The Benign Community comprised small, traditional neighborhoods in which people voluntarily helped one another,
free from government interference. And the Mob at the Gates was
filled with criminals, pornographers, welfare cheats, illegal immigrants, third-world debtors and revolutionaries, ornery trading partners, and Communist aggressors—all of them encouraged by liberal
acquiescence. The Reagan Revolution would discipline "them," to
liberate the Triumphant Individuals in "us." Political choices in this
story were cast as how "hard" or "soft" we should be on "them."
Hard always emerged as the only decent American response.

In the 1988 election, both Michael Dukakis and George Bush 17
tried to claim the American parables for themselves, but Bush wielded
them far more effectively. Dukakis sought to portray Bush as a
wealthy preppy—the Rot at the Top—and himself as a son of immigrants who had lived the American dream of the Triumphant Individual; Dukakis also warned America of the Japanese Mob at the Gates,
and he called for a Benign Community that would ensure good jobs at
good wages for every American. Bush, on the other hand, portrayed
Dukakis as a member of the Harvard liberal intelligentsia—the Rot at
the Top—and himself as a Triumphant Individual who had come to
Texas as a young man to make his fortune. Bush accused Dukakis of
letting criminals out of jail to rob and rape honest Americans (the
Mob at the Gates); and he celebrated America's "thousand points of
light"—the generous, Benign Community of America, which would
help the less fortunate among us through acts of charity rather than
through central government.

Inevitably, the configuration of stories Americans tell one another 18
will change yet again. The "us" and "them" recountings of the present era eventually may be superseded by a new version that reflects a
more complex, interdependent world. Perhaps, in the next version,
the parable of the Benign Community will be expanded to include
more of the earth's peoples, and that of the Triumphant Individual
will embrace our collective aspirations for freedom and dignity. Indeed, it is just possible that Americans already are telling one another
these sorts of stories, and are only waiting for a new set of political
leaders to give them voice.

Meaning

1. What is Reich's main point in this essay? What functions do the parables have? Why is *parables* an appropriate label for these stories?
2. Who does Reich believe ultimately shapes American values, the public or the politicians? Cite sentences to support your answer.
3. If you do not know the meanings of the following words, look them up in a dictionary: distill (paragraph 2); malevolence, rapacious, imperious, muckrakers, malfeasance (3); novellas (4); benign (5); harangues, vigilante (6); discourse, ideologies (7); succinctly (9); oratorical (12); affluence (13); altruism, Keynesian, buoyant, fiscal (14); acquiescence (16); superseded (18).

Purpose and Audience

1. Reich seems to have had at least two purposes in writing this essay: one is evident through paragraph 17, and another becomes evident in paragraph 18. What are these two purposes?
2. Reich undoubtedly expects his many examples to be self-explanatory or already familiar to his readers. Do you think his expectation is reasonable? Which examples do you find particularly clear and effective? Which, if any, do you not understand?
3. To what extent do you agree or disagree with Reich's view of the configuration of parables during the 1988 presidential campaign (paragraph 17)? If you disagree, what configuration do you think would be more accurate?

Method and Structure

1. What common origin do the four classes of political stories share? What criteria does Reich use to distinguish each class from the others?
2. In paragraphs 3–6 Reich provides examples of the representatives or members of each class of story. For instance, "The Triumphant Individual" class includes the stories of Benjamin Franklin, Abraham Lincoln, Horatio Alger, Rocky, and Lee Iacocca (the head of Chrysler Corporation). But Reich also mentions additional members of the classes in discussing the historical periods (paragraphs 9–17). Make a list of all the members of each class discussed by Reich. How do you explain the fact that some members—for instance, businesspeople—fit into different classes at different times? Is this a flaw in Reich's classification? Why, or why not?
3. **Other Methods**   As noted in a previous question, Reich's classification

depends heavily on examples (Chapter 3). Equally notable is the historical narrative (Chapter 2), which begins in paragraph 9. Why is narrative a particularly appropriate method for Reich to use, given his main point and purpose?

Language

1. Analyze and compare the connotations of the four parable labels—"The Rot at the Top," "The Triumphant Individual," "The Benign Community," and "The Mob at the Gates." What attitudes does Reich attribute to the American people characterized by these labels? Locate examples of similarly connotative words within the explanation of each parable (paragraphs 3–6). What effect does Reich achieve by using words such as these? (If necessary, consult the Glossary for an explanation of *connotation*.)
2. Reich refers more than once to "we" or "us" versus "they" or "them" (paragraphs 14, 16, 18). Why does he enclose these pronouns in quotation marks? Judging from Reich's conclusion (18), does he see himself as "us" or "them" or neither? Why?

Writing Topics

1. Think of stories you have read or heard that have taught you something about values—for instance, about being a good student, maintaining a good reputation, being respectful of your elders, caring for those less fortunate, cherishing democratic freedoms, being masculine or feminine. Sort the stories into classes according to some consistent principle, such as the particular values being taught or the sources of the stories or their effects on you. Write an essay in which you explain your classification.
2. Use the library's *New York Times Index* to help you find the text of a political speech, such as a speech made at the Republican or Democratic National Convention in 1988. Write an essay analyzing the speech in terms of Reich's political parables. Which parables seem to underlie the speaker's points, and why? Which, if any, does the speaker not touch on?
3. In "The Frontier Disappears" (p. 118), Ray Allen Billington also discusses forces shaping the American character. Write an essay in which you compare Billington's and Reich's interpretations of important threads in American history. Where do Reich and Billington agree? Where does each disregard forces highlighted by the other? In your opinion, which is the stronger essay, and why? (This topic will require careful reading and summary of both essays. If necessary, see the Introduction, pp. 3–5, and Chapter 7 on comparison and contrast.)

——————— Donald A. Norman ———————

Donald A. Norman is a psychologist specializing in the study of human cognition, or mental activity, and its interaction with the physical world. Born in 1935 in New York City, Norman obtained a B.S. from Massachusetts Institute of Technology (1957) and an M.S. and Ph.D. from the University of Pennsylvania (1959, 1962). He has taught psychology and conducted research at several institutions, including Harvard University, the Center for Advanced Study in the Behavioral Sciences, the British Medical Research Council, and, since 1966, the University of California at San Diego, where he is a professor. In addition to numerous scholarly articles, Norman has written, coauthored, or edited many texts and professional books, among them Perspectives on Cognitive Science *(1981),* Learning and Memory *(1982), and* User-Centered System Design: New Perspectives on Human Computer Interaction *(1986).*

To Err Is Human

The following essay comes from Norman's book The Psychology of Everyday Things *(1988), an illuminating and often amusing study of the relations between human beings and the objects that confound them—swinging doors, computer keyboards, light switches, videocassette recorders. We blame ourselves for being unable to work these things, says Norman in the preface to his book, while "the real culprit—faulty design—goes undetected."*

A colleague reported that he went to his car to drive to work. As 1
he drove away, he realized that he had forgotten his briefcase, so he turned around and went back. He stopped the car, turned off the engine, and unbuckled his wristwatch. Yes, wristwatch, instead of his seatbelt.

Most everyday errors are slips. Intend to do one action, find your- 2
self doing another. Have a person say something clearly and distinctly to you, but "hear" something quite different. The study of slips is the study of the psychology of everyday errors—what Freud[1] called "the psychopathology of everyday life." Some slips may indeed have hid-

---

[1] Sigmund Freud (1856–1939), an Austrian neurologist and psychiatrist, was the father of psychoanalysis. [Editor's note.]

den, darker meanings, but most are accounted for by rather simple events in our mental mechanisms.

Slips show up most frequently in skilled behavior. We don't make so many slips in things we are still learning. In part, slips result from a lack of attention. On the whole, people can consciously attend to only one primary thing at a time. But we often do many things at once. We walk while we talk; we drive cars while we talk, sing, listen to the radio, use a telephone, take notes, or read a map. We can do more than one thing at a time only if most of the actions are done automatically, subconsciously, with little or no need for conscious attention. *3*

Doing several things at once is essential even in carrying out a single task. To play the piano, we must move the fingers properly over the keyboard while reading music, manipulating the pedals, and listening to the resulting sounds. But to play the piano well, we should do these things automatically. Our conscious attention should be focused on the higher levels of the music, on style, and on phrasing. So it is with every skill. The low-level, physical movements should be controlled subconsciously. *4*

Types of Slips

Some slips result from the similarities of actions. Or an event in the world may automatically trigger an action. Sometimes our thoughts and actions may remind us of unintended actions, which we then perform. We can place slips into one of six categories: capture errors, description errors, data-driven errors, associative activation errors, loss-of-activation errors, and mode errors. *5*

CAPTURE ERRORS

"I was using a copying machine, and I was counting pages. I found myself counting '1, 2, 3, 4, 5, 6, 7, 8, 9, 10, Jack, Queen, King.' I have been playing cards recently." *6*

Consider the common slip called the capture error, in which a frequently done activity suddenly takes charge instead of (captures) the one intended. You are playing a piece of music (without too much attention) and it is similar to another (which you know better); suddenly you are playing the more familiar piece. Or you go off to your bedroom to change your clothes for dinner and find yourself in bed. *7*

(This slip was first reported by William James[2] in 1890.) Or you finish typing your thoughts on your word processor or text editing program, turn off the power, and go off to other things, neglecting to save any of your work. Or you get into your car on Sunday to go to the store and find yourself at the office.

The capture error appears whenever two different action se-   8
quences have their initial stages in common, with one sequence being unfamiliar and the other being well practiced. Seldom, if ever, does the unfamiliar sequence capture the familiar one.

DESCRIPTION ERRORS

A former student reported that one day he came home from jog-   9
ging, took off his sweaty shirt, and rolled it up in a ball, intending
to throw it in the laundry basket. Instead he threw it in the toilet.
(It wasn't poor aim: the laundry basket and toilet were in differ-
ent rooms.)

In the common slip known as the description error, the intended   10
action has much in common with others that are possible. As a result,
unless the action sequence is completely and precisely specified, the
intended action might fit several possibilities. Suppose that my tired
student in the example formed a mental description of his intended
action something like "throw the shirt into the opening at the top of
the container." This description would be perfectly unambiguous and
sufficient were the laundry basket the only open container in sight;
but when the open toilet was visible, its characteristics matched the
description and triggered the inappropriate action. This is a description error because the internal description of the intention was not
sufficiently precise. Description errors usually result in performing the
correct action on the wrong object. Obviously, the more the wrong
and right objects have in common, the more likely the errors are to
occur. Description errors, like all slips, are more likely when we are
distracted, bored, involved in other activities, under extra stress, or
otherwise not inclined to pay full attention to the task at hand.

Description errors occur most frequently when the wrong and   11
right objects are physically near each other. People have reported a
number of description errors to me.

---

[2]William James (1842–1910) was an American psychologist and philosopher.
[Editor's note.]

Two clerks in a department store were both on the telephone to 12
verify credit cards while simultaneously dealing with a customer
and filling out a credit card form. One sales clerk had passed in
back of the other to reach the charge forms. When this clerk
finished preparing the sales slip, she hung up the handset on the
wrong telephone, thereby terminating the other clerk's call.

A person intended to put the lid on a sugar bowl, but instead 13
put it on a coffee cup (with the same size opening).

I had a report of someone who planned to pour orange juice 14
into a glass but instead poured it into a coffee cup (adjacent to the
glass).

Another person told me of intending to pour rice from a 15
storage jar into a measuring cup, but instead pouring cooking oil
into the measuring cup (both the oil and the rice were kept in
glass containers on the counter).

Some things seem designed to cause slips. Long rows of identical 16
switches are perfect setups for description errors. Intend to flip one
switch, instead flip a similar-looking one. It happens in industrial
plants, aircraft, homes, anywhere. When different actions have similar
descriptions, there is a good chance of mishap, especially when the
operator is experienced and well practiced and therefore not paying
full attention, and if there are more important things to do.

DATA-DRIVEN ERRORS

"I was assigning a visitor a room to use. I decided to call the 17
department secretary to tell her the room number. I used the
telephone in the alcove outside the room, with the room number
in sight. Instead of dialing the secretary's phone number—
which I use frequently and know very well—I dialed the room
number."

Much human behavior is automatic, for example, brushing away 18
an insect. Automatic actions are data driven—triggered by the arrival
of the sensory data. But sometimes data-driven activities can intrude
into an ongoing action sequence, causing behavior that was not
intended.

ASSOCIATIVE ACTIVATION ERRORS

"My office phone rang. I picked up the receiver and bellowed 19
'Come in' at it."

If external data can sometimes trigger actions, so, too, can internal thoughts and associations. The ringing of the telephone and knocking on the door both signal the need to greet someone. Other errors occur from associations among thoughts and ideas. Associative activation errors are the slips studied by Freud; you think something that ought not to be said and then, to your embarrassment, you say it.

LOSS-OF-ACTIVATION ERRORS

"I have to go the bedroom before I start working in the dining room. I start going there and realize as I am walking that I have no idea why I am going there. Knowing myself, I keep going, hoping that something in the bedroom will remind me. . . . I get there but still cannot recall what I wanted . . . so I go back to the dining room. There I realize that my glasses are dirty. With great relief I go back to the bedroom, get my handkerchief, and wipe my glasses clean."

One of the more common slips is simply forgetting to do something. More interesting is forgetting part of the act, remembering the rest, as in the story above where the goal was forgotten, but the rest of the action continued unimpaired. One of my informants walked all the way through the house to the kitchen and opened the refrigerator door; then he wondered why he was there. Lack-of-activation errors occur because the presumed mechanism—the "activation" of the goals—has decayed. The less technical but more common term would be "forgetting."

MODE ERRORS

"I had just completed a long run from my university to my home in what I was convinced would be record time. It was dark when I got home, so I could not read the time on my stopwatch. As I walked up and down the street in front of my home, cooling off, I got more and more anxious to see how fast I had run. I then remembered that my watch had a built-in light, operated by the upper right-hand button. Elated, I depressed the button to illuminate the reading, only to read a time of zero seconds. I had forgotten that in stopwatch mode, the same button [that in the normal, time-reading mode would have turned on a light] cleared the time and reset the stopwatch."

Mode errors occur when devices have different modes of oper-   24
ation, and the action appropriate for one mode has different meanings
in other modes. Mode errors are inevitable any time equipment is
designed to have more possible actions than it has controls or dis-
plays, so the controls must do double duty. Mode errors are especially
likely where the equipment does not make the mode visible, so the
user is expected to remember what mode has been established, sometimes for many hours.

Mode errors are common with digital watches and computer sys-   25
tems (especially text editors). Several accidents in commercial aviation
can be attributed to mode errors, especially in the use of the automatic
pilots (which have a large number of complex modes). . . .

Design Lessons from the Study of Slips

Two different kinds of design lessons can be drawn, one for prevent-   26
ing slips before they occur and one for detecting and correcting them
when they do occur. In general, the solutions follow directly from the
preceding analyses. For example, mode errors are minimized by minimizing modes, or at least by making modes visible.

Cars provide a number of examples of how design relates to er-   27
ror. A variety of fluids are required in the engine compartment of an
automobile: engine oil, transmission oil, brake fluid, windshield
washer solution, radiator coolant, battery water. Putting the wrong
fluid into a reservoir could lead to serious damage or even an accident. Automobile manufacturers try to minimize these errors (a combination of description and mode errors) by making the different
compartments look different—using different shapes and different-
size openings—and by adding color to the fluids so that they can be
distinguished. Here design by and large prevents errors. But, unfortunately, designers seem to prefer to encourage them.

I was in a taxi in Austin, Texas, admiring the large number of   28
new devices in front of the driver. No more simple radio. In its
place was a computer display, so that messages from the dispatch-
er were now printed on the screen. The driver took great delight
in demonstrating all the features to me. On the radio transmitter I
saw four identical-looking buttons laid out in a row.

"Oh," I said, "you have four different radio channels."   29
"Nope," he replied, "three. The fourth button resets all the   30

*settings. Then it takes me thirty minutes to get everything all set
up properly again."*

"*Hmm,*" I said, "*I bet you hit that every now and then by*   31
accident."

"*I certainly do,*" he replied *(in his own unprintable words).*   32

In computer systems, it is common to prevent errors by requiring   33
confirmation before a command will be executed, especially when the
action will destroy a file. But the request is ill timed; it comes just after
the person has initiated the action and is still fully content with the
choice. The standard interaction goes something like this:

USER: Remove file "My-most-important-work."
COMPUTER: Are you certain you wish to remove the file "My-most-
important-work"?
USER: Yes.
COMPUTER: Are you certain?
USER: Yes, of course.
COMPUTER: The file "My-most-important-work" has been removed.
USER: Oops, damn.

The user has requested deletion of the wrong file but the computer's
request for confirmation is unlikely to catch the error; the user is
confirming the action, not the file name. Thus asking for confirmation
cannot catch all slips. It would be more appropriate to eliminate irreversible actions: in this example, the request to remove a file would be
handled by the computer's moving the file to some temporary holding
place. Then the user would have time for reconsideration and
recovery.

At a research laboratory I once directed, we discovered that peo-   34
*ple would frequently throw away their records and notes, only to
discover the next day that they needed them again. We solved the
problem by getting seven trash cans and labeling them with the
days of the week. Then the trash can labeled Wednesday would
be used only on Wednesdays. At the end of the day it was safely
stored away and not emptied until the next Tuesday, just before it
was to be used again.*

People discovered that they kept neater records and books   35
*because they no longer hesitated to throw away things that they
thought would probably never be used again; they figured it was
safe to throw something away, for they still had a week in which
to change their minds.*

> *But design is often a tradeoff. We had to make room for the* 36
> *six reserve wastebaskets, and we had a never-ending struggle with*
> *the janitorial staff, who kept trying to empty all of the wastebas-*
> *kets every evening. The users of the computer center came to*
> *depend upon the "soft" nature of the wastebaskets and would*
> *discard things that they otherwise might have kept for a while*
> *longer. When there was an error—sometimes on the part of the*
> *janitorial staff, sometimes on our part in cycling the wastebaskets*
> *properly—then it was a calamity. When you build an error-*
> *tolerant mechanism, people come to rely upon it, so it had better*
> *be reliable.*

Meaning

1. What is Norman's main idea? To what does he attribute those actions he calls "slips"? In what situations are we most likely to slip?
2. What does Norman mean by the phrase "design lessons" (paragraph 26)? What two design lessons does he draw from his research? How do these design lessons minimize the chance for slips?
3. If you do not know the meanings of the following words, look them up in a dictionary: psychopathology (paragraph 2); manipulating, phrasing (4); associative, activation, mode (5); unambiguous (10); presumed (22); calamity (36).

Purpose and Audience

1. What seems to be Norman's main purpose in this selection? What passages indicate his purpose?
2. Is Norman addressing an audience of professionals or more general readers? On what evidence do you base your response?
3. Why do you suppose Norman presents such a variety of examples in his essay? How does his choice of examples support his main idea and engage his intended audience?

Method and Structure

1. What principle of classification does Norman use to determine the various types of slips? What are their distinguishing features?
2. Norman follows the same pattern in his discussion of each category: he

opens the section with a quotation or anecdote that illustrates the type of slip and then explains its origins. Why do you think he orders his material this way? Do you think this method is effective in getting his point across? Why, or why not?

3. **Other Methods**   Norman uses several other methods of development in this essay: for instance, he uses many concrete examples (Chapter 3), most of them narratives (Chapter 2), and he defines such phrases as "capture error" and "data-driven error" (Chapter 9). In addition, Norman includes many process analyses that explain how the errors occur (Chapter 6). Referring to two of Norman's categories, explain why process analysis is key to his purpose.

Language

1. Norman uses some technical terms, such as "data-driven" (paragraph 18) and "associative activation" (20). Why do you think he uses them, given his audience? Based on Norman's definitions, can you think of common substitutes for the technical terms? Are they preferable to the terms? Why, or why not?

2. Norman frequently uses pronouns seldom found in academic social science writing, namely the second-person *you* and the first-person *we*, as in "We don't make so many slips" (paragraph 3) and "You are playing a piece of music" (7). Why do you suppose he uses these forms? What effect do they have on his tone and on you as his reader?

Writing Topics

1. Interview several people, asking them to recall some of the slips they have made. Make a list of all the slips, and then try to place them into Norman's categories. Do most of them seem to fit? Do you find the same similarities and differences among slips that Norman found? Using the material from your interviews as examples, write an essay in which you classify slips either to support or to question Norman's conclusions.

2. Norman creates a humorous scene in paragraph 33, recounting the interaction between a computer and a user who is about to make a terrible mistake. Think of some of the problems you've had in interacting with machines, and write a dialogue similar to Norman's. Then write an analysis of a slip you made. Does it fall into one of Norman's categories? What design lesson(s) can you draw from this example?

3. Think of another principle of classifying everyday errors—perhaps according to the emotions they generate (errors that embarrass, annoy, amuse, or enrage), or their nature (errors in looks, words, or movement),

or their effects (minor inconvenience, moderate problem, disaster). Using Norman's essay as a model, write an essay explaining the classification you choose, providing examples of each before you explain the error. In addition to organization and detail, consider the tone you want to establish: familiar or distant, serious or humorous, sympathetic or critical.

Writing Topics

Classification

Choose one of the following topics, or any other topic they suggest, for an essay developed by classification. The topic you decide on should be something you care about so that classification is a means of communicating an idea, not an end in itself.

1. Satisfactions
2. Ways of disciplining children
3. Vacation spots
4. Careers
5. People who use public transportation
6. Young male or female movie stars
7. Homeless people
8. Talk-show hosts
9. Styles of baseball pitching, tennis serving, football tackling, or another sports skill
10. Buildings in a town or in a city neighborhood
11. Ways of practicing religion
12. Junk foods
13. Laundromat users
14. Graffiti
15. Obsessions
16. Comedians
17. Diets
18. Home computers
19. Teachers or students
20. Friends or co-workers
21. Runners
22. Mothers or fathers
23. Television programs
24. Radio stations
25. Dreams
26. Magazines or newspapers
27. Trucks

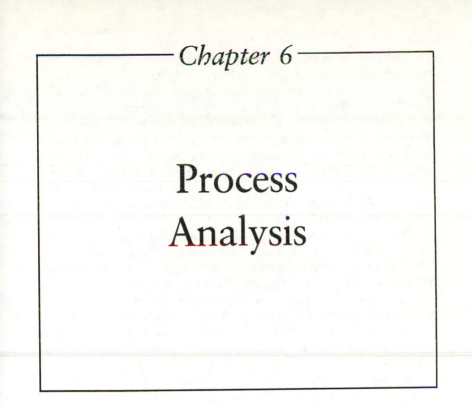

Chapter 6

Process Analysis

Understanding the Method

Game rules, car-repair manuals, cookbooks, science textbooks—these and many other familiar works are essentially process analyses. They explain how to do something (tune a car, play Monopoly), how to make something (a carrot cake), or how something happens (how our hormones affect our behavior, how a computer stores and retrieves data). That is, they explain a sequence of actions with a specified result (the **process**) by dividing it into its component steps (the **analysis**). Almost always, the purpose of process analysis is to explain, but sometimes a parallel purpose is to prove something about the process or to evaluate it: to show how easy it is to change a tire, for instance, or to urge dieters to follow a weight-loss plan on the grounds of its safety and effectiveness.

Process analysis overlaps several other methods discussed in this book. The analysis is actually the method examined in Chapter 4—dividing a thing or concept into its elements. And we analyze a process much as we analyze causes and effects (Chapter 10), except that cause-and-effect analysis asks mainly *why* something happens or *why* it has certain results, whereas process analysis asks mainly *how* something happens. Process analysis also overlaps narration (Chapter 2), for the steps of the process are almost always presented in chronological sequence. But narration emphasizes *what* happens, not *how* it happens. And narration recounts a unique sequence of events with a unique result, whereas process analysis explains a series of steps with the same predictable result. A writer would narrate the sixth game of the 1975 World Series; he or she would analyze the process—the rules—of any baseball game.

Processes occur in several varieties, including mechanical (a car engine), natural (cell division), psychological (acquisition of sex roles), and political (the electoral process). Process analyses generally fall into one of two types. The first, **directive**, tells how to do or make something: bake a cake, repair a bicycle, negotiate a deal, write a process analysis. The writer usually addresses the reader directly, using the second-person *you* ("You should concentrate on the words that tell you what to do") or the imperative (commanding) mood of verbs ("Add one egg yolk and stir vigorously"). The steps in the process are outlined completely so that the reader who follows them can achieve the specified result. The second type of process analysis, **explanatory**, provides the information necessary for readers to understand the process, but more to satisfy their curiosity than to teach them how to perform it. The writer may address the reader directly but more commonly uses the third-person *he, she, it,* and *they*.

Whether directive or explanatory, process analyses usually follow a chronological sequence. Most processes can be divided into phases or stages, and these in turn can be divided into steps. The stages of changing a tire, for instance, may be jacking up the car, removing the flat, putting on the spare, and lowering the car. The steps within, say, jacking up the car may be setting the emergency brake, blocking the other wheels, loosening the bolts, positioning the jack, and raising the car. Following a chronological order, the writer covers the stages in sequence and, within each stage, covers the steps in sequence.

To ensure that the reader can duplicate the process or understand how it unfolds, the writer must fully detail each step and specify the reasons for it. In addition, the writer must be sure that the reader grasps the sequence of steps, their duration, and where they occur. To this end, transitional expressions that signal time and place—such as *after five minutes, meanwhile, to the left,* and *below*—can be invaluable in process analysis.

Though a chronological sequence is usual for process analysis, it sometimes has to be interrupted or modified to suit the material. The writer may need to pause in the sequence to provide definitions of specialized terms or to explain why a step is necessary or how it relates to the preceding and following steps. In an essay on how to change a tire, for instance, the writer might stop briefly to explain that the bolts should be slightly loosened *before* the car is jacked up in order to prevent the wheel from spinning afterward.

For processes consisting of simultaneous steps, the writer may have to sort them out and group them according to what they contribute to the result. In explaining how a computerized video game works, for instance, a writer would be faced with the interdependent and nearly simultaneous operations of the game player and the computer. To make the process clear, the writer could group steps into the player's actions and their results on the screen and then step back to explain how the computer receives the player's instructions and produces images on the screen.

Analyzing Processes in Paragraphs

L. Rust Hills (born 1924) was for many years a magazine editor before turning to writing full-time. The paragraph below comes from "How to Eat an Ice-Cream Cone," which appears in his book *How to Do Things Right* (1972).

In trying to make wise and correct decisions about the ice-cream cone in your hand, you should always keep the objectives in mind. The main objective, of course, is to get the cone under control. Secondarily, one will want to eat the cone calmly and with pleasure. Real pleasure lies not simply in eating the cone but in eating it *right*. Let us assume that you have darted to your open space and made your necessary emergency repairs. The cone is still dangerous— still, so to speak, "live." But you can now proceed with it in an orderly fashion. First, revolve the cone through the full three hundred and sixty degrees, snapping at the loose gobs of ice cream; turn the cone by moving the thumb

Directive process analysis: tells how to eat an ice-cream cone

Goals of the process

Expressions signaling time and place (underlined once)

Imperative verbs or pronoun you (underlined twice)

Process divided into three distinct steps

Process (continued)

<u>away from you</u> and the forefinger <u>toward you,</u> so
the cone moves <u>counterclockwise</u>. <u>Then</u> with the
cone still "wound," which will require the wrist
to be bent at the full <u>right angle toward</u>
<u>you</u>, <u>apply</u> pressure with the mouth and tongue to — *Test for correct perform-ance of step*
accomplish overall realignment, straightening and
settling the whole mess. <u>Then</u>, unwinding the — *Reason for step*
cone back through the full <u>three hundred</u>
<u>and sixty degrees</u>, <u>remove</u> any trickles of ice
cream. <u>From here on</u>, some supplementary repairs — *Result of the process*
may be necessary, but the cone is now defused.

Berton Roueché (born 1911) is a writer of both fiction and nonfiction, especially well known for his reporting on medical detection.
The following paragraph appears in "The Humblest Fruit," an essay
in *The River World and Other Explorations* (1978).

The nature of the banana is as singular as its   *Explanatory process anal-ysis: tells how a banana plant "works"*
history and its shape. Its propagation is unlike
that of any other fruit. The banana plant is not
a tree but a tree-size herb, with a palmlike   *No you or imperative verbs*
crown and a fleshy green stalk that can spring
<u>from the ground</u> and grow <u>to a height</u> of twenty
or thirty, or even forty, feet <u>in little more than a</u>   *Structure of plant*
<u>year</u>. Its visible stalk is not a stem but a tubular
convolution of its unfurling giant leaves, and its
apparent root is not a root but a rhizome. This   *Definition of unfamiliar term*
is a shallow, creeping, tuberous stem that pro-
duces a number of progenitive buds, like the
eyes of a potato. Much as the potato plant
grows from the sprouting seed potato, the banana is grown from planted sections of rhizome.
<u>A few weeks after</u> planting, a leafy stalk sprouts   *Process of growth divided into distinct stages*
<u>from the reproductive bud</u> and begins its labori-
ous simulation of a tree. A truer stalk <u>then</u> appears in the form of a shoot that pushes slowly
<u>up through the hollow center</u> of the spiralling   *Expressions signal-ing time and place (underlined)*
shaft of leaves. The shoot emerges <u>at the crown</u>
of the plant as a flower bud, lengthens, droops,
and <u>slowly</u> opens into a dozen cascading clusters of tiny blossoms. It is from these blossoms

Process (continued)

that the banana's cornucopia of fruit develops. Each female blossom becomes a single banana, or "finger"; each cluster of from ten to twenty upthrusting fingers becomes a "hand"; and the whole bouquet becomes the massive bunch, or "stem," of bananas. The botanically ordained purpose of the banana plant is to produce a bunch of bananas, and when that end is achieved its productive life is over. The cultivated plant is then cut down and a successor shoot takes over.

Developing an Essay by Process Analysis

GETTING STARTED

A subject for process analysis can be any mechanical, natural, psychological, political, or other occurrence that unfolds in a sequence of steps with one predictable result. To find a subject, examine your own interests or hobbies or think of something whose workings you'd like to research in order to understand them better. Explore the subject by listing chronologically all the necessary stages and steps.

While you are exploring your subject, decide on the point of your analysis and express it in a thesis sentence that will guide your writing and tell your readers what to expect. The simplest thesis states what the process is and its basic stages: for instance, "Building a table is a three-stage process of cutting, assembling, and finishing." But you can increase your readers' interest in the process by also conveying your reason for writing about it. You might assert that a seemingly difficult process is actually simple, or vice versa: "Changing a tire does not require a mechanic's skill or strength; on the contrary, a ten-year-old child can do it"; or "Windsurfing may look easy, but it demands the knowledge of the experienced sailor and the balance of an acrobat." You might show how the process demonstrates a more general principle: "The process of getting a bill through Congress illustrates majority rule at work." Or you might assert that a process is inefficient or unfair: "The overly complicated registration procedure forces students to waste two days each semester standing in line."

Remember your readers while you are generating ideas and formulating your thesis. Consider how much background information they need, where specialized terms must be defined, where examples must be given. Especially if you are providing directions, consider

what special equipment readers will need, what hitches they may encounter, and what the interim results should be. To build a table, for
instance, what tools would readers need? What should they do if the
table wobbles even after the corners are braced? What should the
table feel like after the first sanding or the first varnishing?

ORGANIZING

Many successful process analyses begin with an overview of the
process to which readers can relate each step. In such an introduction
you can lead up to your thesis sentence by specifying when or where
the process occurs, why it is useful or interesting or controversial,
what its result is, and the like. Especially if you are providing directions, you can also use the introduction (perhaps a separate paragraph) to provide essential background information, such as the
materials readers will need.

After the introduction, you should present the stages distinctly,
perhaps one or two paragraphs for each, and usually in chronological
order. Within each stage, also chronologically, you then cover the
necessary steps. This chronological sequence helps readers see how a
process unfolds or how to perform it themselves. Try not to deviate
from it unless you have good reason to—perhaps because your process requires you to group simultaneous steps or your readers need
definitions of terms, reasons for steps, connections between separated
steps, and other explanations.

A process essay may end simply with the result. But you might
conclude with a summary of the major stages, with a comment on the
significance or usefulness of the process, or with a recommendation
for changing a process you have criticized. For an essay providing
directions, you might state the standards by which readers can measure their success or give an idea of how much practice may be necessary to master the process.

DRAFTING

While drafting your essay, concentrate on your readers' needs for
precision and clarity. Provide as many details as necessary to help
readers understand the process or perform it. So that readers can see
the relations within the process, tell them how each new step relates to
the one before and how it contributes to the result. In revising you can
always delete unnecessary details and connective tissue if they seem

cumbersome, but in the first draft it's better to overexplain than underexplain.

Use transitional expressions such as *at the same time* and *on the other side of the machine* to indicate when steps start and stop, how long they last, and where they occur. (A list of such expressions appears in the Glossary under *transitions*.) The expressions should be as informative as possible; signals such as *first . . . second . . . third . . . fourteenth* and *next . . . next* do not help indicate movement in space or lapses in time, and they quickly grow tiresome.

Drafting a process analysis is a good occasion to practice a straightforward, concise writing style, for clarity is more important than originality of expression. Stick to plain language and uncomplicated sentences. If you want to dress up your style a bit, you can always do so after you have made yourself clear.

REVISING

When you've finished your draft, ask a friend to read it. If you have explained a process, he or she should be able to understand it. If you have given directions, he or she should be able to follow them, or imagine following them. Then examine the draft yourself by answering the following questions.

1. *Have you adhered to a chronological sequence?* Unless there is a compelling and clear reason to use some other arrangement, the stages and steps of your analysis should proceed in chronological order. If you had to depart from that order—to define or explain or to sort out simultaneous steps—the reasons should be clear to your readers.

2. *Have you included all necessary steps and omitted any unnecessary digressions?* The explanation should be as complete as possible but not cluttered with information, however interesting, that contributes nothing to the readers' understanding of the process.

3. *Have you accurately gauged your readers' need for information?* You don't want to bore readers with explanations and details they don't need. But erring in the other direction is even worse, for your essay will achieve little if readers cannot understand it.

4. *Have you shown readers how each step fits into the whole process and relates to the other steps?* If your analysis seems to break down into the multitude of isolated steps, you may need to organize them more clearly into stages. And you may need more, or more informative, transitions.

5. *Are your pronouns consistent?* Sometimes a writer unconsciously shifts the person of pronouns—for instance, from the third-person *he, she, they* to the second-person *you*—because the original choice ends up feeling awkward. If that has happened to you, revise the earlier pronouns so that they coincide with those you later found more comfortable.

Born in 1952 in Baltimore, Diane Cole is a writer specializing in psychological and career issues. She was educated at Radcliffe College (B.A., 1974) and The Johns Hopkins University (M.A., 1975). Her articles have appeared in many newspapers and periodicals, including The Wall Street Journal, The Washington Post, Newsweek, Mademoiselle, *and* Ms. *She is a contributing editor of* Psychology Today *and the author of* Hunting the Headhunters: A Woman's Guide *(1988) and the forthcoming* After Great Pain: Coping with Loss and Change. *A self-described feminist and humanist, Cole is interested in "why we are who we are, why we do what we do." She lives in New York City with her husband, the writer Peter Baida.*

Don't Just Stand There

In this work of directive process analysis, Cole gives readers several ways of responding to others' expressions of prejudice. The essay first appeared in April 1989 in "A World of Difference," a special supplement to The New York Times *that was sponsored by the Anti-Defamation League of B'nai B'rith as part of a nationwide campaign against bigotry.*

It was my office farewell party, and colleagues at the job I was about to leave were wishing me well. My mood was one of ebullience tinged with regret, and it was in this spirit that I spoke to the office neighbor to whom I had waved hello every morning for the past two years. He smiled broadly as he launched into a long, rambling story, pausing only after he delivered the punch line. It was a very long pause because, although he laughed, I did not: This joke was unmistakably anti-Semitic. 1

I froze. Everyone in the office knew I was Jewish; what could he have possibly meant? Shaken and hurt, not knowing what else to do, I turned in stunned silence to the next well-wisher. Later, still angry, I wondered, what else should I—could I—have done? 2

Prejudice can make its presence felt in any setting, but hearing its nasty voice in this way can be particularly unnerving. We do not know what to do and often we feel another form of paralysis as well: We think, "Nothing I say or do will change this person's attitude, so why bother?" 3

But left unchecked, racial slurs and offensive ethnic jokes "can   4
poison the atmosphere," says Michael McQuillan, adviser for racial/
ethnic affairs for the Brooklyn borough president's office. "Hearing
these remarks conditions us to accept them; and if we accept these, we
can become accepting of other acts."

Speaking up may not magically change a biased attitude, but it   5
can change a person's behavior by putting a strong message across.
And the more messages there are, the more likely a person is to
change that behavior, says Arnold Kahn, professor of psychology at
James Madison University, Harrisonburg, Va., who makes this analogy: "You can't keep people from smoking in *their* house, but you
can ask them not to smoke in *your* house."

At the same time, "Even if the other party ignores or discounts   6
what you say, people always reflect on how others perceive them.
Speaking up always counts," says LeNorman Strong, director of campus life at George Washington University, Washington, D.C.

Finally, learning to respond effectively also helps people feel bet-   7
ter about themselves, asserts Cherie Brown, executive director of the
National Coalition Building Institute, a Boston-based training organization. "We've found that, when people felt they could at least in this
small way make a difference, that made them more eager to take on
other activities on a larger scale," she says. Although there is no
"cookbook approach" to confronting such remarks—every situation
is different, experts stress—these are some effective strategies.

When the "joke" turns on who you are—as a member of an   8
ethnic or religious group, a person of color, a woman, a gay or
lesbian, an elderly person, or someone with a physical handi-
cap—shocked paralysis is often the first response. Then,
wounded and vulnerable, on some level you want to strike back.

Lashing out or responding in kind is seldom the most effective   9
response, however. "That can give you momentary satisfaction, but
you also feel as if you've lowered yourself to that other person's
level," Mr. McQuillan explains. Such a response may further label
you in the speaker's mind as thin-skinned, someone not to be taken
seriously. Or it may up the ante, making the speaker, and then you,
reach for new insults—or physical blows.

"If you don't laugh at the joke, or fight, or respond in kind to the   10
slur," says Mr. McQuillan, "that will take the person by surprise, and
that can give you more control over the situation." Therefore, in

situations like the one in which I found myself—a private conversation in which I knew the person making the remark—he suggests
voicing your anger calmly but pointedly: "I don't know if you realize
what that sounded like to me. If that's what you meant, it really hurt
me."

State how *you* feel, rather than making an abstract statement like, 11
"Not everyone who hears that joke might find it funny." Counsels
Mr. Strong: "Personalize the sense of 'this is how I feel when you say
this.' That makes it very concrete"—and harder to dismiss.

Make sure you heard the words and their intent correctly by 12
repeating or rephrasing the statement: "This is what I heard you say.
Is that what you meant?" It's important to give the other person the
benefit of the doubt because, in fact, he may *not* have realized that the
comment was offensive and, if you had not spoken up, would have
had no idea of its impact on you.

For instance, Professor Kahn relates that he used to include in his 13
exams multiple-choice questions that occasionally contained "incorrect funny answers." After one exam, a student came up to him in
private and said, "I don't think you intended this, but I found a
number of those jokes offensive to me as a woman." She explained
why. "What she said made immediate sense to me," he says. "I apolo-
gized at the next class, and I never did it again."

But what if the speaker dismisses your objection, saying, "Oh, 14
you're just being sensitive. Can't you take a joke?" In that case, you
might say, "I'm not so sure about that, let's talk about that a little
more." The key, Mr. Strong says, is to continue the dialogue, hear the
other person's concerns, and point out your own. "There are times
when you're just going to have to admit defeat and end it," he adds,
"but I have to feel that I did the best I could."

When the offending remark is made in the presence of others—at 15
a staff meeting, for example—it can be even more distressing than an
insult made privately.

"You have two options," says William Newlin, director of field 16
services for the Community Relations division of the New York City
Commission on Human Rights. "You can respond immediately at the
meeting, or you can delay your response until afterward in private.
But a response has to come."

Some remarks or actions may be so outrageous that they cannot 17
go unnoted at the moment, regardless of the speaker or the setting.
But in general, psychologists say, shaming a person in public may
have the opposite effect of the one you want: The speaker will deny

his offense all the more strongly in order to save face. Further, few people enjoy being put on the spot, and if the remark really was not intended to be offensive, publicly embarrassing the person who made it may cause an unnecessary rift or further misunderstanding. Finally, most people just don't react as well or thoughtfully under a public spotlight as they would in private.

Keeping that in mind, an excellent alternative is to take the of- 18 fender aside afterward: "Could we talk for a minute in private?" Then use the strategies suggested above for calmly stating how you feel, giving the speaker the benefit of the doubt, and proceeding from there.

At a large meeting or public talk, you might consider passing the 19 speaker a note, says David Wertheimer, executive director of the New York City Gay and Lesbian Anti-Violence Project: You could write, "You may not realize it, but your remarks were offensive because. . . ."

"Think of your role as that of an educator," suggests James M. 20 Jones, Ph.D., executive director for public interest at the American Psychological Association. "You have to be controlled."

Regardless of the setting or situation, speaking up always raises 21 the risk of rocking the boat. If the person who made the offending remark is your boss, there may be an even bigger risk to consider: How will this affect my job? Several things can help minimize the risk, however. First, know what other resources you may have at work, suggests Caryl Stern, director of the A World of Difference—New York City campaign: Does your personnel office handle discrimination complaints? Are other grievance procedures in place?

You won't necessarily need to use any of these procedures, Ms. 22 Stern stresses. In fact, she advises, "It's usually better to try a one-on-one approach first." But simply knowing a formal system exists can make you feel secure enough to set up that meeting.

You can also raise the issue with other colleagues who heard the 23 remark: Did they feel the same way you did? The more support you have, the less alone you will feel. Your point will also carry more validity and be more difficult to shrug off. Finally, give your boss credit—and the benefit of the doubt: "I know you've worked hard for the company's affirmative action programs, so I'm sure you didn't realize what those remarks sounded like to me as well as the others at the meeting last week. . . ."

If, even after this discussion, the problem persists, go back for 24 another meeting, Ms. Stern advises. And if that, too, fails, you'll know what other options are available to you.

It's a spirited dinner party, and everyone's having a good time, 25
until one guest starts reciting a racist joke. Everyone at the table is
white, including you. The others are still laughing, as you wonder
what to say or do.

No one likes being seen as a party-pooper, but before deciding 26
that you'd prefer not to take on this role, you might remember that
the person who told the offensive joke has already ruined your good
time.

If it's a group that you feel comfortable in—a family gathering, 27
for instance—you will feel freer to speak up. Still, shaming the person
by shouting "You're wrong!" or "That's not funny!" probably won't
get your point across as effectively as other strategies. "If you interrupt people to condemn them, it just makes it harder," says Cherie
Brown. She suggests trying instead to get at the resentments that lie
beneath the joke by asking open-ended questions: "Grandpa, I know
you always treat everyone with such respect. Why do people in our
family talk that way about black people?" The key, Ms. Brown says,
"is to listen to them first, so they will be more likely to listen to
you."

If you don't know your fellow guests well, before speaking up 28
you could turn discreetly to your neighbors (or excuse yourself to help
the host or hostess in the kitchen) to get a reading on how they felt,
and whether or not you'll find support for speaking up. The less alone
you feel, the more comfortable you'll be speaking up: "I know you
probably didn't mean anything by that joke, Jim, but it really offended me. . . ." It's important to say that *you* were offended—not
state how the group that is the butt of the joke would feel. "Otherwise," LeNorman Strong says, "you risk coming off as a goody two-
shoes."

If you yourself are the host, you can exercise more control; you 29
are, after all, the one who sets the rules and the tone of behavior in
your home. Once, when Professor Kahn's party guests began singing
offensive, racist songs, for instance, he kicked them all out, saying,
"You don't sing songs like that in my house!" And, he adds, "they
never did again."

At school one day, a friend comes over and says, "Who do you 30
think you are, hanging out with Joe? If you can be friends with
those people, I'm through with you!"

Peer pressure can weigh heavily on kids. They feel vulnerable and, 31

because they are kids, they aren't as able to control the urge to fight.
"But if you learn to handle these situations as kids, you'll be better
able to handle them as an adult," William Newlin points out.

Begin by redefining to yourself what a friend is and examining   32
what friendship means, advises Amy Lee, a human relations specialist
at Panel of Americans, an intergroup-relations training and educational organization. If that person from a different group fits your
requirement for a friend, ask, "Why shouldn't I be friends with Joe?
We have a lot in common." Try to get more information about whatever stereotypes or resentments lie beneath your friend's statement.
Ms. Lee suggests: "What makes you think they're so different from
us? Where did you get that information?" She explains: "People are
learning these stereotypes from somewhere, and they cannot be
blamed for that. So examine where these ideas came from." Then talk
about how your own experience rebuts them.

Kids, like adults, should also be aware of other resources to back   33
them up: Does the school offer special programs for fighting prejudice? How supportive will the principal, the teachers, or other students be? If the school atmosphere is volatile, experts warn, make sure
that taking a stand at that moment won't put you in physical danger.
If that is the case, it's better to look for other alternatives.

These can include programs or organizations that bring kids from   34
different backgrounds together. "When kids work together across
race lines, that is how you break down the barriers and see that the
stereotypes are not true," says Laurie Meadoff, president of CityKids
Foundation, a nonprofit group whose programs attempt to do just
that. Such programs can also provide what Cherie Brown calls a "safe
place" to express the anger and pain that slurs and other offenses
cause, whether the bigotry is directed against you or others.

In learning to speak up, everyone will develop a different style   35
and a slightly different message to get across, experts agree. But it
would be hard to do better than these two messages suggested by
teenagers at CityKids: "Everyone on the face of the earth has the same
intestines," said one. Another added, "Cross over the bridge. There's
a lot of love on the streets."

Meaning

1. How does Cole's title relate to her main point? Where in the essay is the
    relationship between title and main point clarified? What is to be gained
    by refusing to "just stand there"?

2. According to Cole's source Michael McQuillan, why should we refuse to tolerate ethnic jokes and racial slurs? What can result from such tolerance?
3. According to Cole, what responses are inappropriate when one is confronted with an offensive remark? Why are they inappropriate?
4. At several points in her essay, Cole advocates initiating a dialogue with a person who has made an offensive remark. Where does she discuss this strategy, and in what ways is dialogue beneficial?
5. If you do not know the meanings of the following words, look them up in a dictionary: ebullience, anti-Semitic (paragraph 1); biased (5); ante (9); personalize (11); rift (17); affirmative action (23); discreetly (28); stereotypes (32); volatile (33); bigotry (34).

Purpose and Audience

1. What is Cole's purpose in writing this essay—simply to explain the process of responding to such comments, or something more than that? Explain your response, noting where in the essay her purpose is clarified.
2. What assumptions does Cole make about her audience's attitudes toward offensive remarks? In the "us" versus "them" situation that she sets up, who are "us" and "them"? How does she ally herself with her intended audience? Do you think that an unsympathetic audience might also be influenced by her essay? Why, or why not?
3. In paragraphs 30–34 Cole makes it clear that her audience contains "kids" as well as adults. Do you think that this part of the essay or any earlier part talks down to adult readers in order to reach children and teenagers, or, in contrast, talks over the heads of young readers? Support your answer with reasons and specific passages from Cole's essay.

Method and Structure

1. Although the general subject of Cole's essay is response to offensive remarks, she explains several different processes or strategies for responding, depending on the situation. Outline the processes, and note the common elements shared by all of them.
2. Cole opens her essay with an anecdote about a personal experience (paragraphs 1–2). How does this anecdote lead directly into her process analysis? Is it necessary to the structure of the essay? What other purpose(s) does it serve? How would the effect of the essay change if she were to begin with paragraph 3 instead?
3. Like much writing for newspapers and magazines, Cole's essay contains many short paragraphs to make reading easier in narrow columns. Do

you find the short paragraphs more or less readable than the longer paragraphs used by most of the other writers in this book? As an editing exercise, link Cole's short paragraphs into longer paragraphs wherever such links seem sensible. What specific reasons can you give for each of your changes?

4. **Other Methods**   Cole relies heavily on examples (Chapter 3), relating numerous situations in which offensive remarks may be heard. Why are so many examples necessary for her purpose?

Language

1. Cole gives some of her advice several times. For example, in paragraph 9 she warns readers against "lashing out"; in 17 she warns against "shaming a person in public"; and in 27 she repeats that warning. Why do you think she issues these warnings more than once, and what is the effect of the words she uses?

2. Cole generally uses the second-person *you* or the first-person *we*. Why do you think she prefers these pronouns rather than *one, the offended person, he or she*, and similar alternatives? Do you think the essay is more or less effective as a result of this choice? As support for your response, rewrite paragraph 21 to avoid *you*.

3. Cole frequently provides imaginary dialogue. For example, in paragraph 10 she offers a response to an ethnic joke: "I don't know if you realize. . . ." Locate three or four similar instances. Why do you think Cole uses them?

Writing Topics

1. Cole and several of the experts she cites emphasize that one shouldn't embarrass someone who makes an offensive remark. Do you agree? Or do you think that, as Cole herself acknowledges, "Some remarks or actions may be so outrageous that they cannot go unnoted at the moment" (paragraph 17)? Write an essay in which you argue for either side, supporting your position with detailed examples and clear reasons.

2. In a commentary on his essay "Getting Dirty" (p. 126), Mark Crispin Miller says that some people dismiss analysis such as his of an advertisement "as a case of 'reading too much into it.'" Some might make the same case against reacting to offensive remarks. Write an essay in which you agree or disagree that such remarks are not hurtful or dangerous, using evidence from your own experience, as well as from Cole's essay, to support your view.

3. Think of another unpleasant situation that demands a response—perceived favoritism on the part of a teacher or boss, consistent failure of a roommate to pay his or her share of bills, the discovery that a friend is being dishonest, and so on. Using Cole's essay as a model, write an essay in which you analyze the process(es) of dealing effectively with that situation. Use specific examples to clarify your point, and offer alternative actions the reader can take if one step of the process should prove unsuccessful.

Jessica Mitford

Tough-minded, commonsensical, and witty, Jessica Mitford has been de-scribed by Time *as the "Queen of Muckrakers." She was born in England in 1917, the sixth of Lord and Lady Redesdale's seven children, and was educat-ed entirely at home. Her highly eccentric family is the subject of novels by her sister Nancy Mitford and of her own autobiographical* Daughters and Rebels *(1960). In 1939, a few years after she left home, Mitford took up permanent residence in the United States, becoming a naturalized American citizen in 1944. Shortly afterward, moved by her long-standing antifascism and the promise of equality in a socialist society, she joined the American Communist party; her years as a "Red Menace" are recounted in* A Fine Old Conflict *(1977). In the late 1950s she turned to investigative journalism, and in the years since she has researched and exposed numerous instances of deception, greed, and foolishness in American society. Her articles have appeared in* The Nation, Esquire, The Atlantic Monthly, *and other magazines, and many of them are collected in* Poison Penmanship: The Gentle Art of Muckraking *(1979). Her book-length exposés include* The Trial of Dr. Spock *(1969), on the prosecution of the famous baby doctor for aiding draft resisters during the Vietnam War, and* Kind and Usual Punishment: The Prison Business *(1973), on the American penal system. Her latest book is a novel,* Grace Had an English Heart *(1988), about an ordinary person made into a star by the media. Mitford lives in Oakland, California.*

Embalming Mr. Jones

In 1963 Mitford published The American Way of Death, *a daring, devastat-ing, and influential look at the standard practices of the American funeral industry. Mitford pegs the modern American funeral as "the most irrational and weirdest" custom of our affluent society, in which "the trappings of Gracious Living are transformed, as in a nightmare, into the trappings of Gracious Dying." This excerpt from the book, an analysis of the process of embalming a corpse and restoring it for viewing, demonstrates Mitford's sharp eye for detail, commanding style, and caustic wit.*

The drama begins to unfold with the arrival of the corpse at the mortuary. 1

Alas, poor Yorick![1] How surprised he would be to see how his 2

---

[1] A line from Shakespeare's *Hamlet*, spoken by Hamlet in a graveyard as he con-templates the skull of the former jester in his father's court. [Editor's note.]

counterpart of today is whisked off to a funeral parlor and is in short order sprayed, sliced, pierced, pickled, trussed, trimmed, creamed, waxed, painted, rouged, and neatly dressed—transformed from a common corpse into a Beautiful Memory Picture. This process is known in the trade as embalming and restorative art, and is so universally employed in the United States and Canada that the funeral director does it routinely, without consulting corpse or kin. He regards as eccentric those few who are hardy enough to suggest that it might be dispensed with. Yet no law requires embalming, no religious doctrine commends it, nor is it dictated by considerations of health, sanitation, or even of personal daintiness. In no part of the world but in Northern America is it widely used. The purpose of embalming is to make the corpse presentable for viewing in a suitably costly container; and here too the funeral director routinely, without first consulting the family, prepares the body for public display.

Is all this legal? The processes to which a dead body may be 3 subjected are after all to some extent circumscribed by law. In most states, for instance, the signature of next of kin must be obtained before an autopsy may be performed, before the deceased may be cremated, before the body may be turned over to a medical school for research purposes; or such provision must be made in the decedent's will. In the case of embalming, no such permission is required nor is it ever sought.[2] A textbook, *The Principles and Practices of Embalming*, comments on this: "There is some question regarding the legality of much that is done within the preparation room." The author points out that it would be most unusual for a responsible member of a bereaved family to instruct the mortician, in so many words, to "*embalm*" the body of a deceased relative. The very term "embalming" is so seldom used that the mortician must rely upon custom in the matter. The author concludes that unless the family specifies otherwise, the act of entrusting the body to the care of a funeral establishment carries with it an implied permission to go ahead and embalm.

Embalming is indeed a most extraordinary procedure, and one 4 must wonder at the docility of Americans who each year pay hundreds of millions of dollars for its perpetuation, blissfully ignorant of

[2] In 1984, the Federal Trade Commission began enforcing comprehensive regulations on the funeral industry, including the requirement that funeral providers prepare an itemized price list for their goods and services. The list must include a notice that embalming is not required by law, along with an indication of the charge for embalming and an explanation of the alternatives. Consumers must give permission for embalming before they may be charged for it. [Editor's note.]

what it is all about, what is done, how it is done. Not one in ten thousand has any idea of what actually takes place. Books on the subject are extremely hard to come by. They are not to be found in most libraries or bookshops.

In an era when huge television audiences watch surgical oper-   5
ations in the comfort of their living rooms, when, thanks to the ani-
mated cartoon, the geography of the digestive system has become
familiar territory even to the nursery school set, in a land where the
satisfaction of curiosity about almost all matters is a national pastime,
the secrecy surrounding embalming can, surely, hardly be attributed
to the inherent gruesomeness of the subject. Custom in this regard has
within this century suffered a complete reversal. In the early days of
American embalming, when it was performed in the home of the
deceased, it was almost mandatory for some relative to stay by the
embalmer's side and witness the procedure. Today, family members
who might wish to be in attendance would certainly be dissuaded by
the funeral director. All others, except apprentices, are excluded by
law from the preparation room.

A close look at what does actually take place may explain in large   6
measure the undertaker's intractable reticence concerning a procedure
that has become his major *raison d'être*.[3] Is it possible he fears that
public information about embalming might lead patrons to wonder if
they really want this service? If the funeral men are loath to discuss
the subject outside the trade, the reader may, understandably, be
equally loath to go on reading at this point. For those who have the
stomach for it, let us part the formaldehyde curtain. . . .

The body is first laid out in the undertaker's morgue—or rather,   7
Mr. Jones is reposing in the preparation room—to be readied to bid
the world farewell.

The preparation room in any of the better funeral establishments   8
has the tiled and sterile look of a surgery, and indeed the embalmer–
restorative artist who does his chores there is beginning to adopt the
term "dermasurgeon" (appropriately corrupted by some mortician-
writers as "demisurgeon") to describe his calling. His equipment, consisting of scalpels, scissors, augers, forceps, clamps, needles, pumps,
tubes, bowls and basins, is crudely imitative of the surgeon's, as is his
technique, acquired in a nine- or twelve-month post-high-school
course in an embalming school. He is supplied by an advanced chemical industry with a bewildering array of fluids, sprays, pastes, oils,
powders, creams, to fix or soften tissue, shrink or distend it as needed,

[3] French, meaning "reason for being." [Editor's note.]

dry it here, restore the moisture there. There are cosmetics, waxes, and paints to fill and cover features, even plaster of Paris to replace entire limbs. There are ingenious aids to prop and stabilize the cadaver: a Vari-Pose Head Rest, the Edwards Arm and Hand Positioner, the Repose Block (to support the shoulders during the embalming), and the Throop Foot Positioner, which resembles an old-fashioned stocks.

Mr. John H. Eckels, president of the Eckels College of Mortuary   9
Science, thus describes the first part of the embalming procedure: "In the hands of a skilled practitioner, this work may be done in a comparatively short time and without mutilating the body other than by slight incision—so slight that it scarcely would cause serious inconvenience if made upon a living person. It is necessary to remove the blood, and doing this not only helps in the disinfecting, but removes the principal cause of disfigurements due to discoloration."

Another textbook discusses the all-important time element: "The   10
earlier this is done, the better, for every hour that elapses between death and embalming will add to the problems and complications encountered. . . ." Just how soon should one get going on the embalming? The author tells us, "On the basis of such scanty information made available to this profession through its rudimentary and haphazard system of technical research, we must conclude that the best results are to be obtained if the subject is embalmed before life is completely extinct—that is, before cellular death has occurred. In the average case, this would mean within an hour after somatic death." For those who feel that there is something a little rudimentary, not to say haphazard, about this advice, a comforting thought is offered by another writer. Speaking of fears entertained in early days of premature burial, he points out, "One of the effects of embalming by chemical injection, however, has been to dispel fears of live burial." How true; once the blood is removed, chances of live burial are indeed remote.

To return to Mr. Jones, the blood is drained out through the veins   11
and replaced by embalming fluid pumped in through the arteries. As noted in *The Principles and Practices of Embalming*, "every operator has a favorite injection and drainage point—a fact which becomes a handicap only if he fails or refuses to forsake his favorites when conditions demand it." Typical favorites are the carotid artery, femoral artery, jugular vein, subclavian vein. There are various choices of embalming fluid. If Flextone is used, it will produce a "mild, flexible rigidity. The skin retains a velvety softness, the tissues are rubbery and pliable. Ideal for women and children." It may be blended with B. and

G. Products Company's Lyf-Lyk tint, which is guaranteed to reproduce "nature's own skin texture . . . the velvety appearance of living tissue." Suntone comes in three separate tints: Suntan; Special Cosmetic Tint, a pink shade "especially indicated for young female subjects"; and Regular Cosmetic Tint, moderately pink.

About three to six gallons of a dyed and perfumed solution of   12
formaldehyde, glycerin, borax, phenol, alcohol, and water is soon circulating through Mr. Jones, whose mouth has been sewn together with a "needle directed upward between the upper lip and gum and brought out through the left nostril," with the corners raised slightly "for a more pleasant expression." If he should be bucktoothed, his teeth are cleaned with Bon Ami and coated with colorless nail polish. His eyes, meanwhile, are closed with flesh-tinted eye caps and eye cement.

The next step is to have at Mr. Jones with a thing called a trocar.   13
This is a long, hollow needle attached to a tube. It is jabbed into the abdomen, poked around the entrails and chest cavity, the contents of which are pumped out and replaced with "cavity fluid." This done, and the hole in the abdomen sewn up, Mr. Jones's face is heavily creamed (to protect the skin from burns which may be caused by leakage of the chemicals), and he is covered with a sheet and left unmolested for a while. But not for long—there is more, much more, in store for him. He has been embalmed, but not yet restored, and the best time to start the restorative work is eight to ten hours after embalming, when the tissues have become firm and dry.

The object of all this attention to the corpse, it must be remem-   14
bered, is to make it presentable for viewing in an attitude of healthy repose. "Our customs require the presentation of our dead in the semblance of normality . . . unmarred by the ravages of illness, disease or mutilation," says Mr. J. Sheridan Mayer in his *Restorative Art*. This is a rather large order since few people die in the full bloom of health, unravaged by illness and unmarked by some disfigurement. The funeral industry is equal to the challenge: "In some cases the gruesome appearance of a mutilated or disease-ridden subject may be quite discouraging. The task of restoration may seem impossible and shake the confidence of the embalmer. This is the time for intestinal fortitude and determination. Once the formative work is begun and affected tissues are cleaned or removed, all doubts of success vanish. It is surprising and gratifying to discover the results which may be obtained."

The embalmer, having allowed an appropriate interval to elapse,   15
returns to the attack, but now he brings into play the skill and equip-

ment of sculptor and cosmetician. Is a hand missing? Casting one in plaster of Paris is a simple matter. "For replacement purposes, only a cast of the back of the hand is necessary; this is within the ability of the average operator and is quite adequate." If a lip or two, a nose or an ear should be missing, the embalmer has at hand a variety of restorative waxes with which to model replacements. Pores and skin texture are simulated by stippling with a little brush, and over this cosmetics are laid on. Head off? Decapitation cases are rather routinely handled. Ragged edges are trimmed, and head joined to torso with a series of splints, wires and sutures. It is a good idea to have a little something at the neck—a scarf or high collar—when time for viewing comes. Swollen mouth? Cut out tissue as needed from inside the lips. If too much is removed, the surface contour can easily be restored by padding with cotton. Swollen necks and cheeks are reduced by removing tissue through vertical incisions made down each side of the neck. "When the deceased is casketed, the pillow will hide the suture incisions . . . as an extra precaution against leakage, the suture may be painted with liquid sealer."

The opposite condition is more likely to present itself—that of   16
emaciation. His hypodermic syringe now loaded with massage cream, the embalmer seeks out and fills the hollowed and sunken areas by injection. In this procedure the backs of the hands and fingers and the under-chin area should not be neglected.

Positioning the lips is a problem that recurrently challenges the   17
ingenuity of the embalmer. Closed too tightly they tend to give a stern, even disapproving expression. Ideally, embalmers feel, the lips should give the impression of being ever so slightly parted, the upper lip protruding slightly for a more youthful appearance. This takes some engineering, however, as the lips tend to drift apart. Lip drift can sometimes be remedied by pushing one or two straight pins through the inner margin of the lower lip and then inserting them between the two upper front teeth. If Mr. Jones happens to have no teeth, the pins can just as easily be anchored in his Armstrong Face Former and Denture Replacer. Another method to maintain lip closure is to dislocate the lower jaw, which is then held in its new position by a wire run through holes which have been drilled through the upper and lower jaws at the midline. As the French are fond of saying, *il faut souffrir pour être belle.*[4]

If Mr. Jones has died of jaundice, the embalming fluid will very   18

---

[4] French, meaning "It is necessary to suffer in order to be beautiful." [Editor's note.]

likely turn him green. Does this deter the embalmer? Not if he has intestinal fortitude. Masking pastes and cosmetics are heavily laid on, burial garments and casket interiors are color-correlated with particular care, and Jones is displayed beneath rose-colored lights. Friends will say, "How *well* he looks." Death by carbon monoxide, on the other hand, can be rather a good thing from the embalmer's viewpoint: "One advantage is the fact that this type of discoloration is an exaggerated form of a natural pink coloration." This is nice because the healthy glow is already present and needs but little attention.

The patching and filling completed, Mr. Jones is now shaved, 19 washed and dressed. Cream-based cosmetic, available in pink, flesh, suntan, brunette, and blond, is applied to his hands and face, his hair is shampooed and combed (and, in the case of Mrs. Jones, set), his hands manicured. For the horny-handed son of toil special care must be taken; cream should be applied to remove ingrained grime, and the nails cleaned. "If he were not in the habit of having them manicured in life, trimming and shaping is advised for better appearance—never questioned by kin."

Jones is now ready for casketing (this is the present participle of 20 the verb "to casket"). In this operation his right shoulder should be depressed slightly "to turn the body a bit to the right and soften the appearance of lying flat on the back." Positioning the hands is a matter of importance, and special rubber positioning blocks may be used. The hands should be cupped slightly for a more lifelike, relaxed appearance. Proper placement of the body requires a delicate sense of balance. It should lie as high as possible in the casket, yet not so high that the lid, when lowered, will hit the nose. On the other hand, we are cautioned, placing the body too low "creates the impression that the body is in a box."

Jones is next wheeled into the appointed slumber room where a 21 few last touches may be added—his favorite pipe placed in his hand or, if he was a great reader, a book propped into position. (In the case of little Master Jones a Teddy bear may be clutched.) Here he will hold open house for a few days, visiting hours 10 A.M. to 9 P.M.

Meaning

1. According to Mitford, what is the purpose of embalming and restoration (see paragraphs 2, 6, and 14)? If they are not required by law or religion

or "considerations of health, sanitation, or even of personal daintiness," why are they routinely performed?

2. Why do Americans know so little about embalming (paragraphs 3–6)? Does Mitford blame Americans themselves, the funeral industry, or both?

3. If you do not know the meanings of the following words, look them up in a dictionary: mortuary (paragraph 1); counterpart (2); circumscribed, decedent, bereaved (3); docility, perpetuation (4); inherent, mandatory, apprentices (5); intractable reticence, loath, formaldehyde (6); augers, distend, cadaver (8); rudimentary, haphazard, somatic (10); pliable (11); semblance (14); jaundice (18).

Purpose and Audience

1. What does Mitford reveal about her purpose when she questions whether the undertaker "fears the public information about embalming might lead patrons to wonder if they really want this service" (paragraph 6)? To discover how different the essay would be if Mitford had wanted only to explain the process, reread the essay from the point of view of an undertaker. What comments and details would the undertaker object to or find embarrassing?

2. Mitford's chief assumption about her readers is evident in paragraph 4. What is it?

3. Most readers find Mitford's essay humorous. Assuming you did, too, which details or comments struck you as especially amusing? How does Mitford use humor to achieve her purpose?

Method and Structure

1. Despite the fact that her purpose goes beyond mere explanation, does Mitford explain the process of embalming and restoration clearly enough for you to understand how it's done and what the reasons for each step are? Starting at paragraph 7, what are the main steps in the process?

2. Mitford interrupts the sequence of steps in the process several times. What information does she provide in paragraphs 8, 10, and 14, respectively, to make the interruptions worthwhile?

3. **Other Methods** Mitford occasionally uses other methods to develop her process analysis—for instance, in paragraph 8 she combines description (Chapter 1) and classification (Chapter 5) to present the embalmer's preparation room and tools; and in paragraph 5 she uses contrast (Chapter 7) to note changes in the family's knowledge of embalming. What does this contrast suggest about our current attitudes toward death and the dead?

Language

1. How would you characterize Mitford's tone? Support your answer with specific details, sentence structures, and words in the essay. (If necessary, consult the Glossary for an explanation of *tone*.)
2. Mitford is more than a little ironic—that is, she often says one thing when she means another or deliberately understates her meaning. Here are two examples from paragraph 10: "the all-important time element" in the embalming of a corpse; "How true; once the blood is removed, chances of live burial are indeed remote." What additional examples do you find? What does this persistent irony contribute to Mitford's tone? (For a fuller explanation of *irony*, consult the Glossary.)
3. Mitford's style in this essay is often informal, even conversational, as in "The next step is to have at Mr. Jones with a thing called a trocar" (paragraph 13). But equally often she seems to imitate the technical, impersonal style of the embalming textbooks she quotes so extensively, as in "Another method to maintain lip closure is to dislocate the lower jaw" (17). What other examples of each style do you find? What does each style contribute to Mitford's purpose? Is the contrast effective, or would a consistent style, one way or the other, be more effective? Why?

Writing Topics

1. Think of modern custom or practice that you find ridiculous, barbaric, tedious, or otherwise objectionable. Write an essay in which you analyze the process by which the custom or practice unfolds. Following Mitford's model, explain the process clearly while also conveying your attitude toward it.
2. Elsewhere in her book *The American Way of Death*, Mitford notes that the open casket at funerals, which creates the need for embalming and restoration, is "a custom unknown in other parts of the world. Foreigners are astonished by it." Write an essay in which you explore the possible reasons for the custom in the United States. Or, if you have strong feelings about closed or open caskets at funerals—derived from religious beliefs, family tradition, or some other source—write an essay agreeing or disagreeing with Mitford's treatment of embalming and restoration.
3. Read about funeral customs in another country. (The library's card catalog or a periodical guide such as the *Social Sciences Index* can direct you to appropriate books or articles.) Write an essay in which you analyze the process covered in your source and use it as the basis for agreeing or disagreeing with Mitford's opinion of embalming and restoration.

Alexander Petrunkevitch

One of the foremost zoologists of his time, Alexander Petrunkevitch was also a philosopher, poet, and translator. He was born in Pliski, Russia, in 1875, and educated in Russia and Germany. He came to the United States in 1903 and taught zoology at several universities before taking a position in 1910 at Yale. A popular figure on the Yale campus, Petrunkevitch taught until his retirement in 1944 and then continued his research and writing for many years. He specialized in the study of spiders, inventing techniques for photographing their behavior. Several species of spider have been named after him, and his books on spiders—including Index Catalogue of Spiders of North, Central, and South America *(1911) and* An Inquiry into the Natural Classification of Spiders *(1933)—remain standards in the field. But Petrunkevitch also published a volume of poetry, translated English and Russian poetry, wrote a book on the Russian revolution, and published works on philosophy, including* The Freedom of the Will *(1905) and* Choice and Responsibility *(1947). He died in New Haven, Connecticut, in 1967.*

The Spider and the Wasp

In this essay Petrunkevitch analyzes a natural process, the fatal encounter between a digger wasp and a tarantula. In doing so, he demonstrates how an accomplished scientist who is also a skillful writer with a sense of audience can make a complex subject clear and interesting for anyone. The essay first appeared in Scientific American *in 1952.*

To hold its own in the struggle for existence, every species of animal must have a regular source of food, and if it happens to live on other animals, its survival may be very delicately balanced. The hunter cannot exist without the hunted; if the latter should perish from the earth, the former would, too. When the hunted also prey on some of the hunters, the matter may become complicated.

This is nowhere better illustrated than in the insect world. Think of the complexity of a situation such as the following: There is a certain wasp, *Pimpla inquisitor*, whose larvae feed on the larvae of the tussock moth. *Pimpla* larvae in turn serve as food for the larvae of a second wasp, and the latter in their turn nourish still a third wasp.

187

What subtle balance between fertility and mortality must exist in the case of each of these four species to prevent the extinction of all of them! An excess of mortality over fertility in a single member of the group would ultimately wipe out all four.

This is not a unique case. The two great orders of insects, Hyme- 3
noptera and Diptera, are full of such examples of interrelationship. And the spiders (which are not insects but members of a separate order of arthropods) also are killers and victims of insects.

The picture is complicated by the fact that those species which are 4
carnivorous in the larval stage have to be provided with animal food by a vegetarian mother. The survival of the young depends on the mother's correct choice of food which she does not eat herself.

In the feeding and safeguarding of their progeny the insects and 5
spiders exhibit some interesting analogies to reasoning and some crass examples of blind instinct. The case I propose to describe here is that of the tarantula spiders and their arch-enemy, the digger wasps of the genus Pepsis. It is a classic example of what looks like intelligence pitted against instinct—a strange situation in which the victim, though fully able to defend itself, submits unwittingly to its destruction.

Most tarantulas live in the Tropics, but several species occur in 6
the temperate zone and a few are common in the southern U.S. Some varieties are large and have powerful fangs with which they can inflict a deep wound. These formidable-looking spiders do not, however, attack man; you can hold one in your hand, if you are gentle, without being bitten. Their bite is dangerous only to insects and small mammals such as mice; for a man it is no worse than a hornet's sting.

Tarantulas customarily live in deep cylindrical burrows, from 7
which they emerge at dusk and into which they retire at dawn. Mature males wander about after dark in search of females and occasionally stray into houses. After mating, the male dies in a few weeks, but a female lives much longer and can mate several years in succession. In a Paris museum is a tropical specimen which is said to have been living in captivity for 25 years.

A fertilized female tarantula lays from 200 to 400 eggs at a time; 8
thus it is possible for a single tarantula to produce several thousand young. She takes no care of them beyond weaving a cocoon of silk to enclose the eggs. After they hatch, the young walk away, find convenient places in which to dig their burrows, and spend the rest of their lives in solitude. Tarantulas feed mostly on insects and millipedes. Once their appetite is appeased, they digest the food for several days before eating again. Their sight is poor, being limited to sensing a

change in the intensity of light and to the perception of moving objects. They apparently have little or no sense of hearing, for a hungry tarantula will pay no attention to a loudly chirping cricket placed in its cage unless the insect happens to touch one of its legs.

But all spiders, and especially hairy ones, have an extremely delicate sense of touch. Laboratory experiments prove that tarantulas can distinguish three types of touch: pressure against the body wall, stroking of the body hair, and riffling of certain very fine hairs on the leg called trichobothria. Pressure against the body, by a finger or the end of a pencil, causes the tarantula to move off slowly for a short distance. The touch excites no defensive response unless the approach is from the above, where the spider can see the motion, in which case it rises on its hind legs, lifts its front legs, opens its fangs, and holds this threatening posture as long as the object continues to move. When the motion stops, the spider drops back to the ground, remains quiet for a few seconds, and then moves slowly away.   9

The entire body of a tarantula, especially its legs, is thickly clothed with hair. Some of it is short and woolly, some long and stiff. Touching this body hair produces one of two distinct reactions. When the spider is hungry, it responds with an immediate and swift attack. At the touch of a cricket's antennae the tarantula seizes the insect so swiftly that a motion picture taken at the rate of 64 frames per second shows only the result not the process of capture. But when the spider is not hungry, the stimulation of its hair merely causes it to shake the touched limb. An insect can walk under its hairy belly unharmed.   10

The trichobothria, very fine hairs growing from disklike membranes of the legs, were once thought to be the spider's hearing organs, but we now know that they have nothing to do with sound. They are sensitive only to air movement. A light breeze makes them vibrate slowly without disturbing the common hair. When one blows gently on the trichobothria, the tarantula reacts with a quick jerk of its four front legs. If the front and hind legs are stimulated at the same time, the spider makes a sudden jump. The reaction is quite independent of the state of its appetite.   11

These three tactile responses—to pressure on the body wall, to moving of the common hair, and to flexing of the trichobothria—are so different from one another that there is no possibility of confusing them. They serve the tarantula adequately for most of its needs and enable it to avoid most annoyances and dangers. But they fail the spider completely when it meets its deadly enemy, the digger wasp Pepsis.   12

These solitary wasps are beautiful and formidable creatures.   13
Most species are either a deep shiny blue all over, or deep blue with
rusty wings. The largest have a wingspan of about four inches. They
live on nectar. When excited, they give off a pungent odor—a warning that they are ready to attack. The sting is much worse than that of
a bee or common wasp, and the pain and swelling last longer. In the
adult stage the wasp lives only a few months. The female produces but
a few eggs, one at a time in intervals of two or three days. For each
egg the mother must provide one adult tarantula, alive but paralyzed.
The tarantula must be of the correct species to nourish the larva. The
mother wasp attaches the egg to the paralyzed spider's abdomen.
Upon hatching from the egg, the larva is many hundreds of times
smaller than its living but helpless victim. It eats no other food and
drinks no water. By the time it has finished the single gargantuan meal
and become ready for wasphood, nothing remains of the tarantula
but its indigestible chitinous skeleton.

The mother wasp goes tarantula-hunting when the egg in her   14
ovary is almost ready to be laid. Flying low over the ground late on a
sunny afternoon, the wasp looks for its victim or for the mouth of a
tarantula burrow, a round hole edged by a bit of silk. The sex of the
spider makes no difference, but the mother is highly discriminating as
to species. Each species of Pepsis requires a certain species of tarantula, and the wasp will not attack the wrong species. In a cage with a
tarantula which is not its normal prey the wasp avoids the spider, and
is usually killed by it in the night.

Yet when a wasp finds the correct species, it is the other way   15
about. To identify the species the wasp apparently must explore the
spider with her antennae. The tarantula shows an amazing tolerance
to this exploration. The wasp crawls under it and walks over it without evoking any hostile response. The molestation is so great and so
persistent that the tarantula often rises on all eight legs, as if it were
on stilts. It may stand this way for several minutes. Meanwhile the
wasp, having satisfied itself that the victim is of the right species,
moves off a few inches to dig the spider's grave. Working vigorously
with legs and jaws, it excavates a hole 8 to 10 inches deep with a
diameter slightly larger than the spider's girth. Now and again the
wasp pops out of the hole to make sure that the spider is still there.

When the grave is finished, the wasp returns to the tarantula to   16
complete her ghastly enterprise. First she feels it all over once more
with her antennae. Then her behavior becomes more aggressive. She
bends her abdomen, protruding her sting, and searches for the soft

membrane at the point where the spider's leg joins its body—the only spot where she can penetrate the horny skeleton. From time to time, as the exasperated spider slowly shifts ground, the wasp turns on her back and slides along with the aid of her wings, trying to get under the tarantula for a shot at the vital spot. During all this maneuvering, which can last for several minutes, the tarantula makes no move to save itself. Finally the wasp corners it against some obstruction and grasps one of its legs in her powerful jaws. Now at last the harassed spider tries a desperate but vain defense. The two contestants roll over and over on the ground. It is a terrifying sight and the outcome is always the same. The wasp finally manages to thrust her sting into the soft spot and holds it there for a few seconds while she pumps in the poison. Almost immediately the tarantula falls paralyzed on its back. Its legs stop twitching; its heart stops beating. Yet it is not dead, as is shown by the fact that if taken from the wasp it can be restored to some sensitivity by being kept in a moist chamber for several months.

After paralyzing the tarantula, the wasp cleans herself by drag-   17
ging her body along the ground and rubbing her feet, sucks the drop of blood oozing from the wound of the spider's abdomen, then grabs a leg of the flabby, helpless animal in her jaws and drags it down to the bottom of the grave. She stays there for many minutes, sometimes for several hours, and what she does all that time in the dark we do not know. Eventually she lays her egg and attaches it to the side of the spider's abdomen with a sticky secretion. Then she emerges, fills the grave with soil carried bit by bit in her jaws, and finally tramples the ground all around to hide any trace of the grave from prowlers. Then she flies away, leaving her descendant safely started in life.

In all this the behavior of the wasp evidently is qualitatively dif-   18
ferent from that of the spider. The wasp acts like an intelligent animal. This is not to say that instinct plays no part or that she reasons as man does. But her actions are to the point; they are not automatic and can be modified to fit the situation. We do not know for certain how she identifies the tarantula—probably it is by some olfactory or chemo-tactile sense—but she does it purposefully and does not blindly tackle a wrong species.

On the other hand, the tarantula's behavior shows only confu-   19
sion. Evidently the wasp's pawing gives it no pleasure, for it tries to move away. That the wasp is not simulating sexual stimulation is certain, because male and female tarantulas react in the same way to its advances. That the spider is not anesthetized by some odorless secretion is easily shown by blowing lightly at the tarantula and mak-

ing it jump suddenly. What, then, makes the tarantula behave as stupidly as it does?

No clear, simple answer is available. Possibly the stimulation by 20 the wasp's antennae is masked by a heavier pressure on the spider's body, so that it reacts as when prodded by a pencil. But the explanation may be much more complex. Initiative in attack is not in the nature of tarantulas; most species fight only when cornered so that escape is impossible. Their inherited patterns of behavior apparently prompt them to avoid problems rather than attack them. For example, spiders always weave their webs in three dimensions, and when a spider finds that there is insufficient space to attach certain threads in the third dimension, it leaves the place and seeks another, instead of finishing the web in a single plane. This urge to escape seems to arise under all circumstances, in all phases of life, and to take the place of reasoning. For a spider to change the pattern of its web is as impossible as for an inexperienced man to build a bridge across a chasm obstructing his way.

In a way the instinctive urge to escape is not only easier but more 21 efficient than reasoning. The tarantula does exactly what is most efficient in all cases except in an encounter with a ruthless and determined attacker dependent for the existence of her own species on killing as many tarantulas as she can lay eggs. Perhaps in this case the spider follows its usual pattern of trying to escape, instead of seizing and killing the wasp, because it is not aware of its danger. In any case, the survival of the tarantula species as a whole is protected by the fact that the spider is much more fertile than the wasp.

Meaning

1. What is the main idea of "The Spider and the Wasp"? What, specifically, does Petrunkevitch use process analysis to illustrate? Where is this idea stated explicitly?
2. In what way, according to Petrunkevitch, is the wasp's behavior intelligent (paragraph 18)? What elements of the wasp's behavior, described in paragraphs 13–17, might Petrunkevitch attribute to its intelligence?
3. Summarize Petrunkevitch's explanation for the spider's behaving so "stupidly" (paragraphs 20–21). How is the instinct to escape "more efficient" than reasoning?
4. How does the last sentence of the essay relate to the principle stated in the first two sentences of the essay? What would happen if this species of wasp suddenly became more fertile than this species of tarantula?

5. If you do not know the meanings of the following words, look them up in a dictionary: prey (paragraph 1); larvae (2); carnivorous (4); progeny, crass, unwittingly (5); formidable (6, 13); riffling (9); tactile (12, 18); pungent, gargantuan, chitinous (13); molestation, girth (15); protruding, exasperated, maneuvering (16); secretion, descendant (17); olfactory (18); simulating, anesthetized (19); chasm (20).

Purpose and Audience

1. Petrunkevitch's purpose is clearly explanatory. His original audience — the readers of *Scientific American* magazine—would have consisted of both nonscientists and scientists, most of them unfamiliar with his subject. Locate four or five places where Petrunkevitch defines terms, takes special care with description, or otherwise considers the needs of readers who know little or nothing about his subject. Concentrate especially on information he would *not* have to provide for others like himself who know a lot about tarantulas and digger wasps.

2. If he were writing a report for a scholarly journal, Petrunkevitch would carefully document all the sources of his information. Why does he not do so in this essay? He does, however, refer occasionally to experiments on caged tarantulas, as at the end of paragraph 8. What similar references do you find? What is it about Petrunkevitch's subject that makes these references worthwhile even for a general audience?

3. Petrunkevitch frequently uses informal expressions (such as "wipe out," paragraph 2) and expressions that reflect his subjective impressions (such as "crass," 5). What other similar expressions do you see? Would they be suitable in a report for a scholarly journal? Why, or why not? Why does Petrunkevitch use them in this essay? What effect do they have on you?

Method and Structure

1. Before explaining how the wasp hunts, paralyzes, and buries the spider, Petrunkevitch spends several paragraphs (8–12) describing the spider's sensations and responses. What is the purpose of these paragraphs?

2. Petrunkevitch helps make the process clear with frequent expressions that link sentences and indicate the duration of actions, their sequence, and where they occur—for example, "for several minutes," "Meanwhile," and "a few inches" in paragraph 15. Locate ten such expressions in paragraphs 16–17 and analyze the purpose of each one. (For a discussion and list of such expressions, see *transitions* in the Glossary.)

3. What is the purpose of Petrunkevitch's first four paragraphs?

4. **Other Methods**   Besides process analysis, Petrunkevitch employs several other methods of development: for instance, classification (Chapter 5) in paragraphs 9–12; comparison and contrast (Chapter 7) in paragraphs 18–19; and cause-and-effect analysis (Chapter 10) in paragraphs 20–21. Most notably, however, Petrunkevitch uses the encounter between the spider and the wasp as a single extended example to support his main idea (see Chapter 3). Why does he choose this particular example? Where does he make his reason clear?

Language

1. What attitudes toward the spider, the wasp, and their encounter does Petrunkevitch convey by the more informal and subjective expressions he uses to describe them? Does he ever seem amused by what he is describing? If so, where?
2. Many of Petrunkevitch's words—such as "unwittingly" (paragraph 5), "solitude" (8), and "grave" (15)—would commonly be used in reference to humans, not spiders and wasps. What similar words do you see? Why do you think Petrunkevitch uses them?

Writing Topics

1. Using Petrunkevitch's essay as a model, write an essay that analyzes some process of animal or human behavior by focusing on a single extended example of that behavior. For example, do you have a dog or cat whose behavior has taught you something about the way animals think? Or does a relationship between two people you know well or between two characters in a movie or novel explain something about human relationships in general?
2. What are the differences between the intelligence of the wasp, as Petrunkevitch defines it (paragraph 18), and the intelligence of a human being, as you see it? In an essay, explain the differences, using examples from Petrunkevitch's essay and from your own experience or reading.
3. Petrunkevitch says that the tarantula's "urge to escape is not only easier but more efficient than reasoning" (paragraph 21). Write an essay in which you explore the applications of this statement to the behavior of human beings. For instance, do humans also show an urge to escape their problems? If so, is the urge efficient? Is it healthy? Support your view with specific evidence such as examples or expert opinions.

Writing Topics

Process Analysis

Choose one of the following topics, or any other topic they suggest, for an essay developed by process analysis. The topic you decide on should be something you care about so that process analysis is a means of communicating an idea, not an end in itself.

1. Making a videotape
2. How an engine or other machine works
3. Getting physically fit
4. Making a model car, airplane, or ship
5. Performing a magic trick
6. Shopping efficiently for Christmas
7. How children learn to dress themselves, play with others, read, or write
8. Getting yourself awake in the morning
9. Climbing a mountain
10. Reading a newspaper
11. How an auction works
12. Playing a board or card game, or performing one maneuver in that game
13. Learning a foreign language
14. Throwing a really *bad* party
15. Dieting
16. Offering constructive criticism
17. How a personal computer processes data
18. Driving your parents, brother, sister, friend, or roommate crazy
19. Minimizing sibling rivalry
20. Giving yourself a haircut or a home permanent
21. How solar energy can be converted to electricity
22. Interviewing for a job
23. Playing a sport or a musical instrument
24. Winterizing a car
25. Making great chili or some other dish
26. Succeeding in biology, history, computer science, psychology, or some other course

Chapter 7

Comparison and Contrast

Understanding the Method

An insomniac watching late-night television faces a choice between two World War II movies broadcasting at the same time. To make up his mind, he uses the dual method of comparison and contrast. **Comparison** shows the similarities between two or more subjects: the similar broadcast times of the two movies force the insomniac to choose between them. **Contrast** shows the differences between subjects: the different actors, locations, and reputations of the two movies make it possible for the insomniac to choose one. As in this example, comparison and contrast usually work together because any subjects that warrant side-by-side examination usually resemble each other in some respects and differ in others. (Since comparison and contrast are so closely related, the terms *comparison* and *compare* will be used from now on to designate both.)

Explaining two or more subjects with reference to each other clarifies not only the subjects themselves but also the ideas encompassing them. Thus comparison frequently appears in essays developed by other methods. For instance, a writer will compare two processes, classify items on the basis of their similarities and differences, or argue for one solution to a problem by showing its superiority to another solution. As we saw in Chapter 4, comparison depends on division or analysis as the method of discovering similar or different elements. And, of course, comparison can also serve as the chief means of developing an entire essay.

Most comparative writing has one of two purposes: (1) to explain the similarities and differences between subjects so as to make either or both of them clear; or (2) to evaluate subjects so as to establish their advantages and disadvantages, strengths and weaknesses. The explanatory comparison does not take a position on the relative merits of the subjects; the evaluative comparison does, and it usually concludes with a preference or a suggested course of action. In an explanatory comparison a writer might show how new income-tax laws differ from old laws. In an evaluative comparison on the same subject, a writer might argue that the old laws were more equitable than the new ones are.

Whether explanatory or evaluative, comparisons treat two or more subjects in the same general class or group: tax laws, religions, diseases, advertising strategies, diets, contact sports, friends. A writer may define the class to suit his or her interest—for instance, one writer might focus on Tuesday night's television shows, another on network news programs, another on old situation comedies. The class likeness ensures that the subjects share enough features to make comparison worthwhile. With subjects from different classes, such as an insect and a tree, the similarities are so few and differences so numerous—and both are so obvious—that explaining them would be pointless. (Comparison of subjects in different classes does have a special use, however, as we will see in the next chapter, on analogy.)

The writer of a comparison not only selects subjects from the same class but also, using division or analysis, identifies the features shared by the subjects. These **points of comparison** are the attributes of the class and thus of the subjects within the class. For instance, the points of comparison for diets may be forbidden foods, allowed foods, speed of weight loss, and nutritional quality; for air pollutants they may be sources and dangers to plants, animals, and humans. These points help the writer arrange similarities and differences between subjects, and, more important, they ensure direct comparison rather than a random listing of unrelated characteristics.

In an effective comparison a thesis or controlling idea governs the choice of class, points of comparison, and specific similarities and differences, while also making the comparison worthwhile for the reader. The thesis of an evaluative comparison generally emerges naturally because it coincides with the writer's purpose of supporting a preference for one subject over another: "The two diets result in similarly rapid weight loss, but Harris's requires much more self-discipline and is nutritionally much riskier than Marconi's." In an explanatory comparison, however, the thesis does more than merely reflect the general purpose of explaining. A thesis such as "Rugby and American football are the same in some respects and different in others" is unlikely to interest anyone, even the most avid sports fan; nor can it help determine points of comparison or specific similarities and differences. The writer needs to assert something about the subjects that goes beyond the commonplace and obvious to the significant and unusual—for instance, "Though rugby requires less strength and more stamina than American football, the two games are very much alike in their rules and strategies." Such a thesis promises that the comparison will have a point and forces the writer to deliver on the promise by focusing on the features named.

The examples above also suggest other decisions facing the writer of a comparison: Should the subjects be treated in equal detail, or should one be emphasized over the others? Should the essay focus on similarities or differences or both? The answers depend entirely on the subjects and on the idea that controls the comparison. The thesis on diets suggests an equal treatment of both diets as well as an emphasis on their differences. In contrast, the revised thesis on rugby and football suggests a fuller treatment of rugby and an emphasis on the similarities between the two sports. Generally, writers give the subjects equal emphasis when they are equally familiar or are being evaluated (as the diets are), whereas they stress one subject over the others when it is more unfamiliar (as rugby is in this country). And generally, writers stress similarities and differences equally when all the points of comparison are equally familiar or important, whereas they stress the differences between subjects usually considered similar (such as the diets) or the similarities between subjects usually considered different (such as rugby and American football).

With two or more subjects, several points of comparison, many similarities and differences, and a particular emphasis, comparison clearly requires a firm organizational hand. Most comparisons follow one of two arrangements: **subject-by-subject**, in which the points of comparison are grouped under each subject so that the subjects are covered one at a time; or **point-by-point**, in which the subjects are grouped under each point of comparison so that the points are covered one at a time. The following brief outlines illustrate the different arrangements as they might be applied to diets:

Subject-by-subject	*Point-by-point*
Harris's diet	Speed of weight loss
Speed of weight loss	Harris's diet
Required self-discipline	Marconi's diet
Nutritional risk	
	Required self-discipline
Marconi's diet	Harris's diet
Speed of weight loss	Marconi's diet
Required self-discipline	
Nutritional risk	Nutritional risk
	Harris's diet
	Marconi's diet

Since the subject-by-subject arrangement presents each subject as a coherent unit, it is particularly useful for comparing impressions of subjects: the similar moods of two photographers' work, for instance, or the dissimilar characters of two friends. However, covering the subjects one at a time can break an essay into discrete pieces and strain readers' memories, so this arrangement is usually confined to essays that are short or that compare several subjects briefly. For longer papers requiring precise treatment of the individual points of comparison—say, an evaluation of two proposals for a new student-aid policy or an explanation of the differences between similar breeds of dog—the point-by-point arrangement is more useful. Its chief disadvantage is that the reader can get lost in details and fail to see any subject as a whole. Because each arrangement has its strengths and weaknesses, writers sometimes combine the two in a single work, using the divided arrangement to introduce or summarize overall impressions of the subjects and using the alternating arrangement to deal specifically with the points of comparison.

Whichever arrangement they use, writers help clarify their comparisons by explicitly linking subjects and points of comparison. Transitional expressions such as *similarly* or *in contrast* can help readers pick out similarities and differences. And whole sentences of transition, particularly at the beginnings of paragraphs, can signal changes in direction while also conveying important information: for instance, "Whereas the existing policy thus discriminates against part-time students, the proposed policy is fair to part-timers and full-timers alike" (a shift in subject); or "Though the two policies require similar grade-point averages, they differ markedly in their standards of financial need" (a shift in point of comparison).

Analyzing Comparison and Contrast in Paragraphs

Edward Hoagland (born 1932) writes fiction, books on travel, and essays on nature. The following paragraph comes from "The Ridge-Slope Fox and the Knife Thrower," an essay in his collection *The Tugman's Passage* (1982). In the paragraph preceding this one, Hoagland admits that though he spends much of the year in the country, "I'm a city man and life is short for me."

City people try to buy time as a rule, when they can, whereas country people are prepared to kill time, although both try to cherish in their mind's eye the notion of a better life ahead. Country people do not behave as if they think life is short; they live on the principle that it is long and savor variations of the kind best appreciated if most days are the same. City people crowd life when they have the chance; and it is nonsense to suppose that they have become "less observant," less alert than old-time country people were. Even the pioneer whose lumpy, sharp-roofed log house I have a photo of, and who listened each morning for the location of his big neighbor, the bear, was not more on his toes than the Los Angeles denizens who, four abreast and tailgating, drive the Santa Monica Freeway at seventy miles an hour. His hearing and eyesight may have been better, but the city dweller, it should be borne in mind, wears out his eyes and ears from encountering so much so fast.

Points of comparison:
1. Attitudes toward time

2. Density of life

3. Powers of observation

Purpose of comparison:
to dispute this view

Point-by-point organization, alternating back and forth between city and country

Expressions signal comparison (underlined)

Elizabeth Janeway (born 1913) is a novelist and a social critic. The paragraph below is from one of her books on women's changing roles in society, *Man's World, Woman's Place: A Study in Social Mythology* (1971).

Urbanization and industrialization have changed everyone's way of living, not only that of women; but, as in so many other matters, the changes for men and the changes for women are different. To put it at its simplest, men work in the labor market and they therefore work outside the home—with a very few special exceptions, mostly in the arts. Their work and their homes are separate. Women's lives are divided, too, if they work outside the home, but the division falls in a different place. In their homes they work for the welfare and well-being of their immediate families as their great-grandmother used to do. But if they have to work for money, they can't make it at home. They must turn to the labor market and, like men, work as part of an industrial or commercial enterprise. Whether it is large or small, they work with people to whom they are not related, at a schedule they do not control and usually at a job that bears no relation to what they do in the rest of their working time at home. This experience can be very valuable indeed, if only because it keeps women in touch with the way the world runs. But it means that while men almost all work in just one way, women who work work in two ways. The change from one sort of work to the other may often be stimulating, but it contributes to the part-timeness that is so characteristic of women's lives. They are the original moonlighters.

Purpose of comparison: to explain difference

Subject-by-subject organization:

1. Men's work

2. Women's work

Additional comparison: work at home and in the labor market

Expressions signal comparison (underlined)

A single point of comparison

Developing an Essay by Comparison and Contrast

GETTING STARTED

You are surrounded by subjects for a comparison essay. Your activities, physical environment, political discussions, athletic interests, reading matter, relatives, friends—all provide rich ground for you to dig in. The chief requirements for your subjects are the ones discussed earlier: they must belong to the same class of things, and they must be worth comparing. Until you have gained considerable experience writing comparisons, you may want to compare only two subjects instead of three or four, which are much more difficult to control. (The rest of this discussion assumes a two-subject comparison.) In addition, you should be able to treat your subjects fully in the space and time allowed. If you have a week to complete a three-page paper, don't try to show all the similarities and differences between country-and-western music and rhythm-and-blues. The effort can only frustrate you and irritate your readers. Instead, limit the subjects to a manageable size—for instance, the lyrics of a representative song in each type of music—so that you can develop the comparisons completely and specifically.

To generate ideas for your essay, explore each subject separately to pick out its characteristics, and then explore the subjects together to see what characteristics one suggests for the other. Look for points of comparison. Early on, you can use division or analysis (Chapter 4) to identify points of comparison by breaking the subjects' general class into its elements. A song lyric, for instance, could be divided into story line or plot, basic emotion, and special language such as dialect or slang. After you have explored your subjects fully, you can use classification (Chapter 5) to group their characteristics under the points of comparison. For instance, you might classify characteristics of two proposals for a new student-aid policy into qualifications for aid, minimum and maximum amounts to be made available, and repayment terms.

While you are shaping your ideas, you should begin formulating your controlling idea, your thesis. Do the ideas suggest an explanatory or an evaluative comparison? If explanatory, what point will the comparison make so that it does not merely recite the obvious? If evaluative, what preference or recommendation will you express? As earlier examples illustrated, the thesis should reflect not only your point or preference but also your emphasis: whether you will treat both subjects equally or stress one over the other, and whether you will emphasize differences or similarities or both.

As you gain increasing control over your material, consider also the needs of your readers. Do they know your subjects well, or should you take special care to explain one or both of them? Will your readers be equally interested in similarities and differences, or will they find one more enlightening than the other? If your essay is evaluative, are your readers likely to be biased against your preference? Say you want to recommend that your school's course requirements be expanded to resemble the stricter requirements at another school. If your classmates are your readers, you can probably assume that few of them relish the idea of taking more required courses. Thus you will need to support your case with plenty of reasons for deeming both your school's requirements inadequate and the other school's desirable.

Most readers know intuitively how comparison works, so they will expect you to balance your comparison feature for feature. In other words, all the features you mention for the first subject should be mentioned as well for the second: if you discuss School A's language requirement, you should also discuss School B's. In addition, any features not mentioned for the first subject should not suddenly materialize for the second: if you chose not to discuss School A's health-science requirement, then don't discuss School B's either.

ORGANIZING

Your readers' needs and expectations can also help you plan your essay's organization. An effective introduction to a comparison essay often provides some context for readers—the situation that prompts the comparison, for instance, or the need for the comparison. Placing your thesis in the introduction also informs readers of your purpose and point, and it may help keep you focused while you write.

For the body of the essay, choose the arrangement that will present your material most clearly and effectively. Remember that the subject-by-subject arrangement suits brief essays comparing dominant impressions of the subjects, whereas the point-by-point arrangement suits longer essays requiring emphasis on the individual points of comparison. If you are torn between the two—wanting both to sum up each subject and to show the two side by side—then a combined arrangement may be your wisest choice.

A rough outline like the models on page 199 can help you plan the basic arrangement of your essay and also the order of the subjects and points of comparison. If your subjects are equally familiar to your readers and equally important to you, then it may not matter which subject you treat first, even in a subject-by-subject arrangement. But if one subject is less familiar or if you favor one, then that one should probably come second. For instance, in a point-by-point essay arguing that the existing financial-aid policy should be replaced by a proposed policy, you might treat the existing policy (more familiar, less favored) before the proposed policy (less familiar, more favored) under each point of comparison. You can also arrange the points themselves to reflect their importance and your readers' knowledge: from least to most significant or complex, from most to least familiar. Be sure to use the same order for both subjects.

The conclusion to a comparison essay can help readers see the whole picture: the chief similarities and differences between two subjects compared in a divided arrangement, or the chief characteristics of subjects compared in an alternating arrangement. In addition, you may want to comment on the significance of your comparison, advise readers on how they can use the information you have provided, or recommend a specific course of action for them to follow. As with all other methods of development, the choice of conclusion should reflect the impression you want to leave with readers.

DRAFTING

While you are drafting your essay, try to ensure that each sentence supports your thesis and that readers will see the connection. If a point of comparison or a pair of features seems to be taking you away from your idea, consider dropping it or, if you want to pursue it, rethink your thesis with the new material in mind.

You can use paragraphs to help manage your comparison and also help readers follow your thought. If, in a subject-by-subject arrangement, you devote two paragraphs to the first subject, try also to devote two paragraphs to the second. For both subjects, try to cover the points of comparison in the same order and group the same ones in paragraphs. In a point-by-point arrangement, balance the paragraphs as you move back and forth between subjects. If you treat several points of comparison for the first subject in one paragraph, do the same for the second subject. If you apply a single point of comparison to both subjects in one paragraph, do the same for the next point of comparison. Help your readers further by providing ample links between subjects and between points of comparison. Use transitional expressions such as *also* and *however*. (A list of expressions appears in the Glossary under *transitions*.) And use transitional sentences like those on pages 199–200 to link parts of the essay and to show changes in direction.

As important as balance and transitions are, don't let them overwhelm the subjects themselves. Comparison becomes dull or absurd when a writer marches rigidly through a pattern, devoting a sentence to each point, first for one subject and then for the other, or alternating subjects sentence by sentence through several paragraphs. Let your readers' needs and the complexity of your material determine how much play you give each subject and each point of comparison. As long as your reasons and your presentation are clear, your readers will appreciate the variety that comes from flexibility.

REVISING

When you are revising your draft, ask the following questions to be certain that your essay meets the principal requirements of the comparative method.

1. *Are your subjects drawn from the same class?* The subjects must have notable differences *and* notable similarities to make comparison worthwhile—though, of course, you may stress one group over the other.

2. *Does your essay have a clear purpose and say something significant about the subjects?* Your purpose of explaining or evaluating and the point you are making should be evident in your thesis *and* throughout the essay. A vague, pointless comparison will quickly bore readers.

3. *Do you apply all points of comparison to both subjects?* Even if you emphasize one subject, the two subjects must match feature for feature. An unmatched comparison may leave readers with unanswered questions or weaken their confidence in your authority.

4. *Do organization, paragraphing, and transitions make your comparison clear?* Readers should be able to follow easily as you move among subjects or points of comparison, and they should be able to link related ideas without flipping back and forth in the essay. If you are unsure of your essay's clarity, ask a friend or classmate to read it for you.

Born in 1943 in New York City, where he also lives now, Jeff Greenfield is a writer and television commentator. He graduated from the University of Wisconsin and, in 1967, from Yale Law School. Early in his career he wrote speeches for John Lindsay, then the mayor of New York, and worked as a legislative aide to the late Senator Robert Kennedy. In addition to numerous articles for most of the nation's major magazines, Greenfield has written books on sports, the media, and politics, including Where Have You Gone, Joe DiMaggio? *(1973),* The World's Greatest Team: A Portrait of the Boston Celtics, *(1976),* Television: The First Fifty Years *(1977), and* Playing to Win: An Insider's Guide to Politics *(1980). His most recent book,* The Real Campaign: How the Media Missed the Story of the 1980 Campaign *(1982), derives from his experience as an analyst of politics and the media for CBS News. Currently, he is a correspondent for ABC News and* Nightline.

The Black and White Truth About Basketball

Why is professional basketball dominated by black players? The answer, says Greenfield in this essay, has to do with where the players grew up. First published in Esquire *in 1975, the essay was updated by Greenfield in 1989.*

The dominance of black athletes over professional basketball is beyond dispute. Two-thirds of the players are black, and the number would be greater were it not for the continuing practice of picking white bench warmers for the sake of balance. Over the last two decades, no more than three white players have been among the ten starting players on the National Basketball Association's All-Star team, and in the last quarter century, only two white players—Dave Cowens and Larry Bird of the Boston Celtics—have ever been chosen as the NBA's Most Valuable Player.

And at a time when a baseball executive can lose his job for asserting that blacks lack "the necessities" to become pro sports executives and when the National Football League only in 1989 had its first black head coach, the NBA stands as a pro sports league that hired its first black head coach in 1968 (Bill Russell) and its first black general manager in the early 1970s (Wayne Embry of the Milwaukee Bucks). What discrimination remains—lack of equal opportunity for speaking engagements and product endorsements—has more to do with society than with basketball.

This dominance reflects a natural inheritance: Basketball is a pastime of the urban poor. The current generation of black athletes are heirs to a tradition more than half a century old. In a neighborhood without the money for bats, gloves, hockey sticks and ice skates, or shoulder pads, basketball is an eminently accessible sport. "Once it was the game of the Irish and Italian Catholics in Rockaway and the Jews on Fordham Road in the Bronx," writes David Wolf in his brilliant book, *Foul!* "It was recreation, status, and a way out." But now the ethnic names have been changed: Instead of the Red Holzmans, Red Auerbachs, and the McGuire brothers, there are Julius Ervings and Michael Jordans, Ralph Sampsons and Kareem Abdul-Jabbars. And professional basketball is a sport with national television exposure and million-dollar salaries.

But the mark on basketball of today's players can be measured by more than money or visibility. It is a question of style. For there is a clear difference between "black" and "white" styles of play that is as clear as the difference between 155th Street at Eighth Avenue and Crystal City, Missouri. Most simply (remembering we are talking about culture, not chromosomes), "black" basketball is the use of superb athletic skill to adapt to the limits of space imposed by the game. "White" ball is the pulverization of that space by sheer intensity.[1]

It takes a conscious effort to realize how constricted the space is on a basketball court. Place a regulation court (ninety-four by fifty feet) on a football field, and it will reach from the back of the end zone to the twenty-one-yard line; its width will cover less than a third of the field. On a baseball diamond, a basketball court will reach from home plate to first base. Compared to its principal indoor rival, ice hockey, basketball covers about one-fourth the playing area. More-

3

4

5

---

[1] This distinction has nothing to do with the question of whether whites can play as "well" as blacks. In 1987, the Detroit Pistons' Isaiah Thomas quipped that the Celtics' Larry Bird was "a pretty good player," but would be much less celebrated and wealthy if he were black. As Thomas later said, Bird is one of the greatest pro players in history. Nor is this distinction about "smart," although the Los Angeles Lakers' Magic Johnson is right in saying that too many journalists ascribe brilliant strategy by black players to be solely due to "innate" ability.

over, during the normal flow of the game, most of the action takes place on the third of the court nearest the basket. It is in this dollhouse space that ten men, each of them half a foot taller than the average man, come together to battle each other.

There is, thus, no room; basketball is a struggle for the edge: the   6 half step with which to cut around the defender for a lay-up, the half second of freedom with which to release a jump shot, the instant a head turns allowing a pass to a teammate breaking for the basket. It is an arena for the subtlest of skills: the head fake, the shoulder fake, the shift of body weight to the right and the sudden cut to the left. Deception is crucial to success; and to young men who have learned early and painfully that life is a battle for survival, basketball is one of the few pursuits in which the weapon of deception is a legitimate tactic rather than the source of trouble.

If there is, then, the need to compete in a crowd, to battle for the   7 edge, then the surest strategy is to develop the *unexpected*: to develop a shot that is simply and fundamentally different from the usual methods of putting the ball in the basket. Drive to the hoop, but go under it and come up the other side; hold the ball at waist level and shoot from there instead of bringing the ball up to eye level; leap into the air, but fall away from the basket instead of toward it. All these tactics, which a fan can see embodied in the astonishing play of the Chicago Bulls' Michael Jordan, take maximum advantage of the crowding on the court. They also stamp uniqueness on young men who may feel it nowhere else.

"For many young men in the slums," David Wolf writes, "the   8 school yard is the only place they can feel true pride in what they do, where they can move free of inhibitions and where they can, by being spectacular, rise for the moment against the drabness and anonymity of their lives. Thus, when a player develops extraordinary 'school yard' moves and shots . . . [they] become his measure as a man."

So the moves that begin as tactics for scoring soon become calling   9 cards. You don't just lay the ball in for an uncontested basket; you take the ball in both hands, leap as high as you can, and slam the ball through the hoop. When you jump in the air, fake a shot, bring the ball back to your body, and throw up a shot, all without coming back down, you have proven your worth in uncontestable fashion.

This liquid grace is an integral part of "black" ball, almost exclu-   10 sively the province of the playground player. Some white stars like Bob Cousy, Billy Cunningham, and Doug Collins had it, and the Celtics' Kevin McHale has it now: the body control, the moves to the basket, the free-ranging mobility. Most of them also possessed the surface ease that is integral to the "black" style; an incorporation of the ethic of mean streets—to "make it" is not just to have wealth but to have it without strain. Whatever the muscles and organs are doing, the face of the "black" star almost never shows it. Magic Johnson of the Lakers can bring the ball downcourt with two men on him, whip a pass through an invisible opening, cut to the basket, take a return pass, and hit the shot all with no more emotion than a quick smile. So stoic was San Antonio Spurs' great George Gervin that he earned the nickname "Ice Man." (Interestingly, a black coach like former Celtics' coach K. C. Jones exhibited far less emotion on the bench than a white counterpart like Dick Motta or Jack Ramsey.)

If there is a single trait that characterizes "black" ball it is leaping *11* ability. Bob Cousy, ex-Celtic great and former pro coach, says that "when coaches get together, one is sure to say, 'I've got the one black kid in the country who can't jump.' When coaches see a white boy who can jump or who moves with extraordinary quickness, they say, 'He should have been born black, he's that good.' "

Don Nelson, now a top executive with the Golden State Warriors, *12* recalls that back in 1970, Dave Cowens, then a relatively unknown graduate of Florida State, prepared for his rookie pro season by playing in the Rucker League, an outdoor competition in Harlem playgrounds that pits pros against college kids and playground stars. So ferocious was Cowens's leaping ability, Nelson says, that "when the summer was over, everyone wanted to know who the white son of a bitch was who could jump so high." That's another way to overcome a crowd around the basket—just go over it.

Speed, mobility, quickness, acceleration, "the moves"—all of *13* these are catch-phrases that surround the "black" playground athlete, the style of play. So does the most racially tinged of attributes, "rhythm." Yet rhythm is what the black stars themselves talk about: feeling the flow of the game, finding the tempo of the dribble, the step, the shot. It is an instinctive quality (although it stems from hundreds of hours of practice), and it is one that has led to difficulty between system-oriented coaches and free-form players. "Cats from the street have their own rhythm when they play," said college dropout Bill Spivey, onetime New York high school star. "It's not a matter of somebody setting you up and you shooting. You *feel* the shot. When a coach holds you back, you lose the feel and it isn't fun anymore."

When legendary Brooklyn playground star Connie Hawkins was *14* winding up his NBA career under Laker coach Bill Sharman, he chafed under the methodical style of play. "He's systematic to the point where it begins to be a little too much. It's such an action-reaction type of game that when you have to do everything the same way, I think you lose something."

There is another kind of basketball that has grown up in America. 15 It is not played on asphalt playgrounds with a crowd of kids competing for the court; it is played on macadam driveways by one boy with a ball and a backboard nailed over the garage; it is played in gyms in the frigid winter of the rural Midwest and on Southern dirt courts. It is a mechanical, precise development of skills (when Don Nelson was an Iowa farm boy, his incentive to make his shots was that an errant rebound would land in the middle of chicken droppings). It is a game without frills, without flow, but with effectiveness. It is "white" basketball: jagged, sweaty, stumbling, intense. Where a "black" player overcomes an obstacle with finesse and body control, a "white" player reacts by outrunning or overpowering the obstacle.

By this definition, the Boston Celtics are a classically "white" 16 team. They rarely suit up a player with dazzling moves; indeed such a player would probably make Red Auerbach swallow his cigar. Instead, the Celtics wear you down with execution, with constant running, with the same play run again and again and again. The rebound by Robert Parrish triggers the fast break, as everyone races downcourt; the ball goes to Larry Bird, who pulls up and takes the shot or who drives and then finds Reggie Lewis or Kevin McHale free for an easy basket.

Perhaps the most definitively "white" position is that of the quick 17 forward, one without great moves to the basket, without highly developed shots, without the height and mobility for rebounding effectiveness. So what does he do?

He runs. He runs from the opening jump to the final buzzer. He 18 runs up and down the court, from base line to base line, back and forth under the basket, looking for the opening, the pass, the chance to take a quick step, the high percentage shot. To watch San Antonio's Mark Olberding or Detroit's Bill Lambeer, players without speed or obvious moves, is to wonder what they are doing in the NBA—until you see them swing free and throw up a shot that, without demanding any apparent skill, somehow goes in the basket more frequently than the shots of many of their more skilled teammates. And to have watched the New York Knicks' (now U.S. Senator) Bill Bradley, or the Celtics' John Havlicek, is to have watched "white" ball at its best.

Havlicek or Lambeer, or the former Laker Kurt Rambis, stand in 19 dramatic contrast to Michael Jordan or to the Philadelphia 76ers' legend, Julius Erving. Erving had the capacity to make legends come true, leaping from the foul line and slam-dunking the ball on his way down; going up for a lay-up, pulling the ball to his body, and driving under and up the other side of the rim, defying gravity and probability with impossible moves and jumps. Michael Jordan of the Chicago Bulls has been seen by thousands spinning a full 360 degrees in midair before slamming the ball through the hoop.

When John Havlicek played, by contrast, he was the living em- 20
bodiment of his small-town Ohio background. He would bring the ball downcourt, weaving left, then right, looking for a path. He would swing the ball to a teammate, cut behind the pick, take the pass, and release the shot in a flicker of time. It looked plain, unvarnished. But it was a blend of skills that not more than half a dozen other players in the league possessed.

To former pro Jim McMillian, a black who played quick forward 21
with "white" attributes, "it's a matter of environment. Julius Erving grew up in a different environment from Havlicek. John came from a very small town in Ohio. There everything was done the easy way, the shortest distance between two points. It's nothing fancy; very few times will he go one-on-one. He hits the lay-up, hits the jump shot, makes the free throw, and after the game you look up and say, 'How did he hurt us that much?' "

"White" ball, then, is the basketball of patience, method, and 22
sometimes brute strength. "Black" ball is the basketball of electric self-expression. One player has all the time in the world to perfect his skills, the other a need to prove himself. These are slippery categories, because a poor boy who is black can play "white" and a white boy of middle-class parents can play "black." Bill Cartwright of the Chicago Bulls and Steve Alford of the Golden State Warriors are athletes who seem to defy these categories.

And what makes basketball the most intriguing of sports is how 23
these styles do not necessarily clash; how the punishing intensity of "white" players and the dazzling moves of the "blacks" can fit together, a fusion of cultures that seems more and more difficult in the world beyond the out-of-bounds line.

Meaning

1. What is the main idea of Greenfield's essay, the "black and white truth" of the title? In answering, consider not only the assertion that there are "black" and "white" playing styles but also the reasons for the differ-

ences in style and what they contribute to blacks' dominance of professional basketball.

2. Summarize Greenfield's ideas about the origins of the "black" style and
the elements of the style. Do the same for the origins and elements of the
"white" style. How do the different origins explain the different styles?

3. When it was first published, this essay carried the subtitle "A Skin-Deep
Theory of Style." How does this subtitle relate to Greenfield's statement
that "we are talking about culture, not chromosomes" (paragraph 4)? Is
he also talking about culture when he discusses rhythm (13)? Why does
he say that rhythm is "the most racially tinged of attributes"?

4. If you do not know the meanings of the following words, look them up
in a dictionary: chromosomes, pulverization (paragraph 4); inhibitions,
anonymity (8); integral, ethic, stoic (10); ferocious (12); systematic (14);
macadam, errant, finesse (15).

Purpose and Audience

1. Does Greenfield's purpose seem strictly explanatory, or does he also
seem to express a preference for the "black" style over the "white"?
What passages support your answer?

2. What do you think Greenfield assumes about his readers' familiarity
with basketball? For instance, does a reader have to know the terminology of the game, such as that used in paragraph 6, to appreciate the
different styles of play? Why, or why not? What is your response to this
essay, and to what degree is it influenced by your interest in and knowledge of basketball?

3. Greenfield uses many examples of specific players and quotations from
players and from another sportswriter. Examine a few of these examples
and quotations (such as in paragraphs 8, 10, and 19–21) and analyze
their effectiveness in supporting Greenfield's ideas about style. If you
follow professional basketball, can you think of examples that would
undermine Greenfield's theory? Where, if at all, does he acknowledge
this possibility?

Method and Structure

1. Greenfield's comparison is arranged subject by subject. In which paragraph does he begin explaining the "black" style? In which the "white"
style? Where, in explaining the "white" style, does Greenfield either summarize the differences in style or echo elements of the "black" style to
sharpen the contrast?

2. What is the purpose of each paragraph in the essay's introduction? Con-

sider especially why Greenfield bothers to establish the dominance of blacks in pro basketball (paragraphs 1–2), why he explains the urban appeal of the game (3), and why he describes the size of the basketball court in such detail (5).

3. **Other Methods** Greenfield employs several methods of development besides comparison and contrast. A previous question asked you to examine his use of examples, but can you also locate passages developed by description (Chapter 1), narration (Chapter 2), process analysis (Chapter 6), and cause-and-effect analysis (Chapter 10)?

Language

1. What effect does Greenfield achieve in his descriptions of the players' moves (paragraphs 6–7, 9–10, 13, 16, 18)? In answering, consider especially the verbs and sentence structures in these passages.

2. Greenfield describes basketball as a "battle" in a "dollhouse space" (paragraph 5). From that point on, what other words either denote or connote the ideas of battle, competition, crowding, intensity? How do these words relate to Greenfield's main idea? (If necessary, consult *connotation and denotation* in the Glossary.)

3. Why does Greenfield use quotation marks each time he mentions the "black" or "white" style of play? Should he have used quotation marks as well when referring to the race of the players, as when he identifies Jim McMillian as "a black . . . with 'white' attributes" (paragraph 21)? Why, or why not?

Writing Topics

1. Greenfield says the dominance of black players in professional basketball "reflects a natural inheritance: Basketball is a pastime of the urban poor" (paragraph 3). Consider another sport with which you are familiar— football, car racing, golf, tennis, track, baseball, hockey, gymnastics, swimming—and in an essay explain the degree to which it, too, is dominated by players from certain backgrounds.

2. Write an essay comparing two distinct styles of music, dancing, acting, sports play (in a sport other than basketball), or some other form of art or entertainment. Be sure to limit your subjects so that you have the time and space to be specific about differences and similarities. And be sure your readers see the significance of your comparison.

3. In his final sentence, Greenfield remarks that the meshing of "black" and "white" styles of play on the basketball court is "a fusion of cultures that seems more and more difficult in the world beyond the out-of-bounds

line." To what degree to you think the "fusion of cultures" in professional and amateur sports has contributed or may yet contribute to equality and harmony between races in society as a whole? Write an essay explaining your view. Be sure to support your general statements with specific examples from your experiences, observations, or reading.

An influential art critic and novelist, John Berger was born in 1926 in London and educated in a London art school. He served in the British army during World War II. A decade later he began publishing a long list of innovative writings, including the novels A Painter of Our Time *(1958),* G *(1972), and* Pig Earth *(1979); the screenplays* La Salamandre *and* Jonah Who Will Be 25 in the Year 2000; *the works of social documentation* A Fortunate Man: The Story of a Country Doctor *(1967) and* A Seventh Man: Migrant Workers in Europe *(1975); and the works of art criticism* The Success and Failure of Picasso *(1965),* The Moment of Cubism, and Other Essays *(1969),* Ways of Seeing *(1972), and* About Looking *(1980). Berger, who proclaims himself a Marxist, is intensely interested in how social structures affect individuals and firmly believes that art should reflect social change. He lives and writes in a small peasant village in the French alps.*

Pleasure and Pain

This brief essay comes from And Our Faces, My Heart, Brief as Photos *(1984), a collection of poems, sketches, and speculations about "the devastation and love that face each other in our world." Berger here explores the relation, the commonality, and ultimately the difference between two sensations usually considered merely opposites.*

The existence of pleasure is the first mystery. The existence of pain 1
has prompted far more philosophical speculation. Pleasure and pain
need to be considered together; they are inseparable. Yet the space
filled by each is perhaps different.

Pleasure, defined as a sense of gratification, is essential for nature's 2
workings. Otherwise there would be no impulse to satisfy the needs
which ensure the body's and the species' survival. And survival—for
reasons we do not know—is in-written, inscribed as nature's only
goal. Gratification, or its anticipation, acts as a goad. Pain or the fear
of pain acts as a warning. Both are essential. The difference between
them, considered as opposites, is that pleasure has a constant tendency to exceed its functional purpose, *to not know its place.*

Cats display more pleasure when licking one another than when 3
eating. (There is, it is true, in all animals, except ruminants, an urgency

in eating which displaces pleasure: the pleasure comes as plenitude after the act of eating.) Horses running wild in a field appear to experience more pleasure than when quenching their thirst. The gratification, necessary in order to provoke impulses toward the satisfaction of certain essential needs, produces, even in animals, a capacity for a generalized experience of pleasure. Gratuitous pleasure.

Perhaps this capacity is linked to the fact that all young animals 4 need to play in order to learn. Between play and gratuitous pleasure there is a face in common. Playing implies a distinction between the real and the playful. The world is doubled by play. There is the involuntary world of necessity and the voluntary world of play. In the second world pleasure no longer serves a purpose but becomes gratuitous.

For us, too, the world is doubled by play, but the degree of invention mounts so that play becomes imagination. Imagination doubles and intensifies both pain and pleasure: anxiety and fantasy are born. Nevertheless the same elementary distinction remains. Pain, however much it overflows its source, always has a cause, a center, a locus; whereas pleasure does not necessarily have one.

Human happiness is rare. There are no happy periods, only happy 6 moments. But happiness is precisely a generalized pleasure. And the state of happiness can be defined by an equation whereby, at that moment, the gift of one's well-being equals the gift of the existent. Without a surplus of pleasure over and above functional gratification, such well-being could not exist. Aesthetic experience is the purest expression of this equation.

Traditionally this equation was read as the sign of the existence of 7 a benevolent God or, at least, of a God sometimes capable of benevolence. The arbitrariness of happiness was interpreted as a divine intention. And from this arose the problem of suffering and pain. If pleasure was a gift, if happiness was intended, why should there be pain? The answers are hard.

It has never been easy to relieve pain. The productive recourses 8 have usually been lacking—food, adequate medicines, clothing, shelter. But it has never been difficult to locate the causes of pain: hunger, illness, cold, deprivation. . . . It has always been, in principle, simpler to relieve pain than to give pleasure or make happy. An area of pain is more easily located.

With one enormous exception—the emotional pain of loss, the 9 pain that has broken a heart. Such pain fills the space of an entire life. It may have begun with a single event but the event has produced a surplus of pain. The sufferer becomes inconsolable. Yet, what is this pain, if it is not the recognition that what was once given as pleasure or happiness has been irrevocably taken away?

The gift of pleasure is the first mystery.   *10*

Meaning

1. Berger begins and ends his essay by stating that pleasure is "the first mystery." What is so mysterious about pleasure, and why is it first?
2. According to Berger, what are the essential differences between pleasure and pain? What kind of pain is most similar to pleasure in these attributes?
3. Three times Berger refers to a doubling: "the world is doubled by play" (paragraphs 4, 5), and "Imagination doubles and intensifies both pain and pleasure" (5). What do you think he means?
4. If you do not know the meanings of the following words, look them up in a dictionary: speculation (paragraph 1); gratification, goad (2); ruminants, plenitude, gratuitous (3); existent, aesthetic (6); benevolent, arbitrariness (7); recourses (8); inconsolable, irrevocably (9).

Purpose and Audience

1. Do you consider the main purpose of this comparison to be explanatory or evaluative? On what evidence do you base your response?
2. How would you characterize Berger's intended audience, in terms of such variables as education and assumptions? Where in the essay do you find appeals to that audience?
3. Berger sometimes omits examples of his ideas, apparently assuming that his readers will supply them from their own reading and experience. Alone or with classmates, locate two or three general or abstract statements, such as "There are no happy periods, only happy moments" (paragraph 6), and supply your own supporting examples. Do you think the essay would have been strengthened or weakened by such examples? Why?

Method and Structure

1. What are the points of comparison that Berger employs in discussing pleasure and pain? Why do you think he spends so much more time on pleasure than on pain?

2. Berger makes his comparison point by point rather than subject by subject. Do you think this arrangement serves his purpose well, or would the essay have been more effective the other way? Explain your response.
3. Analyze how Berger links his paragraphs, both explicitly (with transitional expressions and repetitions) and implicitly (with thematic connections). (If necessary, see *coherence* and *transitions* in the Glossary.)
4. **Other Methods**   Berger employs several other methods in his essay, including examples in paragraph 3 of animals experiencing pleasure (Chapter 3), and definition throughout of both pleasure and pain (Chapter 9). Most interesting, however, is his use of cause-and-effect analysis (Chapter 10). Locate examples of cause-and-effect analysis. Why do you think Berger uses it?

Language

1. Berger relies heavily on abstract language—words such as "existence" (paragraph 1) and "gratification" (2). Locate seven or eight other examples, and explain why Berger may have opted for such language. What, for instance, does it contribute to the tone of the essay? (If necessary, see *abstract and concrete words* and *tone* in the Glossary.)
2. Berger's opening line is "The existence of pleasure is the first mystery." His closing line is almost the same: "The gift of pleasure is the first mystery." What is the significance of the word "gift" in place of the word "existence"? Where in the essay can the shift from one to the other be said to occur?

Writing Topics

1. Berger makes a distinction between physical pain caused by such things as hunger or illness and emotional pain caused by the loss of a loved one, stating that an emotional loss produces "a surplus of pain" (paragraph 9). Write an essay in which you compare and contrast physical and emotional pain, focusing on both similarities and differences.
2. Consider another set of opposite feelings: for example, love and hate, fear and courage, excitement and indifference. Using Berger's essay as a model, explore the differences between the two feelings, considering how they function in human life, what causes them, and how various institutions (such as the church or the state) interpret them.
3. In paragraph 8 Berger says, "It has never been easy to relieve pain. The productive recourses have usually been lacking—food, adequate medicines, clothing, shelter." Still, he says, "It has always been, in principle, simpler to relieve pain than to give pleasure." For the past decade or

more, politicians and others have disputed whether food, medicines, shelter, and other potential solutions to social ills are in short supply, are badly distributed, or just don't work. Choose one example of "pain"—for instance, homelessness, AIDS, teenage drug addiction, malnutrition among children—and examine the extent to which its continuation is due to one or a combination of causes: a lack of recourses, a reluctance or inability to use all recourses, or some other factor. Begin research in the library by consulting the *Readers' Guide to Periodical Literature* for recent magazine articles on the problem you choose.

*Born in 1944 in San Francisco to Spanish-speaking Mexican immigrants,
Richard Rodriguez entered school speaking essentially no English and left it
with a Ph.D. in English literature. In between, his increasing assimilation into
the mainstream of American society meant increasing alienation from his
parents and their culture—a simultaneous gain and loss that he often writes
about. Rodriguez was educated in the Catholic schools of Sacramento, California; graduated from Stanford University; and did graduate work at Columbia University, the Warburg Institute in London, and the University of
California at Berkeley, from which he earned his Ph.D. and where he also
taught. Now a lecturer and writer, he has contributed articles to* The American Scholar, Change, The Saturday Review, *and* The New Republic. *Much of
his work concerns the controversial programs of affirmative action and bilingual education, both of which his own experiences have led him to oppose.
On bilingual education he says, "To me, public educators in a public schoolroom have an obligation to teach a public language. . . . The imperative is to
get children away from those languages that increase their sense of alienation
from the public society."*

Private Language,
Public Language

In this excerpt from his memoir Hunger of Memory (1982), *Rodriguez tells of
shuttling between the private language of family and the public language of
society. His family spoke Spanish, his society English, but the distinction
between private and public languages is experienced, he believes, by all
children.*

I remember to start with that day in Sacramento—a California now 1
nearly thirty years past—when I first entered a classroom, able to
understand some fifty stray English words.

The third of four children, I had been preceded to a neighborhood 2
Roman Catholic school by an older brother and sister. But neither of
them had revealed very much about their classroom experiences. Each
afternoon they returned, as they left in the morning, always together,
speaking in Spanish as they climbed the five steps of the porch. And
their mysterious books, wrapped in shopping-bag paper, remained on
the table next to the door, closed firmly behind them.

An accident of geography sent me to a school where all my class- 3
mates were white, many the children of doctors and lawyers and
business executives. All my classmates certainly must have been uneasy on that first day of school—as most children are uneasy—to find
themselves apart from their families in the first institution of their
lives. But I was astonished.

The nun said, in a friendly but oddly impersonal voice, "Boys and 4
girls, this is Richard Rodriguez." (I heard her sound out: *Rich-heard
Road-ree-guess*.) It was the first time I had heard anyone name me in
English. "Richard," the nun repeated more slowly, writing my name
down in her black leather book. Quickly I turned to see my mother's
face dissolve in a watery blur behind the pebbled glass door.

Many years later there is something called bilingual education—a 5
scheme proposed in the late 1960s by Hispanic-American social activ-
ists, later endorsed by a congressional vote. It is a program that seeks
to permit non-English-speaking children, many from lower-class
homes, to use their family language as the language of school. (Such is
the goal its supporters announce.) I hear them and am forced to say
no: It is not possible for a child—any child—ever to use his family's
language in school. Not to understand this is to misunderstand the
public uses of schooling and to trivialize the nature of intimate life—a
family's "language."

Memory teaches me what I know of these matters; the boy 6
reminds the adult. I was a bilingual child, a certain kind—socially
disadvantaged—the son of working-class parents, both Mexican
immigrants.

In the early years of my boyhood, my parents coped very well in 7
America. My father had steady work. My mother managed at home.
They were nobody's victims. Optimism and ambition led them to a
house (our home) many blocks from the Mexican south side of town.
We lived among *gringos*[1] and only a block from the biggest, whitest
houses. It never occurred to my parents that they couldn't live wherever they chose. Nor was the Sacramento of the fifties bent on teaching them a contrary lesson. My mother and father were more annoyed
than intimidated by those two or three neighbors who tried initially to
make us unwelcome. ("Keep your brats away from my sidewalk!")
But despite all they achieved, perhaps because they had so much to
achieve, any deep feeling of ease, the confidence of "belonging" in
public was withheld from them both. They regarded the people at

---

[1] Spanish for "foreigners," especially Americans and the English. [Editor's note.]

work, the faces in crowds, as very distant from us. They were the
others, *los gringos*. That term was interchangeable in their speech
with another, even more telling, *los americanos*. . . .

In public, my father and mother spoke a hesitant, accented, not   8
always grammatical English. And they would have to strain—their
bodies tense—to catch the sense of what was rapidly said by *los
gringos*. At home they spoke Spanish. The language of their Mexican
past sounded in counterpoint to the English of public society. The
words would come quickly, with ease. Conveyed through those
sounds was the pleasing, soothing, consoling reminder of being at
home.

During those years when I was first conscious of hearing, my   9
mother and father addressed me only in Spanish; in Spanish I learned
to reply. By contrast, English (*inglés*), rarely heard in the house, was
the language I came to associate with *gringos*. I learned my first words
of English overhearing my parents speak to strangers. At five years of
age, I knew just enough English for my mother to trust me on errands
to stores one block away. No more.

I was a listening child, careful to hear the very different sounds of   10
Spanish and English. Wide-eyed with learning, I'd listen to sounds
more than words. First, there were English (*gringo*) sounds. So many
words were still unknown that when the butcher or the lady at the
drugstore said something to me, exotic polysyllabic sounds would
bloom in the midst of their sentences. Often the speech of people in
public seemed to me very loud, booming with confidence. The man
behind the counter would literally ask, "What can I do for you?" But
by being so firm and so clear, the sound of his voice said that he was a
gringo; he belonged in public society.

I would also hear then the high nasal tones of middle-class Ameri-   11
can speech. The air stirred with sound. Sometimes, even now, when I
have been traveling abroad for several weeks, I will hear what I heard
as a boy. In hotel lobbies or airports, in Turkey or Brazil, some
Americans will pass, and suddenly I will hear it again—the high
sound of American voices. For a few seconds I will hear it with pleasure, for it is now the sound of my society—a reminder of home. But
inevitably—already on the flight headed for home—the sound fades
with repetition. I will be unable to hear it anymore.

When I was a boy, things were different. The accent of *los gringos*   12
was never pleasing nor was it hard to hear. Crowds at Safeway or at
bus stops would be noisy with sound. And I would be forced to edge
away from the chirping chatter above me.

I was unable to hear my own sounds, but I knew very well that I   *13*
spoke English poorly. My words could not stretch far enough to form
complete thoughts. And the words I did speak I didn't know well
enough to make into distinct sounds. (Listeners would usually lower
their heads, better to hear what I was trying to say.) But it was one
thing for *me* to speak English with difficulty. It was more troubling
for me to hear my parents speak in public: their high-whining vowels
and guttural consonants; their sentences that got stuck with "eh" and
"ah" sounds; the confused syntax; the hesitant rhythm of sounds so
different from the way *gringos* spoke. I'd notice, moreover, that my
parents' voices were softer than those of *gringos* we'd meet. . . .

There were many times like the night at a brightly lit gasoline   *14*
station (a blaring white memory) when I stood uneasily, hearing my
father. He was talking to a teenaged attendant. I do not recall what
they were saying, but I cannot forget the sounds my father made as he
spoke. At one point his words slid together to form one word—
sounds as confused as the threads of blue and green oil in the puddle
next to my shoes. His voice rushed through what he had left to say.
And, toward the end, reached falsetto notes, appealing to his listener's
understanding. I looked away to the lights of passing automobiles. I
tried not to hear anymore. But I heard only too well the calm, easy
tones in the attendant's reply. Shortly afterward, walking toward
home with my father, I shivered when he put his hand on my shoulder. The very first chance that I got, I evaded his grasp and ran on
ahead into the dark, skipping with feigned boyish exuberance.

But then there was Spanish. *Español:* my family's language.   *15*
Español: the language that seemed to me a private language. I'd hear
strangers on the radio and in the Mexican Catholic church across town
speaking Spanish, but I couldn't really believe that Spanish was a
public language, like English. Spanish speakers, rather, seemed related
to me, for I sensed that we shared—through our language—the experience of feeling apart from *los gringos.* It was thus a ghetto Spanish
that I heard and I spoke. Like those whose lives are bound by a barrio,
I was reminded by Spanish of my separateness from *los otros,*[2] *los
gringos* in power. But more intensely than for most barrio children—
because I did not live in a barrio—Spanish seemed to me the language
of home. (Most days it was only at home that I'd hear it.) It became
the language of joyful return.

A family member would say something to me and I would feel   *16*
myself specially recognized. My parents would say something to me

---

[2] Spanish: "the others." [Editor's note.]

and I would feel embraced by the sounds of their words. Those sounds said: *I am speaking with ease in Spanish. I am addressing you in words I never use with* los gringos. *I recognize you as someone special, close, like no one outside. You belong with us. In the family.* (Ricardo.)   17

At the age of five, six, well past the time when most other children   18
no longer easily notice the difference between sounds uttered at home and words spoken in public, I had a different experience. I lived in a world magically compounded of sounds. I remained a child longer than most; I lingered too long, poised at the edge of language—often frightened by the sounds of *los gringos*, delighted by the sounds of Spanish at home. I shared with my family a language that was startlingly different from that used in the great city around us.

For me there were none of the gradations between public and   19
private society so normal to a maturing child. Outside the house was public society; inside the house was private. Just opening or closing the screen door behind me was an important experience. I'd rarely leave home all alone or without reluctance. Walking down the sidewalk, under the canopy of tall trees, I'd warily notice the—suddenly—silent neighborhood kids who stood warily watching me. Nervously, I'd arrive at the grocery store to hear there the sounds of the *gringo*—foreign to me—reminding me that in this world so big, I was a foreigner. But then I'd return. Walking back toward our house, climbing the steps from the sidewalk, when the front door was open in summer, I'd hear voices beyond the screen door talking in Spanish. For a second or two, I'd stay, linger there, listening. Smiling, I'd hear my mother call out, saying in Spanish (words), "Is that you, Richard?" All the while her sounds would assure me: *You are home now; come closer; inside. With us.*

"*Sí,*" I'd reply.   20

Once more inside the house I would resume (assume) my place in   21
the family. The sounds would dim, grow harder to hear. Once more at home, I would grow less aware of that fact. It required, however, no more than the blurt of the doorbell to alert me to listen to sounds all over again. The house would turn instantly still while my mother went to the door. I'd hear her hard English sounds. I'd wait to hear her voice return to soft-sounding Spanish, which assured me, as surely as did the clicking tongue of the lock of the door, that the stranger was gone.

Plainly, it is not healthy to hear such sounds so often. It is not   22
healthy to distinguish public words from private sounds so easily. I

remained cloistered by sounds, timid and shy in public, too dependent on voices at home. And yet it needs to be emphasized: I was an extremely happy child at home. I remember many nights when my father would come back from work, and I'd hear him call out to my mother in Spanish, sounding relieved. In Spanish, he'd sound light and free notes he never could manage in English. Some nights I'd jump up just at hearing his voice. With *mis hermanos*[3] I would come running into the room where he was with my mother. Our laughing (so deep was the pleasure!) became screaming. Like others who know pain of public alienation, we transformed the knowledge of our public separateness and made it consoling—the reminder of intimacy. Excited, we joined our voices in a celebration of sounds. *We are speaking now the way we never speak out in public. We are alone—together*, voices sounded, surrounded to tell me. Some nights, no one seemed willing to loosen the hold sound had on us. At dinner, we invented new words. (Ours sounded Spanish, but made sense only to us.) We pieced together new words by taking, say, an English verb and giving it Spanish endings. My mother's instructions at bedtime would be lacquered with mock-urgent tones. Or a word like *sí* would become, in several notes, able to convey added measures of feeling. Tongues explored the edges of words, especially the fat vowels. And we happily sounded that military drum roll, the twirling roar of the Spanish *r*. Family language: my family's sounds. The voices of my parents and sisters and brothers. Their voices insisting: *You belong here. We are family members. Related. Special to one another. Listen!* Voices singing and sighing, rising, straining, then surging, teeming with pleasure that burst syllables into fragments of laughter. At times it seemed there was steady quiet only when, from another room, the rustling whispers of my parents faded and I moved closer to sleep.

Meaning

1. What is Rodriguez's main idea about public and private language?
2. What did language apparently represent for the young Rodriguez? In answering, consider both his contrasting perceptions of the sounds of English and of Spanish and his contrasting feelings among *los gringos* and among his family.
3. What explanation does Rodriguez give for why his transition from private to public language took longer than most children's (paragraphs

[3] Spanish: "my siblings"—Rodriguez's brother and sisters. [Editor's note.]

18–19)? Given his characterization of himself as a child (especially in paragraph 10), does his slow transition seem attributable solely to his bilingual environment? Why?

4. If you do not know the meanings of the following words, look them up in a dictionary: intimidated (paragraph 7); counterpoint, consoling (8); polysyllabic (10); guttural, syntax (13); falsetto, feigned, exuberance (14); barrio (15); gradations (19); cloistered, lacquered (22).

Purpose and Audience

1. What seems to be Rodriguez's purpose in this piece? Is he primarily expressing his memories of childhood, explaining something about childhood in a bilingual environment and about childhood in general, or arguing against bilingual education? What passages support your answer?

2. Since he writes in English, Rodriguez is presumably addressing English-speaking readers. Why, then, does he occasionally use Spanish words (such as *gringos*, paragraph 7) without translating them? What do these words contribute to the essay?

Method and Structure

1. Rodriguez's comparison of private and public language includes smaller comparisons between himself and other children (paragraphs 3, 15, 18–19), himself as an adult and a child (11–12), and himself and his parents (13). What does each of these smaller comparisons contribute to Rodriguez's portrayal of himself and to his main idea?

2. Where does Rodriguez shift his focus from public language to private language? Why does he treat private language second? What effect does he achieve with the last paragraph?

3. **Other Methods** Rodriguez uses narrative in paragraphs 3–4, 10, 14, and 22. Do you think the experiences and the feelings Rodriguez either expresses or implies are shared by children in one-language environments? What do these narratives contribute to Rodriguez's main idea?

Language

1. Why does Rodriguez spell out his name to reflect its pronunciation with an American accent (paragraph 4)? What does the contrast between this form of his name and the Spanish form (17) contribute to his comparison?

2. Compare the words Rodriguez uses to describe *los gringos* and their speech (paragraphs 4, 7, 10, 12, 14, 19) with those he uses to describe his family and their speech (paragraphs 7, 8, 13, 14, 16, 21, 22). What does his word choice tell you about his childhood attitudes toward each group of people?
3. Notice the figures of speech Rodriguez uses: for instance, "My words could not stretch far enough to form complete thoughts" (paragraph 13); "a blaring white memory" (14). What do these and other figures convey about Rodriguez's feelings? (If necessary, consult the Glossary under *figures of speech*.)

Writing Topics

1. Rodriguez has said, "What I know about language—the movement between private and public society, the distance between sound and words—is a universal experience." Consider a "private" group you feel a part of—for instance, your family, friends, fellow athletes, people who share the same hobby. How do the language, behaviors, and attitudes of the group distinguish it from "public" society? Write an essay in which you compare your perceptions of and feelings toward the two worlds.
2. Recall any difficulties you have had with language—learning English as a second language, learning any other second language, learning to read, overcoming a speech impediment, improving your writing in freshman composition. Write an essay in which you explain the circumstances and their significance for you.
3. In her essay "She's Your Basic L.O.L. in N.A.D." (p. 93), Perri Klass also deals with mastering a new language—in her case, medical jargon. Write an essay in which you compare Klass's and Rodriguez's feelings about their new languages, using quotations from these essays to support your ideas.
4. Many books and articles have been written on the subject of bilingual education in American schools. Consulting the library's card catalog or a periodical index such as *The New York Times Index* or the *Readers' Guide to Periodical Literature*, locate an article or book that presents a variety of opinions on the issue. Or read what Rodriguez says about it in the rest of *Hunger of Memory*. Then write an essay in which you state and support your opinion on whether children whose first language is not English should be taught in English or in their native language.

Writing Topics

Comparison and Contrast

Choose one of the following topics, or any other topic they suggest, for an essay developed by comparison and contrast. The topic you decide on should be something you care about so that the comparison and contrast is a means of communicating an idea, not an end in itself.

1. Two jobs you have held
2. A place as it is now, and as it was years ago
3. Work and play
4. Talent and skill
5. A tornado and a hurricane
6. Patriotism and nationalism
7. Nature in the city and in the country
8. Two styles of teaching
9. Your relationships with two friends
10. The work of two artists or writers, or two works by the same artist or writer
11. Two religions
12. Humanities courses and science and mathematics courses
13. A passive student and an active student
14. Two or more forms of jazz, classical music, or rock music
15. Movies or television today and when you were a child
16. A newspaper account of an event you witnessed or participated in and your own version of the event
17. A novel and a movie or television series on which it's based
18. Two or more candidates for public office (local, state, national)
19. Two or more forms of exercise
20. A high school or college football, baseball, or basketball game and a professional game in the same sport
21. Two cars
22. Contact lenses and glasses
23. A nightmare and a horror movie
24. Two towns or cities
25. Two or more games
26. The advertisements during two very different television programs, or in two very different magazines

Chapter 8

Analogy

Understanding the Method

The physicist Edward Andrade once explained the motion of molecules in a liquid by comparing it to the motion of couples on an overcrowded dance floor: the couples (and the molecules) move continuously within their tight space and jostle each other as they go. This is an **analogy,** a comparison of two essentially unlike subjects that uses some similarities as the basis for establishing other similarities. Andrade's analogy starts with the packed conditions of both the molecules and the dancers and then draws parallels between their movements and their frequent collisions.

Many analogies, like Andrade's, seek to explain an unfamiliar subject by reference to a familiar subject. In fact, analogy is a favorite technique of natural and social scientists and of philosophers who wish to clarify a subject that is unobservable, complex, or abstract. But analogies can serve another purpose as well: to help convince an audience to accept a conclusion by showing similarities to a conclusion the audience already does accept. For instance, an advocate of nuclear disarmament has argued that the United States and the Soviet Union are like two people holding lighted matches while standing knee-deep in gasoline, each threatening to drop a match if the other does. Obviously, neither person will survive if either drops a match, and the analogy invites the same conclusion for the two countries and their use of nuclear weapons. Though an analogy like this one cannot prove an argument, it can cause the audience to view an issue from a new angle, make that view memorable, and perhaps open minds to subsequent conclusions supported by evidence.

Analogies are closely related to **metaphors**, brief equations between unlike subjects that suggest but do not specify the possible similarities. For example, "Most of us are turtles when confronted with the misery of others" suggests the image of a sluggish animal withdrawing into its hard shell at the slightest disturbance. The writer need not spell out the similarities between the turtle and "most of us"; the suggestion alone is enough to make us examine our own behavior toward those in misery. Metaphors can be a powerful means of description (see Chapter 1, p. 30), in part because of their brevity and suggestiveness. But analogies intended to explain or convince generally do not rely so heavily on readers' imaginations. Instead, the writer extends the comparison to make the similarities explicit. In an argument, where such a comparison can vivify but not prove a point, an analogy may occupy only a paragraph. In explanatory writing, an analogy may take a single paragraph—to help explain a process, say, or to help define a word—or it may structure an entire essay.

Though it involves comparison, analogy differs from comparison and contrast, the method discussed in the previous chapter. Whereas an analogy links subjects in different classes (molecules and dancers), comparison and contrast links subjects in the same class (two molecules or two dancers). Whereas analogy concentrates on similarities, comparison and contrast usually treats both similarities and differences. And whereas analogy focuses on one subject, using the other simply to illuminate the first, comparison and contrast often focuses on both subjects equally.

Analogy *is* comparative, however; thus, like comparison and contrast it requires the use of division or analysis (Chapter 4) to discover what features the two subjects can be said to share. Andrade, in explaining the motion of molecules via the motion of dancers, identified several shared features: limited space, continuous movement, jostling. He further likened the male and female dance partners to the atoms of different elements making up a molecule, and he likened the tight links between partners (he imagined them dancing slowly) to the chemical bonds between atoms. The analogy thus establishes enough similarities to help us visualize the motion and even the composition of the molecules. Yet Andrade does not force parallels between all the elements of a dance and a liquid—stretching to compare, say, the rhythm of the dance music to the electrical pulses of the atoms. Thus he does not strain credibility by extending the comparison beyond necessary or logical bounds.

Nor does Andrade ignore crucial differences between the subjects that would undermine his analogy. Of course, there are many, many differences—and big ones—between molecules and people. There will always be more differences than similarities between the two subjects of an analogy, no matter how sound it is, because the subjects come from different classes. The writer's job is to take the analogy as far as logic permits—that is, to a point just before the differences become more significant to the explanation or argument than the similarities. All analogies have such a breaking point. In fact, some break down before they ever get off the ground because the fundamental differences between subjects make the entire explanation or argument unsound. An example of this so-called **false analogy** is one writer's arguing for a monarchy in the United States on the basis of the strength and efficiency of bee societies, which are centered on a queen bee. The analogy rests on an assumption of similarity between bee society and human society, and there it also falls apart: the animals themselves are not comparable in their drives and motivations, nor are their societies comparable in complexity. In a sound analogy, however, the differences between subjects are irrelevant to the explanation or conclusion, just as the similarities are relevant.

Analyzing Analogy in Paragraphs

Sylvia Ashton-Warner (1908–1984) was a New Zealand novelist, teacher, and writer on education. The paragraph below is from her autobiographical *Spearpoint: "Teacher" in America* (1972).

I like the picture of the mind of our child as a house owned by his soul, inhabited by his instincts, his wants, fears, desires, and loves, his hates and happiness. A merry, motley, moving company, some potential homicides, other pure

Purpose of analogy: to explain child's mind

Main subject: child's mind, with varied ideas and urges

Secondary subject: house with occupants

saints, rubbing shoulders and elbows with one another, all together going for it, like a carnival of celebrants dancing madly. At times, from the pressures within, they venture outside into the street for a breath of fresh air, exercise themselves and encounter others, bring back food and something new to talk about, returning somewhat civilised.

Shared features: need for expression, company, new ideas, refinement

Abraham Lincoln (1809–1865) was not only the sixteenth president of the United States but also a gifted writer and speaker with a remarkable capacity for reasoning with an audience. In the following paragraph he uses analogy in the service of an argument to critics who had complained that the government was allowing the Civil War to drag on too long.

Gentlemen, I want you to suppose a case for a moment. Suppose that all the property you were worth was in gold, and you had put it in the hands of Blondin, the famous rope-walker, to carry across the Niagara Falls on a tight rope. Would you shake the rope while he was passing over it, or keep shouting to him, "Blondin, stop a little more! Go a little faster!"? No. I am sure you would not. You would hold your breath as well as your tongue, and keep your hand off until he was safely over. Now, the Government is in the same situation. It is carrying an immense weight across a stormy ocean. Untold treasures are in its hands. It is doing the best it can. Don't badger it! Just keep still, and it will get you safely over.

Purpose of analogy: to convince audience to let government handle the war

The familiar subject: a famous tightrope walker

The readily accepted conclusion

The main subject

The conclusion to be accepted

Developing an Essay by Analogy

GETTING STARTED

Because they help us visualize the unseen, simplify the complex, and grasp the abstract, analogies can be as enlightening for the writer as for the reader. Whether your analogy comes from a writing assignment, a metaphor you have read, or a likeness you have observed, the process of discovering resemblances will lead you to a fresh understanding of your main subject. Say, for example, that you hear a newscaster refer to the race between Japan and the United States to dominate the world's computer and semiconductor markets. You've heard the metaphor of a race applied to this competition before, but this time it suggests the image of two runners leading the pack in an Olympic marathon. Other associations also follow: the training the athletes have undergone, the physical and mental resources they are drawing on, their awareness of each other. Perhaps the technological race between the United States and Japan could be conceived of as a marathon. Perhaps the efforts of the United States to win the race could be compared to those of a runner to win a marathon. At this point, you are beginning to see the technological competition from an entirely new angle. Try to formulate a thesis that states the basic likeness between the two subjects—for instance, "Like an Olympic marathoner, the United States is expending every effort to win the high-technology race against Japan."

Use your thesis to generate more specific similarities between the subjects. The similarities may suggest themselves in pairs, or you may need to identify the relevant features of one subject before finding the comparable features of the other. In developing the marathon analogy, for instance, you might start with what is required of a winning marathoner, such as training, diet, strategy, and concentration. Then you would seek parallel requirements for the United States in its race, perhaps equating education of the work force with training, use of human and natural resources with diet, shrewd and farsighted management with strategy and concentration. If this matching did not seem to complete the main subject, you would identify the missing features and, working in the opposite direction, find parallels for them in the secondary subject of the marathon. For instance, you might consider government support such as research grants and tax breaks for businesses to be crucial to the country's efforts. Searching for similarly essential support of an Olympic marathoner, you might hit on the backing provided by manufacturers of equipment such as running shoes and clothing.

While you are working back and forth between subjects, think also of your readers' needs and expectations. The secondary subject—the one you are drawing on in order to explain—should be something readers know well or can grasp quickly. They may not be familiar with, say, the training required of a marathoner, but they probably understand that training is required. Thus a detailed sentence or two should be adequate to give them the information they need. The more similarities you can specify between the familiar secondary subject and the less familiar primary subject, the more effective your analogy will be. But don't strain to establish similarities; if they are trivial or exaggerated, readers will soon tire of the analogy. And don't hope that a mere statement of similarities will do all the necessary explaining. You need to gauge readers' knowledge of the primary subject and develop explanations where readers require them. After establishing the similarity between the marathoner's training and the education of the work force, for instance, you might describe the efforts of schools, businesses, and the government to prepare students and workers for careers in high technology.

For readers' sake also, watch for the differences between subjects as well as the similarities. Of course, fundamental differences that are relevant to the thesis may force you to rethink your analogy; but if you don't uncover the weaknesses, your readers will. Less important differences may be ignored as long as their absence will not mislead readers. However, you may want to acknowledge minor differences when they help explain something about your primary subject. For instance, you may worry that readers will view government support of high-technology businesses as a handout. To counter this view, you could mention that the equipment manufacturers backing a marathoner derive some publicity but little more, whereas the government reaps concrete rewards such as higher employment and increased exports.

ORGANIZING

When you have found all the relevant similarities between subjects and have at least considered the differences, you should begin arranging your material. In an introduction you might explain what prompts your analogy, mention what readers stand to gain from it, or provide background information on either or both of the subjects. Ending the introduction with your thesis, though it is not essential to do so, can advise readers of your purpose and help keep you focused on the crucial likenesses while you write.

For brief analogies (say, two paragraphs), the body of the essay may treat the known subject entirely before turning to the unknown, as long as you're careful to mention the same features of each. But because this arrangement burdens readers' memories, it is unsuitable for longer analogies. Instead, cover the pairs of similarities one by one, each time touching first the known subject and then the unknown. The similarities themselves can be arranged in one of several ways. The analogy of a marathon almost demands a chronological organization, starting with training and ending with a projected victory. Other topics might suggest an arrangement from least to most important or dramatic features. Depending on the number and complexity of similarities, you can combine them in paragraphs or devote whole paragraphs to them.

An analogy may end without a formal conclusion if it is brief or if the last pair of similarities emphasizes the point of the analogy. But you may want to focus on the primary subject by itself, summarizing what you have said about it or concluding something about its significance, so that readers see it as a whole.

DRAFTING

Since an analogy uses one subject to explain or support another, the first subject should be depicted as concretely and specifically as possible. Don't assume that because the subject is familiar to readers they will be able to imagine it fully. Give them details to create in their minds the image you hold. In the marathon analogy, for example, you might simply say that a runner eats a lot on the eve of a race. But a description of the runner's carbohydrate-loaded dinner—four large plates of spaghetti, a loaf of bread, several beers—would make that point more vividly. And it would set up an even more detailed explanation of the corresponding point in the analogy: the nation's huge demands on human and natural resources to fuel its high-technology industries.

While you are presenting your points of similarity as vividly as possible, also keep your thesis in mind. Focusing sharply on the features encompassed by the thesis will help you resist the distractions posed by irrelevant characteristics of either subject (persistent distractions, though, may signal a need to revise the thesis). And holding a mental picture of the two subjects as wholes will help you make both of them clear to readers.

REVISING

When you are revising your essay, use these questions to ensure that you have avoided the several pitfalls of analogy.

1. *Have you used an analogy as the sole proof of a debatable conclusion?* An analogy can make readers see a subject anew and etch

an impression in their minds, but it cannot function as the only evidence for a conclusion. It must be bolstered with facts and the opinions of experts presented in a framework of sound reasoning (see Chapter 11 on argument and persuasion).

2. *Have you ignored fundamental differences that weaken the analogy?* Recall the earlier example comparing bee society and U.S. society: the differences between the two are directly relevant to the argument about monarchy, and the analogy is false.

3. *Have you strained the analogy beyond logical bounds?* If you push an analogy too far, it will break down. Concentrate on the reasonable and illuminating similarities between subjects, and stop when those similarities run out.

The essay included here has been reprinted often, cited repeatedly in science textbooks, and mined for its message by environmentalists and others. But of its author, James C. Rettie, nothing is known except that he was a conservationist who was once employed with the National Forest Service in suburban Philadelphia.

"But a Watch in the Night": A Scientific Fable

Rettie wrote this compelling analogy in 1948, drawing on a pamphlet published by the federal government about soil erosion. The quotation in the title comes from the Bible, Psalm 90: For a thousand years in thy sight are but . . . a watch in the night."

Out beyond our solar system there is a planet called Copernicus. It came into existence some four or five billion years before the birth of our Earth. In due course of time it became inhabited by a race of intelligent men. 1

About 750 million years ago the Copernicans had developed the motion picture machine to a point well in advance of the stage that we have reached. Most of the cameras that we now use in motion picture work are geared to take twenty-four pictures per second on a continuous strip of film. When such film is run through a projector, it throws a series of images on the screen and these change with a rapidity that gives the visual impression of normal movement. If a motion is too swift for the human eye to see it in detail, it can be captured and artificially slowed down by means of the slow-motion camera. This one is geared to take many more shots per second—ninety-six or even more than that. When the slow-motion film is projected at the normal speed of twenty-four pictures per second, we can see just how the jumping horse goes over a hurdle. 2

What about motion that is too slow to be seen by the human eye? 3

That problem has been solved by the use of the time-lapse camera. In this one, the shutter is geared to take only one shot per second, or one per minute, or even one per hour—depending upon the kind of movement that is being photographed. When the time-lapse film is projected at the normal speed of twenty-four pictures per second, it is possible to see a bean sprout growing up out of the ground. Time-lapse films are useful in the study of many types of motion too slow to be observed by the unaided, human eye.

The Copernicans, it seems, had time-lapse cameras some 757 million years ago and they also had superpowered telescopes that gave them a clear view of what was happening upon this Earth. They decided to make a film record of the life history of Earth and to make it on the scale of one picture per year. The photography has been in progress during the last 757 million years. **4**

In the near future, a Copernican interstellar expedition will arrive **5** upon our Earth and bring with it a copy of the time-lapse film. Arrangements will be made for showing the entire film in one continuous run. This will begin at midnight of New Year's Eve and continue day and night without a single stop until midnight of December 31. The rate of projection will be twenty-four pictures per second. Time on the screen will thus seem to move at the rate of 24 years per second; 1,440 years per minute; 86,400 years per hour; approximately 2 million years per day; and 62 million years per month. The normal life-span of an individual man will occupy about three seconds. The full period of Earth history that will be unfolded on the screen (some 757 million years) will extend from what the geologists call Pre-Cambrian times up to the present. This will, by no means, cover the full time-span of the Earth's geological history, but it will embrace the period since the advent of living organisms.

During the months of January, February and March the picture **6** will be desolate and dreary. The shape of the land masses and the oceans will bear little or no resemblance to those that we know. The violence of geological erosion will be much in evidence. Rains will pour down on the land and promptly go booming down to the seas. There will be no clear streams anywhere except where the rains fall upon hard rock. Everywhere on the steeper ground the stream channels will be filled with boulders hurled down by rushing waters. Raging torrents and dry stream beds will keep alternating in quick succession. High mountains will seem to melt like so much butter in the sun. The shifting of land into the seas, later to be thrust up as new mountains, will be going on at a grand scale.

Early in April there will be some indication of the presence of single-celled living organisms in some of the warmer and sheltered coastal waters. By the end of the month it will be noticed that some of these organisms have become multicellular. A few of them, including the Trilobites, will be encased in hard shells. 7

Toward the end of May, the first vertebrates will appear, but they will still be aquatic creatures. In June about 60 percent of the land area that we know as North America will be under water. One broad channel will occupy the space where the Rocky Mountains now stand. Great deposits of limestone will be forming under some of the shallower seas. Oil and gas deposits will be in the process of formation—also under shallow seas. On land there will still be no sign of vegetation. Erosion will be rampant, tearing loose particles and chunks of rock and grinding them into sand and silt to be spewed out by streams into bays and estuaries. 8

About the middle of July the first land plants will appear and take up the tremendous job of soil building. Slowly, very slowly, the mat of vegetation will spread, always battling for its life against the power of erosion. Almost foot by foot, the plant life will advance, lacing down with its root structures whatever pulverized rock material it can find. Leaves and stems will be giving added protection against the loss of the soil foothold. The increasing vegetation will pave the way for the land animals that will live upon it. 9

Early in August the seas will be teeming with fish. This will be what geologists call the Devonian Period. Some of the races of these fish will be breathing by means of lung tissue instead of through gill tissues. Before the month is over, some of the lung fish will go ashore and take on a crude lizard-like appearance. Here are the first amphibians. 10

In early September the insects will put in their appearance. Some will look like huge dragon flies and will have a wingspread of 24 inches. Large portions of the land masses will now be covered with heavy vegetation that will include the primitive spore-propagating trees. Layer upon layer of this plant growth will build up, later to appear as the coal deposits. About the middle of this month, there will be evidence of the first seed-bearing plants and the first reptiles. Heretofore, the land animals will have been amphibians that could reproduce their kind only by depositing a soft egg mass in quiet waters. The reptiles will be shown to be freed from the aquatic bond because they can reproduce by means of a shelled egg in which the embryo and its nurturing liquids are sealed in and thus protected from destructive 11 evaporation. Before September is over, the first dinosaurs will be seen—creatures destined to dominate the animal realm for about 140 million years and then to disappear.

In October there will be a series of mountain uplifts along what is   *12* now the eastern coast of the United States. A creature with feathered limbs—half bird and half reptile in appearance—will take itself into the air. Some small and rather unpretentious animals will be seen to bring forth their young in a form that is a miniature replica of the parents and to feed these young on milk secreted by mammary glands in the female parent. The emergence of this mammalian form of animal life will be recognized as one of the great events in geologic time. October will also witness the high water mark of the dinosaurs— creatures ranging in size from that of the modern goat to monsters like Brontosaurus that weighed some 40 tons. Most of them will be placid vegetarians, but a few will be hideous-looking carnivores, like Allosaurus and Tyrannosaurus. Some of the herbivorous dinosaurs will be clad in bony armor for protection against their flesh-eating comrades.

November will bring pictures of a sea extending from the Gulf of   *13* Mexico to the Arctic in space now occupied by the Rocky Mountains. A few of the reptiles will take to the air on bat-like wings. One of these, called Pteranodon, will have a wingspread of 15 feet. There will be a rapid development of the modern flowering plants, modern trees, and modern insects. The dinosaurs will disappear. Toward the end of the month there will be a tremendous land disturbance in which the Rocky Mountains will rise out of the sea to assume a dominating place in the North American landscape.

As the picture runs on into December, it will show the mammals   *14* in command of the animal life. Seed-bearing trees and grasses will have covered most of the land with a heavy mantle of vegetation. Only the areas newly thrust up from the sea will be barren. Most of the streams will be crystal clear. The turmoil of geologic erosion will be confined to localized areas. About December 25 will begin the cutting of the Grand Canyon of the Colorado River. Grinding down through layer after layer of sedimentary strata, this stream will finally expose deposits laid down in Pre-Cambrian times. Thus in the walls of that canyon will appear geological formations dating from recent times to the period when the Earth had no living organisms upon it.

The picture will run on through the latter days of December and   *15* even up to its final day with still no sign of mankind. The spectators will become alarmed in the fear that man has somehow been left out. But not so; sometime about noon on December 31 (one million years ago) will appear a stooped, massive creature of man-like proportions. This will be Pithecanthropus, the Java ape man. For tools and weapons he will have nothing but crude stone and wooden clubs. His children will live a precarious existence threatened on the one side by hostile animals and on the other by tremendous climatic changes. Ice sheets—in places 4000 feet deep—will form in the northern parts of North America and Eurasia. Four times this glacial ice will push southward to cover half the continents. With each advance the plant and animal life will be swept under or pushed southward. With each recession of the ice, life will struggle to reestablish itself in the wake of the retreating glaciers. The wooly mammoth, the musk ox, and the caribou all will fight to maintain themselves near the ice line. Sometimes they will be caught and put into cold storage—skin, flesh, blood, bones and all.

The picture will run on through supper time with still very little *16* evidence of man's presence on the Earth. It will be about 11 o'clock when Neanderthal man appears. Another half hour will go by before the appearance of Cro-Magnon man living in caves and painting crude animal pictures on the walls of his dwelling. Fifteen minutes more will bring Neolithic man, knowing how to chip stone and thus produce sharp cutting edges for spears and tools. In a few minutes more it will appear that man has domesticated the dog, the sheep, and, possibly, other animals. He will then begin the use of milk. He will also learn the arts of basket weaving and the making of pottery and dugout canoes.

The dawn of civilization will not come until about five or six *17* minutes before the end of the picture. The story of the Egyptians, the Babylonians, the Greeks, and the Romans will unroll during the fourth, the third, and the second minute before the end. At 58 minutes and 43 seconds past 11:00 P.M. (just 1 minute and 17 seconds before the end) will come the beginning of the Christian era. Columbus will discover the new world 20 seconds before the end. The Declaration of Independence will be signed just 7 seconds before the final curtain comes down.

In those few moments of geologic time will be the story of all that *18* has happened since we became a nation. And what a story it will be! A human swarm will sweep across the face of the continent and take it away from the primitive red men. They will change it far more radically than it has ever been changed before in a comparable time. The great virgin forests will be seen going down before ax and fire. The soil, covered for aeons by its protective mantle of trees and grasses, will be laid bare to the ravages of water and wind erosion. Streams that had been flowing clear will, once again, take up a load of silt and push it toward the seas. Humus and mineral salts, both vital elements of productive soil, will be seen to vanish at a terrifying rate. The railroads and highways and cities that will spring up may divert attention, but they cannot cover up the blight of man's recent activities. In great sections of Asia, it will be seen that man must utilize cow dung and every scrap of available straw or grass for fuel to cook his food. The forests that once provided wood for this purpose will be gone without a trace. The use of these agricultural wastes for fuel, in place of returning them to the land, will be leading to increasing soil impoverishment. Here and there will be seen a dust storm darkening the landscape over an area a thousand miles across. Man-creatures will be shown counting their wealth in terms of bits of printed paper representing other bits of a scarce but comparatively useless yellow metal that is kept buried in strong vaults. Meanwhile, the soil, the only real wealth that can keep mankind alive on the face of this Earth, is savagely being cut loose from its ancient moorings and washed into the seven seas.

We have just arrived upon this Earth. How long will we stay?   19

Meaning

1. What is the primary subject of Rettie's analogy—the subject he is explaining? What does he compare it to?
2. What is Rettie's main idea? Where is it made clear? How is it partly revealed in paragraph 5?
3. What are the main stages into which Rettie divides the evolution of the earth and its forms of life? What are the principal changes in each of these stages?
4. If you do not know the meanings of the following words, look them up in a dictionary: interstellar, geological, advent (paragraph 5); desolate, erosion (6); vertebrates, aquatic, rampant, estuaries (8); pulverized (9); spore, propagating, embryo (11); unpretentious, placid, carnivores, herbivorous (12); sedimentary (14); precarious, climatic (15); domesticated (16); aeons, impoverishment, moorings (18).

Purpose and Audience

1. Rettie calls his analogy a "fable"—that is, a fictional or mythical narrative that often tells the truth or contains a lesson. What is the lesson in Rettie's fable? Where is it revealed? What does it reveal, in turn, about Rettie's purpose in writing this essay?
2. What other instances of human destruction of the earth could Rettie have mentioned in paragraph 18? Given his purpose, why does he not dwell longer on the human phase of evolution?
3. What does Rettie seem to assume about his readers' knowledge of the earth's evolution and of their place in it? What does he seem to assume about their receptiveness to the lesson of his analogy, given where he places it in the essay?

Method and Structure

1. Why do you think Rettie chose to develop his ideas by analogy instead of by some other method? What about his subject makes analogy an effective method of development?
2. How necessary are paragraphs 2 and 3 for understanding Rettie's analogy? Do you think they make the introduction more or less effective, and why?
3. **Other Methods**   Rettie's analogy is presented in a narrative framework (see Chapter 2). Locate the transitional expressions that signal the passage of time—expressions such as "Early in April" and "By the end of the month" (paragraph 7). Which parts of the year-long film does Rettie condense, and which does he dwell on? Why? Why do you think he translates the film's time into actual time only once, in paragraph 5?

Language

1. What force does Rettie describe in paragraph 6? What effect does he create with words like "booming," "hurled," and "raging"? How do these words contrast with those used to describe the opposing process first mentioned in paragraph 9? How is this contrast reflected in paragraph 18, and how does it relate to Rettie's main idea and purpose?
2. For most of the narrative, Rettie seems to view the film and its audience from a distance (see paragraph 15, for instance). Why, in paragraph 18, does he shift to "we"? What is the effect of this shift?
3. What attitude toward human beings and their activities does Rettie convey in the last two sentences of paragraph 18?

Writing Topics

1. Rettie's analogy explains a nearly unimaginable expanse of time to an adult audience. Write a brief analogy that answers one of the questions a child might ask about time: "How long is it until Christmas?" "How long until we get there?" "How long will I have to stay in the hospital?" Try to use an analogy that a child would understand.

2. Do you agree with Rettie that humans are destroying the earth? Or do you think he overlooks positive contributions that humans have made to the earth? Write an essay in which you agree or disagree with Rettie's point, citing specific examples to support your opinion. How does your response to Rettie lead you to answer the question at the end of the essay?

3. Most religions have scenarios for the origins of the earth and life on earth. If you are familiar with one of these accounts, compare it with Rettie's on a few points, such as the amount of time involved, the order of appearance of various life-forms, or the place of human beings in the scheme of things.

Peter Gardella

Peter Gardella was born in 1951 in Derby, Connecticut, where he also grew up. He graduated from Harvard College (B.A., 1973), Harvard Divinity School (M.T.S., 1975), and Yale University (Ph.D., 1983). After teaching at Miami University of Ohio, Indiana University, and Colgate University, Gardella became an associate professor of religion at Manhattanville College in Purchase, New York. In addition to papers delivered before the American Academy of Religion, Gardella has written Innocent Ecstasy: How Christianity Gave America an Ethic of Sexual Pleasure *(1985), an attempt, he says, to combine theology with a history of popular culture in exploring why Americans feel a moral obligation to enjoy themselves sexually. Gardella is now working on a second book, to be titled* Ending the World: American Dreams of Destiny. *He lives in Hamden, Connecticut.*

The Tao of Baseball

With the following analogy Gardella gives new meaning to the national pastime. Originally titled "Baseball Samadhi" (or "state of naked awareness"), this essay first appeared in 1986 in Touchstone, *the daily newspaper of Manhattanville College, and then was reprinted in* Harper's Magazine *with the title used here.*

Baseball diamonds organize space in much the same way as the basilica of St. Peter at Rome, the altar of heaven at Peking, and the great mosque at Mecca.[1] What happens on a baseball diamond may seem to be only a sport, but the pattern of the field and the rules of the game also form a ritual. 1

To look at a baseball diamond, as millions of Americans do for billions of hours every summer, is to contemplate a mandala: a design that aids meditation by drawing attention from its borders toward its center. Within every baseball diamond is a mound of earth, a circle marking the center of a square, to which the focus of the game returns with every pitch. Like the burial mounds of native Americans, the stupas[2] of Theravadin Buddhists, and the earth altars of Hindus, the pitcher's mound is an especially sacred space. 2

---

[1] These three structures are centers of Roman Catholicism, Confucianism, and Islam, respectively. [Editor's note.]
[2] Dome-shaped shrines. [Editor's note.]

Of course, within the base lines all space is sacred; it is "fair"   3
territory, as opposed to the "foul" territory of spectators and reserves.
There are borders around the playing fields of all sports. But unlike
other fields, and like the great mandalas at Mecca and at Rome, a
baseball diamond organizes the whole world. The foul lines go on
forever, so that a ball hit over the fence, out of the stadium, or 10,000
miles away could still be fair. Every home plate is the center of the
earth, where the quarter of the world that is fair territory meets the
three-quarters of the world that is foul.

As a player moves from home to first base, to second, to third,   4
and then home again, the succession of states of consciousness suggests the life cycle. A player is most alert while batting. At first base
the player accepts congratulations and turns into a base runner, still
with many decisions to make but also at the mercy of the batter. At
second the runner relaxes a bit more and usually gives up any thought
of stealing. On third there is almost no chance of independent action;
the runner stands in foul territory and waits to be brought home. The
journey ends with a return into the earth, down the steps of the
dugout.

Fours and threes, the basic units of religious numerology, also   5
inform the ritual of baseball. As Carl Jung[3] pointed out, threes everywhere stand for abstract perfection: the Trinity of Christians and of
Plato, the nine steps between each of the three levels in the Chinese
altar of heaven. Fours mean completeness, or the material reality of
the world, as in the four elements of ancient science.[4] In baseball,
every number that concerns abstract perfection—the three strikes per
batter and the three outs per inning, the nine defensive players, the
unbroken string of twenty-seven outs over nine innings in a "perfect"
game—is a three or a multiple of three. Only when a fourth is added,
when the player walks on four balls or circles all four bases to score a
run, does anything actually happen.

Adding four to three makes seven, the number of creation. And   6
just as God reached the seventh day and rested, so the baseball fan
stands up and stretches in the seventh inning.

What Martin Buber[5] said of religious ritual is also true of base-   7
ball: the game is not in time, but time is in the game. Whether ten

---

[3] Jung (1875–1961) was a Swiss philosopher and psychiatrist. [Editor's note.]
[4] Earth, air, fire, and water. [Editor's note.]
[5] Buber (1878–1965) was an Austrian-born Jewish scholar and philosopher. [Edi-
tor's note.]

minutes or half an hour has passed has no more relevance to a base-ball game than to a Mass or a wedding. Twenty-seven outs for both teams is the standard length of a game, but there are several ways, in theory, for the game to go on forever: by an excess of batting skill, by perfect pitching, or by perfect balance between the teams. In fact, a player's time at bat can last forever if he keeps on hitting foul balls. No other game is so open to infinity. As Yogi Berra said, "It ain't over till it's over."

Meaning

1. What is Gardella's main idea? How is baseball different from other American sports with regard to this main idea?
2. Concepts of space, time, and numerology are central to rituals. How does baseball, according to Gardella, use these three elements in ritualis-tic ways?
3. Look up the meanings of the word *tao* in a dictionary. How does this word in the title apply to Gardella's essay?
4. If you do not know the meanings of the following words, look them up in a dictionary: basilica, mosque (paragraph 1); numerology (5).

Purpose and Audience

1. Most analogies either explain the unfamiliar by using the familiar or support a conclusion by comparing it to another, accepted conclusion. What do you think is Gardella's purpose?
2. Most of Gardella's audience is probably familiar with only Judeo-Christian religious symbols. Why, then, does Gardella cite Confucianism, Buddhism, Hinduism, and Islam in his analogy? How does mention of these religions support his main idea?
3. Does Gardella's essay convince you that baseball is a ritual as well as a sport? Why, or why not?

Method and Structure

1. Within Gardella's central analogy of baseball and religious ritual are several particular analogies. In paragraph 4, for instance, he equates the trip around the bases and the life cycle. Specify what each base stands for. Why do you think Gardella did not make the comparison explicit?
2. In his first three paragraphs, Gardella concentrates on physical similari-

ties between the baseball diamond and several religious structures. Why do you think he chose this way to begin?

3. **Other Methods**   For his analogy to work effectively, Gardella must also employ division or analysis (Chapter 4). State the elements into which he divides baseball, and explain how those particular divisions serve his main idea.

Language

1. To heighten the sense of baseball as ritual, Gardella uses religious terms and metaphors in describing elements of baseball itself. For example, in paragraph 2 he compares the baseball diamond to a mandala. Cite three or four more examples, and comment on how they influence our perception of the analogy.

2. In this essay Gardella frequently uses large numbers and images of great length or distance. Cite several of these images, and explain how they contribute to Gardella's main idea.

3. Authors often refer to important institutions or people in order to support their ideas. Where in the essay does Gardella use this technique, and for what purpose?

Writing Topics

1. Think of another sport that might be explained by an analogy similar to Gardella's (football and a battle, for example). Compose an essay in which you explain the game in terms of the analogy, making sure that you keep your main idea (that the game is more than just a game) in mind.

2. Look up the origins of baseball in an encyclopedia or history of sports. Find out the reasons behind the design of the field, the number of players, and the sequence of outs and innings. Then write an essay in which you counter Gardella's interpretation with an alternative explanation of why the game is designed the way it is.

3. Using Gardella's essay and one or two of the following essays as examples, write a paper in which you explore the attempt to find deep meaning in everyday events and activities: Schjeldahl's "Cyclone!" (p. 49), White's "Once More to the Lake" (p. 70), Miller's "Getting Dirty" (p. 126), and Greenfield's "The Black and White Truth About Basketball" (p. 206). In your essay, address why these authors (and others) search for deep meaning and whether the search is worthwhile.

Writing Topics

Analogy

Choose one of the following topics, or any other topic they suggest, for an essay developed by analogy. The topic you decide on should be something you care about so that analogy is a means of communicating an idea, not an end in itself.

1. An organization you belong to and a family
2. Variety in friends and variety in diet
3. A particular academic course and a surprise package
4. Taking photographs of people and dissecting those people
5. Reading and traveling
6. Style of dress and personality
7. Drug abuse and physical abuse
8. A family and a system of government
9. A friend or relative and an animal such as a rat, mouse, lion, fly, or cat
10. Living one's life and either driving a car wherever one likes or running a train on fixed tracks
11. Suffering grief or humiliation and suffering a physical wound
12. Writing an essay and cultivating a garden, playing someone in chess, or making something out of modeling clay
13. Learning to play a musical instrument and learning to walk
14. Developing a relationship with someone and reading a biography or autobiography
15. Waiting on tables in a restaurant and running a marathon
16. Making an important but risky decision and gambling money on a sporting event or card game
17. A catalog of college courses and a department store or flea market
18. Becoming disillusioned with a friend and learning the truth about Santa Claus
19. Meeting the parents of a girlfriend or boyfriend and going to the dentist
20. Sunday afternoon and a time warp
21. Learning a computer language and learning a language like French or Spanish

Chapter 9

Definition

Understanding the Method

Definition sets the boundaries of a thing, a concept, an emotion, or a value. In answering "What is it?" and also "What is it *not*?" definition specifies the main qualities of the subject and its essential nature. Since words are only symbols, pinning down their precise meanings is essential for us to understand ourselves and one another. Thus we use definition constantly, whether we are explaining a slang word like *nerd* to someone who has never heard it, explaining to ourselves what *nuclear freeze* means before deciding to support or oppose it, or explaining what *culture* means on an essay examination.

There are several kinds of definition, each with different uses. One is the **formal definition**, usually a statement of the general class of things to which the word belongs, followed by the distinction(s) between it and other members of the class. For example:

	General class	*Distinction(s)*
A submarine is	a seagoing vessel	that operates underwater.
A parable is	a brief, simple story	that illustrates a moral or religious principle.
Pressure is	the force	applied to a given surface.
Insanity is	a mental condition	in which a defendant does not know right from wrong.

A formal definition usually gives a standard dictionary meaning of the word (as in the first two examples) or a specialized meaning agreed to by the members of a profession or discipline (as in the last two examples, from physics and criminal law, respectively). It is most useful to explain the basic meaning of a term that readers need to know in order to understand the rest of a discussion. Occasionally, a writer will also use a formal definition as a springboard to a more elaborate, detailed exploration of a word. For instance, a writer might define *pride* simply as "a sense of self-respect" before probing the varied meanings of the word as people actually understand it and then settling on a fuller and more precise meaning of his or her own devising.

This more detailed definition of *pride* could fall into one of two other types of definition: stipulative and extended. A **stipulative definition** clarifies the particular way a writer is using a word: the writer stipulates, or specifies, a meaning to suit a larger purpose; the definition is part of a larger whole. For example, a writer who wants to show how pride can destroy personal relationships might first stipulate a meaning of *pride* that ties in with that purpose. Though a stipulative definition may sometimes take the form of a brief formal definition, most require several sentences or even paragraphs. In a physics textbook, for instance, the physicist's definition of *pressure* quoted above probably would not suffice to give readers a good sense of the term and eliminate all the other possible meanings they may have in mind.

Whereas a formal or stipulative definition is employed for some larger purpose, an **extended definition** is written for the sake of defining—that is, for the purpose of exploring a thing, quality, or idea in its full complexity and drawing boundaries around it until its meaning is complete and precise. Extended definitions usually treat subjects so complex, vague, or laden with emotions or values that people misunderstand or disagree over their meanings. The subject may be an abstract concept like *patriotism*, a controversial phrase like *beginnings* *of life*, a colloquial or slang expression like *hype*, a thing like *micro-computer*, a scientific idea like *natural selection*, even an everyday expression like *nagging*. Besides defining, the writer's purpose may be to persuade readers to accept a definition (for instance, that life begins at conception, or at birth), to explain (what is natural selection?), or to amuse (nagging as exemplified by great nags).

As the variety of possible subjects and purposes may suggest, the writer of an extended definition draws on whatever methods will best accomplish the goal of specifying what the subject encompasses and distinguishing it from similar things, qualities, or concepts. Several strategies are unique to definition. Using **synonyms**, or words of similar meaning, can convey the range of the word's meanings—for example, equating *misery* with *wretchedness* and *distress*. **Negation**, or saying what a word does not mean, can limit the meaning, particularly when the writer wants to focus on only one sense of an abstract term, such as *pride*, that is open to diverse interpretations. Giving the **etymology** of a word—its history—may illuminate its meaning, perhaps by showing the direction and extent of its change (*pride*, for instance, comes from a Latin word meaning "to be beneficial or useful") or by uncovering buried origins that remain implicit in the modern meaning (*patriotism* comes from the Greek word for "father"; *happy* comes from the Old Norse word for "good luck").

These strategies of definition may be used alone or together, and they may occupy whole paragraphs in an essay-length definition; but they rarely provide enough range to surround the subject completely. To do that, writers often draw on the other methods discussed in this book. One or two methods may predominate: an essay on nagging, for instance, might be developed with brief narratives. Or several methods may be combined: a definition of *patriotism* could compare it with *nationalism*, analyze its effects (such as the actions people take on its behalf), and give examples of patriotic individuals. The goal is not to employ every method in a sort of catalog of methods but to use those which best illuminate the subject. By drawing on the appropriate methods, the writer defines and clarifies his or her perspective on the subject so that the reader understands the meaning exactly.

Analyzing Definition in Paragraphs

Nelson W. Aldrich, Jr. (born 1935), is a magazine editor and a writer of nonfiction. The paragraph below is from his book *Old*

Money: The Mythology of America's Upper Class (1988), a look at American myths about inherited versus earned wealth.

Envy is so integral and so painful a part of what animates behavior in market societies that many people have forgotten the full meaning of the word, simplifying it into one of the synonyms of desire. It is that, which may be why it flourishes in market societies: democracies of desire, they might be called, with money for ballots, stuffing permitted. But envy is more or less than desire. It begins with the almost frantic sense of emptiness inside oneself, as if the pump of one's heart were sucking on air. One has to be blind to perceive the emptiness, of course, but that's just what envy is, a selective blindness. *Invidia*, Latin for envy, translates as "nonsight," and Dante had the envious plodding along under cloaks of lead, their eyes sewn shut with leaden wire. What they are blind to is what they have, God-given and humanly nurtured, in themselves.

The common but incomplete definition of envy as desire—and thus the reason for defining it

The qualities of envy (besides desire):

1. Emptiness (defined with a figure of speech)

2. Selective blindness (defined by etymology and by literary citation: Dante Alighieri [1265–1321] was an Italian poet; Aldrich cites his Divine Comedy*)*

Jan Morris (born 1926) is a Welsh journalist who writes insightfully about history and about the people and places she encounters on her travels around the world. The paragraph below is from "The Know-How City," an essay on Los Angeles in Morris's book *Destinations* (1980).

Los Angeles is the city of Know-How. Remember "know-how"? It was one of those vogue words of the forties and fifties, now rather out of fashion. It reflected a whole climate and tone of American thought in the years of supreme American optimism. It stood for skill and experience indeed, but it also expressed the certainty that America's particular genius, the genius for applied logic, for systems, for devices, was inexorably the herald of progress. As the English had thought in the 1840s, so the Americans thought a century later. They held the future in their hands and brains, and this time it *would* work. Their methods and inventions would usher not only America herself but all mankind into another golden age. Know-

The origins of the word

Its commonly understood general meaning

Its narrower meaning

What the word symbolized for Americans

how would be America's great gift to history:
know-how to rescue the poor from their pov-   ⌐*Examples of what know-*
erty, to snatch the colored peoples from their   *how could achieve*
ignominy, to convince the nations that the
American way of free enterprise was the best
and happiest way of all. Nothing was beyond⌐
know-how. Know-how was, if not actually the
substance of God, at least a direct derivative.

Developing an Essay by Definition

GETTING STARTED

As suggested earlier, a subject for a definition essay can be almost
any expression or idea that is complex and either unfamiliar to readers or open to varied interpretations. It should be something you
know and care enough about to explore in great detail and surround
completely. An idea for a subject may come from an overheard conversation (for instance, a reference to someone as "too patriotic"), a
personal experience (a broken marriage you think attributable to one
spouse's pride), or something you've seen or read (another writer's
definition of *jazz*).

Begin exploring your subject by examining and listing its conventional meanings (consulting an unabridged dictionary may help here,
and the dictionary will also give you synonyms and etymology). Also
examine the differences of opinion about the word's meanings—the
different ways, wrong or right, that you have heard or seen it used.
Run through the other methods to see what fresh approaches to the
subject they open up: How can the subject be described? What are
some examples? Can its functions help define it? Can it be divided
into qualities or characteristics? Will comparing and contrasting it
with something else help sharpen its meaning? Will an analogy make
it more familiar to the reader? Do its causes or effects help clarify its
sense? Some of these questions may turn up nothing; but others may
open your eyes to meanings you had not seen.

When you have generated a good list of ideas about your subject,
settle on the purpose of your definition. Do you mostly want to explain a word that is unfamiliar to readers? Do you want to express
your own view so that readers see a familiar subject from a new
angle? Do you want to argue in favor of a particular definition or

perhaps persuade readers to look more critically at themselves or their surroundings? Work your purpose into a thesis sentence that asserts something about the subject—for example, "Though generally considered entirely positive in meaning, *patriotism* in fact reflects selfish, childish emotions that have no place in a global society."

With your thesis formulated, reevaluate your ideas in light of it and pause to consider the needs of your readers. What do they already know about your subject, and what do they need to be told in order to understand it as you do? For instance, in defining *microcomputer* for readers who know little or nothing about computers of any sort, you would have to begin at an elementary level and keep your definition simple and clear, avoiding unnecessary technical terms and carefully explaining necessary ones. In addition, are your readers likely to be biased for or against your subject? If you were defining *patriotism*, for example, you might assume that your readers see the word as representing a constructive, even essential value that contributes to the strength of the country. If your purpose were to contest this view, as implied by the thesis above, you would have to build your case carefully to win readers to your side.

ORGANIZING

The introduction to a definition essay should provide a base from which to expand and at the same time explain to readers why the forthcoming definition is useful, significant, or necessary. You may want to report the incident that prompted you to define, say why the subject itself is important, or specify the common understandings, or misunderstandings, about its meaning. Several devices can serve as effective beginnings: the etymology of the word; a quotation from another writer supporting or contradicting your definition; or an explanation of what the word does *not* mean (negation). (Try to avoid the overused opening that cites a dictionary: "According to *The American Heritage Dictionary*, _____ means. . . ." Your readers have probably seen this opening many times before.) If it is not implied in the rest of your introduction, you may want to state your thesis so that readers know precisely what your purpose and point are.

The body of the essay should then proceed, paragraph by paragraph, to refine the characteristics or qualities of the subject, using the appropriate methods to distinguish it from anything similar and to provide your perspective. You might draw increasingly tight boundaries around the subject. For instance, in defining *microcomputer* you could start with an analogy between all computers and something more familiar to your readers (an adding machine, say, or the human brain), explain the unique construction and uses of the microcomputer, and finally show how all other kinds of computers are excluded from your definition. Or you might arrange your points in order of increasing drama—illustrating *nagging*, say, by arranging the anecdotes to end with the most telling or humorous example. Or you might begin with your own experience of the subject and then show how you see it operating in your surroundings—say, what actions you see citizens or governments taking in the name of patriotism that demonstrate its harmfulness. As these examples illustrate, an extended definition has no set organization but employs whatever arrangement and combination of methods will most clearly and persuasively specify the subject's meaning.

The conclusion to a definition essay is equally a matter of choice. You might summarize your definition, indicate its superiority to other definitions of the same subject, quote another writer whose view supports your own, or recommend that readers make some use of the information you have provided. The choice depends—as it does in any kind of essay—on your purpose and the impression you want to leave with readers.

DRAFTING

While drafting your extended definition, keep your subject vividly in mind. Say too much rather than too little about it to ensure that you capture its essence; you can always cut when you revise. And be sure to provide plenty of details and examples to support your view. Such evidence is particularly important when, as in the earlier example of patriotism, you seek to change readers' perceptions of your subject.

Concrete, specific language is especially important in definition, for abstractions and generalities cannot draw precise boundaries around a subject. Use words and phrases that appeal directly to the senses and experiences of readers. When appropriate, use figures of speech to make meaning inescapably clear; instead of "Patriotism is childish," for example, write "The blindly patriotic person is like a small child who sees his or her parent as a god, all-knowing, always right." The connotations of words—the associations called up in readers' minds by words like *home, ambitious,* and *generous*—can contribute to your definition as well. But be sure that connotative words trigger associations suited to your purpose. And when you are trying to explain something precisely, rely most heavily on words with generally neutral meanings.

REVISING

When you are satisfied that your draft is complete, revise it against the following questions.

1. *Have you surrounded your subject completely and tightly?* Your definition should not leave gaps, nor should the boundaries be so broadly drawn that the subject overlaps something else. For instance, a definition of *hype* that focused on exaggerated and deliberately misleading claims should include all such claims (some political speeches, say, as well as some advertisements), and it should exclude appeals that do not fit the basic definition (some public-service advertising, for instance).

2. *Does your definition reflect the conventional meanings of the word?* Even if you are providing a fresh slant on your subject, you can't change its meaning entirely or you will confuse your readers and perhaps undermine your own credibility. *Patriotism,* for example, could not be defined from the first as "hatred of foreigners," for that definition strays into an entirely different realm. The conventional meaning of "love of country" would have to serve as the starting point, though your essay might interpret that meaning in an original way.

Judy Syfers was born in 1937 in San Francisco. She attended the University of Iowa and graduated with a bachelor's degree in painting in 1962. Married in 1960, by the mid-1960s she was raising two daughters. She began working in the women's movement in 1969 and through it developed an ongoing concern with political and social issues, especially women's rights. She believes that "as long as women continue to tolerate a society which places profits above the needs of people, we will continue to be exploited as workers and as wives." Besides the essay reprinted here, Syfers has written articles for various magazines, and she is compiling a book about "the politics of cancer," based on her own recent struggle with the disease. Divorced from her husband and with, as she says, "little in the way of saleable skills," she works as a secretary in San Francisco.

I Want a Wife

Writing after eleven years of marriage, and before separating from her hus-band, Syfers here pins down the meaning of the word wife *from the perspec-tive of one person who lives the role. This essay was published in the first issue of* Ms. *magazine in December 1971, and it has since been reprinted widely.*

I belong to that classification of people known as wives. I am A Wife. 1
And, not altogether incidentally, I am a mother.

Not too long ago a male friend of mine appeared on the scene 2
fresh from a recent divorce. He had one child, who is, of course, with
his ex-wife. He is looking for another wife. As I thought about him
while I was ironing one evening, it suddenly occurred to me that I,
too, would like to have a wife. Why do I want a wife?

I would like to go back to school so that I can become economi- 3
cally independent, support myself, and, if need be, support those dependent upon me. I want a wife who will work and send me to school.
And while I am going to school I want a wife to take care of my
children. I want a wife to keep track of the children's doctor and
dentist appointments. And to keep track of mine, too. I want a wife to
make sure my children eat properly and are kept clean. I want a wife
who will wash the children's clothes and keep them mended. I want a

wife who is a good nurturant attendant to my children, who arranges for their schooling, makes sure that they have an adequate social life with their peers, takes them to the park, the zoo, etc. I want a wife who takes care of the children when they are sick, a wife who arranges to be around when the children need special care, because, of course, I cannot miss classes at school. My wife must arrange to lose time at work and not lose the job. It may mean a small cut in my wife's income from time to time, but I guess I can tolerate that. Needless to say, my wife will arrange and pay for the care of the children while my wife is working.

I want a wife who will take care of *my* physical needs. I want a   4
wife who will keep my house clean. A wife who will pick up after my children, a wife who will pick up after me. I want a wife who will keep my clothes clean, ironed, mended, replaced when need be, and who will see to it that my personal things are kept in their proper place so that I can find what I need the minute I need it. I want a wife who cooks the meals, a wife who is a *good* cook. I want a wife who will plan the menus, do the necessary grocery shopping, prepare the meals, serve them pleasantly, and then do the cleaning up while I do my studying. I want a wife who will care for me when I am sick and sympathize with my pain and loss of time from school. I want a wife to go along when our family takes a vacation so that someone can continue to care for me and my children when I need a rest and change of scene.

I want a wife who will not bother me with rambling complaints   5
about a wife's duties. But I want a wife who will listen to me when I feel the need to explain a rather difficult point I have come across in my course of studies. And I want a wife who will type my papers for me when I have written them.

I want a wife who will take care of the details of my social life.   6
When my wife and I are invited out by friends, I want a wife who will take care of the babysitting arrangements. When I meet people at school that I like and want to entertain, I want a wife who will have the house clean, will prepare a special meal, serve it to me and my friends, and not interrupt when I talk about things that interest me and my friends. I want a wife who will have arranged that the children are fed and ready for bed before my guests arrive so that the children do not bother us. I want a wife who takes care of the needs of my guests so that they feel comfortable, who makes sure that they have an ashtray, that they are passed the hors d'oeuvres, that they are offered a second helping of the food, that their wine glasses are re-

plenished when necessary, that their coffee is served to them as they like it. And I want a wife who knows that sometimes I need a night out by myself.

I want a wife who is sensitive to my sexual needs, a wife who 7 makes love passionately and eagerly when I feel like it, a wife who makes sure that I am satisfied. And, of course, I want a wife who will not demand sexual attention when I am not in the mood for it. I want a wife who assumes the complete responsibility for birth control, because I do not want more children. I want a wife who will remain sexually faithful to me so that I do not have to clutter up my intellectual life with jealousies. And I want a wife who understands that *my* sexual needs may entail more than strict adherence to monogamy. I must, after all, be able to relate to people as fully as possible.

If, by chance, I find another person more suitable as a wife than 8 the wife I already have, I want the liberty to replace my present wife with another one. Naturally, I will expect a fresh, new life; my wife will take the children and be solely responsible for them so that I am left free.

When I am through with school and have a job, I want my wife to 9 quit working and remain at home so that my wife can more fully and completely take care of a wife's duties.

My God, who *wouldn't* want a wife?   10

Meaning

1. In a few sentences, summarize Syfers's definition of a wife. Consider not only the functions she mentions but also the relationship she portrays.
2. Syfers provides many instances of a double standard of behavior and responsibility for the wife and the wife's spouse. What are the wife's chief responsibilities and expected behaviors? the spouse's?
3. If you do not know the meanings of the following words, look them up in a dictionary: nurturant (paragraph 3); hors d'oeuvres, replenished (6); adherence, monogamy (7).

Purpose and Audience

1. Why do you think Syfers wrote this essay? Was her purpose to explain a wife's duties, to complain about her own situation, to poke fun at men, to attack men, to attack society's attitudes toward women, or what? Was

she trying to provide a realistic and fair definition of *wife*? What passages in the essay support your answers?

2. What does Syfers seem to assume about her readers' gender (male or female) and their attitudes toward women's roles in society, relations between the sexes, and work inside and outside the home? Does she seem to write from the perspective of a particular age-group or social and economic background? If so, what is her perspective? Does she seem to assume that her readers share it? In answering these questions, cite specific passages from the essay.

3. Whatever her assumptions about her readers, Syfers clearly intended to provoke a reaction from them. What is your reaction to this essay: do you think it is realistic or exaggerated, fair or unfair to men, relevant or irrelevant to the 1990s? Why?

Method and Structure

1. Analyze Syfers's essay as a piece of definition, considering its thoroughness, its specificity, and its effectiveness in distinguishing the subject from anything similar.

2. Analyze the introduction to Syfers's essay. What function does paragraph 1 serve? In what way does paragraph 2 confirm Syfers's definition? How does the question at the end of the introduction relate to the question at the end of the essay?

3. **Other Methods** Syfers develops her definition primarily by classification (see Chapter 5). What does she classify, and what categories does she form? What determines her arrangement of these categories?

Language

1. How would you characterize Syfers's tone: whining, amused, angry, contemptuous, or what? What phrases in the essay support your answer? (If necessary, consult the Glossary for a definition of *tone*.)

2. Why does Syfers repeat "I want a wife" in almost every sentence, often at the beginning of the sentence? What does this stylistic device convey about the person who wants a wife? How does it fit in with Syfers's main idea and purpose?

3. Why does Syfers never substitute the personal pronoun "she" for "my wife"? What, if anything, would the essay lose in meaning or effectiveness if Syfers used the pronoun occasionally? Does the effect gained by repeating "my wife" justify the occasionally awkward sentences, such as the last one in paragraph 3?

4. What effect does Syfers achieve with the expressions "of course" (paragraphs 3, 7), "Needless to say" (3), "after all" (7), and "Naturally" (8)?

Writing Topics

1. Think of a role you now fill—friend, son, daughter, brother, sister, student, secretary, short-order cook—and write an essay defining your role as you see it. You could, if appropriate, also follow Syfers's model by showing how your role makes you essential to the other person or people involved.
2. Combine the methods of definition and comparison (Chapter 7) in an essay that compares a wife or a husband you know with Syfers's definition of either role. Be sure that the point of your comparison is clear and that you use specific examples to illustrate the similarities or differences you see.
3. Pick out any of Syfers's points about the husband-wife relationship that you find especially well taken, exaggerated, offensive, untypical, or dated (remember, the essay was first published in 1971). In an essay, explain your reponse to Syfers's essay using these points as evidence and supplying details and examples from your own experiences, observations, and reading.
4. Write an essay similar to Syfers's, but from the point of view of a wife who enjoys her role, a husband who enjoys his role, or a husband who doesn't enjoy his role. Use a tone appropriate to the point you want to make, and support your point with specific details and examples from your experiences, observations, reading, or imagination.

Gloria Naylor

An American novelist and essayist, Gloria Naylor was born in 1950 in New York City. She served as a missionary for Jehovah's Witnesses from 1967 to 1975 and then worked as a hotel telephone operator until 1981. That year she graduated from Brooklyn College of the City of New York with a B.A. and went on to do graduate work in Afro-American studies at Yale University. Since receiving an M.A. from Yale, Naylor has published three novels dealing with the varied histories and life-styles often lumped together as "the black experience": The Women of Brewster Place *(1982), about the lives of eight black women, which won the American Book Award for fiction and was made into a television movie;* Linden Hills *(1985), about a black middle-class neighborhood; and* Mama Day *(1988), about a Georgian woman with visionary powers. In 1989 Naylor became one of the four judges of the Book-of-the-Month Club.*

The Meanings of a Word

From an experience as a third-grader, Naylor develops an essay that not only defines a word but also explores how words acquire their meanings. The essay first appeared in The New York Times *in 1986.*

Language is the subject. It is the written form with which I've managed to keep the wolf away from the door and, in diaries, to keep my sanity. In spite of this, I consider the written word inferior to the spoken, and much of the frustration experienced by novelists is the awareness that whatever we manage to capture in even the most transcendent passages falls far short of the richness of life. Dialogue achieves its power in the dynamics of a fleeting moment of sight, sound, smell, and touch.

I'm not going to enter the debate here about whether it is language that shapes reality or vice versa. That battle is doomed to be waged whenever we seek intermittent reprieve from the chicken and egg dispute. I will simply take the position that the spoken word, like the written word, amounts to a nonsensical arrangement of sounds or letters without a consensus that assigns "meaning." And building from the meanings of what we hear, we order reality. Words themselves are innocuous; it is the consensus that gives them true power.

I remember the first time I heard the word *nigger*. In my third-   3
grade class, our math tests were being passed down the rows, and as I
handed the papers to a little boy in back of me, I remarked that once
again he had received a much lower mark than I did. He snatched his
test from me and spit out that word. Had he called me a nymphomaniac or a necrophiliac, I couldn't have been more puzzled. I didn't
know what a nigger was, but I knew that whatever it meant, it was
something he shouldn't have called me. This was verified when I
raised my hand, and in a loud voice repeated what he had said and
watched the teacher scold him for using a "bad" word. I was later to
go home and ask the inevitable question that every black parent must
face—"Mommy, what does *nigger* mean?"

And what exactly did it mean? Thinking back, I realize that this   4
could not have been the first time the word was used in my presence. I
was part of a large extended family that had migrated from the rural
South after World War II and formed a close-knit network that gravitated around my maternal grandparents. Their ground-floor apartment in one of the buildings they owned in Harlem was a weekend
mecca for my immediate family, along with countless aunts, uncles,
and cousins who brought along assorted friends. It was a bustling and
open house with assorted neighbors and tenants popping in and out
to exchange bits of gossip, pick up an old quarrel, or referee the
ongoing checkers game in which my grandmother cheated shame-
lessly. They were all there to let down their hair and put up their feet
after a week of labor in the factories, laundries, and shipyards of New
York.

Amid the clamor, which could reach deafening proportions—two   5
or three conversations going on simultaneously, punctuated by the
sound of a baby's crying somewhere in the back rooms or out on the
street—there was still a rigid set of rules about what was said and
how. Older children were sent out of the living room when it was time
to get into the juicy details about "you-know-who" up on the third
floor who had gone and gotten herself "p-r-e-g-n-a-n-t!" But my parents, knowing that I could spell well beyond my years, always demanded that I follow the others out to play. Beyond sexual
misconduct and death, everything else was considered harmless for
our young ears. And so among the anecdotes of the triumphs and
disappointments in the various workings of their lives, the word *nig-*

ger was used in my presence, but it was set within contexts and inflections that caused it to register in my mind as something else.

In the singular, the word was always applied to a man who had distinguished himself in some situation that brought their approval for his strength, intelligence, or drive:

"Did Johnny *really* do that?"

"I'm telling you, that nigger pulled in $6,000 of overtime last year. Said he got enough for a down payment on a house."

When used with a possessive adjective by a woman—"my nigger"—it became a term of endearment for her husband or boyfriend. But it could be more than just a term applied to a man. In their mouths it became the pure essence of manhood—a disembodied force that channeled their past history of struggle and present survival against the odds into a victorious statement of being: "Yeah, that old foreman found out quick enough—you don't mess with a nigger."

In the plural, it became a description of some group within the community that had overstepped the bounds of decency as my family defined it. Parents who neglected their children, a drunken couple who fought in public, people who simply refused to look for work, those with excessively dirty mouths or unkempt households were all "trifling niggers." This particular circle could forgive hard times, unemployment, the occasional bout of depression—they had gone through all of that themselves—but the unforgivable sin was a lack of self-respect.

A woman could never be a "nigger" in the singular, with its connotation of confirming worth. The noun *girl* was its closest equivalent in that sense, but only when used in direct address and regardless of the gender doing the addressing. *Girl* was a token of respect for a woman. The one-syllable word was drawn out to sound like three in recognition of the extra ounce of wit, nerve, or daring that the woman had shown in the situation under discussion.

"G-i-r-l, stop. You mean you said that to his face?"

But if the word was used in a third-person reference or shortened so that it almost snapped out of the mouth, it always involved some element of communal disapproval. And age became an important factor in these exchanges. It was only between individuals of the same generation, or from any older person to a younger (but never the other way around), that *girl* would be considered a compliment.

I don't agree with the argument that use of the word *nigger* at this social stratum of the black community was an internalization of racism. The dynamics were the exact opposite: the people in my grandmother's living room took a word that whites used to signify worthlessness or degradation and rendered it impotent. Gathering there together, they transformed *nigger* to signify the varied and complex human beings they knew themselves to be. If the word was to disappear totally from the mouths of even the most liberal of white society, no one in that room was naive enough to believe it would disappear from white minds. Meeting the word head-on, they proved it had absolutely nothing to do with the way they were determined to live their lives.

So there must have been dozens of times that *nigger* was spoken   15
in front of me before I reached the third grade. But I didn't "hear" it until it was said by a small pair of lips that had already learned it could be a way to humiliate me. That was the word I went home and asked my mother about. And since she knew that I had to grow up in America, she took me in her lap and explained.

Meaning

1. What is Naylor's main idea? Where does she express it?
2. In paragraph 14 Naylor disagrees with those who claim that the black community's use of the term *nigger* constitutes "an internalization of racism." What alternative explanation does she offer? Do you agree with her interpretation? Why, or why not?
3. Naylor says in the opening sentence of paragraph 3, "I remember the first time I heard the word *nigger*." At the beginning of paragraph 15 she says that although the word had been spoken in her presence many times, she didn't "hear" it until her classmate called her that name. What does she mean by this statement? Why had she not "heard" the word before?
4. If you do not know the meanings of the following words, look them up in a dictionary: transcendent, dynamics (paragraph 1); intermittent, consensus, innocuous (2); nymphomaniac, necrophiliac, verified, inevitable (3); gravitated, mecca (4); clamor, anecdotes, inflections (5); disembodied (9); unkempt, trifling (10); communal (13); stratum, internalization, rendered, impotent, naive (14).

Purpose and Audience

1. What is Naylor's purpose or purposes in writing this essay: to express

herself? to explain something? to convince readers of something? Support your answer with passages from the essay.
2. Naylor's essay first appeared in *The New York Times*, a daily newspaper whose readers are largely middle-class whites. In what ways does she seem to consider and address this audience?

Method and Structure

1. Naylor supports her main idea by defining two words, *nigger* and *girl*. What factors influence the various meanings of each word?
2. Naylor's essay is divided into sections, each contributing something different to the whole. Identify the sections and their functions.
3. **Other Methods**   Like many writers of definition, Naylor employs a number of other methods of development: for instance, in paragraphs 4 and 5 she describes the atmosphere of her grandparents' apartment (Chapter 1); in 8, 9, and 12 she cites examples of speech (Chapter 3); and in 11–13 she compares and contrasts the two uses of *girl* (Chapter 7). At two points in the essay Naylor relies on a narrative of the same incident (Chapter 2). Where, and for what purpose?

Language

1. In paragraph 3 Naylor uses language to convey a child's perspective. For example, she seems to become the arrogant little girl who "remarked that once again he had received a much lower mark than I did." Locate three or four other uses of language in the essay that emphasize her separation from the world of adults. How does this perspective contribute to the effect of the essay?
2. In paragraph 14 Naylor concludes that her family used *nigger* "to signify the varied and complex human beings they knew themselves to be." This variety and complexity is demonstrated through the words and expressions she uses to describe life in her grandparents' home—"a weekend mecca," "a bustling and open house" (4). Cite five or six other examples of concrete, vivid language in this description. How does this language support Naylor's conclusion in paragraph 14?
3. Occasionally Naylor uses bits of dialogue to support her definitions. In paragraphs 7–8, for example, she demonstrates the approval that accompanies *nigger* by quoting an anonymous conversation. She does the same thing in paragraphs 9 and 12. Do you think the dialogue interferes with Naylor's definitions? enhances them? Explain your response.

Writing Topics

1. Write an essay analyzing the several ways in which Naylor's family confronted and transformed *nigger* so that it served their purposes. Use quotations from the essay itself as evidence for your interpretations.

2. Choose another word whose meanings vary depending on who says it and when (for example, *marriage, ambition, home, loyalty*). Using Naylor's essay as a model, write an essay exploring the various meanings of the word. If you choose a word with strong meaning for you, you can use personal experience and dialogue, as Naylor did, to support your analysis.

3. In "Marrakech" (p. 359), George Orwell describes the attitudes of whites toward North Africans: "The people have brown faces. . . . Are they really the same flesh as yourself? Do they even have names? Or are they merely a kind of undifferentiated brown stuff, about as individual as bees or coral insects?" Write a two- or three-paragraph essay exploring the perspective of Naylor's white third-grade classmate in light of Orwell's words. Consider such questions as how the boy's use of *nigger* reflects his attitude toward black people in general, what characterizes that attitude, and how his action reflects Orwell's comment.

Flora Lewis

Flora Lewis is one of America's most distinguished writers on international affairs. Born in Los Angeles in the 1920s, she graduated in 1941 from the University of California at Los Angeles (B.A.) and in 1942 from Columbia University (M.S.). Her first job in journalism, in 1941, was as a reporter for The Los Angeles Times. Over the next three decades, Lewis reported for the Associated Press, worked as a free-lance reporter, served as a bureau chief for The Washington Post, and wrote a syndicated column for Newsday. In 1972 she moved to The New York Times as Paris bureau chief, and in 1976 she became European diplomatic correspondent. Since 1980 she has been the paper's foreign affairs columnist, working out of Paris. Lewis has received numerous awards and honorary degrees and has also written several books on international politics, among them One of Our H-Bombs Is Missing *(1967) and* Europe: A Tapestry of Nations *(1987).*

Terrorism

In this column for The New York Times *editorial page, Lewis tries to cut through conflicting opinions about terrorism to arrive at a much-needed definition. The essay first appeared in the March 30, 1986 edition, when Ronald Reagan was president. Some of the international situations Lewis refers to have been resolved; others have not. In any case, the problem of terrorism remains.*

Everybody is talking about terrorism, but not everybody means the same thing. For some time, readers have been writing to ask: "What about American aid to the Nicaraguan contras?" "What about Angola's Savimbi?" "What about the Israelis in southern Lebanon?" "What about Afghanistan," both sides?

There are many forms of violence in the world. I consider all of them deplorable, whether a car bomb in Beirut, a plane or ship hijacking, an enforced psychiatric treatment in the Soviet Union, blowing up a Nicaraguan village, the war between Iran and Iraq.

But different systems of violence require different defenses and countermeasures. A major reason for the feeble international response on dealing with terrorism is the failure to reach a specific definition of what is meant. If the term is blurred to mean political violence from opponents, while violence against opponents constitutes "wars of liberation" or "freedom fighters," then there will never be an effective cooperation front against terrorists.

But it should be possible to be clearer, and so to avoid the distasteful alibis for condoning random murder of uninvolved civilians for political reasons. The issue isn't whether war, civil war, assassination, or shooting up tourists at an airport is more or less disgusting. It is what can be done about these excuses for blind killing.   4

Terrorism is a specific form of political violence and requires a specific response, but that cannot be organized without a specific definition. Obviously international cooperation is necessary. There is evidence enough that terrorist groups with quite different causes do cooperate—Libyan, Irish, Iranian, German, Palestinian, and so on— and cannot be foiled by any nation alone.   5

Cooperation of authorities to prevent terrorism, however, has stumbled on disagreement about just what is involved. There has been a tendency to approach the problem in terms of what is considered a just or an unjust cause. This becomes an insuperable obstacle, dragging officials who profess to be the toughest opponents of terrorists into the quagmire.   6

Thus, when Secretary of State George Shultz advocates "moderate use of force" to capture suspects anywhere in the world to bring to trial in the United States, he is suggesting that America go into the kidnapping business to get even with kidnappers.   7

Any useful definition of terrorism is necessarily arbitrary, making a distinction not on the basis of how heinous the crime or wanton the violence, but on the basis of how it is organized. To call one act warfare, another revolution or counterrevolution, and another terrorism should not establish an order of justification but an order of how to organize a response.   8

If categories could be established more clearly, there would be a much better chance that governments could agree at least on trying to suppress one mindless plague.   9

An appropriate definition for terrorism might be the use of force against parties who are not involved in a conflict, who don't even engage themselves or know they are entering a danger zone, in order to make a political statement. Practically all use of force is intended to frighten and intimidate. The question is how directly or indirectly it is applied. Certainly, it is not how admirable or repellent the cause.   10

The importance of arriving at such a non-polemical definition is 11
that it could bring a big advance toward the kind of international
action that might be more effective.

However much they may plan and indulge in violent acts, most 12
governments oppose the uncontrolled use of force for special purposes. Here is a ground for a general approach against terrorists,
providing that a precise, nonpolitical definition can be developed.

This may seem cynical in a world that risks much more destruc- 13
tive violence from the organized forces of government, but the facts of
a balance of power and political relations impose a restraint that does
not now exist on violence without avowed state responsibility.

There have been hints that the Russians, and maybe even the 14
Syrians, who have been targets of domestic terrorism from Arab enemies, would not be averse to cutting off the international opportunities for gangs they may once have aided but who have become self-
propelled. Defining terrorism is the first step to organizing an
international defense.

Meaning

1. According to Lewis, why is it necessary to devise a definition of terrorism? Where in the essay does she make this point clear? What is her
   definition of terrorism, and where does it appear?
2. In paragraph 8 Lewis asserts, "Any useful definition of terrorism is necessarily arbitrary." Why? What steps does Lewis take in previous paragraphs to prepare for this assertion?
3. In paragraph 13 what distinction does Lewis make between state-
   sponsored violence and what we commonly refer to as terrorism? Why is
   the distinction important to her main point?
4. If you do not know the meanings of the following words, look them up
   in a dictionary: deplorable (paragraph 2); countermeasures, front (3);
   alibis, condoning (4); foiled (5); insuperable, quagmire (6); heinous,
   wanton, counterrevolution (8); suppress (9); intimidate, repellent (10);
   non-polemical (11); cynical, avowed (13); averse (14).

Purpose and Audience

1. Lewis has a serious purpose in defining terrorism. What is it? At what
   point in the essay does her purpose become clear?

2. What does Lewis assume about her audience's attitudes toward terrorism? Does she attempt to appeal to people with different views? Does she
   assume that her audience shares any views? Where in the essay does she
   address the issue of audience attitude?
3. Lewis mentions a number of international situations without explaining
   them—for instance, American aid to the Nicaraguan contras and the
   wars in Angola, Lebanon, and Afghanistan (paragraph 1). Is it necessary
   to understand fully all of her references in order to appreciate her essay?
   How much knowledge do you think is necessary to understand her
   point? Why do you think she mentions so many situations?

Method and Structure

1. Lewis's essay is as much about the *need* for definition as it is a work of
   extended definition. What exactly will definition accomplish, according
   to Lewis?
2. Lewis doesn't raise the problem of definition until paragraph 3. What
   function, then, do the first two paragraphs serve?
3. **Other Methods**   Essential to Lewis's definition is an assumption about
   causes and effects (Chapter 10). Restate her main idea in terms of cause
   and effect—that is, in an "If . . . , then . . ." format. Why, according to
   Lewis, is the cause necessary to achieve the desired effect?

Language

1. How do most of the terms Lewis uses for terrorism differ from those she
   uses for violence? What do these terms reveal about her attitude (at least
   for the purposes of her essay) toward both? Why do you think she tries
   to distinguish between violence itself and the idea of terrorism?
2. How would you characterize Lewis's tone in this essay? What attitude
   does she convey toward her audience? toward governments? toward her
   subject? What methods does she use to establish her tone? (If necessary,
   consult the Glossary for a definition of *tone*.)

Writing Topics

1. Do you agree with Lewis that governments, including our own, "blur"
   the term *terrorism* "to mean political violence from opponents, while
   violence against opponents constitutes 'wars of liberation' or 'freedom
   fighters'" (paragraph 3)? Do you think that some forms of political

violence are justified by the cause being fought for? Write an essay in which you argue for or against Lewis's view, making sure that you respond specifically to her points.

2. Read or reread Scott MacLeod's "The Lost Life of Terry Anderson" (p. 79). Do you think Anderson's captors would consider themselves terrorists, based on Lewis's definition? Write a paragraph in which you explain your response. Focus on each element of her definition, making sure to consider the situation from the captors' point of view.

3. Consider another controversial issue that might be better addressed if the key term were more clearly defined—for example, animal rights, cultural literacy, gun control (or the right to bear arms), free trade, right to life, bilingual education, or mandatory drug testing. Using Lewis's editorial as a model, write an essay in which you state the reasons why a clearer definition is needed, provide and explain the meaning on which you wish to focus, and show how your definition fits the need.

Writing Topics

Definition

Choose one of the following topics, or any other topic they suggest, for an essay developed by definition. The topic you decide on should be something you care about so that definition is a means of communicating an idea, not an end in itself.

1. Freedom
2. Poverty
3. Education
4. The Good Life
5. Ignorance
6. Substance abuse
7. Sophistication
8. Prejudice
9. Spirituality or worldliness
10. Jazz or some other kind of music
11. Nostalgia
12. A nightmare
13. Success or failure
14. A good job
15. Self-sacrifice or selfishness
16. Loyalty or disloyalty
17. A good novel, movie, or television program
18. Impressionist painting or some other school of art
19. A good teacher, coach, parent, or friend
20. Feminism
21. Responsibility
22. A good joke
23. Adulthood
24. Religious faith
25. A good sport
26. Hypocrisy
27. An American ethnic group such as blacks, Italians, Mexicans, Wasps, Japanese, Norwegians, Puerto Ricans, or Chinese
28. A key concept in a course you're taking

Chapter 10

Cause-and-Effect Analysis

Understanding the Method

Why did Israel invade Lebanon in 1982, and what did Israel gain from the invasion? Why has free agency become so important in professional baseball, and how is it affecting the sport? What causes the currents of the Pacific Ocean, and how do they affect the earth's weather? We answer questions like these with **cause-and-effect analysis**, the method of dividing occurrences into their elements to find relationships among them. Cause-and-effect analysis is a specific kind of division or analysis, the method discussed in Chapter 4.

When we analyze **causes**, we discover which of the events preceding a specified outcome actually made it happen: What caused Adolf Hitler's rise in Germany? Why is the nation caught up in a health craze? What caused the rift between a woman and her parents? When we analyze **effects**, we discover which of the events following a specified occurrence actually resulted from it: What do we do for (or to) drug addicts when we imprison them? What happens to our foreign policy when the president's advisers disagree over its conduct? How does the conflict between a woman and her parents affect the other members of the family? These are existing effects of past or current situations, but effects are often predicted for the future: How would a cure for cancer affect the average life expectancy of men and women? How might our Latin American policies affect our relations with the Soviet Union? How will the rift between a woman and her parents affect the woman's children? And causes and effects can also be analyzed together, as the questions opening this chapter illustrate.

Cause-and-effect analysis is found in just about every discipline and occupation, including history, social science, natural science, engineering, medicine, law, business, and sports. In any of these fields, as well as in writing done for college courses, the purpose of the analysis may be to explain or to persuade. In explaining why something happened or what its outcome was or will be, the writer tries to order experience and pin down the connections in it. In arguing with cause-and-effect analysis, the writer may try to demonstrate why one explanation of causes is more accurate than another or how a proposed action will produce desirable or undesirable consequences.

The possibility of arguing about causes and effects points to the main challenge of this method. Related events sometimes overlap, sometimes follow one another immediately, and sometimes connect over gaps in time. They vary in their duration and complexity. They vary in their importance. Thus analyzing causes and effects requires not only identifying them but also discerning their relationships accurately and weighing their significance fairly.

Causes and effects often do occur in a sequence, each contributing to the next in what is called a **causal chain**. For instance, an unlucky man named Jones ends up in prison, and the causal chain leading to his imprisonment can be outlined as follows: Jones's neighbor, Smith, dumped trash on Jones's lawn. In reprisal, Jones set a small brushfire in Smith's yard. A spark from the fire accidentally ignited Smith's house. Jones was prosecuted for the fire and sent to jail. In this chain each event is the cause of an effect, which is turn is the cause of another effect, and so on to the unhappy conclusion.

Identifying a causal chain in related events partly involves distinguishing the **immediate** causes or effects—those occurring nearest an event—from the **remote** causes or effects—those occurring further away in time. For instance, the immediate cause of a town's high unemployment rate may be the closing of a large manufacturing plant where many of the townspeople worked. But the remote cause of the unemployment may be a drastic decline in the company's sales or (more remote) the weak regional or national economy.

Besides sorting events out in time, analyzing causes and effects also requires distinguishing their relative importance in the sequence. Regardless of when they occur, causes and effects may be either **major** or **minor** in relation to one another and to the event or situation being analyzed. The manufacturing plant may have closed not only because a weak economy reduced its sales but also because it could not afford to make necessary repairs to its machines. The weak economy is the *major* cause because it is responsible for poor sales and thus for the lack of funds to make repairs. The lack of funds is a *minor* cause (also called a **contributory** cause) because it merely contributed to the plant shutdown. As these examples illustrate, time and significance can overlap in analyzing causes and effects: the weak economy, for instance, is both a remote and a major cause; the lack of funds for repairs is both an immediate and a minor cause.

Since most cause-and-effect relationships are complex, the writer must take care to avoid several pitfalls in analyzing and presenting them. One is a confusion of coincidence and cause—that is, an assumption that because one event preceded another, it must have caused the other. This error is nicknamed **post hoc**, from the Latin *post hoc, ergo propter hoc*, meaning "after this, therefore because of this." Superstitions often illustrate post hoc: a basketball player believes that a charm once ended his shooting slump, so he now wears the charm whenever he plays. But post hoc also occurs in more serious matters. For instance, the office of a school administrator is vandalized, and he blames the incident on a recent speech by the student-government president criticizing the administration. But the administrator has no grounds for his accusation unless he can prove that the speech incited the vandals. In the absence of proof, the administrator commits the error of post hoc by asserting that the speech caused the vandalism simply because the speech preceded the vandalism.

Another potential problem in cause-and-effect writing is **oversimplification**. In analyzing causes and effects, the writer must consider not just the ones that seem obvious or important but all the possibilities: remote as well as immediate, minor as well as major. One form of oversimplification is confusing a necessary cause with a sufficient cause. As the term implies, a **necessary** cause is one that must happen in order for an effect to come about; an effect can have more than one necessary cause. A **sufficient** cause, in contrast, is one that brings about the effect *by itself*. Suppose a writer has evidence that the high rate of illness in a neighborhood is caused by emissions from a nearby chemical plant. The emissions are thus a *necessary* cause of the illness.

But they are not a *sufficient* cause unless all other possible causes—such as water pollution or infection—can be eliminated. The writer would be oversimplifying if she attributed the illnesses solely to the emissions without examining and eliminating the other possible causes.

Oversimplification can also occur when the writer allows opinions or emotions to cloud the interpretation of evidence. Suppose that a writer is examining the reasons why a gun-control bill he supported was defeated in the state legislature. Some of his evidence strongly suggests that a key member of the legislature, a vocal opponent of the bill, was unduly influenced by lobbyists. But if the writer attributed the defeat of the bill solely to this legislator, he would be exaggerating the significance of a single legislator and he would be ignoring the opinions of the many other legislators who also voted against the bill. To achieve a balanced analysis, the writer would have to put aside his own feelings and consider all possible causes for the defeat of the bill.

Analyzing Causes and Effects in Paragraphs

Ruth Rosen (born 1945) teaches history at the University of California at Davis and writes about feminist issues. The following paragraph comes from her essay "Search for Yesterday," which originally appeared in an anthology of essays, *Watching Television* (1986).

It should not be surprising that all sorts of Americans—not only the bed- and house-ridden—find solace in the mythically stable communities of soap operas. Some soap communities, after all, have lasted over thirty years. All potential viewers are members of a society that has been in constant transformation through geographic mobility and the loss of extended families. Loneliness, we are repeatedly told, has become pandemic in America, and the longing for community is a palpable need. Whether through religion, clubs, associations, or support groups—or through daily immersion in a favorite soap—many Americans search for some kind of communal life to counter varying degrees of social isolation and alienation.

The effect to be examined: the comfort of soap opera communities

The causes: long-lived and stable soap communities . . .

1. . . . contrast with constant change

2. . . . relieve loneliness

3. . . . provide a kind of communal life

Peter Matthiessen (born 1927) is a novelist and an eloquent observer of the natural world. His book *The Tree Where Man Was Born* (1972) provides a human and natural history of East Africa. The following paragraph from the book explains a complex causal sequence begun by elephants, humans, and fires in the Serengeti Plain, a vast East African grassland populated by wildlife and nomadic cattle herders such as the Maasai, whom Matthiessen mentions. The sentence numbers to the right make it possible to trace the causal relationships in the diagram that immediately follows at the top of page 280.

Elephants, with their path-making and tree-splitting propensities, <u>will alter</u> the character of the densest bush in very short order; probably they rank with man and fire as the greatest force for habitat change in Africa. In the Serengeti,	1 *Verb forms (underlined) specify relationships among events*
the herds <u>are destroying</u> many of the taller trees which are thought to have risen at the beginning of the century, in a long period without grass fires that <u>followed</u> plague, famine, and an absence of the Maasai. Dry season fires, often <u>set</u>	2
purposely <u>by</u> poachers and pastoral peoples, <u>encourage</u> grassland by <u>suppressing</u> new woody growth; when <u>accompanied by</u> drought, and <u>fed by</u> a woodland tinder of elephant-killed trees, they <u>do</u> lasting <u>damage</u> to the soil and the whole environment. Fires <u>waste</u> the dry grass that is	3
<u>used</u> by certain animals, and the regrowth <u>exhausts</u> the energy in the grass roots that <u>is needed</u> for good growth in the rainy season. In the Serengeti in recent years, fire and elephants together <u>have converted</u> miles and miles	4
of acacia wood to grassland, and <u>damaged</u> the stands of yellow-bark acacia or fever tree along the water courses. The range of the plains game <u>has</u>	5
<u>increased</u>, but the much less numerous woodland species such as the roan antelope and oribi <u>become</u> ever more difficult to see.	6

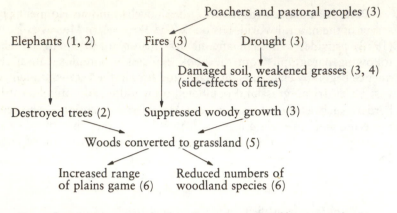

Developing an Essay by Cause-and-Effect Analysis

GETTING STARTED

A subject for cause-and-effect analysis can be just about anything that unfolds over time: ideas, events, conditions; past, present, future. The subject may come from your own experiences, from observations of others, from your course work, or from your reading outside school. Anytime you find yourself wondering what happened or why or what if, you may be onto an appropriate subject. Just remember that your treatment of causes or effects or both must be thorough; thus your subject must be manageable within the constraints of time and space imposed on you. No matter how interesting you find subjects like the causes of the decline in American industrial productivity or the effects of college students' preoccupation with careers, avoid them. These broad subjects would require substantial research and perhaps whole volumes to sort out their complexities. If they interest you, limit them to something you can cover adequately: perhaps the causes of decreasing productivity on one assembly line, or the effects of students' preoccupation with careers on the curriculum at your college.

Whether your subject suggests a focus on causes or effects or both, list as many of them as you can from memory or, if necessary, from further reading. If the subject does not suggest a focus, then ask yourself questions to begin exploring it: Why did it happen? What contributed to it? What were or are its results? What might its consequences be? One or more of these questions should lead you to a focus and, as you explore further, to a more complete list of ideas.

But you cannot stop with a simple list, for you must arrange the causes or effects in sequence and weigh their relative importance: Do the events sort out into a causal chain? Besides the immediate causes and effects, are there also less obvious, more remote ones? Besides the major causes or effects, are there also minor ones? At this stage, you may find that diagraming relationships helps you see them more clearly. The diagram below illustrates the earlier example of the plant closing (see pp. 276–77):

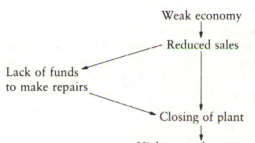

Though uncomplicated, the diagram does sort out the causes and effects and show their relationships and sequence.

While you are developing a clear picture of your subject, you should also be anticipating the expectations and needs of your readers. As with the other methods of essay development, consider especially what your readers already know about your subject and what they need to be told: Do they require background information? Are they likely to be familiar with some of the causes or effects you are analyzing, or should you explain every one completely? Consider as well any bias your readers may have toward your subject or your perspective on it: Which causes or effects might they already accept? Which ones might they disagree with? If, for instance, the plant closing affected many of your readers—putting them or their friends or relatives out of work—they might blame the plant's directors rather than economic forces beyond the directors' control. To convince your readers that the directors were essentially blameless, you would have to address readers' preconceptions and provide plenty of evidence for your own interpretation.

To help manage your ideas and information, develop a thesis that states your subject, your perspective on it, and your purpose. The thesis should reflect your judgments about the relative significance of possible causes or effects. For instance, the thesis for an explanatory essay might read, "Being caught in the middle of a family quarrel has affected not only my feelings about my family but also my relations with friends." For a persuasive essay, the thesis might read, "Contrary to local opinion, the many people put out of work by the closing of Windsor Manufacturing were victims not of the directors' incompetence but of the nation's weak economy."

ORGANIZING

The introduction to a cause-and-effect essay can pull readers in by describing the situation whose causes or effects you plan to analyze, such as the defeat of a bill in the legislature or a town's high unemployment rate. The introduction may also provide background, such as a brief narrative of a family quarrel; or it may summarize the analysis of causes or effects that the essay disputes, such as the townspeople's blaming the directors for a plant's closing. If your thesis is not already apparent in the introduction, stating it explicitly can tell readers exactly what your purpose is and which causes or effects or both you plan to highlight. But if you anticipate that readers will oppose your thesis, you may want to withhold it for the end of the essay, after you have provided the evidence to support it.

The arrangement of the body of the essay depends primarily on your material and your emphasis. If events unfold in a causal chain with each effect becoming the cause of another effect, and if stressing these links coincides with your purpose, then a simple chronological sequence will probably be clearest. But if events overlap and vary in significance, their organization will require more planning. Probably the most effective way to arrange either causes or effects is in order of increasing importance. Such an arrangement helps readers see which causes or effects you consider minor and which major, while it also reserves your most significant (and probably most detailed) point for last. The groups of minor or major events may then fit into a chronological framework. If not, however, they may require a climactic arrangement of their own or some other organization (such as more to less familiar) that suits the material.

To avoid being preoccupied with organization while you are drafting your essay, prepare some sort of outline before you start writing. The outline need not be detailed so long as you have written the details elsewhere or can retrieve them easily from your mind. But it should show all the causes or effects you want to discuss and the order in which you will cover them.

To conclude your essay, you may want to restate your thesis—or state it, if you deliberately withheld it for the end—so that readers are left with the point of your analysis. If your analysis is complex, readers may also benefit from a summary of the relationships you have identified. And depending on your purpose, you may want to specify why your analysis is significant, what use your readers can make of it, or what action you hope they will take.

DRAFTING

While drafting your essay, strive primarily for clarity and specificity. To be clear the essay must be logically organized, but it should also signal the sequence and relative importance of events with transitional expressions such as *for this reason, thus*, or *as a result; first, second*, and *third; at the same time* or *within a year; equally important* or *even more crucial*. These expressions and scores of others like them pinpoint causes or effects, show the steps in a sequence, link events in time and specify their duration, and indicate the weights you have assigned events. Without them, even the most logical organization would be difficult for the reader to follow. (A list of transitional expressions appears in the Glossary under *transitions*.)

Clarity also comes in part from specificity—from sharp details, strong examples, concrete explanations. To make readers see not only *what* you see but also *why* you see it, you can draw on just about any method of writing discussed in this book. For instance, you might narrate the effect of a situation on one person, analyze a process, compare and contrast two interpretations of cause, or draw an analogy between familiar and unfamiliar situations. Particularly if your thesis is debatable (like the earlier example asserting the directors' blamelessness for the plant's closing), you will need accurate, representative facts to back up your interpretation, and you may also need quotations from experts such as witnesses and scholars. If you do not support your assertions specifically, your readers will have no reason to believe them. (For more on evidence in persuasive writing, see p. 312.)

REVISING

While revising your draft, ask yourself the following questions to be sure your analysis is clear and sound.

1. *Have you explained causes or effects clearly and specifically?* Readers will need to see the pattern of causes or effects—their se-

quence and relative importance. And readers will need facts, examples, and other evidence to understand and accept your analysis.

2. *Have you demonstrated that causes are not merely coincidences?* Avoid the error of post hoc, of assuming that one event caused another just because it preceded the other. To be convincing, a claim that one event caused another must be supported with ample evidence.

3. *Have you considered all the possible causes or effects?* Your analysis should go beyond what is most immediate or obvious so that you do not oversimplify the cause-and-effect relationships. Your readers will expect you to present the relationships in all their complexity.

4. *Have you represented the cause-and-effect relationships honestly?* Don't deliberately ignore or exaggerate causes or effects in a misguided effort to strengthen your essay. If a cause fails to support your thesis but still does not invalidate it, mention the cause and explain why you believe it to be unimportant. If a change you are proposing will have bad effects as well as good, mention the bad effects and explain how they are outweighed by the good. As long as your reasoning and evidence are sound, such admissions will not weaken your essay; on the contrary, readers will appreciate your fairness.

K. C. Cole

K. C. Cole is a journalist and essayist who writes mainly about science and women's issues. She was born in 1946 in Detroit, Michigan, and received a B.A. in 1968 from Columbia University. She began her journalism career as a specialist in Eastern European affairs, working as a reporter in Czechoslovakia, Hungary, and the Soviet Union. In the early 1970s, back in the United States, she began writing about science for the Exploratorium, a science museum in San Francisco. She has published several books with the Exploratorium, including Facets of Light: Colors and Images and Things That Glow in the Dark *(1980). Cole has also held editorial and writing posts with* Saturday Review *and* Newsday *and has published articles on education, science, and women in those periodicals and in* The New York Times, Lear's, *and others. Her two most recent books are* Between the Lines *(1982), a collection of her essays on women and women's issues, and* Sympathetic Vibrations: Physics as a Way of Life *(1984), a look at what physics can tell us about ourselves and our world. She has held fellowships to teach science writing at Yale and Wesleyan Universities.*

Women in Science

In this essay Cole joins her primary writing interests—science and women—as she explores why so few women choose science as a career. The essay first appeared in The New York Times *in 1981.*

I know few other women who do what I do. What I do is write about science, mainly physics. And to do that, I spend a lot of time reading about science, talking to scientists, and struggling to understand physics. In fact, most of the women (and men) I know think me quite queer for actually liking physics. "How can you write about that stuff?" they ask, always somewhat askance. "I could never understand that in a million years." Or more simply, "I hate science."

I didn't realize what an odd creature a woman interested in physics was until a few years ago when a science magazine sent me to Johns Hopkins University in Baltimore for a conference on an electrical phenomenon known as the Hall effect. We sat in a huge lecture hall and listened as physicists talked about things engineers didn't understand, and engineers talked about things physicists didn't understand. What *I* didn't understand was why, out of several hundred young students of physics and engineering in the room, less than a handful were women.

Sometime later, I found myself at the California Institute of Technology reporting on the search for the origins of the universe. I interviewed physicist after physicist, man after man. I asked one young administrator why none of the physicists were women. And he answered: "I don't know, but I suppose it must be something innate. My seven-year-old daughter doesn't seem to be much interested in science."

It was with that experience fresh in my mind that I attended a conference in Cambridge, Massachusetts, on science literacy, or rather the worrisome lack of it in this country today. We three women—a science teacher, a young chemist, and myself—sat surrounded by a company of august men. The chemist, I think, first tentatively raised the issue of science illiteracy in women. It seemed like an obvious point. After all, everyone had agreed over and over again that scientific knowledge these days was a key factor in economic power. But as soon as she made the point, it became clear that we women had committed a grievous social error. Our genders were suddenly showing; we had interrupted the serious talk with a subject unforgivably silly.

For the first time, I stopped being puzzled about why there weren't any women in science and began to be angry. Because if science is a search for answers to fundamental questions then it hardly seems frivolous to find out why women are excluded. Never mind the economic consequences.

A lot of the reasons women are excluded are spelled out by the Massachusetts Institute of Technology experimental physicist Vera Kistiakowsky in a recent article in *Physics Today* called "Women in Physics: Unnecessary, Injurious, and Out of Place?" The title was taken from a nineteenth-century essay written in opposition to the appointment of a female mathematician to a professorship at the University of Stockholm. "As decidedly as two and two make four," a woman in mathematics is a "monstrosity," concluded the writer of the essay.

Dr. Kistiakowsky went on to discuss the factors that make women in science today, if not monstrosities, at least oddities. Contrary to much popular opinion, one of those is *not* an innate difference in the scientific ability of boys and girls. But early conditioning does play a stubborn and subtle role. A recent *Nova* program, "The Pinks and the

Blues," documented how girls and boys are treated differently from birth—the boys always encouraged in more physical kinds of play, more active explorations of their environments. Sheila Tobias, in her book, *Math Anxiety*, showed how the games boys play help them to develop an intuitive understanding of speed, motion, and mass.

The main sorting out of the girls from the boys in science seems to happen in junior high school. As a friend who teaches in a science museum said, "By the time we get to electricity, the boys already have had some experience with it. But it's unfamiliar to the girls." Science books draw on boys' experiences. "The examples are all about throwing a baseball at such and such a speed," said my stepdaughter, who barely escaped being a science drop-out. 8

The most obvious reason there are not many more women in science is that women are discriminated against as a class, in promotions, salaries, and hirings, a conclusion reached by a recent analysis by the National Academy of Sciences. 9

Finally, said Dr. Kistiakowsky, women are simply made to feel out of place in science. Her conclusion was supported by a Ford Foundation study by Lynn H. Fox on the problems of women in mathematics. When students were asked to choose among six reasons accounting for girls' lack of interest in math, the girls rated this statement second: "Men do not want girls in the mathematical occupations." 10

A friend of mine remembers winning a Bronxwide mathematics competition in the second grade. Her friends—both boys and girls—warned her that she shouldn't be good at math: "You'll never find a boy who likes you." My friend continued nevertheless to excel in math and science, won many awards during her years at the Bronx High School of Science, and then earned a full scholarship to Harvard. After one year of Harvard science, she decided to major in English. 11

When I asked her why, she mentioned what she called the "macho mores" of science. "It would have been O.K. if I'd had someone to talk to," she said. "But the rules of comportment were such that you never admitted you didn't understand. I later realized that even the boys didn't get everything clearly right away. You had to stick with it until it had time to sink in. But for the boys, there was a payoff in suffering through the hard times, and a kind of punishment—a shame—if they didn't. For the girls it was O.K. not to get it, and the only payoff for sticking it out was that you'd be considered a freak." 12

Science is undeniably hard. Often, it can seem quite boring. It is   13
unfortunately too often presented as laws to be memorized instead of
mysteries to be explored. It is too often kept a secret that science, like
art, takes a well-developed esthetic sense. Women aren't the only ones
who say, "I hate science."

That's why everyone who goes into science needs a little help   14
from friends. For the past ten years, I have been getting more than a
little help from a friend who is a physicist. But my stepdaughter—
who earned the highest grades ever recorded in her California high
school on the math Scholastic Aptitude Test—flunked calculus in her
first year at Harvard. When my friend the physicist heard about it, he
said, "Harvard should be ashamed of itself."

What he meant was that she needed that little extra encourage-   15
ment that makes all the difference. Instead, she got that little extra
discouragement that makes all the difference.

"In the first place, all the math teachers are men," she explained.   16
"In the second place, when I met a boy I liked and told him I was
taking chemistry, he immediately said: 'Oh, you're one of those
science types.' In the third place, it's just a kind of a social thing.
The math clubs are full of boys and you don't feel comfortable join-
ing."

In other words, she was made to feel unnecessary, injurious, and   17
out of place.

A few months ago, I accompanied a male colleague from the   18
science museum where I sometimes work to a lunch of the history of
science faculty at the University of California. I was the only woman
there, and my presence for the most part was obviously and rudely
ignored. I was so surprised and hurt by this that I made an extra effort
to speak knowledgeably and well. At the end of the lunch, one of the
professors turned to me in all seriousness and said: "Well, K.C., what
do the women think of Carl Sagan?" I replied that I had no idea what
"the women" thought about anything. But now I know what I should
have said: I should have told him that his comment was unnecessary,
injurious, and out of place.

Meaning

1. Explain in a sentence what Cole sees as the basic cause of women's not
   entering science. To what extent does this basic cause underlie the specific causes she mentions in the essay? Why do you think she does not
   state this basic cause directly?

2. Why was it a "grievous social error" to ask specifically about science illiteracy among women (paragraph 4)? What male attitudes did this experience make Cole aware of?
3. If you do not know the meaning of the following words, look them up in a dictionary: askance (paragraph 1); phenomenon (2); innate (3); august, grievous (4); frivolous (5); conditioning (7); macho, mores, comportment (12); esthetic (13).

Purpose and Audience

1. What seems to be Cole's primary purpose in this essay: to encourage more women to become scientists? to make men ashamed of their attitudes? to express her anger? to make readers aware of this kind of sexism? Do you think Cole accomplishes her purpose? Why, or why not?
2. Cole admits that "science is undeniably hard" (paragraph 13) and that she spends "a lot of time . . . struggling to understand physics" (1). Why does she admit this difficulty? Do you think her emphasis on the difficulty of science weakens her case? Why, or why not?
3. In the conclusion of the essay, quoting a conversation between herself and a male professor, Cole writes: "I replied that I had no idea what 'the women' thought about anything." What does her response reveal about her ultimate goals? What does her last sentence suggest as a way of reaching these goals?

Method and Structure

1. List the several causes Cole identifies as contributing to the exclusion of women from science. How are these causes arranged by Cole?
2. Cole borrows much of her analysis from Vera Kistiakowsky's article in *Physics Today* (paragraphs 6–10). Which of the points made in this section of the essay are Kistiakowsky's? What does Cole contribute to the analysis? What does she gain by citing Kistiakowsky?
3. **Other Methods** In addition to cause-and-effect analysis, Cole relies mainly on narration (Chapter 2) and example (Chapter 3). Analyze the contributions made to the essay by the narrative passages (paragraphs 2, 3, 4, 11–12, 18) and by the examples of her stepdaughter (8, 14–16) and her friend from the Bronx (11–12).

Language

1. At the conference on science literacy, Cole reports, she became angry about the problem of women in science (paragraph 5). What kind of anger does Cole express through her words and sentence structures:

rage? irritation? bitterness? sarcasm? controlled anger? impatience? something else? How and to what extent did the anger affect your response to the essay?

2. Why did Cole write this essay in the first person, using *I*? How would the essay have differed if she had avoided *I*?

Writing Topics

1. Write a narrative account of your most significant experiences with science and mathematics, in an attempt to discover why you have the attitudes you do about them. To help focus on significant experiences, consider the following questions: Who encouraged or discouraged your study of science? To what extent was science related to the real world in your elementary and high school education? What measures were taken to help students through the hard parts? Was there a science club? If so, who belonged and what kinds of activities did it sponsor? Did you encounter science anywhere besides school—in a museum program, for instance, or at summer camp?

2. Think of ways in which experience with sports could contribute to the study of science. Cole mentions "an intuitive understanding of speed, motion, and mass" (paragraph 7); other contributions might include patience and perseverance, an appreciation for method and technique, or a liking for statistics. Using as many specific examples as you can, develop an essay explaining the positive effect of sports participation on the study of science. Your purpose may be explanatory or persuasive—for instance, you might argue for expanding your school's sports programs for women.

3. Ask the reference librarian at your library to help you find information (statistics and opinions) about the changing role of women in some profession other than science (business or medicine, for example). Write an essay explaining when, how, and to what extent women have participated in that profession; to what extent women have been accepted by men; and what degree of sexual discrimination still remains in the profession. Alternatively, you could explore minority participation in the profession, addressing the same questions about the roles of, say, blacks or Hispanics or Asians.

Margarita Chant Papandreou

An ardent socialist and feminist, Margarita Chant Papandreou is a writer and a political activist. She was born in Oak Park, Illinois, in 1923 and attended the University of Minnesota, earning a B.A. in 1946 and a Master of Public Health degree in 1955. After several years in public relations, Papandreou worked for the U.S. Public Health Service as a roving health educator. From 1951 to 1989 she was married to Andreas Papandreou, a Greek politician who was the prime minister of Greece for most of the 1980s. Margarita Papandreou has written extensively on political issues, including a book, Nightmare in Athens (1970), about the turmoil in Greece in the 1960s and the American role in it. To that period and situation she attributes her "political 'education.'" Papandreou is now the head of World Women Parliamentarians for Peace and president of the Women's Union of Greece.

Causes and Cures
of Anti-Americanism

As someone with strong ties to both the United States and Greece, Papandreou is in a unique position to explain each culture to the other. Here she tells Americans why their country is often unpopular, not only in Greece but in many other countries as well. The essay first appeared in The Nation *in March 1986. The American policies it discusses have not changed substantially.*

One of the questions I am most frequently asked back in the States is, Why is Greece anti-American? The next two questions are, Will Greece get out of NATO? and Will you keep American bases?[1] In feminist circles there are also queries about our progressive measures toward equality for women. I seldom get questions about socialism in Greece, although if I happen to mention that we have a socialist government, the listener turns pale. No one, however, seems to be interested in our conflicts with Turkey, the Cyprus problem, or our peace initiatives.

[1]Greece has threatened to withdraw from NATO (the North Atlantic Treaty Organization) and to shut down American military bases on its territory. [Editor's note.]

The questions regarding Greece's intentions toward the North 2
Atlantic Treaty Organization and the U.S. bases seem to reflect a
keener awareness of national security issues in the States than existed
during the years after World War II. But the one about anti-Americanism comes from the heart; people are pained and puzzled by it.
Some time ago Administration officials talked about launching a public relations program to dispel anti-American attitudes in Europe, a
truly naive idea. There are substantial reasons for such attitudes and
feelings, and unless those reasons are understood and responded to,
no media campaign, no exchange-student program, no cultural or
scientific collaboration, will change them.

Anti-Americanism does not mean hostility toward the American 3
people. Nor does it signify dislike of American culture. Blue jeans,
rock-and-roll, Big Macs, films, and television serials are generally
popular and are the United States' best and most powerful ambassa-
dors. They are opposed nowadays, particularly by fundamentalist societies, as symbols of modernity, corruption, and cultural intervention, but they are not in any way the cause of anti-American attitudes.
Anti-Americanism is most prevalent in the underdeveloped and developing world (not, interestingly enough, in the Eastern bloc countries[2]), where people feel that U.S. economic forces have exploited
them, military forces have tried to control them, and political forces
have supported unpopular, undemocratic establishments.

The Philippines is the most recent example. Washington seems to 4
have supported Ferdinand Marcos[3] because it considered him the
most reliable guarantor of the U.S. military bases there. Although
intelligence reports must have indicated long ago the existence of the
growing nationalist movement and the people's dissatisfaction with
Marcos and his corrupt government, U.S. policy-makers seemed unable to decide on a course that would honor the Filipinos' right to
determine their own destiny and that would dissociate the Administration from the dictator. As a result, public demonstrations during
and after the elections bristled with signs and banners castigating the
United States.

In Greece all the goodwill that the United States built up during 5
the war, and immediately afterward with a massive aid program that

---

[2]The Eastern bloc comprises the countries of Eastern Europe that are aligned with
the Soviet Union, including East Germany, Poland, Hungary, Czechoslovakia, Bulgaria,
and Romania. [Editor's note.]

[3]Until elections in 1986, Marcos (1917–1989) was the president of the Philippines. He was succeeded by the current president, Corazon Aquino. [Editor's note.]

put the economy back on its feet, was slowly dissipated as the nation became more and more dependent on the United States.[4] Washington collaborated first with the Greek monarchy in deciding domestic political matters, then with the rightist government, in 1961, by recognizing fraudulent elections, and finally with the colonels, in 1967, by accepting and eventually strengthening their seven-year dictatorship.

Anti-Americanism reached its peak in 1974, when the dictatorship of the colonels fell; it has diminished considerably since then, as the Pasok government follows a pro-Greek independent foreign policy that is grudgingly accepted by the Reagan Administration. The Greeks watch what the United States does in the rest of the world and draw their own conclusions. During the dictatorial rule in Greece, when the United States was involved in the Vietnam War, a war which pitted a giant industrial military machine against a peasant society, even the colonels found it difficult to give open and enthusiastic support to the American side.

Central Intelligence Agency interventions overseas, support for "friendly" dictators, the overthrow of the Allende government in Chile,[5] Watergate, the efforts to overthrow the Sandinista regime,[6] the nuclear arms buildup—all have served to strengthen the image of the United States as an aggressive, ruthless, and unethical nation. For Americans to understand anti-Americanism they must take off their cultural blinders and see their country as others see it. They must recognize that America's vast military and economic power does not give it the right to interfere in other nations' development or to frustrate their efforts to achieve independence. To the contrary, it antagonizes their people.

---

[4]After World War II (the "war" Papandreou refers to), Greece reverted to a monarchy with a series of conservative governments. In 1967 the political situation grew increasingly unstable, the military took over the government, and the king fled the country. This dictatorship collapsed in 1974, and a republic was proclaimed. Andreas Papandreou became prime minister in the 1981 election of his Panhellenic Socialist Movement (Pasok). His government was defeated in democratic elections in 1989. [Editor's note.]

[5]In 1973 the Marxist government of Salvador Allende was overthrown in Chile, and Allende died. It is widely assumed that the CIA had a hand in the overthrow and perhaps in Allende's death. A repressive military regime replaced the Allende government, but with a national vote in 1988 the country began a transition to elected democracy. [Editor's note.]

[6]The Sandinistas are the current rulers of Nicaragua who assumed power in 1979. The United States supports the Sandinistas' rebel opponents, called contras. [Editor's note.]

This does not mean that millions of people in the world would   8
not want to live in America. The American way of life, insofar as it
applies to those who live in America, continues to be envied. America
still stands for opportunity and individual freedom. It means diversity,
natural beauty, creativity, dynamism, vitality. But that is not the
point, though it may be why Americans are distressed and puzzled
about anti-Americanism. They are so convinced that their society is
unique, just, and good—and this is a conviction that permeates the
consciousness of many who grow up in the United States—that they
fail to understand criticism of their government's international
actions.

The way to fight anti-Americanism is with an enlightened policy   9
of international relations that would seek to break down the global
war system and establish a permanent peace; that would avoid intervention in the affairs of other nations but provide moral support to
popular democratic forces; and that would rein in the military industrial complex,[7] which affects so many things—the trade balance, the
direction of industrial growth, the choice of technology, the rate at
which natural resources are extracted, the status of women, even the
culture, values, and aspirations of people.

These are not unrealistic proposals. One could make the case that   10
they advance "national security interests." They are unworkable only
in that there may not be the kind of leadership in Washington that
wants to pursue them or that the vested interests opposing them are
too deeply entrenched. But given the situation today—a world economic crisis, social unrest and turmoil, and an arms race that is driving the world toward oblivion—these are the only realistic policies.
They will make it possible for the world to see the United States with
new eyes.

Meaning

1. Papandreou characterizes attempts to launch pro-American public relations campaigns as "naive" (paragraph 2). Why does she say this? How
   does this statement lead to her main idea? What does she say is the real
   cause of anti-American feelings abroad?
2. In paragraph 2 Papandreou says that Americans are "pained and puz-

---

[7]The complicated network of the U.S. military establishment and the private industries that conduct much of its research and supply its arms and equipment. [Editor's
note.]

zled" by anti-American attitudes. Why might Americans feel this way? Where in the essay does Papandreou suggest the answer?
3. What does Papandreou think is the "cure" for anti-Americanism? What obstacles does she see to changes in international attitudes?
4. If you do not know the meanings of the following words, look them up in a dictionary: dispel, naive (paragraph 2); fundamentalist, prevalent (3); guarantor, castigating (4); dissipated, fraudulent (5); grudgingly (6); antagonizes (7); permeates (8); aspirations (9); vested, oblivion (10).

Purpose and Audience

1. What does Papandreou seem to want readers to take away from her essay? Where in the essay do you find evidence indicating this intention?
2. Whom does Papandreou seem to be addressing in this essay: Europeans? Americans? government officials? citizens? Where do you find indications of her intended audience? Why do you think she chooses not to address her audience directly?
3. List places in the essay where Papandreou evidently assumes her readers' familiarity with key events in international politics. If she were to miscalculate her audience's knowledge, would the essay's thesis be undermined? Why, or why not?

Method and Structure

1. Papandreou's essay concerns the causes of anti-Americanism throughout the world, but she details the particular situation of Greek-American relations in a causal chain (paragraphs 5–6). List the links in the chain, and explain how the entire sequence supports Papandreou's main point.
2. While Papandreou explains the causes of anti-American feeling, she also projects the effects that U.S. foreign policy could have in the future. What, according to Papandreou, might be the effects of a change in policy? What might be the effects if the policy does not change?
3. **Other Methods**   Much of the evidence Papandreou offers for her cause-and-effect analysis is historical narration (Chapter 2). Locate two extended examples of narration, and explain what each contributes to Papandreou's main idea.

Language

1. In paragraph 7 Papandreou uses a vivid metaphor, calling on Americans to "take off their cultural blinders and see their country as others see it." How does this metaphor work? What are blinders usually used for? How can Americans be said to wear cultural blinders?

2. Although she was born in the United States, Papandreou is obviously sympathetic with the anti-American sentiments of many non-Americans. Cite five or six examples of words whose connotations reflect this bias. (If necessary, consult *connotation and denotation* in the Glossary.)

Writing Topics

1. Think of a pervading sentiment against some group or activity—for example, community fears of heavy-metal rock concerts, public mistrust of used-car salespeople, or mainstream suspicion of religious cults. (Make sure to choose a subject with which you are familiar.) Using Papandreou's essay as a model, write an essay explaining the causes of the sentiment and suggesting possible cures for it. Your essay should make clear whether or not you think the sentiment is valid.

2. Imagine that you are perversely advising the American president on just how to create anti-American sentiment abroad. Recast Papandreou's essay into a step-by-step process analysis (see Chapter 6), a recipe in your own words for generating and sustaining ill will. (You will have to rearrange the elements of Papandreou's essay.)

3. Papandreou presents an image of the United States as supporting "unpopular, undemocratic establishments" (paragraph 3) run by "'friendly' dictators" (7). Consider Joan Didion's "Death in El Salvador" (p. 43) in light of this characterization. (Note that the United States has long supported the Salvadoran government.) Write a brief essay in which you use Didion's descriptions as examples of Papandreou's statements.

4. Papandreou discusses the fall of the Philippine president Ferdinand Marcos in paragraph 4, claiming that the Filipino people had good reason to blame the United States for the abuses of the Marcos regime. Research the Marcos fall in the library, consulting at least three or four newspaper and magazine accounts of the events surrounding the election of Corazon Aquino on February 25, 1986. (Consult *The New York Times Index* and the *Readers' Guide to Periodical Literature*.) Write an essay analyzing the role played by the United States and concluding whether the incident supports Papandreou's argument.

Mark Twain

One of America's best-loved writers, and generally regarded as our greatest humorist, Mark Twain was born Samuel Langhorne Clemens in Florida, Missouri, in 1835. He grew up in Hannibal, Missouri, on the banks of the Mississippi, and left school at the age of twelve. He learned to be a printer, traveled widely in the eastern United States, and in 1857 ended up on the Mississippi again as a steamboat pilot. (His pen name is river pilots' slang for "two fathoms deep.") At the outbreak of the Civil War, Twain volunteered for the Confederacy but left soon after to prospect for gold in the West. When the venture failed, he wrote for newspapers in Nevada and California. Made famous by "The Celebrated Jumping Frog of Calaveras County," a story published in 1865, Twain began delivering the humorous lectures that, as much as his novels, stories, and essays, would make him a folk hero in his time. Twain's best-known books are The Adventures of Tom Sawyer *(1876) and* The Adventures of Huckleberry Finn *(1884); the latter, especially, is unsurpassed in its humor, characterizations, and ear for American speech. Twain also wrote other enduring novels, including* The Prince and the Pauper *(1881) and* A Connecticut Yankee in King Arthur's Court *(1889). And he published several autobiographical works, such as* Life on the Mississippi *(1883), about his years as a river pilot, and* The Innocents Abroad *(1869), an account of his travels through Europe and the Middle East. In his later years, troubled by debts and a sense of personal failure and perhaps most of all by the deaths of two daughters and his wife, Twain developed a pessimistic outlook on life that expressed itself in bitter satire. He died in 1910 at his home in Redding, Connecticut.*

The Turning-Point in My Life

This essay originally appeared in Harper's Bazaar *in 1909, the year before Twain died. The essay amply illustrates the wit and lively colloquial style for which Twain remains famous. But is also reflects the disillusionment of his later years and his corresponding view of human beings, including himself, as victims or beneficiaries of "circumstance." Refusing to identify a single turning point in his life, Twain instead outlines a complex causal chain starting way before he was born.*

If I understand the idea, the *Bazaar* invites several of us to write upon   1
the above text.[1] It means the change in my life's course which introduced what must be regarded by me as the most *important* condition
of my career. But it also implies—without intention, perhaps—that
that turning-point *itself* was the creator of the new condition. This
gives it too much distinction, too much prominence, too much credit.
It is only the *last* link in a very long chain of turning-points commis-
sioned to produce the cardinal result; it is not any more important
than the humblest of its ten thousand predecessors. Each of the ten
thousand did its appointed share, on its appointed date, in forwarding
the scheme, and they were all necessary; to have left out any one of
them would have defeated the scheme and brought about *some other*
result. I know we have a fashion of saying "such and such an event
was the turning-point of my life," but we shouldn't say it. We should
merely grant that its place as *last* link in the chain makes it the most
conspicuous link; in real importance it has no advantage over any one
of its predecessors.

Perhaps the most celebrated turning-point recorded in history   2
was the crossing of the Rubicon.[2] Suetonius says:

> Coming up with his troops on the banks of the Rubicon, he halted
> for a while, and, revolving in his mind the importance of the step he was
> on the point of taking, he turned to those about him and said, "We may
> still retreat; but if we pass this little bridge, nothing is left for us but to
> fight it out in arms."

This was a stupendously important moment. And all the inci-   3
dents, big and little, of Caesar's previous life had been leading up to it,
stage by stage, link by link. This was the *last* link—merely the last
one, and no bigger than the others; but as we gaze back at it through
the inflating mists of our imagination, it looks as big as the orbit of
Neptune.

You, the reader, have a *personal* interest in that link, and so have   4
I; so has the rest of the human race. It was one of the links in your life-
chain, and it was one of the links in mine. We may wait, now with

---

[1] Twain refers to the title of the essay. [Editor's note.]

[2] In 49 B.C. Julius Caesar was in command of the Roman provinces north of
ancient Italy. Though ordered not to march against his political rival Pompey, whom
the Roman senate supported, Caesar defied the order by crossing a small stream, the
Rubicon, into Italy. In doing so, Caesar committed himself to conquer or be conquered,
and "crossing the Rubicon" has since meant taking an irreversible step. Caesar's step
led to his becoming dictator of Rome in 44 B.C. and then to his assassination in the
same year. Suetonius, in the next sentence, was a Roman historian. [Editor's note.]

bated breath, while Caesar reflects. Your fate and mine are involved in his decision.

While he was thus hesitating, the following incident occurred. A person remarked for his noble mien and graceful aspect appeared close at hand, sitting and playing upon a pipe. When not only the shepherds, but a number of soldiers also, flocked to listen to him, and some trumpeters among them, he snatched a trumpet from one of them, ran to the river with it, and, sounding the advance with a piercing blast, crossed to the other side. Upon this, Caesar exclaimed: "Let us go whither the omens of the gods and the iniquity of our enemies call us. *The die is cast*." 5

So he crossed—and changed the future of the whole human race, for all time. But that stranger was a link in Caesar's life-chain, too; and a necessary one. We don't know his name, we never hear of him again; he was very casual; he acts like an accident; but he was no accident, he was there by compulsion of *his* life-chain, to blow the electrifying blast that was to make up Caesar's mind for him, and thence go piping down the aisles of history forever. 6

If the stranger hadn't been there! But he *was*. And Caesar crossed. With such results! Such vast events—each a link in the *human* race's life-chain; each event producing the next one, and that one the next one, and so on: the destruction of the republic; the founding of the empire; the breaking up of the empire; the rise of Christianity upon its ruins; the spread of the religion to other lands—and so on; link by link took its appointed place at its appointed time, the discovery of America being one of them; our Revolution another; the inflow of English and other immigrants another; their drift westward (my ancestors among them) another; the settlement of certain of them in Missouri, which resulted in *me*. For I was one of the unavoidable results of the crossing of the Rubicon. If the stranger, with his trumpet blast, had stayed away (which he *couldn't*, for he was an appointed link) Caesar would not have crossed. What would have happened, in that case, we can never guess. We only know that the things that did happen would not have happened. They might have been replaced by equally prodigious things, of course, but their nature and results are beyond our guessing. But the matter that interests me personally is that I would not be *here* now, but somewhere else; and probably black—there is no telling. Very well, I am glad he crossed. And very really and thankfully glad, too, though I never cared anything about it before. 7

To me, the most important feature of my life is its literary feature. I have been professionally literary something more than forty years. 8

There have been many turning-points in my life, but the one that was the last link in the chain appointed to conduct me to the literary guild is the most *conspicuous* link in that chain. *Because* it was the last one. It was not any more important than its predecessors. All the other links have an inconspicuous look, except the crossing of the Rubicon; but as factors in making me literary they are all of the one size, the crossing of the Rubicon included.

I know how I came to be literary, and I will tell the steps that led   9
up to it and brought it about.

The crossing of the Rubicon was not the first one, it was hardly   10
even a recent one; I should have to go back ages before Caesar's day to find the first one. To save space I will go back only a couple of generations and start with an incident of my boyhood. When I was twelve and a half years old, my father died. It was in the spring. The summer came, and brought with it an epidemic of measles. For a time, a child died almost every day. The village was paralyzed with fright, distress, despair. Children that were not smitten with the disease were imprisoned in their homes to save them from the infection. In the homes there were no cheerful faces, there was no music, there was no singing but of solemn hymns, no voice but of prayer, no romping was allowed, no noise, no laughter, the family moved spectrally about on tiptoe, in a ghostly hush. I was a prisoner. My soul was steeped in this awful dreariness—and in fear. At some time or other every day and every night a sudden shiver shook me to the marrow, and I said to myself, "There, I've got it! and I shall die." Life on these miserable terms was not worth living, and at last I made up my mind to get the disease and have it over, one way or the other. I escaped from the house and went to the house of a neighbor where a playmate of mine was very ill with the malady. When the chance offered I crept into his room and got into bed with him. I was discovered by his mother and sent back into captivity. But I had the disease; they could not take that from me. I came near to dying. The whole village was interested, and anxious, and sent for news of me every day; and not only once a day, but several times. Everybody believed I would die; but on the four-teenth day a change came for the worse and they were disappointed.

This was a turning-point of my life. (Link number one.) For when   11
I got well my mother closed my school career and apprenticed me to a printer. She was tired of trying to keep me out of mischief, and the adventure of the measles decided her to put me into more masterful hands than hers.

I became a printer, and began to add one link after another to the   12
chain which was to lead me into the literary profession. A long road,

but I could not know that; and as I did not know what its goal was, or even that it had one, I was indifferent. Also contented.

A young printer wanders around a good deal, seeking and finding   13
work; and seeking again, when necessity commands. N.B.[3] Necessity is a *Circumstance;* Circumstance is man's master—and when Circumstance commands, he must obey; he may argue the matter—that is his privilege, just as it is the honorable privilege of a falling body to argue with the attraction of gravitation—but it won't do any good, he must *obey*. I wandered for ten years, under the guidance and dictatorship of Circumstance, and finally arrived in a city of Iowa, where I worked several months. Among the books that interested me in those days was one about the Amazon. The traveler told an alluring tale of his long voyage up the great river from Para to the sources of the Madeira, through the heart of an enchanted land, a land wastefully rich in tropical wonders, a romantic land where all the birds and flowers and animals were of the museum varieties, and where the alligator and the crocodile and the monkey seemed as much at home as if they were in the Zoo. Also, he told an astonishing tale about *coca*, a vegetable product of miraculous powers, asserting that it was so nourishing and so strength-giving that the native of the mountains of the Madeira region would tramp up hill and down all day on a pinch of powdered coca and require no other sustenance.[4]

I was fired with a longing to ascend the Amazon. Also with a   14
longing to open up a trade in coca with all the world. During months I dreamed that dream, and tried to contrive ways to get to Para and spring that splendid enterprise upon an unsuspecting planet. But all in vain. A person may *plan* as much as he wants to, but nothing of consequence is likely to come of it until the magician *Circumstance* steps in and takes the matter off his hands. At last Circumstance came to my help. It was in this way. Circumstance, to help or hurt another man, made him lose a fifty-dollar bill in the street; and to help or hurt me, made me find it. I advertised the find, and left for the Amazon the same day. This was another turning-point, another link.

Could Circumstance have ordered another dweller in that town   15
to go to the Amazon and open up a world-trade in coca on a fifty-dollar basis and been obeyed? No, I was the only one. There were other fools there—shoals and shoals of them—but they were not of my kind. I was the only one of my kind.

Circumstance is powerful, but it cannot work alone; it has to   16

---

[3] Abbreviation for the Latin *nota bene*, meaning "note well." [Editor's note.]
[4] The leaves of the coca tree contain the narcotic cocaine. [Editor's note.]

have a partner. Its partner is man's *temperament*—his natural disposition. His temperament is not his invention, it is *born* in him, and he has no authority over it, neither is he responsible for its acts. He cannot change it, nothing can change it, nothing can modify it—except temporarily. But it won't stay modified. It is permanent, like the color of the man's eyes and the shape of his ears. Blue eyes are gray in certain unusual lights; but they resume their natural color when that stress is removed.

A Circumstance that will coerce one man will have no effect upon   17
a man of a different temperament. If Circumstance had thrown the bank-note in Caesar's way, his temperament would not have made him start for the Amazon. His temperament would have compelled him to do something with the money, but not that. It might have made him advertise the note—and *wait*. We can't tell. Also, it might have made him go to New York and buy into the Government, with results that would leave Tweed[5] nothing to learn when it came his turn.

Very well, Circumstance furnished the capital, and my tempera-   18
ment told me what to do with it. Sometimes a temperament is an ass. When that is the case the owner of it is an ass, too, and is going to remain one. Training, experience, association, can temporarily so polish him, improve him, exalt him that people will think he is a mule, but they will be mistaken. Artificially he *is* a mule, for the time being, but at bottom he is an ass yet, and will remain one.

By temperament I was the kind of person that *does* things. Does   19
them, and reflects afterward. So I started for the Amazon without reflecting and without asking any questions. That was more than fifty years ago. In all that time my temperament has not changed, by even a shade. I have been punished many and many a time, and bitterly, for doing things and reflecting afterward, but these tortures have been of no value to me: I still do the thing commanded by Circumstance and Temperament, and reflect afterward. Always violently. When I am reflecting, on those occasions, even deaf persons can hear me think.

I went by the way of Cincinati, and down the Ohio and Missis-   20
sippi. My idea was to take ship, at New Orleans, for Para. In New Orleans I inquired, and found there was no ship leaving for Para.

---

[5] William Marcy Tweed (1823–1878), nicknamed Boss Tweed, was a New York City politician who made a fortune defrauding the city and eventually died in jail. [Editor's note.]

Also, that there never had *been* one leaving for Para. I reflected. A policeman came and asked me what I was doing, and I told him. He made me move on, and said if he caught me reflecting in the public street again he would run me in.

After a few days I was out of money. Then Circumstance arrived, 21 with another turning-point of my life—a new link. On my way down, I had made the acquaintance of a pilot. I begged him to teach me the river, and he consented. I became a pilot.

By and by Circumstance came again—introducing the Civil War, 22 this time, in order to push me ahead another stage or two toward the literary profession. The boats stopped running, my livelihood was gone.

Circumstance came to the rescue with a new turning-point and a 23 fresh link. My brother was appointed secretary to the new Territory of Nevada, and he invited me to go with him and help in his office. I accepted.

In Nevada, Circumstance furnished me the silver fever and I went 24 into the mines to make a fortune, as I supposed; but that was not the idea. The idea was to advance me another step toward literature. For amusement I scribbled things for the Virginia City *Enterprise*. One isn't a printer ten years without setting up acres of good and bad literature, and learning—unconsciously at first, consciously later—to discriminate between the two, within his mental limitations; and meantime he is unconsciously acquiring what is called a "style." One of my efforts attracted attention, and the *Enterprise* sent for me and put me on its staff.

And so I became a journalist—another link. By and by Circum- 25 stance and the Sacramento *Union* sent me to the Sandwich Islands for five or six months, to write up sugar. I did it; and threw in a good deal of extraneous matter that hadn't anything to do with sugar. But it was this extraneous matter that helped me to another link.

It made me notorious, and San Francisco invited me to lecture. 26 Which I did. And profitably. I had long had a desire to travel and see the world, and now Circumstance had most kindly and unexpectedly hurled me upon the platform and furnished me the means. So I joined the "Quaker City Excursion."

When I returned to America, Circumstance was waiting on the 27 pier—with the *last* link—the conspicuous, the consummating, the victorious link: I was asked to *write a book*, and I did it, and called it *The Innocents Abroad*. Thus I became at last a member of the literary guild. That was forty-two years ago, and I have been a member ever since. Leaving the Rubicon incident away back where it belongs, I can say with truth that the reason I am in the literary profession is because I had the measles when I was twelve years old.

Meaning

1. Briefly, what is the main idea of Twain's essay? Consider not only his introductory paragraph but also the points he makes later about circumstance and temperament.
2. What is the significance to Twain's essay of Caesar's crossing the Rubicon (paragraphs 2–7)? Why does Twain embellish the incident (5–6)?
3. Twain focuses on his bout with measles as the personal beginning of his writing career (paragraph 10). Given his theory of circumstances, could Twain just as well have chosen any other incident in his life? If not, why? If so, why does he focus on this particular episode?
4. Summarize Twain's views of circumstance (starting in paragraph 13) and of temperament (starting in 16). How do circumstance and temperament relate to Twain's main idea? How are they compatible with his view of linked causes?
5. If you do not know the meanings of the following words, look them up in the dictionary: cardinal (paragraph 1); mien, iniquity (5); prodigious (7); predecessors (8); smitten, spectrally (10); apprenticed (11); alluring (13); shoals (15); coerce (17); extraneous (25); notorious (26); consummating (27).

Purpose and Audience

1. How does the first paragraph reveal that Twain's purpose is not simply to explain how he became a writer but to convince his readers to accept an idea?
2. What passages in the essay do you find humorous? Why does Twain use humor: to indicate that he does not take his main idea seriously, to indicate that he does not take himself seriously, to make his messages easier for readers to digest and accept, or simply to amuse readers? Explain your answer.
3. How convincing do you find Twain's essay? Does his embellishment of the tale of Caesar (paragraphs 5–6) strengthen or weaken the essay, and why? Does his recounting of events in his own life (10–15, 18–27) demonstrate the roles of circumstance and temperament—at least in his life—to your satisfaction? Why, or why not?

Method and Structure

1. Twain identifies a causal chain, with each effect becoming the cause of another effect. Outline or diagram the causal chain that led to Twain's becoming a writer, starting with the epidemic of measles (paragraph 10). At what points does circumstance intervene? At what points does temperament intervene?

2. **Other Methods** Twain uses many other methods to develop his cause-and-effect analysis. Locate at least one instance each of description, narration, example, process analysis, comparison and contrast, analogy, and definition. How does each use of another method contribute to Twain's analysis?

Language

1. What do the following features of Twain's essay convey about his attitudes toward his subject and toward himself: italic type (as in paragraph 1); "should" (1), "must" (13), and similar words; the combination of formal and informal expressions and sentence structures such as "A person remarked for his noble mien and graceful aspect appeared close at hand . . . " (5) and "at last I made up my mind to get the disease and have it over, one way or the other" (10); and exaggeration, such as "When I am reflecting, . . . even deaf persons can hear me think" (19). How would you characterize the overall tone of the essay? (If necessary, see *tone* in the Glossary.)

2. Twain uses figures of speech to make his ideas clear: for instance, "as we gaze back at it through the inflating mists of our imagination, it looks as big as the orbit of Neptune" (paragraph 3). Locate four or five other figures and explain their meaning in the context of Twain's essay. (If necessary, see *figures of speech* in the Glossary.)

3. Twain says, "Circumstance, to help or hurt another man, made him lose a fifty-dollar bill in the street; and to help or hurt me, made me find it" (paragraph 14). Look at the verbs and other words used by Twain to explain the workings and effects of circumstance in his own life. Do those words indicate that Twain views circumstance primarily as a helpful or a hurtful force in his life?

Writing Topics

1. Think of an event or a sequence of events in your own life that has significantly affected what you do, how you feel about yourself, or how

you relate to others. In an essay, analyze the causes and effects of the event or the sequence. Be sure to clarify precisely why it was significant: how is your life different because of it?

2. Twain's essay expresses the philosophy of determinism—the belief that circumstances or existing conditions control human actions and decisions. Opposed to determinism is a belief in free will, in the power of human beings to make free choices independent of circumstances or necessity. Think of an important incident in your life when circumstances determined what happened or, alternatively, when your conscious choices—your will—shaped events. Write a narrative essay about the incident, selecting events and explaining them so as to express and support your own view of determinism versus free will.

Writing Topics

Cause-and-Effect Analysis

Choose one of the following questions, or any other question they suggest, and answer it in an essay developed by analyzing causes or effects. The question you decide on should concern a topic you care about so that your analysis of causes or effects is a means of communicating an idea, not an end in itself.

1. Why does the United States spend so much money on defense?
2. What are the possible effects of rising college tuition costs?
3. Why are educated citizens important in a democracy?
4. Why do teenagers like rock music?
5. Why have art museums become so popular?
6. What makes a professional sports team succeed in a new city?
7. Why is (or was) a particular television show or movie so popular?
8. Why does the United States support El Salvador?
9. Why is a past or present politician, athlete, or actor considered a hero?
10. Why is writing difficult?
11. How can a long period of involuntary unemployment affect a person?
12. At what age should a person start working for pay, and why?
13. What causes eating disturbances such as anorexia nervosa or bulimia?
14. How has a professional sports team been affected by the free-agent system?
15. Why is a college education important?
16. Why do marriages among teenagers fail more often than marriages among people in other age groups?
17. Why do people root for the underdog?
18. How does a person's alcohol or drug dependency affect others in his or her family?
19. Why do Americans buy so many foreign cars?
20. How does rock music shape the attitudes of its fans?
21. What are the possible effects of widespread adult illiteracy on American society?

Chapter 11

Argument and Persuasion

Understanding the Method

Since we argue all the time—with relatives, with friends, with the auto mechanic or the shop clerk—a chapter devoted to argument and persuasion may at first seem unnecessary. But arguing with an auto mechanic over the cost of repairs is quite a different process from arguing with readers over a complex issue. In both cases we are trying to get our audience to change views and even to act as we wish. But the mechanic is in front of us; we can shift our tactics in response to his or her gestures, expressions, and words. The reader, in contrast, is "out there"; we have to anticipate those gestures, expressions, and words in the way we structure the argument, the kinds of evidence we use to support it, even the way we conceive of the subject.

A great many assertions that are worth making are debatable at some level—whether over the facts on which the assertion is based or over the values it implies. Two witnesses to an accident cannot agree on what they saw; two scientists cannot agree on what an experiment shows; two economists cannot agree on what measures will reduce unemployment; two doctors cannot agree on what constitutes life or death. Making an effective case for our opinions requires upholding certain responsibilities and attending to several established techniques of argumentation, most of them dating back to ancient Greece.

Technically, argument and persuasion are two different processes. **Argument** appeals mainly to an audience's sense of reason in order to win agreement with a claim; it is the method of a columnist who defends a president's foreign policy on the grounds of economics and defense strategy. **Persuasion**, in contrast, appeals mainly to an audience's feelings and values in order to compel some action, or at least support for an action; it is the method of a mayoral candidate who urges voters to support her because she is sensitive to the poor. In fact, however, argument and persuasion so often mingle that we will use the one term *argument* to mean a deliberate appeal to an audience's reason and emotions in order to win agreement or compel action.

Depending on his or her purpose, the writer of an argument may draw on classification, comparison, or any other rhetorical method to develop the entire essay or to introduce evidence or strengthen a conclusion. For instance, in a paper arguing for raising a college's standards of admission, the writer might contrast the existing standards with the proposed standards, analyze a process for raising the standards over a period of years, and predict the effects of the new standards on future students' preparedness for college work.

In such an essay, the writer would also employ the elements that all arguments share. The first of these is an **assertion** or **proposition**, often expressed up front in a thesis statement, that makes a debatable claim about the subject. The thesis may defend or attack a position, suggest a solution to a problem, recommend a change in policy, or challenge a value or belief. Here are a few examples:

> The college should give first priority for on-campus jobs to students who need financial aid.

> School prayer has been rightly declared unconstitutional and should not be reinstituted in any form.

> Smokers who wish to poison themselves should be allowed to do so, but not in any place where their smoke will poison others.

Of course, a mere assertion cannot convince. Thus an argument is broken down into subclaims, and each of these is supported by evidence. Significant opposing arguments are also raised and dispensed with, again with the support of evidence. All elements of the argument are woven into a clear, tight structure that pushes steadily toward the conclusion.

Most arguments combine three kinds of appeals to readers: ethical, emotional, and rational. The **ethical appeal** is often not explicit in an argument, yet it pervades the whole. It is the sense of the writer's expertise and character projected by the reasonableness of the argument, by the use and quality of evidence, and by tone. A reasonable argument and strong evidence convey the writer's knowledge, credibility, and fairness; they will be discussed further below. Tone conveys the writer's attitudes toward the subject and toward the audience through choice of words and sentence structures. How readers perceive the writer's balance and goodwill can be crucial to the success of an argument. Thus a sincere tone is generally more effective than a flippant one, respectfulness is more effective than arrogance, and calmness is more effective than shrillness.

The **emotional appeal** in argument aims directly for readers' hearts—for the complex of beliefs, values, and feelings deeply embedded in all of us. We are just as often motivated by these ingrained ideas and emotions as by our intellects. Even scientists, who stress the rational interpretation of facts above all else, are sometimes influenced in their interpretations by emotions deriving from, say, competition with other scientists. And the willingness of a nation's citizens to go to war may result more from their fear and pride than from their reasoned considerations of risks and gains. An emotional appeal in argument attempts to tap such feelings in order to heighten the responsiveness of readers, inspire them to new beliefs, compel them to act, or simply assure them that their values remain unchallenged. For instance, a writer arguing against capital punishment might appeal to readers' religious values by citing the Bible's Sixth Commandment, "Thou shalt not kill." Or a writer arguing that people should arrange to have their organs donated after death might appeal to readers' compassion by offering examples of patients whose lives are in jeopardy for lack of donated organs. An emotional appeal can also be less obvious than these examples suggest, because individual words may have connotations that elicit emotional responses from readers. For instance, one writer may characterize an environmental group as "a well-organized team representing diverse interests," while another may call the same group "a hodgepodge of nature lovers and irresponsible businesspeople." The first appeals to readers' preference for order and balance, the second to readers' fear of extremism and disdain for unsound business practices.

The use of emotional appeals requires care. To appeal to an audience's beliefs and feelings, the writer obviously must know something about them. A misdirected appeal, based on incorrect assumptions about readers' emotions, is one of the surest ways to weaken an argument. But even when the appeal is properly directed, it can miss the mark if it is presented so passionately that readers must doubt the writer's fairness in the rest of the argument. In addition, an appeal must be appropriate to the subject and to the argument. In arguing against a pay raise for city councilors, a writer might appeal to readers' resentment and distrust of wealthy people by pointing out that two of the councilors are rich enough to work for nothing. But such an appeal would divert attention from the issue of whether the pay raise is justified for all councilors on the basis of the work they do and the city's ability to pay the extra cost.

Carefully used, emotional appeals can have great force, particularly when they contribute to an argument based largely on sound reasoning and evidence. The appropriate mix of emotion and reason in a given essay is entirely dependent on the subject, the writer's purpose, and the audience. Emotional appeals are out of place in most arguments in the natural and social sciences, where rational interpretations of factual evidence are all that will convince readers of the truth of an assertion. But emotional appeals may be essential when a writer wants an audience to support or take an action, for emotion is a stronger motivator than reason.

Rational appeals have been saved for last because their form and substance are most complicated. A **rational appeal** is one that, as the name implies, addresses the rational faculties of readers—their capacity to reason logically about a problem. The writer establishes the truth of a proposition or claim by moving through a series of related subclaims, each supported by evidence. In doing so, he or she follows processes of reasoning that are natural to all of us and thus are expected by readers. These processes are induction and deduction.

Inductive reasoning moves from the particular to the general, from evidence to a generalization or conclusion about the evidence. It is a process we begin learning in infancy and use daily throughout our lives: a child burns herself the three times she touches a stove, so she concludes that stoves burn; we have liked four movies produced by George Lucas, so we form the generalization that George Lucas makes good movies. Inductive reasoning is also very common in argument: a writer offers facts showing that chronic patients in the state's mental hospitals receive only drugs as treatment, and then she concludes that the state's hospitals rely exclusively on drugs to treat chronic patients.

The movement from particular to general is called an **inductive leap** because the arguer must make something of a jump to conclude that what is true of some instances (the chronic patients whose records were available) is also true of all other instances in the class (the rest of the chronic patients). In the ideal world we could perhaps avoid the inductive leap by pinning down every conceivable instance, but in the real world such thoroughness is usually impractical and often impossible. Instead, we gather enough evidence to make our generalizations probable.

The evidence for induction may be facts—statistics or other hard data that are verifiable or, failing that, attested to by reliable sources (for instance, the number of drug doses per chronic patient and the absence of any other kind of treatment, derived from hospital records). Or the evidence may be the opinions of recognized experts on the subject, opinions that are themselves conclusions based on research and observation (for instance, the testimony of an experienced hospital doctor or of an authority on mental health care in the state). Sometimes examples or analogies may also aid induction; but they can only illustrate or illuminate a conclusion, not support an inductive leap. (See Chapter 3 on example and Chapter 8 on analogy, especially p. 231 on false analogy.)

Since induction does involve a leap from specific to general, an inductive conclusion is only as sound as its evidence. Sometimes writers leap to conclusions on the basis of inadequate or unrepresentative data. These so-called **hasty generalizations** are responsible for many of our worst stereotypes: handicapped people are mentally retarded; blacks are good dancers; Italians are volatile. And sometimes writers commit **oversimplification**, ignoring inconsistencies or complexities in their data that, if heeded, would weaken the conclusion or suggest an entirely different one. The more evidence a writer has and the more cautious the leap from it to a conclusion, the sounder that conclusion will be.

A sound inductive conclusion can form the basis for the second reasoning process, **deductive reasoning.** Working from the general to the particular, the writer starts with such a conclusion and applies it to a new situation in order to draw a conclusion about that situation. Like induction, deduction is a process we use constantly to order our experience. The child who learns from three experiences that all stoves burn then sees a new stove and concludes that this stove also will burn. The child's thought process can be written in the form of a **syllogism**, a three-step outline of deductive reasoning:

> All stoves burn me.
> This is a stove.
> Therefore, this stove will burn me.

The first statement, the generalization derived from induction, is called the **major premise**. The second statement, a more specific assertion about some element of the major premise, is called the **minor premise**. And the third statement, an assertion of the logical connection between premises, is called the **conclusion**. The following syllogism takes the earlier example about mental hospitals one step further:

> The state hospitals' treatment of chronic patients relies exclusively on drugs. (The major premise, a generalization based on evidence.)
>
> Drugs do not cure chronic patients. (The minor premise, a more specific generalization, based on a different set of evidence, about one element of the major premise.)
>
> Therefore, the state hospitals' treatment of chronic patients will not cure them. (The conclusion, a logical connection between premises.)

Unlike an inductive conclusion, which requires a leap, the deductive conclusion derives necessarily from the premises: as long as the reasoning process is valid and the premises are accepted as true, then the conclusion must also be true. To be valid, the reasoning must conform to the process outlined above. The following syllogism is *not* valid, even though the premises are true:

> All radicals want to change the system.
> Georgia Allport wants to change the system.
> Therefore, Georgia Allport is a radical.

The flaw in this syllogism is that not *only* radicals want to change the system, so Allport does not *necessarily* fall within the class of radicals just because she wants to change the system. The conclusion, then, is invalid.

A syllogism can be valid without being true if either of the premises is untrue. For example:

> All people who want political change are radicals.
> Georgia Allport wants political change.
> Therefore, Georgia Allport is a radical.

The conclusion here is valid because Allport falls within the class of people who want political change. But the conclusion is untrue because the major premise is untrue. As commonly defined, a radical seeks extreme change, often by revolutionary means. But other forms and means of change are also possible; Allport, for instance, may be interested in improving the delivery of services to the poor and in achieving passage of tougher environmental-protection laws—both political changes, to be sure, but neither radical.

In arguments, syllogisms are rarely spelled out as neatly as in these examples. Sometimes the order of the statements is reversed, as in this sentence paraphrasing a 1983 Supreme Court decision: "The state may not imprison a man just because he is too poor to pay a fine; the only justification for imprisonment is certain danger to society, and poverty does not constitute certain danger." The buried syllogism can be stated thus: The state may imprison only those who are a certain danger to society (major premise); a man who is too poor to pay a fine is not a certain danger to society (minor premise); therefore, the state cannot imprison a man just because he is too poor to pay a fine (conclusion). And often one of the premises or even the conclusion is implied but not expressed. Each of the following sentences omits one part of the same syllogism: "All five students cheated, so they should be expelled" (implied major premise: cheaters should be expelled); "Cheaters should be punished by expulsion, so all five students should be expelled" (implied minor premise: all five students cheated); "Cheaters should be punished by expulsion, and all five students cheated" (implied conclusion: all five students should be expelled).

Partly because the statements of a syllogism can be reversed or omitted entirely, deductive reasoning requires special attention to the truth of the premises and the validity of the conclusion derived from those premises. Several logical fallacies—that is, failures in reasoning—present special traps for the careless. One is **begging the question**: assuming a conclusion in the statement of a premise, and thus begging readers to accept the conclusion—the question—before it is proved. For example, "We can trust the president not to neglect the needy, because he is a compassionate man" asserts in a circular fashion that the president is not uncompassionate because he is compassionate. He may indeed be compassionate, but this is the question that needs addressing.

Another fallacy is **ignoring the question**, introducing an issue or consideration that shifts the argument away from the real issue. Offering an emotional appeal as a premise in a logical argument is a form of ignoring the question. The following sentence, for instance, appeals to pity, not to logic: "The mayor was badly used by people he loved and trusted, so we should not blame him for the corruption in his administration." And writers also ignore the question when they attack the opponents instead of the opponents' arguments—for example, "O'Brien is married to a convict, so her proposals for prison reform should not be taken seriously." This argument is called **ad hominem,** Latin for "to the man."

A third fallacy is **either-or,** requiring that readers choose between two interpretations or actions when in fact the choices are more numerous: "Either we imprison all drug users, or we will become a nation of addicts." Though there may be some correlation between imprisoning drug users and reducing drug addiction, the factors contributing to drug addiction, and the choices for dealing with it, are obviously more complex than this statement suggests. Not all either-or arguments are invalid, for sometimes the alternatives encompass all the possibilities. But when they do not, the argument is false.

Another logical fallacy is the **non sequitur,** Latin for "it does not follow." The non sequitur is a conclusion derived illogically or erroneously from stated or implied premises. For instance, the sentence "Young children are too immature to engage in sex, so they should not be taught about it" implies one of two meanings, both of them illogical: only the sexually active can learn anything about sex, or teaching young children about sex will cause them to engage in it. Akin to the non sequitur is the **post hoc** fallacy, discussed in the previous chapter on cause-and-effect analysis (see p. 277). A post hoc conclusion assumes that because one thing preceded another, it must have caused the other—for example, "After the town banned smoking in closed public places, the incidence of vandalism went up." Many things may have caused the rise in vandalism, including improved weather and a climbing unemployment rate. It does not follow that the ban on smoking, and that alone, caused the rise.

Analyzing Argument and Persuasion in Paragraphs

Bruno Bettelheim (born 1903) is a noted child psychologist and the author of many important books in his field. He came to the United States from his native Austria in 1939, after a year's imprisonment in concentration camps run by the German Nazis. The following paragraph appears in "The Holocaust—One Generation After," an essay in Bettelheim's *Surviving and Other Essays* (1979) that looks back on the mass murder of Jews committed by the Nazis during

World War II. The argument of the paragraph is deductive, based on a syllogism. Despite the highly emotional topic, the appeal of the argument is almost wholly ethical and rational.

By calling the victims of the Nazis "martyrs," we falsify their fate. The true meaning of "martyr" is: "one who voluntarily undergoes the penalty of death for refusing to renounce his faith" (*Oxford English Dictionary*). The Nazis made sure that nobody could mistakenly think that their victims were murdered for their religious beliefs. Renouncing their faith would have saved none of them. Those who had converted to Christianity were gassed, as were those who were atheists, and those who were deeply religious Jews. They did not die for any conviction, and certainly not out of choice.

The assertion of the argument and the conclusion of the syllogism: it is inaccurate to call the Nazis' victims "martyrs"

Major premise: martyrs die voluntarily for refusing to renounce faith

Minor premise: the Nazis' victims did not die for religion or voluntarily

David Bruck (born 1949) is an attorney specializing in the representation of persons facing death sentences. The following paragraph comes from one of his many writings against capital punishment, "The Death Penalty," originally published in *The New Republic* in May 1985. (The data given were current as of that time.) The argument is inductive, based on examples. The appeal is largely ethical and rational.

The death penalty states are also learning that the death penalty is easier to advocate than it is to administer. In Florida, where executions have become almost routine, the governor reports that nearly a third of his time is spent reviewing the clemency requests of condemned prisoners. The Florida Supreme Court is hopelessly backlogged with death cases. Some have taken five years to decide, and the rest of the Court's work waits in line behind the death appeals. Florida's death row currently holds more than 230 prisoners. State officials are reportedly considering building a special "death prison" devoted entirely to the isolation and electrocution of the condemned. The state is also considering the creation of a special public defender unit that will do nothing else but handle death penalty appeals. The death penalty, in short, is spawning death agencies.

The generalization: the death penalty burdens resources

Evidence: in Florida the death penalty . . .

. . . takes the governor's time

. . . clogs the court

. . . overloads the prisons

. . . taxes the public defender system

Developing an Argumentative and Persuasive Essay

GETTING STARTED

You probably have at least one subject for an argumentative essay already: a behavior or policy that irks you, an opinion you want to defend, a change you would like to see implemented, a way to solve a problem. The subject should be something you know about from your own experience or observations, from class discussions, or from reading, though you may want to do further research as well. It should be limited to a topic you can treat thoroughly in the space and time available to you—for instance, the quality of computer instruction at your school rather than in the whole nation. And it should be something you feel strongly about so that you can make a convincing case. However, it's best to avoid subjects that you cannot view with some objectivity, seeing the opposite side as well as your own; otherwise, you may not be open to flaws in your argument, and you may not be able to represent the opposition fairly.

With your subject in hand, you should develop your thesis, for it will influence the rest of the writing process. Make the thesis as clear and specific as possible. Don't resort to a vague generality ("Computer instruction is important") or to a nondebatable statement of fact ("The school's investment in computer instruction is less than the average investment of the nation's colleges and universities"). Instead, state the precise opinion you want readers to accept or the precise action you want them to take or support: perhaps "Money designated for investment in dormitories and athletic facilities should be diverted to constructing computer facilities and hiring a first-rate computer faculty." Since the thesis is essentially a conclusion from evidence, you may have to do some preliminary reading to be sure the evidence exists. This step is especially important with an issue like welfare cheating or tax advantages for the wealthy that we all tend to have opinions about whether we know the facts or not. But don't feel you have to prove your thesis at this early stage; fixing it too firmly may make you unwilling to reshape it if further evidence, your audience, or the structure of your argument so demands.

Once you have framed a tentative thesis, the next step is to begin gathering evidence in earnest. You should consult as broad a range of sources as necessary to uncover the facts and opinions supporting not only your view but also any opposing views. Though it may be tempting to ignore your opposition in the hope that readers know nothing of it, it is dishonest and probably futile to do so. Acknowledging and, whenever possible, refuting significant opposing views will enhance your credibility with readers. If you find that some counterarguments damage your own argument too greatly, then you will have to revise your thesis or abandon it entirely.

Where to seek evidence depends on the nature of your thesis. For a thesis derived from your own experiences and observations, such as a recommendation that all students work part-time for the education if not for the money, gathering evidence will be primarily a matter of searching your own thoughts and perhaps consulting others to uncover opposing views. Some arguments derived from personal experience can also be strengthened by the judicious use of facts and opinions from other sources; an essay arguing in favor of vegetarianism, for instance, could mix the benefits you have felt with those demonstrated by scientific data. Of course, the evidence of other sources becomes increasingly crucial the further removed the subject is from your realm and the more controversial it is. Though you might strongly favor or oppose a massive federal investment in solar-energy research, your opinions would count little if they were not supported with facts and the opinions of experts.

As you generate or collect evidence, it should suggest the reasons that will support the claim of your thesis—essentially the minor arguments that bolster the main argument. In an essay favoring federal investment in solar-energy research, for instance, the minor arguments might include the need for solar power, the feasibility of its widespread use, and its cost and safety compared with the cost and safety of other energy sources. It is in developing these minor arguments that you are most likely to use induction and deduction consciously—generalizing from specifics or applying generalizations to new information. Thus the minor arguments provide the entry points for your evidence, and together they should encompass all the relevant evidence you find.

As we have already seen, knowledge of readers' needs and expectations is absolutely crucial in argumentation. In explanatory writing, detail and clarity alone may accomplish your purpose; but you cannot hope to move readers in a certain direction unless you have some idea of where they stand. You need a sense of their background in your subject, of course. But even more, you need a good idea of their values and beliefs, their attitudes toward your subject—in short, their willingness to be convinced by your argument. In a composition class, your readers will probably be your instructor and your classmates, a small but diverse group. Some readers may agree with you from the start, and these you need not worry much about. Others may be passionately hostile to your view, especially if it represents values they oppose, and these you probably cannot convince. A good target when you are addressing a diverse audience is the reader who is neutral or mildly biased one way or the other toward your thesis. This person you can hope to influence as long as your argument is reasonable, your evidence is thorough and convincing, your treatment of opposing views is fair, and your appeals to readers' emotions are appropriate to your purpose, your subject, and especially your readers' values and feelings.

ORGANIZING

Once you have formulated your thesis, gathered reasons and the evidence to support them, and evaluated these against the needs and expectations of your audience, you should plan how you will arrange your argument. The introduction to your essay should draw readers into your framework, making them see how the subject affects them and predisposing them to consider your argument. Sometimes, a forthright approach works best, but an eye-opening anecdote or quotation can also be effective. Usually, your thesis sentence should end your introduction. But if you think readers will not even entertain your thesis until they have seen all your evidence, then withhold it for your conclusion.

The main part of the essay consists of your minor arguments or reasons and your evidence for them. Unless the minor arguments form a chain, with each growing out of the one before, their order should be determined by their potential effects on readers. In general, it is most effective to arrange the reasons in order of increasing importance or strength so as to finish powerfully. But to engage readers in the argument from the start, try to begin with a reason that they will find compelling or that they already know and accept; that way, the weaker reasons will be sandwiched between a strong beginning and an even stronger ending.

The views opposing yours can be raised and dispensed with wherever it seems most appropriate to do so. If a counterargument pertains to just one of your minor arguments, then dispose of it at that point. But if the counterarguments are more basic, pertaining to your whole thesis, you should dispose of them either after the introduction or shortly before the conclusion. Use the former strategy if the opposition is particularly strong and you fear that readers will be disinclined to listen unless you address their concerns first. Use the latter strategy when the counterarguments are generally weak or easily dispensed with once you've presented your case.

In the conclusion to your essay, you may summarize the main point of your argument and state your thesis for the first time, if you have saved it for the end, or restate it from your introduction. An effective quotation, an appropriate emotional appeal, or a call for support or action can often provide a strong finish to an argumentative essay.

DRAFTING

While you are drafting the essay, keep the needs of your readers uppermost in mind. Make your reasoning clear by showing how each bit of evidence relates to the reason or minor argument being discussed, and how each minor argument relates to the main argument contained in the thesis. In working through the reasons and evidence, you may find it helpful to state each reason as the first sentence in a paragraph and then support it in the following sentences. If this scheme seems too rigid or creates overlong paragraphs, you can always make changes after you have got the draft down on paper. Draw on a range of methods to clarify your points. For instance, define specialized terms or those you use in a special sense; compare and contrast one policy or piece of evidence with another; carefully analyze causes or effects; introduce an analogy when it will help reinforce a point.

When presenting evidence, use specific, concrete words, sharp details, and vivid examples, because an argument that is entirely general and abstract is unlikely to succeed. Also watch the connotations of your words, and the associations they trigger in readers. Don't use *childlike* when you mean *childish*, *stubborn* when you mean *resolute*. And strive for a moderate, sincere tone that conveys fairness toward the opposition. This, remember, is part of your ethical appeal: the sense you convey of being reasonable, trustworthy, and knowledgeable.

REVISING

When your draft is complete, revise it against the following questions.

1. *Is every part of the argument fair and reasonable?* Check for shrillness, plaintiveness, or misplaced sarcasm in the way you word claims, dispute opposing views, and present evidence. Search out every emotional appeal (some may have crept in accidentally) to be sure it is appropriate to the subject, your purpose, and especially the audience. Watch closely for places where you might have used emotional appeals to construct a deductive argument.

2. *Have you slipped into any logical fallacies?* Detecting fallacies in your own work can be difficult, but your readers will find them if you don't. Look for the following fallacies discussed earlier (pp. 312–15): hasty generalization; oversimplification; begging the question; ignoring the question, including ad hominem arguments; either-or; non sequitur; and post hoc arguments. (All of these are also listed in the Glossary under *logical fallacies*.)

3. *Have you proved your thesis?* Is your evidence specific, representative, and adequate to support each minor argument, and does each minor argument support the central claim? In behalf of your readers, question every sentence you have written to be sure it connects with the one before and contributes to the point you are making and to the argument as a whole.

—————— *Martin Luther King, Jr.* ——————

Born in 1929 in Atlanta, Georgia, the son of a Baptist minister, Martin Luther King, Jr., was a revered and powerful leader of the black civil rights movement during the 1950s and 1960s. He was ordained in his father's church before he was twenty and went on to earn degrees at Morehouse College (B.A. in 1948), Crozer Theological Seminary (B.D. in 1951), and Boston University (Ph.D. in 1955). In 1955 and 1956, while he was pastor of a church in Montgomery, Alabama, King attracted national attention to the plight of Southern blacks by leading a boycott that succeeded in desegregating the city's buses. He was elected the first president of the Southern Christian Leadership Conference and continued to organize demonstrations for equal rights in other cities. By the early 1960s his efforts had helped raise the national consciousness so that the landmark Civil Rights Act of 1964 and Voting Rights Act of 1965 could be passed by Congress. In 1964 King was awarded the Nobel Peace Prize. When leading sit-ins, boycotts, and marches, King always insisted on nonviolent resistance "because our end is a community at peace with itself." But his nonviolence often met with violent opposition. Over the years he was jailed, beaten, stoned, and stabbed. His house in Montgomery was bombed. And on April 4, 1968, at a motel in Memphis, Tennessee, he was assassinated. He was not yet forty years old.

I Have a Dream

One August 28, 1963, one hundred years after Abraham Lincoln's Emancipation Proclamation had freed the slaves, 200,000 black and white Americans marched on Washington, D.C., to demand equal rights for blacks. It was the largest crowd ever to assemble in the capital in behalf of a cause, and the high point of the day was this speech delivered by King on the steps of the Lincoln Memorial. Always an eloquent and inspirational speaker, King succeeded in articulating the frustrations and aspirations of America's blacks in a way that gave hope to the oppressed and opened the eyes of many oppressors.

Five score years ago, a great American, in whose symbolic shadow 1
we stand, signed the Emancipation Proclamation. This momentous decree came as a great beacon light of hope to millions of Negro slaves who had been seared in the flames of withering injustice. It came as a joyous daybreak to tend the long night of captivity.

But one hundred years later, we must face the tragic fact that the 2
Negro is still not free. One hundred years later, the life of the Negro is still sadly crippled by the manacles of segregation and the chains of

discrimination. One hundred years later, the Negro lives on a lonely island of poverty in the midst of a vast ocean of material prosperity. One hundred years later, the Negro is still languishing in the corners of American society and finds himself an exile in his own land. So we have come here today to dramatize an appalling condition.

In a sense we have come to our nation's capital to cash a check. 3 When the architects of our republic wrote the magnificent words of the Constitution and the Declaration of Independence, they were signing a promissory note to which every American was to fall heir. This note was a promise that all men—yes, black men as well as white men—would be guaranteed the unalienable rights of life, liberty, and the pursuit of happiness.

It is obvious today that America has defaulted on this promissory 4 note insofar as her citizens of color are concerned. Instead of honoring this sacred obligation, America has given the Negro people a bad check, a check which has come back marked "insufficient funds." But we refuse to believe that there are insufficient funds in the great vaults of opportunity of this nation. So we have come to cash this check—a check that will give us upon demand the riches of freedom and the security of justice. We have also come to this hallowed spot to remind America of the fierce urgency of *now*. This is no time to engage in the luxury of cooling off or to take the tranquilizing drugs of gradualism. *Now* is the time to make real the promises of Democracy. *Now* is the time to rise from the dark and desolate valley of segregation to the sunlit path of racial justice. *Now* is the time to open the doors of opportunity to all of God's children. *Now* is the time to lift our nation from the quicksands of racial injustice to the solid rock of brotherhood.

It would be fatal for the nation to overlook the urgency of the 5 moment and to underestimate the determination of the Negro. This sweltering summer of the Negro's legitimate discontent will not pass until there is an invigorating autumn of freedom and equality; 1963 is not an end, but a beginning. Those who hope that the Negro needed to blow off steam and will now be content will have a rude awakening if the nation returns to business as usual. There will be neither rest nor tranquility in America until the Negro is granted his citizenship rights. The whirlwinds of revolt will continue to shake the foundations of our nation until the bright day of justice emerges.

But there is something that I must say to my people who stand on 6 the warm threshold which leads into the palace of justice. In the process of gaining our rightful place we must not be guilty of wrongful deeds. Let us not seek to satisfy our thirst for freedom by drinking from the cup of bitterness and hatred. We must forever conduct our struggle on the high plane of dignity and discipline. We must not allow our creative protest to degenerate into physical violence. Again and again we must rise to the majestic heights of meeting physical force with soul force. The marvelous new militancy which has engulfed the Negro community must not lead us to a distrust of all white people, for many of our white brothers, as evidenced by their presence here today, have come to realize that their destiny is tied up with our destiny and their freedom is inextricably bound to our freedom. We cannot walk alone.

And as we walk, we must make the pledge that we shall march   7
ahead. We cannot turn back. There are those who are asking the devotees of civil rights, "When will you be satisfied?" We can never be satisfied as long as the Negro is the victim of the unspeakable horrors of police brutality. We can never be satisfied as long as our bodies, heavy with the fatigue of travel, cannot gain lodging in the motels of the highways and the hotels of the cities. We cannot be satisfied as long as the Negro's basic mobility is from a smaller ghetto to a larger one. We can never be satisfied as long as a Negro in Mississippi cannot vote and a Negro in New York believes he has nothing for which to vote. No, no, we are not satisfied, and we will not be satisfied until justice rolls down like waters and righteousness like a mighty stream.

I am not unmindful that some of you have come here out of great   8
trials and tribulations. Some of you have come fresh from narrow jail cells. Some of you have come from areas where your quest for freedom left you battered by the storms of persecution and staggered by the winds of police brutality. You have been the veterans of creative suffering. Continue to work with the faith that unearned suffering is redemptive.

Go back to Mississippi, go back to Alabama, go back to South   9
Carolina, go back to Georgia, go back to Louisiana, go back to the slums and ghettos of our northern cities, knowing that somehow this situation can and will be changed. Let us not wallow in the valley of despair.

I say to you today, my friends, that in spite of the difficulties and   10
frustrations of the moment I still have a dream. It is a dream deeply rooted in the American dream.

I have a dream that one day this nation will rise up and live out   11
the true meaning of its creed: "We hold these truths to be self-evident, that all men are created equal."

I have a dream that one day on the red hills of Georgia the sons of 12
former slaves and the sons of former slaveowners will be able to sit
down together at the table of brotherhood.

I have a dream that one day even the state of Mississippi, a desert 13
state sweltering with the heat of injustice and oppression, will be
transformed into an oasis of freedom and justice.

I have a dream that my four little children will one day live in a 14
nation where they will not be judged by the color of their skin but by
the content of their character.

I have a dream today. 15

I have a dream that one day the state of Alabama, whose gover- 16
nor's lips are presently dripping with the words of interposition and
nullification, will be transformed into a situation where little black
boys and black girls will be able to join hands with little white boys
and white girls and walk together as sisters and brothers.

I have a dream today. 17

I have a dream that one day every valley shall be exalted, every 18
hill and mountain shall be made low, the rough places will be made
plain, and the crooked places will be made straight, and the glory of
the Lord shall be revealed, and all flesh shall see it together.[1]

This is our hope. This is the faith with which I return to the 19
South. With this faith we will be able to hew out of the mountain of
despair a stone of hope. With this faith we will be able to transform
the jangling discords of our nation into a beautiful symphony of
brotherhood. With this faith we will be able to work together, to pray
together, to struggle together, to go to jail together, to stand up for
freedom together, knowing that we will be free one day.

This will be the day when all of God's children will be able to sing 20
with new meaning

> My country, 'tis of thee,
> Sweet land of liberty,
>   Of thee I sing:
> Land where my fathers died,
> Land of the pilgrims' pride,
> From every mountainside,
>   Let freedom ring.

So let freedom ring from the prodigious hilltops of New Hamp- 21
shire. Let freedom ring from the mighty mountains of New York. Let
freedom ring from the heightening Alleghenies of Pennsylvania. Let

[1]This paragraph quotes the Bible, Isaiah 40:4–5. [Editor's note.]

freedom ring from the snowcapped Rockies of Colorado. Let freedom ring from the curvaceous peaks of California.

But not only that. Let freedom ring from Stone Mountain of   22 Georgia. Let freedom ring from Lookout Mountain of Tennessee. Let freedom ring from every hill and molehill of Mississippi. From every mountainside, let freedom ring.

When we let freedom ring, when we let it ring from every village   23 and every hamlet, from every state and every city, we will be able to speed up that day when all of God's children, black men and white men, Jews and Gentiles, Protestants and Catholics, will be able to join hands and sing in the words of the old Negro spiritual, "Free at last! Free at last! Thank God almighty, we are free at last!"

Meaning

1. In a sentence, state the main point of King's speech.
2. How does King depict the general condition of the nation's black people? What specific injustices does he cite?
3. What reasons does King give for refusing to resort to violence? What comfort does he offer those who have been jailed or beaten?
4. Summarize the substance of King's dream. What does he mean when he says, "It is a dream deeply rooted in the American dream" (10)?
5. If you do not know the meanings of the following words, look them up in a dictionary: manacles, languishing (paragraph 2); promissory note, unalienable (3); defaulted, gradualism (4); degenerate, inextricably (6); tribulations, redemptive (8); interposition, nullification (16); prodigious, curvaceous (21); hamlet (23).

Purpose and Audience

1. What do you think King wanted to achieve with this speech? How does each part of the speech relate to his purpose?
2. What group of people does King seem to be addressing primarily in this speech? Where does he seem to assume that they agree with his ideas? Where does he seem to assume that they have reservations or need reassurance?
3. What about King's purpose and audience leads him to rely primarily on emotional appeal? Where does he appeal specifically to his listeners' pride and dignity? to their religious beliefs? to their patriotism?
4. Where does King seem to suppose that doubters and opponents of the civil rights movement might also hear his speech? What messages about the goals and determination of the movement does he convey to these hearers?

Method and Structure

1. Analyze the organization of King's speech. What is the main subject of paragraphs 3–5? 6–9? 10–23? How does this structure suit King's purpose?
2. Why does King's first paragraph refer to the hope generated by Lincoln's Emancipation Proclamation? Is the contrast King develops in paragraphs 1 and 2 an effective introduction to the speech? Why, or why not?
3. **Other Methods**   Paragraph 3 and the first half of paragraph 4 are developed by analogy (Chapter 8). What are the main points of the analogy, and what purpose does it serve? Do you think it is effective? Why, or why not?

Language

1. In paragraph 6 King says, "Let us not seek to satisfy our thirst for freedom by drinking from the cup of bitterness and hatred." To what extent in this speech does King follow his own suggestion? How would you characterize his attitudes toward oppression and segregation? Choose words and phrases in the speech to support your answer.
2. King depends heavily on two stylistic devices: repetition of sentence openings, as in "I have a dream" (paragraphs 11–18); and parallelism within sentences, as in "the manacles of segregation and the chains of discrimination" (2). Locate other instances of these two related devices. How do they contribute to King's purpose? (If necessary, consult the Glossary for an explanation of *parallelism*.)
3. King's speech abounds in metaphors, such as the "manacles of segregation" and the "chains of discrimination" in the sentence quoted above. Locate as many metaphors as you can (consulting the Glossary under *figures of speech* if necessary), and analyze what five or six of them contribute to King's meaning. Which metaphors are repeated or restated, and how does this repetition help link portions of the speech?

Writing Topics

1. King's speech had a tremendous impact when it was first delivered in 1963, and it remains influential to this day. Pick out the elements of the speech that seem most remarkable and powerful to you: ideas, emotional appeals, figures of speech, repetition and parallelism, or whatever you choose. Write an essay in which you cite these elements and analyze their effectiveness.
2. Reread paragraph 6, where King outlines a strategy for achieving racial justice. In an essay, briefly explain an unjust situation that affects you

directly—in school, in your family, at work, in your community—and propose a strategy for correcting the injustice. Be specific about the steps in the strategy, and explain how each one relates to the final goal you want to achieve.

3. King says that his dream is "deeply rooted in the American dream" (paragraph 10). Write an essay in which you provide your own definition of the American dream. Draw on the elements of King's dream as you see fit. Make your definition specific with examples and details from your experiences, observations, and reading.

Ethan A. Nadelmann

A political scientist, Ethan Nadelmann was born in 1957 in New York City and grew up north of the city. He has earned numerous degrees: a B.A. from McGill University (1979), an M.S. in international relations from the London School of Economics (1980), and both a law degree (1984) and a Ph.D. (1987) from Harvard University. In his extensive research and writing, Nadelmann has focused on international crime and law enforcement and especially on U.S. drug policy. He has published many scholarly articles in such journals as Foreign Policy *and* The Public Interest *that explore the possibility of controlled legalization of drugs in the United States. In addition, he has spoken about drug policy and legalization before a congressional committee, to diverse groups in North and South America, and on television news programs such as* Nightline. *Since 1987 Nadelmann has been an assistant professor of politics and public affairs in Princeton University's politics department and Woodrow Wilson School of Public and International Affairs. He lives with his family in Princeton, New Jersey.*

Legalize Drugs

Nadelmann here condenses his scholarly work into a succinct argument for considering legalization as a serious alternative in the war on drugs. The essay first appeared under the title "Shooting Up" in The New Republic *on June 13, 1988. The essay after this one, by Morton Kondracke (p. 336), responds to Nadelmann's argument.*

Hamburgers and ketchup. Movies and popcorn. Drugs and crime. 1

Drugs and crime are so thoroughly intertwined in the public mind 2 that to most people a large crime problem seems an inevitable consequence of widespread drug use. But the historical link between the two is more a product of drug laws than of drugs. There are four clear connections between drugs and crime, and three of them would be much diminished if drugs were legalized. This fact doesn't by itself make the case for legalization persuasive, of course, but it deserves careful attention in the emerging debate over whether the prohibition of drugs is worth the trouble.

The first connection between drugs and crime—and the only one 3 that would remain strong after legalization—is the commission of violent and other crimes by people under the influence of illicit drugs.

329

It is this connection that most infects the popular imagination. Obviously some drugs do "cause" people to commit crimes by reducing normal inhibitions, lessening the sense of responsibility, and unleashing aggressive and other antisocial tendencies. Cocaine, particularly in the form of "crack," has earned such a reputation in recent years, just as heroin did in the 1960s and 1970s and marijuana did in the years before that.

Crack's reputation may or may not be more deserved than those   4
of marijuana and heroin. Reliable evidence isn't yet available. But no illicit drug is as widely associated with violent behavior as alcohol. According to Justice Department statistics, 54 percent of all jail inmates convicted of violent crimes in 1983 reported having used alcohol just prior to committing the offense. The impact of drug legalization on this drug-crime connection is hard to predict. Much would depend on overall rates of drug abuse and changes in the nature of consumption, both imponderables. It's worth noting, though, that any shift in consumption from alcohol to marijuana would almost certainly reduce violent behavior.

This connection between drugs and antisocial behavior—which is   5
inherent and may or may not be substantial—is often confused with a second link between the two that is definitely substantial and not inherent: many illicit drug users commit crimes such as robbery, burglary, prostitution, and numbers-running to earn enough money to buy drugs. Unlike the millions of alcoholics who support their habits for modest amounts, many cocaine and heroin addicts spend hundreds, maybe even thousands, of dollars a week. If these drugs were significantly cheaper—if either they were legalized or drug laws were not enforced—the number of crimes committed by drug addicts to pay for their habits would drop dramatically. Even if the drugs were taxed heavily to discourage consumption, prices probably would be much lower than they are today.

The third drug-crime link—also a byproduct of drug laws—is the   6
violent, intimidating, and corrupting behavior of the drug traffickers. Illegal markets tend to breed violence, not just because they attract criminally minded people but also because there are no legal institutions for resolving disputes. During Prohibition[1] violent struggles be-

---

[1] Prohibition was the period from 1920 to 1933 during which the Eighteenth Amendment to the Constitution prohibited the manufacture and sale of alcoholic beverages. Bootleggers were violators of the law. The amendment was repealed in 1933. [Editor's note.]

tween bootlegging gangs and hijackings of booze-laden trucks were frequent and notorious. Today's equivalents are the booby traps that surround marijuana fields; the pirates of the Caribbean, who rip off drug-laden vessels en route to the United States; and the machine-gun battles and executions of the more sordid drug mafias—all of which occasionally kill innocent people. Most authorities agree that the dramatic increase in urban murder rates over the past few years is almost entirely due to the rise in drug-dealer killings, mostly of one another.

Perhaps the most unfortunate victims of drug prohibition laws 7 have been the residents of America's ghettos. These laws have proved largely futile in deterring ghetto-dwellers from becoming drug abusers, but they do account for much of what ghetto residents identify as the drug problem. Aggressive, gun-toting drug dealers often upset law-abiding residents far more than do addicts nodding out in doorways. Meanwhile other residents perceive the drug dealers as heroes and successful role models. They're symbols of success to children who see no other options. At the same time the increasingly harsh criminal penalties imposed on adult drug dealers have led drug traffickers to recruit juveniles. Where once children started dealing drugs only after they had been using them for a few years, today the sequence is often reversed. Many children start using drugs only after working for older drug dealers for a while.

The conspicuous failure of law enforcement agencies to deal with 8 the disruptive effect of drug traffickers has demoralized inner-city neighborhoods and police departments alike. Intensive crackdowns in urban neighborhoods, like intensive anti-cockroach efforts in urban dwellings, do little more than chase the menace a short distance away to infect new areas. By contrast, legalization of drugs, like legalization of alcohol in the early 1930s, would drive the drug-dealing business off the streets and out of apartment buildings and into government-regulated, tax-paying stores. It also would force many of the gun-toting dealers out of the business and convert others into legitimate businessmen. Some, of course, would turn to other types of criminal activities, just as some of the bootleggers did after Prohibition's repeal. Gone, though, would be the unparalleled financial gains that tempt people from all sectors of society into the drug-dealing business.

Gone, too, would be the money that draws police into the world 9 of crime. Today police corruption appears to be more pervasive than at any time since Prohibition. In Miami dozens of law enforcement officials have been charged with accepting bribes, ripping off drug dealers, and even dealing drugs themselves. In small towns and rural communities in Georgia, where drug smugglers from the Caribbean and Latin America pass through, dozens of sheriffs have been implicated in corruption. In one New York police precinct, drug-related corruption has generated the city's most far-reaching police scandal since the late 1960s. Nationwide, over 100 cases of drug-related corruption are now prosecuted each year. Every one of the federal law enforcement agencies with significant drug enforcement responsibilities has seen an agent implicated.

It isn't hard to explain the growth of this corruption. The financial temptations are enormous relative to other opportunities, legitimate or illegitimate. Little effort is required. Many police officers are demoralized by the scope of drug traffic, the indifference of many citizens, a frequent lack of appreciation for their efforts, and the seeming futility of it all; even with the regular jailing of drug dealers, there always seem to be more to fill their shoes. Some police also recognize that their real function is not so much to protect victims from predators as to regulate an illicit market that can't be suppressed but that much of society prefers to keep underground. In every respect, the analogy to Prohibition is apt. Repealing drug prohibition laws would dramatically reduce police corruption. By contrast, the measures currently being proposed to deal with the growing problem, including more frequent and aggressive internal inspection, offer little promise and cost money. 10

The final link between drugs and crime is the tautological connection: producing, selling, buying, and consuming drugs is a crime in and of itself that occurs billions of times each year nationwide. Last year alone, about 30 million Americans violated a drug law, and about 750,000 were arrested, mostly for mere possession, not dealing. In New York City almost half of the felony indictments were on drug charges, and in Washington, D.C., the figure was more than half. Close to 40 percent of inmates in federal prisons are there on drug-dealing charges, and that population is expected to more than double within 15 years. 11

Clearly, if drugs were legalized, this drug-crime connection— which annually accounts for around $10 billion in criminal justice costs—would be severed. (Selling drugs to children would, of course, continue to be prosecuted.) And the benefits would run deeper than that. We would no longer be labeling as criminals the tens of millions of people who use drugs illicitly, subjecting them to the risk of arrest, and inviting them to associate with drug dealers (who may be crimi- 12 nals in many more senses of the word). The attendant cynicism toward the law in general would diminish, along with the sense of hostility and suspicion that otherwise law-abiding citizens feel toward police. It was costs such as these that strongly influenced many of Prohibition's more conservative opponents. As John D. Rockefeller[2] wrote in explaining why he was withdrawing his support of Prohibition:

> That a vast array of lawbreakers has been recruited and financed on a colossal scale; that many of our best citizens, piqued at what they regarded as an infringement of their private rights, have openly and unabashedly disregarded the 18th Amendment; that as an inevitable result respect for all law has been greatly lessened; that crime has increased to an unprecedented degree—I have slowly and reluctantly come to believe.

Meaning

1. What is the proposition with which Nadelmann would like his audience to agree? How and why does he qualify his proposition?
2. What does Nadelmann mean in paragraph 5 by "inherent"? If necessary, look up the word in a dictionary, and then explain how the connection between drugs and antisocial behavior sometimes is and sometimes is not inherent.
3. While most people involved in the war on drugs emphasize the harmful effects of drugs on children, Nadelmann argues that legalizing drugs may actually help children. Where in the essay does he make this assertion, and what are his reasons for it?
4. If you do not know the meanings of the following words, look them up in a dictionary: illicit, inhibitions (paragraph 3); imponderables (4); intimidating, sordid (6); deterring (7); conspicuous, demoralized (8); implicated (9); predators, apt (10); tautological (11); cynicism, colossal, piqued, infringement, unabashedly (12).

Purpose and Audience

1. What is Nadelmann's purpose? Does he want his readers to embrace the idea of legalizing drugs? Support your answer with evidence from the essay.

[2] Rockefeller (1839–1937) was an industrialist, financier, and philanthropist, the first of the prominent American Rockefellers. [Editor's note.]

2. Based on his argument, how would you characterize Nadelmann's audience? Is he addressing supporters, opponents, or undecideds? Explain your response.
3. Why does Nadelmann choose John D. Rockefeller's words about Prohibition to close his essay? Why is Rockefeller significant for Nadelmann's purpose?

Method and Structure

1. In organizing his argument, Nadelmann cites four connections between drugs and crime. His first connection, however, does not support his main point. What is that connection, and what is the effect of its placement?
2. Nadelmann uses both inductive and deductive reasoning in his essay. Find evidence of both types of reasoning, and comment on their effectiveness.
3. **Other Methods** Nadelmann's references to Prohibition constitute an analogy (Chapter 8). Explain Nadelmann's use of the Prohibition analogy. Does it seem strained at any point? Do you find it effective? Why, or why not?

Language

1. How would you characterize Nadelmann's tone in this essay? How does his language contribute to his tone? Do you think the tone is effective for his purpose? (If necessary, consult *tone* in the Glossary.)
2. Compare Nadelmann's language with Rockefeller's (paragraph 12). How do you characterize and explain the difference?
3. Identify several instances in which Nadelmann uses statistics to support his argument, and analyze their effect. What would be the effect of eliminating the statistics?

Writing Topics

1. Rewrite paragraph 7 of Nadelmann's essay to appeal more to readers' emotions—that is, use emotional language, and draw on readers' feelings. Then write a paragraph saying what this exercise tells you about appeals in arguments.
2. According to Nadelmann, legalizing drugs would eliminate the problem of "labeling as criminals . . . people who use drugs illicitly" and prevent

"otherwise law-abiding citizens" from becoming increasingly cynical toward the law and hostile toward police (paragraph 12). Write an essay in which you support or oppose this position, based on your personal experience, observations, reading, and viewing of television or film documentaries.

3. Nadelmann expanded on his argument in a much longer essay, "The Case for Legalization," appearing in the Summer 1988 issue of *The Public Interest*. Read that essay, and compare it with "Legalize Drugs." Consider the following in your comparison essay: How do the audiences for the two essays differ? What is Nadelmann's purpose in each essay? What type of appeal does he make in each essay? Which do you think is the more effective argument, and why?

4. During the Reagan administration, a vigorous antidrug campaign aimed at young people was conducted, using the slogan "Just Say No." Consult the *Readers' Guide to Periodical Literature* and *The New York Times Index* for the years 1982 to 1988 to research the campaign and its perceived effectiveness. Write an essay in which you either defend or criticize the campaign. Be sure to offer evidence in support of your view.

Morton M. Kondracke

Morton Kondracke was born in 1939 in Chicago and graduated from Dartmouth College (B.A., 1960). He was a Nieman Fellow at Harvard University in 1973–1974. He began his career in journalism in the 1960s, serving as a reporter and then as White House correspondent for The Chicago Sun-Times. *For eight years he was executive editor of* The New Republic *and then in 1985–1986 was Washington bureau chief for* Newsweek. *He is now a senior editor of* The New Republic, *writing mainly on foreign policy. He also writes for* The Wall Street Journal *and is a syndicated columnist with United Features. A broadcast journalist as well, Kondracke is a commentator on National Public Radio and appears regularly on* This Week with David Brinkley *on ABC television.*

Don't Legalize Drugs

The following essay appeared in The New Republic *on June 27, 1988, two weeks after Ethan A. Nadelmann's "Legalize Drugs" (p. 329). Kondracke believes that his essay was "the first attempt to put any numbers on the human and economic costs of legalized drugs." The essay was written during the presidency of Ronald Reagan (hence the references to his administration). President Bush proposed a significant escalation in the war against drugs.*

The next time you hear that a drunk driver has slammed into a 1
school bus full of children or that a stoned railroad engineer has killed 16 people in a train wreck, think about this: if the advocates of legalized drugs have their way, there will be more of this, a lot more. There will also be more unpublicized fatal and maiming crashes, more job accidents, more child neglect, more of almost everything associated with substance abuse: babies born addicted or retarded, teenagers zonked out of their chance for an education, careers destroyed, families wrecked, and people dead of overdoses.

The proponents of drug legalization are right to say that some 2
things will get better. Organized crime will be driven out of the drug business, and there will be a sharp drop in the amount of money (currently about $10 billion per year) that society spends to enforce the drug laws. There will be some reduction in the cost in theft and injury (now about $20 billion) by addicts to get the money to buy prohibited drugs. Internationally, Latin American governments presumably will stop being menaced by drug cartels and will peaceably export cocaine as they now do coffee.

336

However, this is virtually the limit of the social benefits to be *3*
derived from legalization, and they are far outweighed by the costs,
which are always underplayed by legalization advocates such as the
Economist, Princeton scholar Ethan A. Nadelmann, economist Mil-
ton Friedman and other libertarians, columnists William F. Buckley
and Richard Cohen, and Mayors Keith Schmoke of Baltimore and
Marion Barry of Washington, D.C. In lives, money, and human woe,
the costs are so high, in fact, that society has no alternative but to
conduct a real war on the drug trade, although perhaps a smarter one
than is currently being waged.

Advocates of legalization love to draw parallels between the drug *4*
war and Prohibition. Their point, of course, is that this crusade is as
doomed to failure as the last one was, and that we ought to surrender
now to the inevitable and stop wasting resources. But there are some
important differences between drugs and alcohol. Alcohol has been
part of Western culture for thousands of years; drugs have been the
rage in America only since about 1962. Of the 115 million Americans
who consume alcohol, 85 percent rarely become intoxicated; with
drugs, intoxication is the whole idea. Alcohol is consistent chemically,
even though it's dispensed in different strengths and forms as beer,
wine, and "hard" liquor; with drugs there's no limit to the variations.
Do we legalize crack along with snortable cocaine, PCPs as well as
marijuana, and LSD and "Ecstasy" as well as heroin? If we don't—
and almost certainly we won't—we have a black market, and some
continued crime.

But Prohibition is a useful historical parallel for measuring the *5*
costs of legalization. Almost certainly doctors are not going to want
to write prescriptions for recreational use of harmful substances, so if
drugs ever are legalized they will be dispensed as alcohol now is—in
government-regulated stores with restrictions on the age of buyers,
warnings against abuse (and, probably, with added restrictions on
amounts, though this also will create a black market).

In the decade before Prohibition went into effect in 1920, alcohol *6*
consumption in the United States averaged 2.6 gallons per person per
year. It fell to 0.73 gallons during the Prohibition decade, then doubled to 1.5 gallons in the decade after repeal, and is now back to 2.6
gallons. So illegality suppressed usage to a third or a fourth of its
former level. At the same time, incidence of cirrhosis of the liver fell
by half.

So it seems fair to estimate that use of drugs will at least double, *7*
and possibly triple, if the price is cut, supplies are readily available,

and society's sanction is lifted. It's widely accepted that there are now 16 million regular users of marijuana, six million of cocaine, a half million of heroin, and another half million of other drugs, totaling 23 million. Dr. Robert DuPont, former director of the National Institutes of Drug Abuse and an anti-legalization crusader, says that the instant pleasure afforded by drugs—superior to that available with alcohol—will increase the number of regular users of marijuana and cocaine to about 50 or 60 million and heroin users to ten million.

Between ten percent and 15 percent of all drinkers turn into alco-   8
holics (ten million to 17 million), and these drinkers cost the economy an estimated $117 billion in 1983 ($15 billion for treatment, $89 billion in lost productivity, and $13 billion in accident-related costs). About 200,000 people died last year as a result of alcohol abuse, about 25,000 in auto accidents. How many drug users will turn into addicts, and what will this cost? According to President Reagan's drug abuse policy adviser, Dr. David I. McDonald, studies indicate that marijuana is about as habit-forming as alcohol, but for cocaine, 70 percent of users become addicted, as many as with nicotine.

So it seems reasonable to conclude that at least four to six million   9
people will become potheads if marijuana is legal, and that coke addicts will number somewhere between 8.5 million (if regular usage doubles and 70 percent become addicted) and 42 million (if DuPont's high estimate of use is correct). An optimist would have to conclude that the number of people abusing legalized drugs will come close to those hooked on alcohol. A pessimist would figure the human damage as much greater.

Another way of figuring costs is this: the same study (by the   10
Research Triangle Institute of North Carolina) that put the price of alcoholism at $117 billion in 1983 figured the cost of drug abuse then at $60 billion—$15 billion for law enforcement and crime, and $45 billion in lost productivity, damaged health, and other costs. The updated estimate for 1988 drug abuse is $100 billion. If legalizing drugs would save $30 billion now being spent on law enforcement and crime, a doubling of use and abuse means that other costs will rise to $140 billion or $210 billion. This is no bargain for society.

If 200,000 people die every year from alcohol abuse and 320,000   11
from tobacco smoking, how many will die from legal drugs? Government estimates are that 4,000 to 5,000 people a year are killed in drug-related auto crashes, but this is surely low because accident victims are not as routinely blood-tested for drugs as for alcohol. Legalization advocates frequently cite figures of 3,600 or 4,100 as the

number of drug deaths each year reported by hospitals, but this number too is certainly an understatement, based on reports from only 75 big hospitals in 27 metropolitan areas.

If legalization pushed the total number of drug addicts to only   *12*
half the number of alcoholics, 100,000 people a year would die. That's the figure cited by McDonald. DuPont guesses that, given the potency of drugs, the debilitating effects of cocaine, the carcinogenic effects of marijuana, and the AIDS potential of injecting legalized heroin, the number of deaths actually could go as high as 500,000 a year. That's a wide range, but it's clear that legalization of drugs will not benefit human life.

All studies show that those most likely to try drugs, get hooked,   *13*
and die—as opposed to those who suffer from cirrhosis and lung cancer—are young people, who are susceptible to the lure of quick thrills and are terribly adaptable to messages provided by adult society. Under pressure of the current prohibition, the number of kids who use illegal drugs at least once a month has fallen from 39 percent in the late 1970s to 25 percent in 1987, according to the annual survey of high school seniors conducted by the University of Michigan. The same survey shows that attitudes toward drug use have turned sharply negative. But use of legal drugs is still strong. Thirty-eight percent of high school seniors reported getting drunk within the past two weeks, and 27 percent said they smoke cigarettes every day. Drug prohibition is working with kids; legalization would do them harm.

And, even though legalization would lower direct costs for drug   *14*
law enforcement, it's unlikely that organized crime would disappear. It might well shift to other fields—prostitution, pornography, gambling or burglaries, extortion, and murders-for-hire—much as it did in the period between the end of Prohibition and the beginning of the drug era. As DuPont puts it, "Organized crime is in the business of giving people the things that society decides in its own interest to prohibit. The only way to get rid of organized crime is to make everything legal." Even legalization advocates such as Ethan Nadelmann admit that some street crimes will continue to occur as a result of drug abuse—especially cocaine paranoia, PCP insanity, and the need of unemployable addicts to get money for drugs. Domestic crime, child abuse, and neglect surely would increase.

Some legalization advocates suggest merely decriminalizing mari-   *15*
juana and retaining sanctions against other drugs. This would certainly be less costly than total legalization, but it would still be no

favor to young people, would increase traffic accidents and productivity losses—and would do nothing to curtail the major drug cartels, which make most of their money trafficking in cocaine.

Legalizers also argue that the government could tax legal drug 16 sales and use the money to pay for anti-drug education programs and treatment centers. But total taxes collected right now from alcohol sales at the local, state, and federal levels come to only $13.1 billion per year—which is a pittance compared with the damage done to society as a result of alcohol abuse. The same would have to be true for drugs—and any tax that resulted in an official drug price that was higher than the street price would open the way once again for black markets and organized crime.

So, in the name of health, economics, and morality, there seems 17 no alternative but to keep drugs illegal and to fight the criminals who traffic in them. Regardless of what legalization advocates say, this is now the overwhelming opinion of the public, the Reagan administration, the prospective candidates for president, and the Congress—not one of whose members has introduced legislation to decriminalize any drug. Congress is on the verge of forcing the administration to raise anti-drug spending next year from $3 billion to $5.5 billion.

There is, though, room to debate how best to wage this war. A 18 consensus is developing that it has to be done both on the supply side (at overseas points of origin, through interdiction at U.S. borders and criminal prosecution of traffickers) and on the demand side (by discouraging use of drugs through education and treatment and/or by arrest and urine testing at workplaces). However, there is a disagreement about which side to emphasize and how to spend resources. Members of Congress, especially Democrats, want to blame foreigners and the Reagan administration for the fact that increasing amounts of cocaine, heroin, and marijuana are entering the country. They want to spend more money on foreign aid, use the U.S. military to seal the borders, and fund "nice" treatment and education programs, especially those that give ongoing support to professional social welfare agencies.

Conservatives, on the other hand, want to employ the military to 19 help foreign countries stamp out drug laboratories, use widespread drug testing to identify—and, often, punish—drug users, and spend more on police and prisons. As Education Secretary William Bennett puts it, "How can we surrender when we've never actually fought the war?" Bennett wants to fight it across all fronts, and those who have seen drafts of a forthcoming report of the White House Conference for a Drug Free America say this will be the approach recommended by the administration, although with muted emphasis on use of the U.S. military, which is reluctant to get involved in what may be another thankless war.[1]

However, Dupont and others, including Jeffrey Eisenach of the Heritage Foundation, make a strong case that primary emphasis ought to be put on the demand side—discouraging use in the United States rather than, almost literally, trying to become the world's policeman. Their argument, bolstered by a study conducted by Peter Reuter of the RAND Corporation, is that major profits in the drug trade are not made abroad (where the price of cocaine triples from farm to airstrip), but within the United States (where the markup from entry point to street corner is 12 times), and that foreign growing fields and processing laboratories are easily replaceable at low cost.

They say that prohibition policy should emphasize routine random urine testing in schools and places of employment, arrests for possession of drugs, and "coercive" treatment programs that compel continued enrollment as a condition of probation and employment. DuPont thinks that corporations have a right to demand that their employees be drug-free because users cause accidents and reduce productivity. He contends that urine testing is no more invasive than the use of metal detectors at airports.

"Liberals have a terrible time with this," says DuPont. "They want to solve every problem by giving people things. They want to love people out of their problems, while conservatives want to punish it out of them. What we want to do is take the profits out of drugs by drying up demand. You do that by raising the social cost of using them to the point where people say, 'I don't want to do this.' This isn't conservative. It's a way to save lives."

It is, and it's directly parallel to the way society is dealing with drunk driving and cigarette smoking—not merely through advertising campaigns and surgeon general's warnings, but through increased penalties, social strictures—and prohibitions. Random testing for every employee in America may be going too far, but testing those holding sensitive jobs or workers involved in accidents surely isn't, nor is arresting users, lifting driver's licenses, and requiring treatment.

[1] The first "thankless war" was the one fought in Vietnam. [Editor's note.]

These are not nosy, moralistic intrusions on people's individual rights, but attempts by society to protect itself from danger.

In the end, they are also humane and moral. There is a chance, 24 with the public and policy-makers aroused to action, that ten years from now drug abuse might be reduced to its pre-1960s levels. Were drugs to be legalized now, we would be establishing a new vice—one that, over time, would end or ruin millions of lives. Worse yet, we would be establishing a pattern of doing the easy thing, surrendering, whenever confronted with a difficult challenge.

Meaning

1. Kondracke's thesis actually encompasses two closely related arguments, one negative, the other positive. What are these two arguments, and where in the essay is each articulated? How are the two linked?
2. In paragraph 4 Kondracke states that "there are some important differences between drugs and alcohol." What are these differences, and why does Kondracke stress them? Are you convinced of his point in this paragraph? Why, or why not?
3. Paragraphs 2–16 of Kondracke's argument indirectly answer Ethan Nadelmann's argument for the legalization of drugs in the previous essay (beginning on p. 329). Outline the parallel arguments on a piece of paper. Where does Kondracke refute Nadelmann directly? Where does he introduce points not considered by Nadelmann? Where does he ignore points raised by Nadelmann? Do you think Kondracke's response is effective? How do the different interests of the two authors dictate the points they raise?
4. If you do not know the meanings of the following words, look them up in a dictionary: proponents, cartels (paragraph 2); advocates, libertarians (3); black market (5); cirrhosis (6); understatement (11); potency, debilitating, carcinogenic (12); susceptible, adaptable (13); decriminalizing (15); pittance (16); consensus, interdiction (18); coercive (21).

Purpose and Audience

1. Kondracke's title points to one purpose of his essay, but his argument against legalization serves as a springboard for another purpose. What is it? Why do you think he chose not to focus exclusively on legalization?
2. Whom does Kondracke seem to be addressing in this essay: Nadelmann and the other legalization advocates mentioned in paragraph 3? legalization advocates in general? opponents of legalization? those who haven't

made up their minds? some other group? What influence does Kondracke apparently hope to have on his readers' opinions? To what extent did he influence your opinion on legalization and Nadelmann's argument supporting it?

3. More than Nadelmann, Kondracke uses paraphrases and quotations of experts to support his argument. Why do you think he chose to cite Robert DuPont (paragraphs 7, 12, 14, 20–22), David McDonald (8, 12), and William Bennett (19)? To what extent are they biased or unbiased experts? How convincing do you find their opinions, and why?

Method and Structure

1. Where in his essay does Kondracke state his thesis? What kind of information precedes the thesis? Why do you suppose Kondracke opens the essay this way?
2. Kondracke opens his essay with a clearly emotional appeal. Where in the essay do you see rational and ethical appeals?
3. Three times Kondracke begins a paragraph with "So . . ."—in 7, 9, and 17. In each case the word signals a transition, a shift from one part of the essay to another. What ideas in the essay are linked by these transitions?
4. **Other Methods** Kondracke's argument involves considerable cause-and-effect analysis (Chapter 10). How does Kondracke use cause-and-effect analysis in paragraphs 6–13, and for what purpose?

Language

1. How does the tone of Kondracke's opening paragraph compare with that of the rest of his essay? How does he create the tone of this paragraph? (If necessary, consult *tone* in the Glossary.)
2. Kondracke uses statistics to an even greater extent than Nadelmann does. Cite several examples. From a reader's perspective, what is the advantage of being given such statistics? the disadvantage?

Writing Topics

1. Write an essay in which you analyze Kondracke's comparison, in paragraph 4, between drugs and alcohol. Begin by stating his purpose in making the comparison, and then discuss each point, noting both his reason for making the point and your response. In your response, consider whether Kondracke has made a valid comparison, whether his rea-

sons for making it are sound, and whether the comparison is relevant to his purpose.

2. Consider another controversial issue, such as motorcycle helmet laws, seat-belt laws, the link between financial aid and draft registration, or the legal drinking age. Write an essay analyzing the problem reasonably, supporting your assertions, and offering a solution on practical rather than moral terms. Make sure to state your position clearly early in the essay.

3. In the Summer 1988 issue of *The Public Interest* (the same issue in which Nadelmann's longer essay appears), John Kaplan argues against legalization in an essay titled "Taking Drugs Seriously." Read Kaplan's article, and write an essay comparing it with Kondracke's. Consider the following questions: Are the two addressing similar audiences? If not, how do the audiences differ? How do the writers' purposes differ? What arguments or evidence does either include that the other does not? Which is the more convincing essay, and why?

4. Kondracke's case for escalating the war on the *demand* for drugs (paragraphs 20–24) involves what many people would deem invasions of privacy: "testing [the urine of] those holding sensitive jobs or workers involved in accidents . . . , arresting users, lifting driver's licenses, and requiring treatment" (23). Kondracke claims that "these are not nosy, moralistic intrusions on people's individual rights." Do you agree or disagree? Write an essay in which you argue for or against this part of Kondracke's solution to the drug problem, either drawing on your own experiences and observations or researching the issues in the library. (The *Readers' Guide to Periodical Literature* for recent years can direct you to articles on drug testing and related issues.)

Jonathan Swift

Jonathan Swift was an Anglican priest, a poet, and a political pamphleteer, but he is best known as a satirist with a sharp wit and a sense of outrage at human folly and cruelty. He was born in 1667 in Dublin, Ireland, to English parents. After receiving a diploma from Trinity College in Dublin, he went to England in 1689 and there became involved in the political and literary life of London. He was ordained in the Church of Ireland in 1694 and in 1713 became dean of St. Patrick's Cathedral in Dublin, where he served until his death in 1745. Several of Swift's works, including The Tale of a Tub *and* The Battle of the Books *(both 1704), ridicule the religious extremism and literary pretensions of his day.* Gulliver's Travels *(1726), his most famous book, is often abridged for children into a charming fantasy about tiny people and giants and a wise race of horses; but unabridged it takes a bitter swipe at humankind's lack of humanity and abuse of reason.*

A Modest Proposal

In Swift's time Ireland had already suffered almost two centuries of exploitation by the English. Mostly from abroad, the English controlled much of Ireland's farmland, exacted burdensome taxes from the Irish, and repressed the people in countless other ways. Swift, who had often lashed out at the injustices he saw, was moved in 1729 to his most vicious attack. Several years of crop failures had resulted in widespread starvation among the Irish poor, yet the government of England, the English landowners, and the well-to-do Irish had done nothing to help. In response, Swift wrote "A Modest Proposal," subtitled "For Preventing the Children of the Poor People in Ireland from Being a Burden to Their Parents or Country, and for Making Them Beneficial to Their Public." The essay is a model of satire, the combination of wit and criticism to mock or condemn human foolishness or evil. Like much satire, the essay is also heavily ironic, saying one thing but meaning another. (Satire and irony are both explained more fully in the Glossary.) Assuming the role of a thoughtful and sympathetic observer, Swift proposes a solution to the troubles of the Irish that, in the words of the critic Gilbert Highet, is "couched in terms of blandly persuasive logic, but so atrocious that no one could possibly take it as serious."

It is a melancholy object to those who walk through this great town[1] or travel in the country, when they see the streets, the roads, and

[1] Dublin. [This note and all other notes in the essay have been added by the editor.]

345

cabin doors, crowded with beggars of the female sex, followed by three, four, or six children, all in rags and importuning every passenger for an alms. These mothers, instead of being able to work for their honest livelihood, are forced to employ all their time in strolling to beg sustenance for their helpless infants, who, as they grow up, either turn thieves for want of work, or leave their dear native country to fight for the Pretender in Spain, or sell themselves to the Barbados.[2]

I think it is agreed by all parties that this prodigious number of children in the arms, or on the backs, or at the heels of their mothers, and frequently of their fathers, is in the present deplorable state of the kingdom a very great additional grievance; and therefore whoever could find out a fair, cheap, or easy method of making these children sound, useful members of the commonwealth would deserve so well of the public as to have his statue set up for a preserver of the nation.

But my intention is very far from being confined to provide only for the children of professed beggars; it is of a much greater extent, and shall take in the whole number of infants at a certain age who are born of parents in effect as little able to support them as those who demand our charity in the streets.

As to my own part, having turned my thoughts for many years upon this important subject, and maturely weighed the several schemes of other projectors,[3] I have always found them grossly mistaken in their computation. It is true, a child just dropped from its dam may be supported by her milk for a solar year, with little other nourishment; at most not above the value of two shillings,[4] which the mother may certainly get, or the value in scraps, by her lawful occupation of begging; and it is exactly at one year that I propose to provide for them in such a manner as instead of being a charge upon their parents or the parish, or wanting food and raiment for the rest of their lives, they shall on the contrary contribute to the feeding, and partly to the clothing, of many thousands.

There is likewise another great advantage in my scheme, that it will prevent those voluntary abortions, and that horrid practice of women murdering their bastard children, alas, too frequent among us, sacrificing the poor innocent babes, I doubt, more to avoid the ex-

---

[2] The Pretender was James Stuart (1688–1766). He laid claim to the English throne from exile in Spain, and many Irishmen joined an army in support of his cause. Irishmen also shipped out for the British colony of Barbados, in the Caribbean, exchanging several years' labor there for their passage.

[3] People who develop projects or schemes.

[4] A shilling was then worth less than twenty-five cents.

pense than the shame, which would move tears and pity in the most savage and inhuman breast.

The number of souls in this kingdom being usually reckoned one million and a half, of these I calculate there may be about two hundred thousand couples whose wives are breeders; from which number I subtract thirty thousand couples who are able to maintain their own children, although I apprehend there cannot be so many under the present distress of the kingdom; but this being granted, there will remain an hundred and seventy thousand breeders. I again subtract fifty thousand of those women who miscarry, or whose children die by accident or disease within the year. There only remain an hundred and twenty thousand children of poor parents annually born. The question therefore is, how this number shall be reared and provided for, which, as I have already said, under the present situation of affairs, is utterly impossible by all the methods hitherto proposed. For we can neither employ them in handicraft or agriculture; we neither build houses (I mean in the country) nor cultivate land. They can very seldom pick up a livelihood by stealing till they arrive at six years old, except where they are of towardly parts;[5] although I confess they learn the rudiments much earlier, during which time they can however be looked upon only as probationers, as I have been informed by a principal gentleman in the country of Cavan, who protested to me that he never knew above one or two instances under the age of six, even in a part of the kingdom so renowned for the quickest proficiency in that art.

I am assured by our merchants that a boy or a girl before twelve years old is no salable commodity; and even when they come to this age they will not yield above three pounds; or three pounds and half a crown at most on the Exchange;[6] which cannot turn to account either to the parents or the kingdom, the charge of nutriment and rags having been at least four times that value.

I shall now therefore humbly propose my own thoughts, which I hope will not be liable to the least objection.

I have been assured by a very knowing American of my acquaintance in London, that a young healthy child well nursed is at a year old a most delicious, nourishing, and wholesome food, whether stewed, roasted, baked, or boiled; and I make no doubt that it will equally serve in a fricassee or a ragout.

6

7

8

9

---

[5] Natural abilities.
[6] A pound consisted of twenty shillings; a crown consisted of five shillings.

I do therefore humbly offer it to public consideration that of the   *10*
hundred and twenty thousand children, already computed, twenty
thousand may be reserved for breed, whereof only one fourth part to
be males, which is more than we allow to sheep, black cattle, or
swine; and my reason is that these children are seldom the fruits of
marriage, a circumstance not much regarded by our savages, therefore
one male will be sufficient to serve four females. That the remaining
hundred thousand may at a year old be offered in sale to the persons
of quality and fortune through the kingdom, always advising the
mother to let them suck plentifully in the last month, so as to render
them plump and fat for a good table. The child will make two dishes
at an entertainment for friends; and when the family dines alone, the
fore or hind quarter will make a reasonable dish, and seasoned with a
little pepper or salt will be very good boiled on the fourth day, especially in winter.

I have reckoned upon a medium that a child just born will weigh   *11*
twelve pounds, and in a solar year if tolerably nursed increaseth to
twenty-eight pounds.

I grant this food will be somewhat dear, and therefore very   *12*
proper for landlords, who, as they have already devoured most of the
parents, seem to have the best title to the children.

Infant's flesh will be in season throughout the year, but more   *13*
plentiful in March, and a little before and after. For we are told by a
grave author, an eminent French physician,[7] that fish being a prolific
diet, there are more children born in Roman Catholic countries about
nine months after Lent than at any other season; therefore, reckoning
a year after Lent, the market will be more glutted than usual, because
the number of popish infants is at least three to one in this kingdom;
and therefore it will have one other collateral advantage, by lessening
the number of Papists among us.

I have already computed the charge of nursing a beggar's child (in   *14*
which list I reckon all cottagers, laborers, and four-fifths of the farmers) to be about two shillings per annum, rags included; and I believe
no gentleman would repine to give ten shillings for the carcass of a
good fat child, which, as I have said, will make four dishes of excellent nutritive meat, when he hath only some particular friend or his
own family to dine with him. Thus the squire will learn to be a good
landlord, and grow popular among the tenants; the mother will have
eight shillings net profit, and be fit for work till she produces another
child.

---

[7] François Rabelais, a sixteenth-century French humorist.

Those who are more thrifty (as I must confess the times require) 15
may flay the carcass; the skin of which artifically[8] dressed will make
admirable gloves for ladies, and summer boots for fine gentlemen.

As to our city of Dublin, shambles[9] may be appointed for this 16
purpose in the most convenient parts of it, and butchers we may be
assured will not be wanting; although I rather recommend buying the
children live, and dressing them hot from the knife as we do roasting
pigs.

A very worthy person, a true lover of his country, and whose 17
virtues I highly esteem, was lately pleased in discoursing on this matter to offer a refinement upon my scheme. He said that many gentlemen of his kingdom, having of late destroyed their deer, he conceived
that the want of venison might be well supplied by the bodies of
young lads and maidens, not exceeding fourteen years of age nor
under twelve, so great a number of both sexes in every county being
now ready to starve for want of work and service; and these to be
disposed of by their parents, if alive, or otherwise by their nearest
relations. But with due deference to so excellent a friend and so deserving a patriot, I cannot be altogether in his sentiments; for as to the
males, my American acquaintance assured me from frequent experience that their flesh was generally tough and lean, like that of our
schoolboys, by continual exercise, and their taste disagreeable; and to
fatten them would not answer the charge. Then as to the females, it
would, I think with humble submission, be a loss to the public, because they soon would become breeders themselves; and besides, it is
not improbable that some scrupulous people might be apt to censure
such a practice (although indeed very unjustly) as a little bordering
upon cruelty; which, I confess, hath always been with me the strongest objection against any project, how well soever intended.

But in order to justify my friend, he confessed that this expedient 18
was put into his head by the famous Psalmanazar,[10] a native of the
island Formosa, who came from thence to London above twenty
years ago, and in conversation told my friend that in his country when
any young person happened to be put to death, the executioner sold
the carcass to persons of quality as a prime dainty; and that in his
time the body of a plump girl of fifteen, who was crucified for an
attempt to poison the emperor, was sold to his Imperial Majesty's
prime minister of state, and other great mandarins of the court, in

[8] Artfully.

[9] Slaughterhouses.

[10] Georges Psalmanazar was a Frenchman who gulled London society into thinking he was an exotic Formosan.

joints from the gibbet, at four hundred crowns. Neither indeed can I deny that if the same use were made of several plump young girls in this town, who without one single groat to their fortunes cannot stir abroad without a chair,[11] and appear at the playhouse and assemblies in foreign fineries which they never will pay for, the kingdom would not be the worse.

Some persons of a desponding spirit are in great concern about   19 the vast number of poor people who are aged, diseased, or maimed, and I have been desired to employ my thoughts what course may be taken to ease the nation of so grievous an encumbrance. But I am not in the least pain upon the matter, because it is very well known that they are every day dying and rotting by cold and famine, and filth and vermin, as fast can be reasonably expected. And as to the younger laborers, they are now in almost as hopeful a condition. They cannot get work, and consequently pine away for want of nourishment to a degree that if any time they are accidentally hired to common labor, they have not strength to perform it; and thus the country and themselves are happily delivered from the evils to come.

I have too long digressed, and therefore shall return to my sub-   20 ject. I think the advantages by the proposal which I have made are obvious and many, as well as of the highest importance.

For first, as I have already observed, it would greatly lessen the   21 number of Papists, with whom we are yearly overrun, being the principal breeders of the nation as well as our most dangerous enemies; and who stay at home on purpose to deliver the kingdom to the Pretender, hoping to take their advantage by the absence of so many good Protestants, who have chosen rather to leave their country than to stay at home and pay tithes against their conscience to an Episcopal curate.

Secondly, the poorer tenants will have something valuable of their   22 own, which by law may be made liable to distress,[12] and help to pay their landlord's rent, their corn and cattle being already seized and money a thing unknown.

Thirdly, whereas the maintenance of an hundred thousand chil-   23 dren, from two years old and upwards, cannot be computed at less than ten shillings a piece per annum, the nation's stock will be thereby increased fifty thousand pounds per annum, besides the profit of a

---

[11] A groat was a coin worth a few pennies. In a sedan chair, one person is carried about by two others on foot.
[12] Seizure for payment of debts.

new dish introduced to the tables of all gentlemen of fortune in the kingdom who have any refinement in taste. And the money will circulate among ourselves, the goods being entirely of our own growth and manufacture.

Fourthly, the constant breeders, besides the gain of eight shillings 24 sterling per annum by the sale of their children, will be rid of the charge of maintaining them after the first year.

Fifthly, this food would likewise bring great custom to taverns, 25 where the vintners will certainly be so prudent as to procure the best receipts[13] for dressing it to perfection, and consequently have their houses frequented by all the fine gentlemen, who justly value themselves upon their knowledge in good eating; and a skillful cook, who understands how to oblige his guests, will contrive to make it as expensive as they please.

Sixthly, this would be a great inducement to marriage, which all 26 wise nations have either encouraged by rewards or enforced by laws and penalties. It would increase the care and tenderness of mothers toward their children, when they were sure of a settlement for life to the poor babes, provided in some sort by the public, to their annual profit instead of expense. We should see an honest emulation among the married women, which of them could bring the fattest child to the market. Men would become as fond of their wives during the time of their pregnancy as they are now of their mares in foal, their cows in calf, or sows with they are ready to farrow; nor offer to beat or kick them (as is too frequent a practice) for fear of a miscarriage.

Many other advantages might be enumerated. For instance, the 27 addition of some thousand carcasses in our exportation of barreled beef, the propagation of swine's flesh, and improvements in the art of making good bacon, so much wanted among us by the great destruction of pigs, too frequent at our tables, which are no way comparable in taste or magnificence to a well-grown, fat, yearling child, which roasted whole will make a considerable figure at a lord mayor's feast or any other public entertainment. But this and many others I omit, being studious of brevity.

Supposing that one thousand families in this city would be con- 28 stant customers for infants' flesh, besides others who might have it at merry meetings, particularly weddings and christenings, I compute that Dublin would take off annually about twenty thousand carcasses,

[13] Recipes.

and the rest of the kingdom (where probably they will be sold somewhat cheaper) the remaining eighty thousand.

I can think of no one objection that will possibly be raised against   29
this proposal, unless it should be urged that the number of people will
be thereby much lessened in the kingdom. This I freely own, and it
was indeed one principal design in offering it to the world. I desire the
reader will observe, that I calculate my remedy for this one individual
kingdom of Ireland and for no other that ever was, is, or I think ever
can be upon earth. Therefore let no man talk to me of other expedients: of taxing our absentees at five shillings a pound: of using
neither clothes nor household furniture except what is of our own
growth and manufacture: of utterly rejecting the materials and instruments that promote foreign luxury: of curing the expensiveness of
pride, vanity, idleness, and gaming in our women: of introducing a
vein of parsimony, prudence, and temperance: of learning to love our
country, in the want of which we differ even from Laplanders and the
inhabitants of Topinamboo:[14] of quitting our animosities and factions, nor acting any longer like the Jews, who were murdering one
another at the very moment their city was taken:[15] of being a little
cautious not to sell our country and conscience for nothing: of teaching landlords to have at least one degree of mercy toward their tenants: lastly, of putting a spirit of honesty, industry, and skill into our
shopkeepers; who, if a resolution could not be taken to buy only our
native goods, would immediately unite to cheat and exact upon us in
the price, the measure, and the goodness, nor could ever yet be
brought to make one fair proposal of just dealing, though often and
earnestly invited to it.

Therefore I repeat, let no man talk to me of these and the like   30
expedients, till he hath at least some glimpse of hope that there will be
some hearty and sincere attempt to put them in practice.

But as to myself, having been wearied out for many years with   31
offering vain, idle, visionary thoughts, and at length utterly despairing
of success, I fortunately fell upon this proposal, which, as it is wholly
new, so it hath something solid and real, of no expense and little
trouble, full in our own power, and whereby we can incur no danger
in disobliging England. For this kind of commodity will not bear

[14]Lapland is the northernmost part of Scandinavia, above the Arctic Circle. The
primitive tribes of Topinamboo, in Brazil, were notorious in Swift's day for their
savagery.
[15]Jerusalem was seized by the Romans in A.D. 70.

exportation, the flesh being of too tender a consistence to admit a long continuance in salt, although perhaps I could name a country which would be glad to eat up our whole nation without it.

After all, I am not so violently bent upon my own opinion as to reject any offer proposed by wise men, which shall be found equally innocent, cheap, easy, and effectual. But before something of that kind shall be advanced in contradiction to my scheme, and offering a better, I desire the author or authors will be pleased maturely to consider two points. First, as things now stand, how they will be able to find food and raiment for an hundred thousand useless mouths and backs. And secondly, there being a round million of creatures in human figure throughout this kingdom, whose sole subsistence put into a common stock would leave them in debt two millions of pounds sterling, adding those who are beggars by profession to the bulk of farmers, cottagers, and laborers, with their wives and children who are beggars in effect; I desire those politicians who dislike my overture, and may perhaps be so bold to attempt an answer, that they will first ask the parents of these mortals whether they would not at this day think it a great happiness to have been sold for food at a year old in this manner I prescribe, and thereby have avoided such a perpetual scene of misfortunes as they have since gone through by the oppression of landlords, the impossibility of paying rent without money or trade, the want of common sustenance, with neither house nor clothes to cover them from the inclemencies of the weather, and the most inevitable prospect of entailing the like or greater miseries upon their breed forever.

I profess, in the sincerity of my heart, that I have not the least personal interest in endeavoring to promote this necessary work, having no other motive than the public good of my country, by advancing our trade, providing for infants, relieving the poor, and giving some pleasure to the rich. I have no children by which I can propose to get a single penny; the youngest being nine years old, and my wife past childbearing.

Meaning

1. In your own words, explain Swift's "modest proposal," the chief problems it is designed to solve, and how it would solve those problems.
2. What reasonable solutions does Swift mention to Ireland's problems? Why does he reject these solutions in favor of his outrageous one?

3. If you do not know the meanings of the following words, look them up in a dictionary: importuning, alms, sustenance (paragraph 1); prodigious, deplorable (2); dam, raiment (4); rudiments, probationers (6); commodity (7); eminent, prolific, popish, collateral, Papists (13); cottagers, repine (14); flay (15); discoursing, deference, scrupulous, censure (17); expedient, mandarins, gibbet (18); desponding, encumbrance, vermin (19); tithes, curate (21); vintners, prudent, procure, contrive (25); emulation, farrow (26); propagation (27); parsimony, prudence, temperance, animosities (29); incur, disobliging (31); inclemencies, entailing (32).

Purpose and Audience

1. Like all satirists, Swift writes on two levels: as his narrator, the *I* of the essay, and as himself. What is the narrator's purpose? What is Swift's real purpose? Where do these two purposes overlap? Where do they diverge?

2. Ever since this essay was first published, many readers have failed to grasp its irony and have condemned Swift for his inhumanity. Yet Swift provides clues that make his true intentions clear, as in his statement that the landlords, "as they have already devoured most of the parents, seem to have the best title to the children" (paragraph 12). What other such clues do you find after that point? Why do you think Swift provides them?

3. What was your own reaction to Swift's essay? Did you appreciate the irony? To what extent—and in what ways—did the repulsiveness of the proposal affect your willingness to accept his argument? What do your own responses and those of your classmates suggest about the advantages and disadvantages of satire as a technique of argument?

Method and Structure

1. Swift casts his essay in a fairly standard argumentative structure. Outline the essay roughly to see its parts, and analyze what each part contributes to the whole.

2. What steps does Swift take to establish the ethical appeal of his narrator? Cite sentences or passages that seem designed to gain the reader's trust and confidence in the author.

3. **Other Methods**   Swift furthers his argument through skillful use of several methods of development, including process analysis (Chapter 6) and cause-and-effect analysis (Chapter 10). Locate one example of each of these methods, and explain what each contributes to the persuasiveness of the argument.

Language

1. Locate several passages where Swift's irony strikes you as particularly apt or intriguing, and explain the contrast between their ironic and literal meanings. At whom is the ironic barb directed? Is it bitter or humorous? (If necessary, consult the Glossary for a definition of *irony*.)

2. Swift refers to the poor people of Ireland in terms normally reserved for livestock—for example, "breeders" (paragraph 6) and "fore or hind quarter" (10). Locate other expressions or sentences in this vein. What do they lend to the satire?

3. How would you characterize Swift's writing style? Give examples to support your answer. To what extent does his style contribute to or detract from your appreciation of the essay, and why? (See *style* in the Glossary if you need a definition.)

Writing Topics

1. Just as Swift was outraged by conditions in Ireland, you may be similarly moved by some current condition—perhaps nuclear-arms proliferation, increasing crime, a newly discovered health hazard, or a dangerous traffic intersection the authorities persist in ignoring. Imitate Swift's strategy and write a "modest proposal" to end the condition. Like Swift's, your proposal should be fairly simple and argued with the most careful and detailed logic you can muster.

2. Ireland's problems did not end with the publication of Swift's essay but in fact have endured. Consult an encyclopedia such as *The New Encyclopaedia Britannica* to find an overview of the history of Ireland and its relations with England from Swift's time until the present. Focus on one of the specific problems Swift mentions—prejudices against "Papists," for example, or food shortages or absentee landlords—and research it in at least several other sources (your library's reference librarian or card catalog can help you find sources). Write an essay explaining the origins of the problem, the extent of its persistence, the attempts to resolve it, and the results of those attempts.

3. In analyzing Swift's essay, you have observed many of the elements of good satire. Using what you now know about satire, write an essay examining the strategy and effectiveness of one of the other satiric essays in this book, such as Neil Postman's "Megatons for Anthromegs" (p. 99), Jessica Mitford's "Embalming Mr. Jones" (p. 178), Judy Syfers's "I Want a Wife" (p. 258), or Barbara Ehrenreich's "Blocking the Gates to Heaven" (p. 364).

Writing Topics

Argument and Persuasion

Choose one of the following statements, or any other statement they suggest, and support *or* refute it in an argumentative essay. The statement you decide on should concern a topic you care about so that argument is a means of convincing readers to accept an idea, not an end in itself.

1. Pornographic magazines and books should be banned.
2. Professional athletes should be allowed to compete in the Olympics.
3. Private automobiles should be restricted in cities.
4. The elderly are entitled to unlimited free medical care.
5. Private institutions have the right to make rules that would be unconstitutional outside those institutions.
6. Health care should be nationalized in the United States.
7. Laboratory experiments on dogs, cats, and primates should be banned.
8. Students caught in any form of academic cheating should be expelled.
9. Violence and sex should be prohibited from television.
10. Advertisements for consumer products (or political candidates) should be recognized as serving useful purposes.
11. Students should not be granted high-school diplomas until they can demonstrate reasonable competence in writing and mathematics.
12. The school's costly athletic programs should be eliminated in favor of improving the academic curriculum.
13. Children should be able to sue their parents for negligence or abuse.
14. Smoking should be banned in all indoor public places.
15. Like high school textbooks, college textbooks should be purchased by the school and loaned to students for the duration of a course.
16. A citizen ought to be able to buy and keep a handgun for protection without having to register it.
17. When they turn eighteen, adopted children should have free access to information about their birth parents.
18. The owners of a professional sports team should be able to sell or move the team as they see fit, without obtaining the approval of the league.
19. Rock music albums should be specially labeled if their lyrics contain violent or sexual images.

Chapter 12

Combining Methods of Development

ESSAYS FOR FURTHER READING

Though each essay in the preceding chapters illustrates one overall method of development, all the essays also illustrate other methods at the level of passages or paragraphs. (Follow-up questions labeled "Other Methods" have highlighted these varied strategies.) In fact, an essay is rarely developed by a single method alone. Even when writers are purposefully comparing or classifying, say, they also describe, narrate, define, or employ other methods. And often writers use no dominant method at all but select whatever methods they need, in whatever sequence, to achieve their purpose.

Combining methods usually adds texture and substance to an essay, for the methods provide different approaches to a subject, different ways to introduce the details and other evidence needed to interest and convince readers. Sometimes the appropriate methods may suggest themselves, but at other times it can help to explore them deliberately. The introductory discussion of the writing process includes a set of questions derived from the methods of development that can aid such a deliberate search (see p. 15). Say you are writing a paper on owls. Right off several methods suggest themselves: a classi-

357

fication of kinds of owls, a description of each kind of owl, a process analysis of an owl's life cycle or hunting behavior. But you want your paper to go beyond the facts to convey your fascination with owls. Running through the list of questions, you find that "How did the subject happen?" suggests a narrative of your first encounter with a barn owl, when your own awe and fear recalled the owl's reputation for wisdom and bad luck. Other questions then lead you further along this path: for instance, "How can the subject be illustrated?" calls forth examples of myths and superstitions involving owls; and "Why did the subject happen?" leads you to consider why people see owls as symbols and omens. In the course of asking the questions, you have moved from a straightforward look at owls to a more imaginative and complex examination of their meaning and significance for human beings.

The more you use the methods of development—alone or in combination—the more comfortable you will be with them and the better they will serve you. The three essays in this chapter illustrate how the methods may be combined in any way the author chooses to express ideas and achieve a purpose. (Brief annotations accompanying each essay point out some of the methods.) All the essays demonstrate how much the authors gain from having a battery of techniques and strategies to employ at will.

George Orwell

A masterful novelist, essayist, journalist, and critic, George Orwell was a highly political writer with little tolerance for authoritarianism, deceit, or pretension. He was born Eric Arthur Blair in 1903 in Bengal, India, where his father held a position in the British civil service. After attending school in England, in 1922 Orwell returned to the East as an officer with the British police in Burma. Five years later he left government service with a lasting contempt for the injustices of imperialism. He had believed since childhood that he should be a writer, so he returned to Europe to become one. His next years of wandering, odd jobs, and poverty were chronicled in Down and Out in Paris and London *(1933), his first book and the occasion for assuming his pen name. Other books followed, including* Burmese Days *(1934), a novel based on his colonial experiences, and* Homage to Catalonia *(1938), a memoir of fighting against the fascists in the Spanish Civil War in 1936. Orwell's best-known works are two satirical novels,* Animal Farm *(1945) and* Nineteen Eighty-Four *(1949), both attacks on totalitarian government. He wrote, he said, largely from political purpose, from a "desire to push the world in a certain direction, to alter other people's ideas of the kind of society that they should strive for." Orwell died in 1950, at the age of forty-six, from a lung ailment. The four-volume* Collected Essays, Journalism, and Letters of George Orwell, *coedited by his widow, Sonia Orwell, was published in 1968.*

Marrakech

Marrakech is a city in Morocco, a North African country that was a French colony in 1939, when Orwell wrote this essay. Claiming to be "merely pointing to a fact," Orwell instead produces a sharp indictment of his own and other white people's insensitivity to the sufferings of brown and black people everywhere.

The annotations indicate the use of nearly every method of development discussed in this book. The essay is often classified as a work of description, and indeed Orwell does take care to convey the impressions of the senses. But the essay can also be seen as an argument against the kind of insensitivity Orwell finds in himself and other white people.

As the corpse went past the flies left the restaurant table in a cloud and rushed after it, but they came back a few minutes later.   1

Description and example

The little crowd of mourners—all men and boys, no 2 women—threaded their way across the market-place be- *Description and example* tween the piles of pomegranates and the taxis and the cam- els, wailing a short chant over and over again. What really appeals to the flies is that the corpses here are never put into coffins, they are merely wrapped in a piece of rag and carried on a rough wooden bier on the shoulders of four friends. When the friends get to the burying-ground they *Process analysis* hack an oblong hole a foot or two deep, dump the body in it and fling over it a little of the dried-up, lumpy earth, which is like broken brick. No gravestone, no name, no iden- tifying mark of any kind. The burying-ground is merely a huge waste of hummocky earth, like a derelict building- lot. After a month or two no one can even be certain where his own relatives are buried.

When you walk through a town like this—two hun- 3 dred thousand inhabitants, of whom at least twenty thou- sand own literally nothing except the rags they stand up in—when you see how the people live, and still more how *Cause-and-effect* easily they die, it is always difficult to believe that you are *analysis* walking among human beings. All colonial empires are in reality founded upon that fact. The people have brown faces—besides, there are so many of them! Are they really the same flesh as yourself? Do they even have names? Or are they merely a kind of undifferentiated brown stuff, about as individual as bees or coral insects? They rise out of the earth, they sweat and starve for a few years, and then they sink back into the nameless mounds of the grave- yard and nobody notices that they are gone. And even the graves themselves soon fade back into the soil. Sometimes, out for a walk, as you break your way through the prickly pear, you notice that it is rather bumpy underfoot, and only a certain regularity in the bumps tells you that you are walking over skeletons.

I was feeding one of the gazelles in the public gardens. 4
Gazelles are almost the only animals that look good to 5 eat when they are still alive, in fact, one can hardly look at their hindquarters without thinking of mint sauce. The ga- *Narration* zelle I was feeding seemed to know that this thought was *and example* in my mind, for though it took the piece of bread I was

holding out it obviously did not like me. It nibbled rapidly at the bread, then lowered its head and tried to butt me, then took another nibble and then butted again. Probably its idea was that if it could drive me away the bread would somehow remain hanging in midair.

An Arab navvy working on the path nearby lowered his heavy hoe and sidled towards us. He looked from the gazelle to the bread and from the bread to the gazelle, with a sort of quiet amazement, as though he had never seen anything quite like this before. Finally he said shyly in French:

"*I* could eat some of that bread."

I tore off a piece and he stowed it gratefully in some secret place under his rags. This man is an employee of the Municipality. . . .

All people who work with their hands are partly invisible, and the more important the work they do, the less visible they are. Still, a white skin is always fairly conspicuous. In northern Europe, when you see a labourer ploughing a field, you probably give him a second glance. In a hot country, anywhere south of Gibraltar or east of Suez, the chances are that you don't even see him. I have noticed this again and again. In a tropical landscape one's eye takes in everything except the human beings. It takes in the dried-up soil, the prickly pear, the palm-tree and the distant mountain, but it always misses the peasant hoeing at his patch. He is the same colour as the earth, and a great deal less interesting to look at.

It is only because of this that the starved countries of Asia and Africa are accepted as tourist resorts. No one would think of running cheap trips to the Distressed Areas. But where the human beings have brown skins their poverty is simply not noticed. What does Morocco mean to a Frenchman? An orange-grove or a job in government service. Or to an Englishman: Camels, castles, palm-trees, Foreign Legionnaires, brass trays, and bandits. One could probably live here for years without noticing that for nine-tenths of the people the reality of life is an endless, back-breaking struggle to wring a little food out of an eroded soil.

[Marginal annotations:]

Narration and example

6

7

8

9

Comparison

Example

Example

10

Cause-and-effect analysis

Example

Most of Morocco is so desolate that no wild animal   11
bigger than a hare can live on it. Huge areas which were   *Description*
once covered with forest have turned into a treeless waste
where the soil is exactly like broken-up brick. Nevertheless
a good deal of it is cultivated, with frightful labour. Everything is done by hand. Long lines of women, bent double
like inverted capital Ls, work their way slowly across the
fields, tearing up the prickly weeds with their hands, and
the peasant gathering lucerne for fodder pulls it up stalk by   *Process*
stalk instead of reaping it, thus saving an inch or two on   *analysis*
each stalk. The plough is a wretched wooden thing, so frail
that one can easily carry it on one's shoulder, and fitted
underneath with a rough iron spike which stirs the soil to a
depth of about four inches. This is as much as the strength
of the animals is equal to. It is usual to plough with a cow
and a donkey yoked together. Two donkeys would not be
quite strong enough, but on the other hand two cows
would cost a little more to feed. The peasants possess no
harrows, they merely plough the soil several times over in
different directions, finally leaving it in rough furrows,
after which the whole field has to be shaped with hoes into
small oblong patches, to conserve water. Except for a day
or two after the rare rainstorms there is never enough water. Along the edges of the fields channels are hacked out
to a depth of thirty or forty feet to get at the tiny trickles
which run through the subsoil.

Every afternoon a file of very old women passes down   12
the road outside my house, each carrying a load of firewood. All of them are mummified with age and the sun,
and all of them are tiny. It seems to be generally the case in
primitive communities that the women, when they get beyond a certain age, shrink to the size of children. One day
a poor old creature who could not have been more than
four feet tall crept past me under a vast load of wood. I
stopped her and put a five-sou piece (a little more than a
farthing) into her hand. She answered with a shrill wail,   *Narration and*
almost a scream, which was partly gratitude but mainly   *example*
surprise. I suppose that from her point of view, by taking
any notice of her, I seemed almost to be violating a law of
nature. She accepted her status as an old woman, that is to

say as a beast of burden. When a family is travelling it is quite usual to see a father and a grown-up son riding ahead on donkeys, and an old woman following on foot, carrying the baggage.

But what is strange about these people is their invisi- 13 bility. For several weeks, always at about the same time of day, the file of old women had hobbled past the house with their firewood, and though they had registered themselves on my eyeballs I cannot truly say that I had seen them. Firewood was passing—that was how I saw it. It was only that one day I happened to be walking behind them, and the curious up-and-down motion of a load of wood drew my attention to the human being underneath it. Then for the first time I noticed the poor earth-coloured bodies, bodies reduced to bones and leathery skin, bent double under the crushing weight. Yet I suppose I had not been five minutes on Moroccan soil before I noticed the overloading of the donkeys and was infuriated by it. There is no question that the donkeys are damnably treated. The Moroccan donkey is hardly bigger than a St. Bernard dog, it carries a load which in the British army would be considered too much for a fifteen-hands mule,[1] and very often its pack-saddle is not taken off its back for weeks together. But what is peculiarly pitiful is that it is the most willing creature on earth, it follows its master like a dog and does not need either bridle or halter. After a dozen years of devoted work it suddenly drops dead, whereupon its master tips it into the ditch and the village dogs have torn its guts out before it is cold.

This kind of thing makes one's blood boil, whereas— 14 on the whole—the plight of the human beings does not. I am not commenting, merely pointing to a fact. People with brown skins are next door to invisible. Anyone can be sorry for the donkey with its galled back, but it is generally owing to some kind of accident if one even notices the old woman under her load of sticks.

---

[1] A mule measuring sixty inches high at the base of the neck. [Editor's note.]

Barbara Ehrenreich

Barbara Ehrenreich is a leading voice in the movements for women's rights and against nuclear arms. She was born in 1941 in Butte, Montana, and educated at Reed College (B.A., 1963) and Rockefeller University (Ph.D. in biology, 1968). As a writer, she says, she is "motivated by a commitment to social justice." Her essays on health policy, the economic condition of women, the nuclear-arms race, and related issues appear regularly in Ms. *magazine, where she is a contributing editor, as well as in* The New York Times Magazine, The Nation, Monthly Review, *and other periodicals. She has written or coauthored a number of books, including* The American Health Empire *(1970), with her first husband, John E. Ehrenreich;* The Hearts of Men: American Dreams and the Flight from Commitment *(1983); and* Toward Economic Justice for Women: A National Agenda of Change *(1985). Ehrenreich's latest book is* Fear of Falling: The Inner Life of the Middle Class *(1989), an examination of the sources and manifestations of anxiety in the American middle class.*

Blocking the Gates to Heaven

With the ironic tone that figures in much of her writing, Ehrenreich here explores the meaning and effect of a changing view of the universe. Her inspiration and target is Star Wars, the nickname given to the controversial Strategic Defense Initiative. Conceived during the presidency of Ronald Reagan, Star Wars calls for the use of satellites in space to "shield" the United States by directing rockets, laser beams, and other weapons toward enemy missiles. Since Ehrenreich published this essay in Mother Jones *in 1986, the plan has been altered and delayed under President George Bush, but it is still a significant element of defense policy.*

Ehrenreich's entire essay illustrates cause-and-effect analysis: she seeks the causes for what amounts to a loss of respect for the universe, a change that allows us to view the universe as a battlefield. Within that framework, she uses many other methods of development, some indicated by the annotations.

W hen I was the age my children are now, that is, old 1
enough to know everything but still young enough to be   *Narration and*
dissatisfied with the limited information available, the   *comparison*
night sky meant a lot more than a connect-the-dots lesson

in ancient Roman mythology. It was a threshold leading to better worlds, where, according to my monthly *Galaxy* magazine, humanoids of great strength and surpassing intelligence drove about purposefully from star to star. In sci-fi convention, life-forms that hadn't developed space travel were mere prehistory—the horseshoe crabs of the cosmic scene—and something of the humiliation of being stuck on a provincial planet in a galactic backwater has stayed with me ever since. But now, with the prospect of Star Wars, I am beginning to feel claustrophobic. It is bad enough that the heavens are still inaccessible, but they are about to become a "shield," which means, for all practical purposes, a lid.

Narration and comparison

This is no idle metaphor, for NASA[1] is already so compromised by military priorities that we might never really get off the ground. What was the ill-fated shuttle for, if not to show the Russians that we're honing the capacity to pelt them with warheads from beyond the Van Allen belt? Unfortunately, all the shuttle demonstrated is that NASA (and hence, no doubt, the Pentagon) is still stuck at the balsa wood and airplane glue level of technology, in which the key engineering question is whether part A will stay attached to part B, even in the cold and without a rubber band.

2

Example

Perhaps, though, in some subtle and unacknowledged way, we've been losing interest in the universe. From an entertainment point of view, the Solar System has been a bust. None of the planets turns out to have any real-estate potential, and most of them are probably even useless for filming *Dune*[2] sequels. We may also be despairing of finding any friends out there, and America badly needs friends,

3

Cause of change: loss of excitement and interest

[1] NASA is the National Aeronautics and Space Administration. The "ill-fated shuttle" in the next sentence refers to the space-shuttle program; when Ehrenreich was writing, the shuttle program had been halted by the explosion of the *Challenger*, which killed all seven crew members, in 1986. Later in the same sentence, "the Van Allen belt" refers to a band of radiation extending from 400 to 40,000 miles above the earth. The last sentence in the paragraph refers to the rubber seals that proved defective in cold weather and caused the *Challenger* explosion. [Editor's note.]

[2] A science-fiction novel (1965) by Frank Herbert that was made into a movie. [Editor's note.]

since so many of the ones we have on earth are either bad-tempered tyrants or wealthy vagrants who have been forced to leave the tyrant business. A few years ago, Hollywood promised us a universe populated by short, sensitive fellows who would, at the very least, be ideal companions for single mothers. But the search for extraterrestrial intelligence (SETI, to us insiders) has so far only proved that no matter what you beam up—the Pythagorean theorem, pictures of attractive nude people, etc.—the big 800 number in the sky does not return calls. So, in the cinematic imagination, ET was replaced by a batch of gremlins and ghosts, all of unknown provenance and dubious morality.

Comparison and example

It could be, though I hesitate to suggest it, that the universe is simply going out of style. It was big in the '50s, with the likes of Asimov and Clarke[3] promoting it, and before we had fully realized that Einstein was serious about a cosmic speed limit that would put even the nearest star about three light-years[4] away by express flight. Black holes, when they came along in the late 1960s, seemed to solve the problem. If you were willing to forgive them for their shrewlike capacity for guzzling whole nebulae and occasional solid matter like stars and planets, they looked as if they could have been put to use as secret passages through which a crew might burrow from galaxy to galaxy before Alzheimer's set in. Such luminaries of sci-fi and sci-fact as Joan D. Vinge and Carl Sagan have already employed black holes as cosmic mass transit systems; and if you don't mind being chewed down to your bosons and spat out on the other side of creation, I suppose it beats staying at home and watching *Star Trek* reruns.

4

Narration

Recent discoveries, though, may have made us wonder whether it's worth the effort. Just a few months ago there was the unsettling news that the universe has, as a result of explosions subsidiary to the big bang, a "bubble structure"—that is, the galaxies seem to be arrayed on the sur-

5 *Cause of change: peculiar theories*

Example

Definition

[3]Isaac Asimov (born 1920) and Arthur C. Clarke (born 1917) are prominent science-fiction writers. Albert Einstein (1879–1955), cited later in the sentence, is the famous physicist. [Editor's note.]

[4]A light-year is the distance light travels in one year: 5,878 trillion miles. [Editor's note.]

face of massive bubbles, more or less like dust specks on beer foam. Now, this is not the kind of thing we were brought up to expect from the universe. A great deal of human tradition and prejudice says that big things are automatically majestic and only small things can be silly. So how are we to comprehend such megascale frivolity? It was hard enough to adjust to a grim and indifferent universe that had some purpose other than giving tips to astrologers. But are we ready for a carbonated universe, potentially as "lite" as a dinner from Lean Cuisine or a *USA Today* story on African starvation?

Definition

Example

Another bit of bad PR for the universe was the discovery in January [1986] of "bizarre structures"—described as threads, loops, and shells—within our own galaxy. We are not talking about some fuzz left on a telescope lens; the threads alone are 100 light-years long by a light-year wide. There must be an explanation, of course, and astronomers are already blaming the big bang, which started the universe, but it is hard to be filled with reverence toward a firmament filled with objects that look like pasta.

6

Definition

Then there's the big bang itself. If that's how it all started, then we might as well face the fact that what's left out there is a great deal of shrapnel and a whole bunch of cinders (one of which is, fortunately, still hot enough and close enough to be good for tanning). Trying to find some sense and order in this mess may be as futile as trying to understand the culture of Japan from the wreckage of Hiroshima,[5] or trying to reconstruct the economy of Iowa from a bowl of popcorn.

7

Analogy

So I can well imagine the top scientists at NASA pouring a rare dollop of gin into their Tang and deciding that the universe no longer has the right stuff. Maybe that was when they decided to drop "manned" space travel in the classic sense and fill the available shuttle seats with women, blacks, Jews, Asians, and members of the traditionally Democratic teachers' union. Maybe, a few dollops later,

8 | *Cause of change: arrogance*

Narration (imaginary)

[5]Hiroshima, Japan, is the city on which Americans dropped the first atomic bomb in 1945. [Editor's note.]

these same famous scientists decided that the noblest course for "man" would be to emulate that great and witty Engineer who designed the universe (with some help, no doubt, from the likes of Morton Thiokol and Bechtel[6]) and go out with the biggest little bang we can muster. Hence Star Wars, an ingenious, trillion-dollar technology designed to squelch all meaningful arms talks, subvert the space program, and generate the national arrogance required for that essential first strike.

Narration (imaginary)

There are still a few of us left, though, who don't feel we're too good for the universe, no matter how much it lets us down. Maybe it isn't a vast demonstration of eternal law and order put up there for our edification. Maybe it's more like a room after an all-night party, strewn with random debris by Someone whose idea of a good time we can never hope to fathom. I'd still like to know, still like to meet whoever's out there, still like to think my descendants won't be stuck here forever, toiling away on a large rock near a small-sized star. And for the time being, when I look up at night, I want to sense the huge, untidy humor of infinity—not a gravestone of our own making pressing down on us.

9

Analogy

[6]Both of these firms are government contractors. Morton Thiokol manufactured the parts of the space shuttle *Challenger* that malfunctioned, causing the explosion. [Editor's note.]

Maxine Hong Kingston

Born of Chinese immigrant parents in 1940 in Stockton, California, Maxine Hong Kingston grew up there amid the Chinese-American community. Her parents, well educated in China, worked in this country as laborers and laundry operators. Kingston graduated from the University of California at Berkeley in 1962, taught language arts and English at high schools in California and Hawaii, and taught creative writing at the University of Hawaii before turning to writing full-time. She has published poems, stories, and nonfiction in The New Yorker, The New York Times Magazine, Ms., *and other periodicals. In 1989 she published a novel,* Tripmaster Monkey: His Fake Book, *centered in the youth and art culture of 1960s San Francisco. Before that, her best-known works had been two related books of autobiography:* The Woman Warrior: Memoirs of a Childhood Among Ghosts *(1976) and* China Men *(1980). Both books draw on the "talk-stories" Kingston heard from her elders—Chinese myths, legends about China, family tales—and her own memories of growing up in an immigrant community. "Sometimes," Kingston says, "our lives have plots like stories; sometimes we're affected by the stories or we try to live up to them or the stories give a color and an atmosphere to life." She describes her work as an attempt to sort out the legends and the reality.*

No Name Woman

In this selection from The Woman Warrior, *Kingston recalls and embellishes one of the cautionary tales told by her mother. The rapt attention to family legend, the shifts between reality and fantasy, and the powerful, often dreamlike voice are typical of Kingston's work.*

The annotations to Kingston's essay indicate only some of the methods of development she uses. Description, for example, is too pervasive to be noted at every appearance; only a few powerful instances are marked. The entire essay is in essence a comparison between two narratives—that of Kingston's mother and that imagined by Kingston herself—in order to discover the causes of a death and its cover-up. (All three of these methods also come into play at the paragraph level, and some instances are noted.) By the end of the essay, Kingston's invented story has gained all the strength and sureness of her mother's eyewitness account.

"You must not tell anyone," my mother said, "What I am about to tell you. In China your father had a sister who | 1 | *Narration*

killed herself. She jumped into the family well. We say that   *Narration*
your father has all brothers because it is as if she had never
been born.

"In 1924 just a few days after our village celebrated   2
seventeen hurry-up weddings—to make sure that every
young man who went 'out on the road' would responsibly
come home—your father and his brothers and your grandfather and his brothers and your aunt's new husband
sailed for America, the Gold Mountain. It was your grandfather's last trip. Those lucky enough to get contracts
waved good-bye from the decks. They fed and guarded the
stowaways and helped them off in Cuba, New York, Bali,
Hawaii. 'We'll meet in California next year,' they said. All
of them sent money home.

"I remember looking at your aunt one day when she   3
and I were dressing; I had not noticed before that she had
such a protruding melon of a stomach. But I did not think,
'She's pregnant,' until she began to look like other pregnant women, her shirt pulling and the white tops of her
black pants showing. She could not have been pregnant,
you see, because her husband had been gone for years. No
one said anything. We did not discuss it. In early summer
she was ready to have the child, long after the time when it
could have been possible.

"The village had also been counting. On the night the   4
baby was to be born the villagers raided our house. Some
were crying. Like a great saw, teeth strung with lights, files
of people walked zigzag across our land, tearing the rice.   *Description*
Their lanterns doubled in the disturbed black water, which
drained away through the broken bunds. As the villagers
closed in, we could see that some of them, probably men
and women we knew well, wore white masks. The people
with long hair hung it over their faces. Women with short
hair made it stand up on end. Some had tied white bands
around their foreheads, arms, and legs.

"At first they threw mud and rocks at the house. Then   5
they threw eggs and began slaughtering our stock. We
could hear the animals scream their deaths—the roosters,
the pigs, a last great roar from the ox. Familiar wild heads
flared in our night windows; the villagers encircled us.

Some of the faces stopped to peer at us, their eyes rushing   *Narration*
like searchlights. The hands flattened against the panes,
framed heads, and left red prints.

"The villagers broke in the front and the back doors at   6
the same time, even though we had not locked the doors
against them. Their knives dripped with the blood of our
animals. They smeared blood on the doors and walls. One
woman swung a chicken, whose throat she had slit, splat-
tering blood in red arcs about her. We stood together in
the middle of our house, in the family hall with the pictures and tables of the ancestors around us, and looked
straight ahead.

"At that time the house had only two wings. When the   7
men came back, we would build two more to enclose our
courtyard and a third one to begin a second courtyard.
The villagers pushed through both wings, even your
grandparents' rooms, to find your aunt's, which was also
mine until the men returned. From this room a new wing
for one of the younger families would grow. They ripped
up her clothes and shoes and broke her combs, grinding
them underfoot. They tore her work from the loom. They
scattered the cooking fire and rolled the new weaving in it.
We could hear them in the kitchen breaking our bowls and
banging the pots. They overturned the great waist-high
earthenware jugs; duck eggs, pickled fruits, vegetables
burst out and mixed in acrid torrents. The old woman
from the next field swept a broom through the air and
loosed the spirits-of-the-broom over our heads. 'Pig.'
'Ghost.' 'Pig,' they sobbed and scolded while they ruined
our house.

"When they left, they took sugar and oranges to bless   8
themselves. They cut pieces from the dead animals. Some
of them took bowls that were not broken and clothes that
were not torn. Afterward we swept up the rice and sewed
it back up into sacks. But the smells from the spilled pre-
serves lasted. Your aunt gave birth in the pigsty that night.
The next morning when I went up for the water, I found
her and the baby plugging up the family well.

"Don't let your father know that I told you. He denies   9
her. Now that you have started to menstruate, what hap-

pened to her could happen to you. Don't humiliate us. You wouldn't like to be forgotten as if you had never been born. The villagers are watchful."

Whenever she had to warn us about life, my mother told stories that ran like this one, a story to grow up on. She tested our strength to establish realities. Those in the emigrant generations who could not reassert brute survival died young and far from home. Those of us in the first American generations have had to figure out how the invisible world the emigrants built around our childhoods fit in solid America.

10

Cause-and-effect analysis

The emigrants confused the gods by diverting their curses, misleading them with crooked streets and false names. They must try to confuse their offspring as well, who, I suppose, threaten them in similar ways—always trying to get things straight, always trying to name the unspeakable. The Chinese I know hide their names; sojourners take new names when their lives change and guard their real names with silence.

11

Chinese-Americans, when you try to understand what things in you are Chinese, how do you separate what is peculiar to childhood, to poverty, insanities, one family, your mother who marked your growing with stories, from what is Chinese? What is Chinese tradition and what is the movies?

12

If I want to learn what clothes my aunt wore, whether flashy or ordinary, I would have to begin, "Remember Father's drowned-in-the-well sister?" I cannot ask that. My mother has told me once and for all the useful parts. She will add nothing unless powered by Necessity, a riverbank that guides her life. She plants vegetable gardens rather than lawns; she carries the odd-shaped tomatoes home from the fields and eats food left for the gods.

13

Example

Whenever we did frivolous things, we used up energy; we flew high kites. We children came up off the ground over the melting cones our parents brought home from work and the American movie on New Year's Day—*Oh, You Beautiful Doll* with Betty Grable one year, and *She Wore a Yellow Ribbon* with John Wayne another year.

14

After the one carnival ride each, we paid in guilt; our tired   *Example*
father counted his change on the dark walk home.

Adultery is extravagance. Could people who hatch   15
their own chicks and eat the embryos and the heads for
delicacies and boil the feet in vinegar for party food, leaving only the gravel, eating even the gizzard lining—could   *Cause-and-effect*
such people engender a prodigal aunt? To be a woman, to   *analysis (imagined*
causes)
have a daughter in starvation time was a waste enough.
My aunt could not have been the lone romantic who gave
up everything for sex. Women in the old China did not
choose. Some man had commanded her to lie with him   *Comparison*
and be his secret evil. I wonder whether he masked himself   *(alternative*
explanations)
when he joined the raid on her family.

Perhaps she encountered him in the fields or on the   16
mountain where the daughters-in-law collected fuel. Or
perhaps he first noticed her in the marketplace. He was not
a stranger because the village housed no strangers. She had
to have dealings with him other than sex. Perhaps he
worked an adjoining field, or he sold her the cloth for the
dress she sewed and wore. His demand must have surprised, then terrified her. She obeyed him; she always did
as she was told.

When the family found a young man in the next vil-   17
lage to be her husband, she stood tractably beside the best
rooster, his proxy, and promised before they met that she
would be his forever. She was lucky that he was her age
and she would be the first wife, an advantage secure now.
The night she first saw him, he had sex with her. Then he
left for America. She had almost forgotten what he looked
like. When she tried to envision him, she only saw the
black and white face in the group photograph the men had
had taken before leaving.

The other man was not, after all, much different from   18
her husband. They both gave orders: she followed. "If you
tell your family, I'll beat you. I'll kill you. Be here again
next week." No one talked sex, ever. And she might have
separated the rapes from the rest of living if only she did
not have to buy her oil from him or gather wood in the
same forest. I want her fear to have lasted just as long as

rape lasted so that the fear could have been contained. No *Cause-and-effect*
drawn-out fear. But women at sex hazarded birth and *analysis*
hence lifetimes. The fear did not stop but permeated every- *Comparison*
where. She told the man, "I think I'm pregnant." He organized the raid against her.

On nights when my mother and father talked about 19
their life back home, sometimes they mentioned an "outcast table" whose business they still seemed to be settling,
their voices tight. In a commensal tradition, where food is *Definition*
precious, the powerful older people made wrongdoers eat
alone. Instead of letting them start separate new lives like
the Japanese, who could become samurais and geishas, the
Chinese family, faces averted but eyes glowering sideways,
hung on to the offenders and fed them leftovers. My aunt
must have lived in the same house as my parents and eaten
at an outcast table. My mother spoke about the raid as if
she had seen it, when she and my aunt, a daughter-in-law
to a different household, should not have been living together at all. Daughters-in-law lived with their husbands'
parents, not their own; a synonym for marriage in Chinese *Process analysis*
is "taking a daughter-in-law." Her husband's parents
could have sold her, mortgaged her, stoned her. But they
had sent her back to her own mother and father, a mysterious act hinting at disgraces not told me. Perhaps they had
thrown her out to deflect the avengers.

She was the only daughter; her four brothers went 20
with her father, husband, and uncles "out on the road"
and for some years became western men. When the goods
were divided among the family, three of the brothers took *Comparison*
land, and the youngest, my father, chose an education.
After my grandparents gave their daughter away to her
husband's family, they had dispensed all the adventure and
all the property. They expected her alone to keep the traditional ways, which her brothers, now among the barbar-
ians, could fumble without detection. The heavy, deep-
rooted women were to maintain the past against the flood,
safe for returning. But the rare urge west had fixed upon
our family, and so my aunt crossed boundaries not delin-
eated in space.

The work of preservation demands that the feelings   21
playing about in one's guts not be turned into action. Just
watch their passing like cherry blossoms. But perhaps my
aunt, my forerunner, caught in a slow life, let dreams grow
and fade and after some months or years went toward
what persisted. Fear at the enormities of the forbidden
kept her desires delicate, wire and bone. She looked at a
man because she liked the way the hair was tucked behind
his ears, or she liked the question-mark line of a long torso
curving at the shoulder and straight at the hip. For warm
eyes or a soft voice or a slow walk—that's all—a few
hairs, a line, a brightness, a sound, a pace, she gave up
family. She offered us up for a charm that vanished with
tiredness, a pigtail that didn't toss when the wind died.
Why, the wrong lighting could erase the dearest thing
about him.

Cause-and-effect analysis (imagined causes)

Comparison (alternative explanations)

It could very well have been, however, that my aunt   22
did not take subtle enjoyment of her friend, but, a wild
woman, kept rollicking company. Imagining her free with
sex doesn't fit, though. I don't know any women like that,
or men either. Unless I see her life branching into mine, she
gives me no ancestral help.

To sustain her being in love, she often worked at her-   23
self in the mirror, guessing at the colors and shapes that
would interest him, changing them frequently in order to
hit on the right combination. She wanted him to look
back.

Comparison

On a farm near the sea, a woman who tended her   24
appearance reaped a reputation for eccentricity. All the
married women blunt-cut their hair in flaps about their
ears or pulled it back in tight buns. No nonsense. Neither
style blew easily into heart-catching tangles. And at their
weddings they displayed themselves in their long hair for
the last time. "It brushed the backs of my knees," my
mother tells me. "It was braided, and even so, it brushed
the backs of my knees."

At the mirror my aunt combed individuality into her   25
bob. A bun could have been contrived to escape into black
streamers blowing in the wind or in quiet wisps about her

face, but only the older women in our picture album wear
buns. She brushed her hair back from her forehead, tuck-
ing the flaps behind her ears. She looped a piece of thread,
knotted into a circle between her index fingers and
thumbs, and ran the double strand across her forehead.
When she closed her fingers as if she were making a pair of
shadow geese bite, the string twisted together catching the
little hairs. Then she pulled the thread away from her skin,
ripping the hairs out neatly, her eyes watering from the
needles of pain. Opening her fingers, she cleaned the
thread, then rolled it along her hairline and the tops of her
eyebrows. My mother did the same to me and my sisters
and herself. I used to believe that the expression "caught
by the short hairs" meant a captive held with a depilatory
string. It especially hurt at the temples, but my mother said
we were lucky we didn't have to have our feet bound when
we were seven. Sisters used to sit on their beds and cry
together, she said, as their mothers or their slave removed
the bandages for a few minutes each night and let the
blood gush back into their veins. I hope that the man my
aunt loved appreciated a smooth brow, that he wasn't just
a tits-and-ass man.

Cause-and-effect analysis

Process analysis

   Once my aunt found a freckle on her chin, at a spot   26
that the almanac said predestined her for unhappiness. She
dug it out with a hot needle and washed the wound with
peroxide.

   More attention to her looks than these pullings of   27
hairs and pickings at spots would have caused gossip
among the villagers. They owned work clothes and good
clothes, and they wore good clothes for feasting the new
seasons. But since a woman combing her hair hexes beginnings, my aunt rarely found an occasion to look her best.
Women looked like great sea snails—the corded wood,
babies, and laundry they carried were the whorls on their
backs. The Chinese did not admire a bent back; goddesses
and warriors stood straight. Still there must have been a
marvelous freeing of beauty when a worker laid down her
burden and stretched and arched.

Comparison

   Such commonplace loveliness, however, was not   28
enough for my aunt. She dreamed of a lover for the fifteen

days of New Year's, the time for families to exchange vis- *Comparison*
its, money, and food. She plied her secret comb. And sure
enough she cursed the year, the family, the village, and
herself.

Even as her hair lured her imminent lover, many other 29
men looked at her. Uncles, cousins, nephews, brothers
would have looked, too, had they been home between
journeys. Perhaps they had already been restraining their *Cause-and-effect analysis*
curiosity, and they left, fearful that their glances, like a
field of nesting birds, might be startled and caught. Poverty hurt, and that was their first reason for leaving. But
another, final reason for leaving the crowded house was
the never-said.

She may have been unusually beloved, the precious 30
only daughter, spoiled and mirror gazing because of the
affection the family lavished on her. When her husband
left, they welcomed the chance to take her back from the
in-laws; she could live like the little daughter for just a
while longer. There are stories that my grandfather was
different from other people, "crazy ever since the little Jap
bayoneted him in the head." He used to put his naked *Narration*
penis on the dinner table, laughing. And one day he
brought home a baby girl, wrapped up inside his brown
western-style greatcoat. He had traded one of his sons, probably my father, the youngest, for her. My grandmother
made him trade back. When he finally got a daughter of
his own, he doted on her. They must have all loved her,
except perhaps my father, the only brother who never
went back to China, having once been traded for a girl.

Brothers and sisters, newly men and women, had to 31
efface their sexual color and present plain miens. Disturbing hair and eyes, a smile like no other, threatened the
ideal of five generations living under one roof. To focus *Cause-and-effect analysis*
blurs, people shouted face to face and yelled from room to
room. The immigrants I know have loud voices, unmodu-
lated to American tones even after years away from the
village where they called their friendships out across the
fields. I have not been able to stop my mother's screams in *Comparison and example*
public libraries or over telephones. Walking erect (knees
straight, toes pointed forward, not pigeon-toed, which is

Chinese-feminine) and speaking in an inaudible voice, I   *Comparison and*
have tried to turn myself American-feminine. Chinese   *example*
communication was loud, public. Only sick people had to
whisper. But at the dinner table, where the family members came nearest one another, no one could talk, not the
outcasts nor any eaters. Every word that falls from the   *Description*
mouth is a coin lost. Silently they gave and accepted food
with both hands. A preoccupied child who took his bowl
with one hand got a sideways glare. A complete moment
of total attention is due everyone alike. Children and
lovers have no singularity here, but my aunt used a secret
voice, a separate attentiveness.

She kept the man's name to herself throughout her 32
labor and dying; she did not accuse him that he be punished with her. To save her inseminator's name she gave
silent birth.

He may have been somebody in her own household, 33
but intercourse with a man outside the family would have
been no less abhorrent. All the village were kinsmen, and
the titles shouted in loud country voices never let kinship
be forgotten. Any man within visiting distance would have   *Cause-and-effect*
been neutralized as a lover—"brother," "younger broth-   *analysis*
er," "older brother"—one hundred and fifteen relationship titles. Parents researched birth charts probably not so
much to assure good fortune as to circumvent incest in a
population that has but one hundred surnames. Everybody
has eight million relatives. How useless then sexual mannerisms, how dangerous.

As if it came from an atavism deeper than fear, I used 34
to add "brother" silently to boys' names. It hexed the
boys, who would or would not ask me to dance, and made
them less scary and as familiar and deserving of benevolence as girls.

But, of course, I hexed myself also—no dates. I should 35
have stood up, both arms waving, and shouted out across
libraries, "Hey, you! Love me back." I had no idea,
though, how to make attraction selective, how to control
its direction and magnitude. If I made myself American-
pretty so that the five or six Chinese boys in the class fell in
love with me, everyone else—the Caucasian, Negro, and

Japanese boys—would too. Sisterliness, dignified and honorable, made much more sense.

Cause-and-effect analysis

Attraction eludes control so stubbornly that whole societies designed to organize relationships among people cannot keep order, not even when they bind people to one another from childhood and raise them together. Among the very poor and the wealthy, brothers married their adopted sisters, like doves. Our family allowed some romance, paying adult brides' prices and providing dowries so that their sons and daughters could marry strangers. Marriage promises to turn strangers into friendly relatives—a nation of siblings.

In the village structure, spirits shimmered among the live creatures, balanced and held in equilibrium by time and land. But one human being flaring up into violence could open up a black hole, a maelstrom that pulled in the sky. The frightened villagers, who depended on one another to maintain the real, went to my aunt to show her a personal, physical representation of the break she made in the "roundness." Misallying couples snapped off the future, which was to be embodied in true offspring. The villagers punished her for acting as if she could have a private life, secret and apart from them.

Description

If my aunt had betrayed the family at a time of large grain yields and peace, when many boys were born, and wings were being built on many houses, perhaps she might have escaped such severe punishment. But the men—hungry, greedy, tired of planting in dry soil, cuckolded—had been forced to leave the village in order to send food-money home. There were ghost plagues, bandit plagues, wars with the Japanese, floods. My Chinese brother and sister had died of an unknown sickness. Adultery, perhaps only a mistake during good times, became a crime when the village needed food.

The round moon cakes and round doorways, the round tables of graduated size that fit one roundness inside another, round windows and rice bowls—these talismans had lost their power to warn this family of the law: a family must be whole, faithfully keeping the descent line by having sons to feed the old and the dead who in turn

look after the family. The villagers came to show my aunt   *Cause-and-effect*
and lover-in-hiding a broken house. The villagers were   *analysis*
speeding up the circling of events because she was too
shortsighted to see that her infidelity had already harmed
the village, that waves of consequences would return un-
predictably, sometimes in disguise, as now, to hurt her.
This roundness had to be made coin-sized so that she
would see its circumference: punish her at the birth of her
baby. Awaken her to the inexorable. People who refused
fatalism because they could invent small resources insisted
on culpability. Deny accidents and wrest fault from the
stars.

After the villagers left, their lanterns now scattering in   *40*
various directions toward home, the family broke their
silence and cursed her. "Aiaa, we're going to die. Death is
coming. Death is coming. Look what you've done. You've   *Narration*
killed us. Ghost! Dead Ghost! Ghost! You've never been
born." She ran out into the fields, far enough from the
house so that she could no longer hear their voices, and
pressed herself against the earth, her own land no more.
When she felt the birth coming, she thought that she had
been hurt. Her body seized together. "They've hurt me too
much," she thought. "This is gall, and it will kill me."
With forehead and knees against the earth, her body con-
vulsed and then relaxed. She turned on her back, lay on
the ground. The black well of sky and stars went out and   *Description*
out and out forever; her body and her complexity seemed
to disappear. She was one of the stars, a bright dot in
blackness, without home, without a companion, in eternal
cold and silence. An agoraphobia rose in her, speeding
higher and higher, bigger and bigger; she would not be
able to contain it; there would be no end to fear.

Flayed, unprotected against space, she felt pain return,   *41*
focusing her body. This pain chilled her—a cold, steady
kind of surface pain. Inside, spasmodically, the other pain,
the pain of the child, heated her. For hours she lay on the
ground, alternately body and space. Sometimes a vision of
normal comfort obliterated reality: she saw the family in
the evening gambling at the dinner table, the young people
massaging their elders' backs. She saw them congratulat-
ing one another, high joy on the mornings the rice shoots

came up. When these pictures burst, the stars drew yet   *Narration*
further apart. Black space opened.   *Description*

  She got to her feet to fight better and remembered that 42
old-fashioned women gave birth in their pigsties to fool
the jealous, pain-dealing gods, who do not snatch piglets.
Before the next spasms could stop her, she ran to the pigsty, each step a rushing out into emptiness. She climbed
over the fence and knelt in the dirt. It was good to have a
fence enclosing her, a tribal person alone.

  Laboring, this woman who had carried her child as a   43
foreign growth that sickened her every day, expelled it at
last. She reached down to touch the hot, wet, moving
mass, surely smaller than anything human, and could feel
that it was human after all—fingers, toes, nails, nose. She *Description*
pulled it up on to her belly, and it lay curled there, butt in
the air, feet precisely tucked one under the other. She
opened her loose shirt and buttoned the child inside. After
resting, it squirmed and thrashed and she pushed it up to
her breast. It turned its head this way and that until it
found her nipple. There, it made little snuffling noises. She
clenched her teeth at its preciousness, lovely as a young
calf, a piglet, a little dog.

  She may have gone to the pigsty as a last act of respon- 44
sibility: she would protect this child as she had protected
its father. It would look after her soul, leaving supplies on
her grave. But how would this tiny child without family
find her grave when there would be no marker for her   *Cause-and-effect*
anywhere, neither in the earth nor the family hall? No one *analysis*
would give her a family hall name. She had taken the child
with her into the wastes. At its birth the two of them had
felt the same raw pain of separation, a wound that only
the family pressing tight could close. A child with no descent line would not soften her life but only trail after her,
ghost-like, begging her to give it purpose. At dawn the
villagers on their way to the fields would stand around the
fence and look.

  Full of milk, the little ghost slept. When it awoke, she 45
hardened her breasts against the milk that crying loosens.
Toward morning she picked up the baby and walked to
the well.

  Carrying the baby to the well shows loving. Otherwise   46

abandon it. Turn its face into the mud. Mothers who love
their children take them along. It was probably a girl;
there is some hope of forgiveness for boys.

"Don't tell anyone you had an aunt. Your father does   47
not want to hear her name. She has never been born." I
have believed that sex was unspeakable and words so
strong and fathers so frail that "aunt" would do my father
mysterious harm. I have thought that my family, having
settled among immigrants who had also been their neighbors in the ancestral land, needed to clean their name, and
a wrong word would incite the kinspeople even here. But
there is more to this silence: they want me to participate in
her punishment. And I have.

In the twenty years since I heard this story I have not   48
asked for details nor said my aunt's name; I do not know
it. People who comfort the dead can also chase after them
to hurt them further—a reverse ancestor worship. The real
punishment was not the raid swiftly inflicted by the villagers, but the family's deliberately forgetting her. Her betrayal so maddened them, they saw to it that she would
suffer forever, even after death. Always hungry, always
needing, she would have to beg food from other ghosts,
snatch and steal it from those whose living descendants
give them gifts. She would have to fight the ghosts massed
at crossroads for the buns a few thoughtful citizens leave
to decoy her away from village and home so that the ancestral spirits could feast unharassed. At peace, they could
act like gods, not ghosts, their descent lines providing them
with paper suits and dresses, spirit money, paper houses,
paper automobiles, chicken, meat, and rice into eternity—
essences delivered up in smoke and flames, steam and in-
cense rising from each rice bowl. In an attempt to make
the Chinese care for people outside the family, Chairman
Mao encourages us now to give our paper replicas to the
spirits of outstanding soldiers and workers, no matter
whose ancestors they may be. My aunt remains forever
hungry. Goods are not distributed evenly among the dead.

My aunt haunts me—her ghost drawn to me because   49
now, after fifty years of neglect, I alone devote pages of

paper to her, though not origamied into houses and clothes. I do not think she always means me well. I am telling on her, and she was a spite suicide, drowning herself in the drinking water. The Chinese are always very frightened of the drowned one, whose weeping ghost, wet hair hanging and skin bloated, waits silently by the water to pull down a substitute.

ACKNOWLEDGMENTS
(*Continued from page iv*)

Barbara Lazear Ascher, "The Box Man." Excerpts from *Playing After Dark* by Barbara Lazear Ascher. Copyright © 1986 by Barbara Lazear Ascher. Used by permission of Doubleday, a division of Bantam, Doubleday, Dell Publishing Group, Inc.

Sylvia Ashton-Warner, from *Spearpoint: "Teacher" in America.* Copyright © 1972 by Sylvia Ashton-Warner. Reprinted by permission of Alfred A. Knopf, Inc.

John Berger, "Pleasure and Pain." From *And Our Faces, My Heart, Brief as Photos* by John Berger. Copyright © 1984 by John Berger. Reprinted by permission of Pantheon Books, a Division of Random House, Inc.

Bruno Bettelheim, from "The Holocaust—One Generation After." From *Surviving and Other Essays* by Bruno Bettelheim. Copyright 1952, © 1960, 1962, 1969 by Bruno and Trude Bettelheim, as trustees. Reprinted by permission of Alfred A. Knopf, Inc.

Ray Allen Billington, "The Frontier Disappears." From *The American Story*, Earl Schenck Miers, editor. Copyright © 1956 by The United States Capitol Historical Society. Reprinted by permission.

David Bruck, from "The Death Penalty." Reprinted by permission of *The New Republic*, May 20, 1985. © 1985, The New Republic, Inc.

William H. Calvin, from *The Throwing Madonna: Essays on the Brain*, published by McGraw-Hill Book Company. Copyright © 1983 by William H. Calvin. Reprinted by permission of the author.

Benjamin Capps, from *The Old West: The Great Chiefs* by the Editors of Time-Life Books with text by Benjamin Capps. © 1975 Time-Life Books Inc. Reprinted by permission.

Diane Cole, "Don't Just Stand There." From *The New York Times*, April 16, 1989. Reprinted by permission of the author.

K. C. Cole, "Women in Science." From *The New York Times*, December 3, 1981. Copyright © 1981 by The New York Times Company. Reprinted by permission.

Joan Didion, "Death in El Salvador." From *Salvador* by Joan Didion. Copyright © 1983 by Joan Didion. Reprinted by permission of Simon & Schuster, Inc.

Annie Dillard, "In the Jungle." From *Teaching a Stone to Talk* by Annie Dillard. Copyright © 1982 by Annie Dillard. Reprinted by permission of Harper & Row, Publishers, Inc.

Barbara Ehrenreich, "Blocking the Gates to Heaven." Originally published in the June 1986 issue of *Mother Jones*. Reprinted by permission of the author.

Peter Gardella, "The Tao of Baseball." From *Harper's*, May 1986, as excerpted from an article appearing in the Manhattanville College newspaper, *Touchstone*, February 5, 1986. Reprinted by permission of the author.

Glossary

abstract and concrete words An **abstract** word refers to an idea, quality, attitude, or state that we cannot perceive with our senses: *beauty, liberty, hate, anxious, brave, idealistic*. A **concrete** word, in contrast, refers to an object, person, place, or state that we can perceive with our senses: *newspaper, police officer, Mississippi River, red-faced, tangled, screeching.* Though abstract words are useful to convey general concepts or impressions, they are too vague to create distinct sensory impressions in readers' minds. To make meaning precise and vivid, writers support abstractions with concrete words that appeal directly to readers' senses of sight, hearing, touch, taste, and smell. See also *general and specific words.*

allusion A brief reference to a real or fictitious person, place, object, or event. An allusion can convey considerable meaning with few words, as when a writer describes a movie as "potentially this year's *Star Wars*" to imply both that the movie is a space adventure and that it may be a blockbuster. But to be effective, the allusion must refer to something readers know well.

analogy An extended comparison of two unlike subjects that uses some similarities as the basis for establishing other similarities. The purpose of an analogy may be explanatory or argumentative. See Chapter 8 on analogy, p. 229.

analysis See *division or analysis.*

anecdote A brief narrative that recounts an episode from a person's experience. See, for instance, Twain, paragraph 10, p. 300. See also Chapter 2 on narration, p. 57.

argument The form of writing that appeals to readers' reason and emotions in order to win agreement with a claim or to compel some action. This definition encompasses both argument in a narrower sense—the appeal to reason to win agreement—and persuasion—the appeal to emotion to compel action. See Chapter 11 on argument and persuasion, p. 308.

audience A writer's audience is the group of readers for whom a particular work is intended. To communicate effectively, the writer should estimate readers' knowledge of the subject, their interests in it, and their biases toward it and should then consider these needs and expectations in choosing what to say and how to say it. For further discussion of audience, see pp. 2, 9, 16.

cause-and-effect analysis The method of development in which occurrences are divided into their elements to find what made an event happen (its causes) and what the consequences were (its effects). See Chapter 10 on cause-and-effect analysis, p. 275.

chronological order A pattern of organization in which events are arranged as they occurred over time, earliest to latest. Narratives often follow a chronological order; see Chapter 2, p. 58.

classification   The method of development in which the members of a group are sorted into classes or subgroups according to shared characteristics. See Chapter 5 on classification, p. 137.

cliché   An expression that has become tired from overuse and that therefore deadens rather than enlivens writing. Examples: *tried and true, in over their heads, turn over a new leaf, march to a different drummer, as heavy as lead, as clear as a bell.*

climactic order   A pattern of organization in which elements—words, sentences, examples, ideas—are arranged in order of increasing importance or drama.

coherence   The quality of effective writing that comes from clear, logical connections among all the parts, so that the reader can follow the writer's thought process without difficulty. Coherence is largely a matter of logic, ensuring that each point develops naturally out of the ones before, and of organization, arranging material in the way that best focuses and directs the reader's attention. But writers can also improve coherence with special devices that link sentences and paragraphs clearly and smoothly; see *parallelism* and *transitions*. See also *unity*.

colloquial language   The language of conversation, including contractions (*don't , can't*) and informal words and expressions (*hot* for new or popular, *boss* for employer, *ad* for advertisement, *get away with it, flunk the exam*). Most dictionaries label such words and expressions *colloquial* or *informal*. Colloquial language is inappropriate when the writing situation demands precision and formality, as a college term paper or a business report does. But in other situations it can be used selectively to relax a piece of writing and reduce the distance between writer and reader. (See, for instance, Schjeldahl, p. 49; Hughes, p. 65; and Twain, p. 297.) See also *diction*.

comparison and contrast   The method of development in which the similarities and differences between subjects are examined. Comparison examines similarities and contrast examines differences, but the two are generally used together. See Chapter 7 on comparison and contrast, p. 196.

conclusions   The endings of written works—the sentences that bring the writing to a close. A conclusion provides readers with a sense of completion, with a sense that the writer has finished. Sometimes the final point in the body of an essay may accomplish this purpose, especially if it is very important or dramatic (for instance, see White, p. 76). But usually a separate conclusion is needed to achieve completion. It may be a single sentence or several paragraphs, depending on the length and complexity of the piece of writing. And it may include one of the following, or a combination, depending on the writer's subject and purpose.

1. A summary of the main points of the essay (see Billington, p. 123; Twain, p. 303; Kondracke, p. 342).
2. A statement of the main idea of the essay, if it has not been stated

before (see Klass, p. 96), or a restatement of the main idea incorporating information from the body of the essay (see Will, p. 106; Greenfield, p. 211; Lewis, p. 271).

3. A comment on the significance or implications of the subject (see Miller, p. 132; Reich, p. 147).
4. A suggestion or recommendation that readers support a proposal or action, or that they take some action themselves (see Papandreou, p. 294).
5. A prediction for the future (see King, p. 326).
6. An example, anecdote, question, or quotation that reinforces the point of the essay (see MacLeod, p. 83; Rettie, p. 242; Gardella, p. 246–47; K. C. Cole, p. 288; Nadelmann, p. 332–33).

Excluded from this list are several endings that should be avoided because they tend to weaken the overall effect of an essay: (1) an example, fact, or quotation that pertains to only part of the essay; (2) an apology for the writer's ideas, for the quality of the writing, or for omissions; (3) an attempt to enhance the significance of the essay by overgeneralizing from its ideas and evidence; (4) a new idea that requires the support of an entirely different essay.

concrete words See *abstract and concrete words.*

connotation and denotation A word's **denotation** is its literal meaning: *dog* denotes a four-legged domestic canine; *bawling* denotes loud crying; *famous* denotes the quality of being well known. A word's **connotations** are the associations or suggestions that go beyond its literal meaning. Some connotations are personal, varying according to an individual's experiences. *Dog,* for instance, may connote a particular dog and may further connote warm or unpleasant feelings about that dog. Other connotations are more general, calling up basically the same associations for all who use or hear the word. *Bawling* connotes crying that is not only loud but uncontrolled and undignified; we do not sympathize with bawlers. Many groups of words with essentially the same denotation vary in their connotations. *Famous, eminent,* and *notorious* all denote the quality of being well known; but *famous* connotes celebrity and popularity among contemporaries (*famous actor*), *eminent* connotes recognition for outstanding qualities or contributions (*eminent physician*), and *notorious* connotes sensational, even unfavorable, recognition (*notorious thief*). Each of these words can help shape a reader's responses to the person being described. But connotative words will backfire if they set off inappropriate associations—if, for instance, a writer describes a respected figure as "a notorious teacher and scholar." Habitual use of a dictionary is the best safeguard against such mistakes.

contrast See *comparison and contrast.*

deductive reasoning The method of reasoning that moves from the general to the specific. See Chapter 11 on argument and persuasion, especially pp. 312–15.

definition   An explanation of the meaning of a word. An extended definition may serve as the primary method of developing an essay. See Chapter 9 on definition, p. 250.

denotation   See *connotation and denotation.*

description   The form of writing that conveys the perceptions of the senses— sight, hearing, smell, taste, touch—to make a person, place, object, or state of mind vivid and concrete. See Chapter 1 on description, p. 28.

diction   The choice of words made by a writer to achieve a purpose and make meaning clear. Effective diction conveys the writer's meaning exactly, emphatically, and concisely, and it is appropriate to the writer's intentions and audience. **Standard English,** the written language of educated native speakers, is expected in all writing for college, business and the professions, and publication. The vocabulary of standard English is large and varied, encompassing, for instance, both *comestibles* and *food* for edible things, both *paroxysm* and *fit* for a sudden seizure. In some writing situations, standard English may also include words and expressions typical of conversation (see *colloquial language*). But it excludes other levels of diction that only certain groups understand or find acceptable. Most dictionaries label expressions at these levels as follows:

Nonstandard: words spoken among particular social groups, such as *ain't, them guys, hisself,* and *nowheres.*

Slang: words that are usually short-lived and that may not be understood by all readers, such as *tanked* for drunk, *bread* for money, and *honcho* for one in charge.

Regional or **dialect:** words spoken in a particular region but not in the country as a whole, such as *poke* for a sack or bag, *holler* for a hollow or small valley.

Obsolete: words that have passed out of use, such as *cleam* for smear or stain.

See also *connotation and denotation.*

division or analysis   The method of development in which a subject is separated into its elements or parts and then reassembled into a new whole. See Chapter 4 on division or analysis, p. 110.

dominant impression   The central idea or feeling conveyed by a description of a person, place, object, or state of mind. See Chapter 1 on description, especially p. 28.

effect   See *cause-and-effect analysis.*

emotional appeal   In argumentative and persuasive writing, the appeal to readers' values, beliefs, or feelings in order to win agreement or compel action. See pp. 310–11.

essay   A prose composition on a single nonfictional topic or idea. An essay usually reflects the personal experiences and opinions of the writer.

ethical appeal   In argumentative and persuasive writing, the sense of the writer's expertise and character projected by the reasonableness of the argument, the use and quality of evidence, and tone. See p. 310.

evidence   The details, examples, facts, statistics, or expert opinions that support any general statement or claim. See p. 312 on the use of evidence in argumentative writing.

example   An instance or representative of a general group or an abstract concept or quality. One or more examples may serve as the primary method of developing an essay. See Chapter 3 on example, p. 87.

exposition   The form of writing that explains or informs. Most of the essays in this book are primarily expository, and some essays whose primary purpose is self-expression or persuasion employ exposition to clarify ideas.

figures of speech   Expressions that imply meanings beyond or different from their literal meanings in order to achieve vividness or force. Some of the more common figures of speech are simile, metaphor, personification, and hyperbole. A **simile** compares two unlike things and makes the comparison explicit with *like* or *as*: "The car spun around like a top"; "Coins as bright as sunshine lay glinting in the chest." A **metaphor** also compares two unlike things, but more subtly, by equating them without *like* or *as*: "Her words shattered my fragile self-esteem"; "The laboratory was his prison, the beakers and test tubes his guards." **Personification** is a kind of simile or metaphor that attributes human qualities or powers to things or abstractions: "The breeze sighed and whispered in the grasses"; "The city embraced me gently at first but then began squeezing too tightly." **Hyperbole** is deliberate overstatement or exaggeration: "The movie lasts forever"; "The children's noise shook the walls and rafters." (The opposite of hyperbole is understatement, discussed under *irony*.)

formal style   See *style*.

general and specific words   A **general** word refers to a group or class: *buildings, colors, apparel*. A **specific** word refers to a particular member of a group or class: *courthouse, red, gloves*. General and specific are not exclusive categories but relative terms, as illustrated by the following chain from the most general to the most specific: *apparel, hand warmers, gloves, leather gloves, Uncle Joe's gray kid gloves*. Though general words are essential for referring to entire groups or classes, they contribute little to vividness, and they often leave meaning unclear. Usually, the more specific a word is, the more interesting it will be for readers. See also *abstract and concrete words*.

generalization   A statement about a group or a class derived from knowledge of some or all of its members: for instance, "Dolphins can be trained to count" or "Television news rarely penetrates beneath the headlines." The more instances the generalization is based on, the more accurate it is likely to be. A generalization is the result of inductive reasoning; see pp. 311–12.

hyperbole   See *figures of speech*.

image   A verbal representation of sensory experience—that is, of something seen, heard, felt, tasted, or smelled. Images may be literal: "Snow stuck to her eyelashes"; "The red car sped past us." Or they may be figurative: "Her eyelashes were snowy feathers"; "The car rocketed past us like a red missile." (See *figures of speech*.) Through images, a writer touches the reader's experiences, thus sharpening meaning and adding immediacy. See also *abstract and concrete words*.

inductive reasoning   The method of reasoning that moves from the particular to the general. See Chapter 11 on argument and persuasion, especially pp. 311–12.

informal style   See *style*.

introductions   The openings of written works, the sentences that set the stage for what follows. An introduction to an essay identifies and restricts the subject while establishing the writer's attitude toward it. Accomplishing these purposes may require anything from a single sentence to several paragraphs, depending on the writer's purpose and how much readers need to know before they can begin to grasp the ideas in the essay. The introduction often includes a thesis sentence stating the main idea of the essay (see *thesis*). To set up the thesis sentence, or as a substitute for it, any of the following openings, or a combination, may be effective.

1. Background on the subject that establishes a time or place or that provides essential information (see Didion, pp. 43–44; Billington, pp. 118–19; Miller, pp. 126–27; Swift, pp. 345–46).

2. An anecdote or other reference to the writer's experience that forecasts or illustrates the main idea or that explains what prompted the essay (see White, pp. 70–71; Diane Cole, p. 169; Rodriguez, pp. 220–21; Syfers, p. 258; Ehrenreich, pp. 364–65).

3. An explanation of the significance of the subject (see Reich, pp. 143–44; Petrunkevitch, pp. 187–88; Naylor, pp. 263–64).

4. An outline of the situation or problem that the essay will address, perhaps using interesting facts or statistics (see Postman, p. 99; King, pp. 322–23; Nadelmann, p. 329).

5. A statement or quotation of an opinion that the writer will modify or disagree with (see Will, p. 104).

6. An example, quotation, or question that reinforces the main idea (see MacLeod, p. 79; Klass, p. 93; Kondracke, p. 336).

A good introduction does not mislead readers by exaggerating the significance of the subject or the essay, and it does not bore readers by saying more than is necessary. In addition, a good introduction avoids two openings that are always clumsy: (1) beginning with "The purpose of this essay is . . ." or something similar; and (2) referring to the title of the essay in the first sentence, as in "This is not as hard as it looks" or "This is a serious problem."

irony   In writing, irony is the use of words to suggest a meaning different
from their literal meaning. Mitford's "Embalming Mr. Jones" contains
considerable irony, as when she notes that making a corpse "presentable
for viewing in an attitude of healthy repose . . . is rather a large order [for
the undertaker] since few people die in the full bloom of health, unravaged by illness or unmarked by some disfigurement" (paragraph 14, p.
182). Mitford is not sympathizing with the undertaker's difficult job but
pointing out the absurdity of trying to restore a corpse at all, much less to
"an attitude of healthy repose." Mitford's irony derives from **understatement**, from saying less than is meant. But irony can also derive from
hyperbole, or exaggerating meaning (see *figures of speech*), and from
reversal, or saying the opposite of the actual meaning. Reversal pervades
Swift's "A Modest Proposal" (p. 345). Irony can be witty, teasing, biting,
or cruel. At its most humorless and heavily contemptuous, it becomes
sarcasm: "Thanks a lot for telling Dad we stayed out all night; that was
really bright of you." For other essays using irony, see Postman (p. 99)
and Ehrenreich (p. 364).

logical fallacies   Flaws in reasoning that weaken or invalidate an argument.
Some of the most common fallacies are listed below (the page numbers
refer to further discussion in the text).

1. **Oversimplification,** overlooking or ignoring inconsistencies or complexities in evidence: "The problems in Northern Ireland would be
   solved if the British would just go home" (pp. 277–78, 312).
2. **Hasty generalization,** leaping to a conclusion on the basis of inadequate or unrepresentative evidence: "Every one of the twelve students polled supports the change in the grading system, so the
   administration should implement it" (p. 312).
3. **Begging the question,** assuming the truth of a conclusion that has not
   been proved: "Acid rain does not do serious damage, so it is not a
   serious problem" (p. 314).
4. **Ignoring the question,** shifting the argument away from the real issue:
   "A fine, churchgoing man like Charles Harold would make an excellent mayor" (pp. 314–15).
5. **Ad hominem** ("to the man") **argument,** attacking an opponent instead of the opponent's argument: "She is just a student, so we need
   not listen to her criticisms of foreign policy" (p. 315).
6. **Either-or,** presenting only two alternatives when the choices are more
   numerous: "If you want to do well in college, you have to cheat a
   little" (p. 315).
7. **Non sequitur** ("it does not follow"), deriving a wrong or illogical
   conclusion from stated premises: "Since students are actually in
   school, they should be the ones to determine our educational policies"
   (p. 315).
8. **Post hoc** (from *post hoc, ergo propter hoc,* "after this, therefore be-

cause of this"), assuming that one thing caused another simply because it preceded the other: "Two students left school in the week after the new policies were announced, proving that the policies will eventually cause a reduction in enrollments" (pp. 277, 315).

metaphor See *figures of speech.*

narration The form of writing that tells a story, relating a sequence of events. See Chapter 2 on narration, p. 57.

nonstandard English See *diction.*

paragraph A group of related sentences, set off by an initial indention, that develops an idea. By breaking continuous text into units, paragraphing helps the writer manage ideas and helps the reader follow those ideas. Each paragraph makes a distinct contribution to the main idea governing the entire piece of writing. The idea of the paragraph itself is often stated explicitly in a topic sentence, and it is supported with sentences containing specific details, examples, and reasons. Like the larger piece of writing to which it contributes, the paragraph should be easy to follow and clearly focused (see *coherence* and *unity*). For examples of well-developed paragraphs, see the paragraph analyses in the middle section of each chapter introduction.

parallelism The use of similar grammatical form for ideas of equal importance. Within a sentence, two or more elements of equal function and importance should always be parallel to avoid confusing or jarring readers: "The doctor recommends swimming, bicycling, or walking" is clearer and easier to read than "The doctor recommends swimming, bicycling, or that patients walk." But parallelism can also be an emphatic stylistic device either within or among sentences: "*Now* is the time to lift our nation from the quicksands of racial injustice to the solid rock of brotherhood" (King, paragraph 4, p. 323); "She dreamed of a lover. . . . She plied her secret comb. And sure enough she cursed the year, the family, the village, and herself" (Kingston, paragraph 28, pp. 376–77). When used among sentences, parallelism also clarifies the relations among ideas (see *coherence*).

personification See *figures of speech.*

persuasion See *argument.*

point of view The position of the writer in relation to the subject. In description, point of view depends on the writer's physical and psychological relation to the subject (see p. 30). In narration, point of view depends on the writer's place in the story and on his or her relation to it in time (see p. 59). More broadly, point of view can also mean the writer's particular mental stance or attitude. For instance, an employee and employer might have different points of view toward the employee's absenteeism or the employer's sick-leave policies.

premise The generalization or assumption on which an argument is based. See *syllogism.*

process analysis   The method of development in which a sequence of actions with a specified result is divided into its component steps. See Chapter 6 on process analysis, p. 161.

purpose   The reason for writing, the goal the writer wants to achieve. The purpose may be primarily to explain the subject so that readers understand it or see it in a new light; to convince readers to accept or reject an opinion or to take a certain action; to entertain readers with a humorous or exciting story; or to express the thoughts and emotions triggered by a revealing or instructive experience. The writer's purpose overlaps the main idea—the particular point being made about the subject. In effective writing, the two together direct and control every choice the writer makes. See also *thesis* and *unity*.

rational appeal   In argumentative and persuasive writing, the appeal to readers' rational faculties—to their ability to reason logically—in order to win agreement or compel action. See pp. 311–15.

rhetoric   The art of using words effectively to communicate with an audience, or the study of that art. To the ancient Greeks, rhetoric was the art of the *rhetor*—orator, or public speaker—and included the art of persuasion. Later the word shifted to mean elegant language, and a version of that meaning persists in today's occasional use of *rhetoric* to mean pretentious or hollow language, as in "Their argument was mere rhetoric."

sarcasm   See *irony*.

satire   The combination of wit and criticism to mock or condemn human foolishness or evil. The intent of satire is to arouse readers to contempt or action, and thus it differs from comedy, which seeks simply to amuse. Much satire relies on irony—saying one thing but meaning another (see *irony*). Swift's "A Modest Proposal" (p. 345) is a model of ironic satire: in coolly recommending an appalling solution to the problems of the Irish poor, Swift attacks the greed and inhumanity of those who were exploiting the poor and ignoring their plight.

simile   See *figures of speech*.

slang   See *diction*.

specific words   See *general and specific words*.

standard English   See *diction*.

style   The *way* something is said, as opposed to *what* is said. Style results primarily from a writer's characteristic word choices and sentence structures. A person's writing style, like his or her voice or manner of speaking, is distinctive. Style can also be viewed more broadly as ranging from formal to informal. A very formal style adheres strictly to the conventions of standard English (see *diction*), tends toward long sentences with sophisticated structures, and relies on learned words such as *malodorous* and *psychopathic*. A very informal style, in contrast, is more conversational (see *colloquial language*); tends toward short, uncomplicated sentences; and relies on words typical of casual speech, such as *smelly* or *crazy*. Among the writers represented in this book, Swift (p. 345) writes the most formally, Hughes (p. 65) the most informally; the others fall in between. The formality of style may often be modified to suit a particular audience or occasion: a college term paper, for instance, demands a more formal style than an essay narrating a personal experience. See also *tone*.

syllogism The basic form of deductive reasoning, in which a conclusion derives necessarily from proven or accepted premises. For example: *The roof always leaks when it rains* (the major premise). *It is raining* (the minor premise). *Therefore, the roof will leak* (the conclusion). See Chapter 11 on argument and persuasion, especially pp. 313–14.

symbol A person, place, or thing that represents an abstract quality or concept. A red heart symbolizes love; the Golden Gate Bridge symbolizes San Francisco's dramatic beauty; a cross symbolizes Christianity.

thesis The main idea of a piece of writing, to which all other ideas and details relate. The main idea is often stated in a **thesis sentence**, which asserts something about the subject and conveys the writer's purpose. The thesis sentence is often included near the beginning of an essay, especially when the purpose is explanatory or persuasive. Even when the writer does not state the main idea and purpose, they govern all the ideas and details in the essay. See pp. 15–16. See also *unity*.

tone The attitude toward the subject, and sometimes toward the audience and the writer's own self, expressed in choice of words and sentence structures as well as in what is said. Tone in writing is similar to tone of voice in speaking, from warm to serious, amused to angry, joyful to sorrowful, sympathetic to contemptuous. For examples of strong tone in writing, see, for instance, Didion (p. 43), Schjeldahl (p. 49), White (p. 70), Mitford (p. 178), Syfers (p. 258), and King (p. 322). See also *style*.

transitions Links between sentences and paragraphs that relate ideas and thus contribute to clarity and smoothness (see *coherence*). Some transitions are echoes of previous material that tie parts together and subtly indicate relationships: repetition and restatement can stress important words or phrases; pronouns such as *he, she, it,* and *they* can substitute for and refer back to earlier nouns; and parallelism can highlight ideas of similar importance (see *parallelism*). Other transitions are more obvious, stating the connections explicitly: transitional sentences beginning paragraphs or brief transitional paragraphs can help shift the focus or introduce new ideas; and transitional expressions can signal and specify relationships. Some common transitional expressions—by no means all—are listed below.

Space: above, below, beyond, farther away, here, nearby, opposite, there, to the right

Time: afterward, at last, earlier, later, meanwhile, simultaneously, soon, then

Illustration: for example, for instance, specifically, that is

Comparison: also, likewise, similarly

Contrast: but, even so, however, in contrast, on the contrary, still, yet

Addition or repetition: again, also, finally, furthermore, in addition, moreover, next, that is

Cause or effect: as a result, consequently, equally important, hence, then, therefore, thus

Summary or conclusion: all in all, in brief, in conclusion, in short, in summary, therefore, thus

Intensification: indeed, in fact, of course, truly

understatement See *irony.*

unity The quality of effective writing that occurs when all the parts relate to the main idea and contribute to the writer's purpose. Digressions and aimlessness irritate and confuse readers. A piece of writing must have a point, that point must be clear to readers, and they must see how every sentence relates to it. See *purpose* and *thesis.* See also *coherence.*